After the Cosmopolitan?

D0219762

The majority of the world's population now lives in cities. The social, cultural and economic problems and opportunities that are generated by this extraordinary concentration of people have become symbolic of the contemporary human condition. This burgeoning of city life has in particular led to progressively greater concentrations of demographic groups from increasingly diverse backgrounds and resulted in new forms of cultural conflict and cultural dialogue.

In *After the Cosmopolitan?* Michael Keith argues that both racial divisions and intercultural dialogue can only be understood in the context of the urbanism through which they are realised. The author addresses debates in cultural theory and urban studies about the growth of cultural industries and the marketing of cities, the debates around social exclusion and violence, the big debate in the States around the nature of the ghetto, the cross disciplinary conceptualisation of cultural hybridity and the politics of third way social policy. Through this Keith considers the ways in which race is played out in the streets of some of the world's most eminent cities and argues that neither the utopian naiveté of some invocations of cosmopolitan democracy nor the pessimism of multicultural hell can adequately make sense of the changing nature of contemporary metropolitan life.

This authoritative book will be of interest to advanced undergraduates, post-graduates and researchers across the disciplines of anthropology, architecture, cultural studies, geography, politics, social policy and sociology.

Michael Keith is Professor of Sociology and Director of the Centre for Urban and Community Research, Goldsmiths College, University of London. His research focuses on the interplay of contemporary urbanism and the forms and politics of city change and cultural production. He has published several books including *Race, Riots, and Policing: Lore and Disorder in a Multi-Racist Society*.

WITHDRAWN
UTSA LIBRARIES

After the Cosmopolitan?

Multicultural cities and the future of racism

Michael Keith

Routledge
Taylor & Francis Group

LONDON AND NEW YORK

Library
University of Texas
at San Antonio

First published 2005
by Routledge
2 Park Square, Milton Park, Abingdon, Oxon OX14 4RN

Simultaneously published in the USA and Canada
by Routledge
270 Madison Ave, New York, NY 10016

Routledge is an imprint of the Taylor & Francis Group

© 2005 Michael Keith

Typeset in Baskerville by
Book Now Ltd, London
Printed and bound in Great Britain by
TJ International Ltd, Padstow, Cornwall

All rights reserved. No part of this book may be reprinted or reproduced or
utilised in any form or by any electronic, mechanical, or other means, now
known or hereafter invented, including photocopying and recording, or in
any information storage or retrieval system, without permission in writing
from the publishers.

British Library Cataloguing in Publication Data
A catalogue record for this book is available from the British Library

Library of Congress Cataloging in Publication Data
Keith, Michael, 1960–
    After the cosmopolitan?: multicultural cities and the future of racism/
Michael Keith.– 1st ed.
        p. cm.
    Includes bibliographical references and index.
    1. Sociology, Urban. 2. Pluralism (Social sciences) 3. Racism. I. Title.
    HT151.K37 2005
    307.76–dc22   2004023608

ISBN 0–415–34168–X (hbk)
ISBN 0–415–34169–8 (pbk)

Library
University of Texas
at San Antonio

Contents

Acknowledgements

This book attempts to synthesise an approach to cities research in a manner that is committed to both empirical labour and theoretical reflection. In this context several of the chapters are based on collaborative research, and I am indebted to many who have worked on a number of projects over the last decade. These include a large number of colleagues who have collaborated with me and tolerated me on long-term projects based at the Centre for Urban and Community Research (CUCR) at Goldsmiths College, University of London, without whose support this book would not have been written. They include Les Back, Phil Cohen, Marjorie Mayo, Nikolas Rose and John Solomos. In particular Les Back and John Solomos have been sources of patience, humour and encouragement. Other colleagues who have offered advice and support at many different times include David Goldberg, Barnor Hesse, Roger Hewitt, Azra Khan, Karim Murji, Steve Pile, Michael Stone, Scott Lash and Kalbir Shukra.

Graduates students have provided a constant source of inspiration and dialogue, and in particular I would like to thank Jo Hadley, George Mavromatis, Yasmeen Narayan, Heidi Seetzen, Ben Gidley, Mutmahim Roaf and Jo Sadler. Other colleagues at CUCR who at have various times provided support, both moral and otherwise, include Diane Blanc, Emma Haughton, Carole Keegan, Sarah Newlands, Lande Pratt, Chen Li Vaultier and Bridget Ward. The work is also informed by an engagement with both the parochial and the global world of South London and again a large number of individuals have provided steady support, research help and a patient ear, including Susan Angoy, Jo Montgomery, Paul Maslin and Bayo Kelekun.

The work is informed by first-hand involvement in the sometimes slightly murky – but also commonly honourable – world of municipal politics and local government in the United Kingdom. In this sense there is too long a list of the many people that have taught me politics in Liverpool and London. Selectively, though, it is only fair to recognise the help and influence of, in particular, the Wapping Mafia for their robust moral and at times physical defence of things forgiven but never forgotten. Others in the East End, including Christine Gilbert, Denise Jones, Eleanor Kelly, Sunawar Ali, Ayob Ali, Ranu Miah and Hasina Zaman, are owed in different ways. Most of all there are debts and respect to Rajan Uddin Jalal, whose translation of democracy into the rule of 51 per cent at times reached an art form, and those such as Muksood Shaikh who studiously eschewed the 51 per cent of political power. And then there are both the unnamed who taught me inadvertently the horrors of violence in politics, and those nameless ones who once as friends taught so much about the working of political machines until – sadly – they got greedy and ended up on the wrong side of the law. All of this engagement has taken place in situations where acute forms of racism sit alongside moments of transcultural dialogue, communication and progressive moments of optimism. In this spirit both the volume itself and its routes emerge from a sense of the simultaneous worry and joy of the realities of multicultural urbanism and Samuel Beckett's injunction to 'fail again, fail better'.

1 Introduction

Globalisation, urbanism and cosmopolitanism fever

At the outset of the twentieth century 10 per cent of the population of the world lived in cities. In 2000 this proportion had risen to just over 50 per cent, and by 2025 the total urban population of the world is predicted to increase again in relative terms and to grow in absolute terms to a figure in excess of 5 billion worldwide.[1] These urban concentrations invariably involve flows of culture that challenge the ethical settlement of the city, become a key driver of economic change, raise massive questions about the nature of city transformation, and become the fault lines of various kinds of social division.

The process of urbanisation foregrounds encounter and contact in the metropolis. Through both the demographic movements of migration that generate the multiracial metropolis and the globalising networks of sentiment and identification that link places of residence to a transnational sensibility, the cities of the 21st century will increasingly be characterised by the challenges of multiculturalism. In this sense the analysis and dynamics of metropolitan cultural change has never been of more pressing importance for the research agenda of the social sciences. This volume attempts to conceptualise these dynamics.

It does so by framing the problems of multiculturalism within the languages of urbanism and city change. In doing so, it is consciously attempting to study culture from 'up close', but placing it within a context that is common, if not exactly universal to the challenges of multiculturalism across the globe. There has been a tendency to privilege national context (most commonly the United States or Britain in the anglophone academy), with relatively little attention paid to cross-national comparison[2] in attempts to generalise about contemporary multiculturalism. Such exceptionalism can tend to privilege the parochial. However, it is equally the case that attempts to work comparatively at an international level can alternatively privilege either that which is easily measurable or generalisations about 'racial' or 'ethnic' groupings that border on caricature or stereotypes.[3] Culture and the dynamics of cultural change demand sensitive engagement and description, frequently over extended periods of time where nuances of language and meaning not only signify but are also causally significant. The book attempts to address this by suggesting that, by placing cultural change within international contexts of city transformation and common understandings of urbanism, it is possible to 'frame' the cosmopolitan city transnationally. Debates that address the configurations of citizenship, belonging and identity (or racism, intolerance and social exclusion) may emerge through academic engagements that may be largely ethnographic in nature and rooted in specific sites, but simultaneously invite comparative analysis.

The relation between national and transnational is changing. These changes disrupt, displace and dislocate conventional models of national sovereignty. This does not mean national sovereignty is eclipsed; even within contemporary models of transnational justice the nation state remains central to both the practice and the theorising of what David Held has described as cosmopolitan democracy.[4] However, the disruptions to notions of national sovereignty create new problematisations of how we think about urbanism, and the realisation of cultural difference in patterns of residence, work and social organisation. The contemporary metropolis is consequently one key to the narratives through which twenty-first-century multiculturalism will become visible. Consequently, this volume attempts to develop a framework for analysing the specificity of particular urban settings whilst not losing sight of the routed nature of urbanism and the contingencies of forces of ethnic identity formation and racist intolerance.

Processes of globalisation have been examined across a range of disciplines, most commonly within a principally economistic frame of reference.[5] Yet in recent years – across the stakeholder communities of the cities of the world – there has been a growing recognition of the role that culture plays in determining the boundaries of political debate, driving economic transformation, structuring urban citizens' understanding of their homeplace and creating forms of social division. In this context there has been a growing fascination in the academy, in disciplines of political theory, cultural studies, anthropology, geography and sociology, with the nature and the potential of the category of the cosmopolitan.[6]

Cosmopolitanism fever

The provenance of this interest in the cosmopolitan is varied. In political theory the search for new forms of liberal government in the face of intensifying forces of economic globalisation reinvigorate a debate about the international order and the political settlement at different geographical scales of analysis below it.[7] In cultural theory and anthropology the routed nature of cultural flows reconfigures theorisations of the location of cultural production and the forms, norms and ethics of cultural creolisation.[8] Globalisation reconfigures the ethnographic locale.[9] The flows of migration frame the debate slightly differently,[10] whilst the concerns of postcolonial theory challenge both the dominant cartographies of knowledge and cultural value and the metaphors of the 'west and the rest' that are sometimes deployed to make sense of them.[11]

What such debate foregrounds is the sense in which transnational alliances and multicultural demographics reconfigure relationships between forms of social organisation and senses of unity. The degree to which new political imaginaries (at global, transnational, national, regional or metropolitan scales of analysis) are necessary under conditions of globalisation, for some might suggest the need for a *constitutional patriotism* or even what Craig Calhoun has described as a level of 'peopleness'.[12] For others the very appeal to the global creates a horizon of possibilities that transcends the limits of nationalism and appeals to what can be described as 'cosmopolitics'.[13]

All of these slightly different concerns share a routing through debates that foreground the ethical settlement of *the good society* in contexts of global flows of people, capital and values. They draw on an understanding of the times and places when languages of solidarity displace, disrupt and fracture, or reinforce, complement or amplify, languages of rights. To do so in turn demands taking seriously the spaces and the times when these languages become speakable, effective or causally significant, and the times and places when these languages are silenced. Given the epochal move towards an accelerated urbanism, this locates such debate within the contemporary city. An understanding of the dynamics of contemporary urbanism is consequently imperative for a consideration of both the potential of the cosmopolitan and its actually existing realisations.

Perhaps most importantly, such thinking points towards a reinsertion of the ethically contested nature of the cosmopolitan city in both its local and international realisations. *Locally*, the city does not merely curate the exotica of difference, it realises transnational (or global) politics in its streets and neighbourhoods, and reveals the contested and limited nature of the national settlement in its schoolrooms and town halls. Likewise, the nature of the local settlement of the multicultural highlights the limits of various sovereignties that stretch from the domestic arrangements of marriage through the public arenas of education to the welfare state rights of migrant minorities and the relatives of second- and third-generation diaspora communities.

Internationally, as Chetan Bhatt and Amy Chua[14] have pointed out, geopolitical realities (rarely discussed) undermine both casual theorisation of 'the west and the rest' and sloppy descriptions of the curatorial metropolis of difference. Transnational political traces inhabit the cultures of diaspora populations of the contemporary metropolis. For Bhatt the tensions of the BJP's incipient nationalism stray into the second- and third-generation politics of migrant communities from India. The routed traces of American and Saudi money underscore some forms of transnational Wahhabi radicalisation and international responses to it. For Chua the privileged positions of ethnic or migrant minorities within the crony capitalisms of South-East Asia or the post-communist world of Iron Curtain nations creates explosive tensions between democracy, ethnic hatred and economic transition. Majority rule and ethnicised minority affluence sit uneasily alongside one another. Similarly, the contemporary realisations of politics in Central America and postcolonial regimes in Africa play directly to the flows of migration in Europe and North America, cutting across the sometime spurious distinctions of refugee movements and economic migrants. The temporalities and spatialities of the postcolonial consequently disrupt a transparent understanding of time and space through the legacies of old empire in the crevices of the city and the architectures of city power in the structuring of 'progress'.[15] The metaphor of the new empire refigures both the theorisation of the global and the explanations of forms of twenty-first-century intervention in Afghanistan and Iraq.[16]

The cosmopolitan city?

Although the city marks the most intense points of transnational collisions of culture and demography produced by globalising change, the loosely convened interdisciplinary field of urban studies has been relatively slow to consider the problems of cosmopolitanism. This is interesting, because in a search for alternative geographical scales of analysis, in a world where the nation state is at least weakened, the city is commonly invoked as an alternative register of political analysis. This is most prominent in discussions that consider the ethical challenge cosmopolitanism raises for social organisation and political action.[17]

Because transnational and global flows bring together very different ways of thinking, value and self-organisation, a notion of ethical contest is central to conceptualising the cosmopolitan, but also to a description of the forms of cultural encounter that characterise the cities of the twenty-first century. Yet in contemporary human sciences both the *ethical* and the *cultural* are two of the most contested terms in the vocabulary of the academy.

If we accept that the banal demography of global city change brings together both different peoples and different cultures, the challenge of cosmopolitan cities will inevitably become one that is simultaneously about both values and analytical rigour. In this sense the city is made visible through an analytic lens of the academic that may not only consider the political economy of migration, but also either erase or privilege the markers of minor difference triggered by processes of migration. A focus on religious practice, lifestyle, taste, sexuality, diasporic sentiment, community organisation, cuisine, aesthetic and cultural production and reproduction foregrounds certain kinds of difference. This process of making visible is a relation of power, as it is likewise when precisely the same differences are either stigmatised or erased in languages and practices of intolerance and racism.[18]

Hence for Jacques Derrida, when we consider the cosmopolitan future, 'ethics is hospitality' and is linked to the notions of the state after the end of sovereignty, and is tied explicitly to the future of the city after globalisation.[19] Consequently, whilst globalisation promotes multicultural diversity, multicultural diversity brings with it a debate about the contesting of the social and political settlement of the city that runs throughout the chapters of this volume.

In this sense the book is not straightforwardly demographic. It takes as a first starting point that races, ethnicities and identities cannot be taken for granted as objects to be studied, precisely because the meanings of race, ethnicity and identity are context-dependent. A language of ethnicity privileges processes of collective identity formation. A language of race foregrounds the manner in which visible and cultural differences are recognised as source of both stigma and collective rights. The book takes as a second starting point that the urban is similarly empirically straightforward but conceptually chimeric. Concentrations of settlement in the metropolis bring to the fore challenges about the manner in which we think about, regulate and conceptualise the metropolis itself.

Such a stance foregrounds the relationship between empirical research that engages with the rapidly changing flux of the city and the theoretical apparatus that is used to make sense of this flux. This book attempts to address concerns that transcend the single city but are distinctive features of contemporary urbanism. In doing so it is necessary to conceptualise the particular relationship between empirical specificity, categoric generalisation and social and cultural theory. The spirit in which it is written attempts to combine a Chicago School commitment to the city's empirical detail with a Frankfurt School commitment to the notion of critique.[20] The book argues for the necessity of combining deep empirical engagement with the material objects of city cultures with an awareness of the situation of such *objets trouvés* within the systems of cataloguing and taxonomising that is the nature of academic research.

In this sense the book draws on a sense of perennial wonder at the ability of the contemporary city to generate new forms of social organisation, new forms of cultural expression that draw on forms of global connection and local expression. Such a wonder demands an academic engagement with the empirical complexity and political creativity of the manner in which individuals and groups shape the frequently invisible spaces of the city. The rapidly accelerated pace of twenty-first-century city change provides what Pierre Bourdieu represented as a multiplicity of forms of *bodily hexis*: certain styles and forms of life mediated by culture within the city. The *habitus* of cultural forms in the contemporary city is consequently plural-ised at a rate of change that can defy academic categorisation and generalisation. In this sense the book argues that we should be suspicious of an analytical approach that privileges the chronological ordering of city life. The notion that space might be *authored* by time is potentially undermined by an analytical focus that recognises as well the different temporalities of the spaces of contemporary urbanism. A study of the spaces of the city might generate different chronologies simultaneously present within the flux of urbanism. Such a stance leads to an examination of the two starting points of the volume and the research that informs the substance of subsequent chapters.

Starting point 1. Race thinking and the city: the mimetic nature of cultural difference and racism

This book is written against a notion that leaves culture as a mere residual effect of the great forces of capitalist modernity, against a notion that underplays the significance of socially constructed divisions. But it is also written against the sort of analytical perspective that, by studying the object of cultural difference bound up in the concept of the multicultural city, turns that object into a thing in itself.

In this sense a key theme that echoes throughout the chapters of this book is the process of iteration, a notion that ethnic specificity and cultural difference are invariably on the move. What is seen at the heart of processes of race making and race thinking is the process of mimesis, a process that in principle has no beginning and no end. It involves an endless iteration between identification and categor-isation, commonalities casting themselves as differences, different trajectories becoming visible and then disappearing.

Common sense might suggest to us that if the experience of multiculture is common to the world then it should be possible in a laboratory-like fashion to compare the different experiences of cosmopolitanism that define the contemporary nations of the world.[21] Yet such a model would suggest a notion of firm demographic units coming into contact with receiving societies where the relative paths of success and failure, assimilation and rejection, model and stigma, might be tracked back historically and geographically to be explained analytically in terms of a quasi-chemical relationship between the variables of migrant culture and receiving societies. Such a logic generally takes a notion of assimilation as (explicitly or implicitly) teleological – an end point of the social processes of migration.

In contrast, this volume takes as a starting point the notion that demography is more fragile than this. It also suggests that in the spirit of critical theory the temporal and the spatial constitution of city life are themselves subject to analytical scrutiny.[22] Consequently, throughout the volume I explore the tensions between languages of belonging and forces of power that make racial subjects visible. The city is commonly crucial to the mediation of such tensions. The forms of collective identity and the fabrication of racial subjects (or *subjectification*) that result are not necessarily commensurable one with another in any particular setting. But their incommensurabilities are mediated by the settings within specific patterns of labour demand and residential settlement.

The book questions efforts to generalise from the experiences of migrant minorities in the increasingly multicultural cities of the world. It is a book that attempts to suggest a slightly different understanding of the purpose of both theoretical labour and empirical investigation, whilst valorising the significance of both analytical debate and extended empirical engagement with the perplexing and contradictory realities of contemporary multicultural urbanism. It is also a volume that, through assuming the centrality of notions of intentionality, power and meaning, demands a fundamentally interpretative understanding of the cultural manifestations of ethnic and racial difference. Such difference may be causally rooted in forms of material exploitation, political subordination or voluntaristic articulation, but is invariably mediated by structures of sensibility and representation that demand a qualitative understanding of the nature of contemporary multiculture.

We are invariably talking of the choreography of the 'mirror dance'. If we choose to look we shall find. The attribution of causal significance to differences we find must be justified.[23] Ethnic categories can conceal the nature of their fabrication. A debate has consequently long raged as to the alternative powers of explanation given to conceptual categories of race and ethnicity.[24] What such debates can conceal is the banal truth that alternative collective identities may be simultaneously relevant in different contexts for different realisations of city life.

One example can be taken from the traumatised vocabularies that are used to describe the experiences of diasporic communities that moved from the Caribbean to Britain – largely, though far from completely – in the post-1945 era of migrant labour demand that was common to the economic expansions of the industrial north of Europe and North America. Variously described in academic and political debate as black, West Indian, Afro-Caribbean, African Caribbean and black

British the categoric challenge of the vocabulary invariably offends some, distorts the complexity of Caribbean pluralism, excludes others unthinkingly and may conceal a simpler truth. In London differences between Barbados, Jamaica, Guyana and the smaller islands are meaningful historically in determining the temporalities of chain migration to the (almost) postcolonial cities of Britain. They are meaningful geographically in describing patterns of residential settlement within the city. There are also some minor differences that at times have less concrete roots but become significant within the circuits of rumour and gossip. The particular nature of the Cheddi Jagan/Forbes Burnham masque in postwar Guyana is said sometimes to have led to a different class profile of Guyanese migrants to Britain than the predominantly less affluent settings from which many Jamaicans came to the country. Such changes are sometimes held up anecdotally or analytically as causally significant in the differences in achievement between first-, second- or third-generation migrants from the islands, even if they were constitutively absent in the scopic regimes that informed police stop-and-search practices at the same time. The legacies of island identities differ from the forms of political solidarity forged in the face of forms of British postwar racism. They do not compete in a mercantilist identity politics sum whereby the strengthening of one form of identification necessarily detracts from another.

For the coordinates of British racism in the middle decades of the twentieth century had little space for the narcissism of such minor, minor differences. The creation of a subject position of blackness within the great Fordist industrial apparatuses of collective consumption in social housing, in state-controlled education and – perhaps most significantly of all – in the criminal justice system had no time to discriminate between such niceties. The mechanisms of institutional racism are specific and worthy of study within each historical context, but overwhelmingly throughout the latter half of the twentieth century *blackness* becomes central to the figuring of the racist imagination and the mundane realities of everyday racist practice in restricting access to welfare services, in underachievement in schools and the spiralling antagonism with the police. Yet this category of blackness – even in the eyes of the powerful institutions – is seen to map uneasily into the ethnic pluralities of the contact zones of the cities. It both works and does not work to explain the experiences of other migrant minorities in the United Kingdom – Irish, Jewish, Maltese, Chinese, Italian, Punjabi, Sylheti. All occasionally are bracketed within singular analytical understandings of British racism and then do not quite fit.

In this context one analytical problem is straightforward and echoes the dilemma of Northrop Frye's critic concerned to place what interests him most into a causal relationship with what interests him least. Intra- or inter-ethnic difference may be significant in some places and at some times in connection with some things. Yet whilst to erase the cultural differences of class and geography between different strands of migration from the West Indies to the United Kingdom is problematic, to place such differences into specific causal relations is potentially analytically spurious and commonly politically dangerous.

A similar reading can be traced through almost any migrant experience to almost any city of the world. From the difference between West End and East End Jews in the London of the turn of the nineteenth/twentieth centuries, to the different migration streams that moved to Karachi after the Partition of India in 1948, to the massive variations bound up in the notion of 'Latino' or Hispanic migration to the cities of North America, the tension between commonalities of origin and cultural specificity are invariably set against the institutional and ideological framing of the migrant within the 'receiving' cities and nations.

The categories of intolerance and bigotry are also inverted and translated into forms of identification and solidarity. 'Black' and 'nigger' are reappropriated; Banglatown is turned from an abusive stigma of East London's ghetto to a celebration of placed ethnicity. In the United Kingdom the political category of blackness consequently becomes both a rallying cry of the 1970s and 1980s and an object of critique in the ethnic plurality of the 1990s onwards. In the USA Stokeley Carmichael's invocation of institutional racism and the civil rights struggle for affirmative action results decades on in struggle over the definition of the categories of ethnic subject worthy of recognition within such systems of minority privilege.[25] Invariably ethnic and racial categorisation sits alongside the play of identity politics in specific contexts.

Moreover, the terms of the dialogue between the pieces of the multicultural mosaic produces a new set of dilemmas, from the categoric uncertainties of the 'mixed race' or 'multiple heritage' experience to the forms of cultural exchange that result in newness emerging in the crucibles of the city.[26] The forms of politics that crosses North American unionism with Mexican cultural networks is celebrated in Ken Loach's 1999 film *Bread and Roses*; the politics of multiculture are espoused in the music that draws together global routes through expressive syncretism. In the United Kingdom bands such as Joi, Fundamental and Asian Dub Foundation draw together Indian bhangra and Afro-Caribbean takes on African-American expressive cultures that are themselves subject to complex geographical genealogies that reinscribe the Caribbean in their lineage.[27] Apache Indian becomes a star in India as well as in his native Birmingham (United Kingdom), in part through an alliance with African-Caribbean reggae star Maxi Priest.[28] Such models set precedents for neologisms of cosmopolitan wordplay, as 'ragamuffin' translates into *bhangramuffin* to *banglamuffin*; the bricolage of cultural exchange can be both politically powerful in drawing together groups of many different backgrounds and ethically nugatory in the promotion of a sloppy feel-good rhetoric of melting-pot harmony.[29] Such hybridities are exemplary of the 'way newness comes into the world'[30] but also exemplary of the way that cultural differences themselves at the heart of the multicultural city are consistently changing. Multiculturalism is consequently taken throughout this volume not as a municipal project of the 1970s but as a challenge to the ethical settlement of the city and a product of cultural globalisation that involves demographic movements of migration and cultural networks of transnational sentiment.[31]

Yet, as with the minor or major differences between migrant flows, the causal significance of such processes of creolisation and hybridisation must be considered in detail rather than asserted arbitrarily. At the heart of this volume is the simple understanding that cultures invariably change through time and space. The pace of change may vary between one historical moment and another. The degree of difference is not (as Robert Park once famously suggested) a direct correlate of spatial proximity. Jewish communities in the diasporic setting of late nineteenth-century London maintained loyalties and sentiments that tied them simultaneously to the Pale and to the East End.[32] They maintained a sense of citizenship that was simultaneously highly local and powerfully global in its reach.

So in part the process of iteration between the recognition of metropolitan institutions and forms of collective identification is one that has invariably characterised the migrant experience, whether we are talking about single migration from Ireland and Scotland to parts of Tudor London, or the mass movements of the twentieth century; whether we are talking about the new migrations of US twenty-first-century post-Fordism or the twice migrant African-American settlement of the cities of the USA that was traced on the historicity of the middle passage. In each case a demographic flow carries the traces of its own history and its own translation into the newly produced spaces of the city.

Through particular institutional contexts both racial difference and multiculture are imprinted in particular ways on the geography of the city of settlement. The *historicity* of the former and the *spatiality* of the latter become the focus of attention of the governing gaze of the city. And so the mirror dance begins, between the expectations of the institutions of the urban system and the strategies, tactics, successes and failures of the migrant minorities of first, second and subsequent generations. This process has been at the heart of every city characterised by migration.

Sometimes such histories are made visible; at other times they are not. The fact that London can be narrated as a succession of migrant flows and settlements has only relatively recently been acknowledged. The banishing of Danes to an area of London east of the River Lee by King Alfred, the segregation of Welsh, Scots and Irish in the medieval metropolis, and the antagonism between a Saxon city state and the contested legitimacy of the Norman nation throughout the long reign of Henry III, are just some of the moments of history that are rarely rendered visible through a lens of ethnic and racial studies. Colonial echoes disrupt the notion of historical progress through homogeneous, empty time or a spatial science of the metropolis as much in London as in Delhi.

Consequently race-making sits between historically complex demographic trajectories and highly spurious systems of categorisation. Temporalities and spatialities are consequently not just the context of these processes, they are instead a constitutive feature of them. As cultures, identities and forms of political subjectivity are transformed, the nature of the multicultural changes likewise.

International comparison

There is a paradox here that speaks to the paradigmatic heart of this volume. If the broad conditions of multiculturalism and globalising urbanisation tend to the universal, it might be thought to create the ideal comparative framing. Multicultural urbanism might be compared on a spectrum of the world's cities test case by test case. But, as we have already explored, malleable demography and the cultural routes of the city lexicon complicate this. In the spirit of critical theory and at the heart of our problem, the subjects that we examine – ethnicity, urbanism, collective identities, forms of government – and the metropolitan time-spaces in which they are realised share familial similarities and differences but are quite literally not the same 'things' at different times and places.[33] Capitalist evolution, colonial and postcolonial legacies haunt the present and infest the spaces of the city, but in turn these metropolitan time-spaces are not merely produced, they also mediate analysis itself.

Consequently, Chapters 2 and 3 of this book attempt to provide a conceptual framing for the volume as a whole through the argument that the spatialisation of urban cultures in particular places at specific times is central to an understanding of the manner in which cities mediate the cosmopolitan. This does not diminish the value of international comparison at all, but it does change the register in which it is developed. Straightforwardly, quantitative analyses of migrant minorities in specific cities across the world may be helpful as elementary description but will not be able to consider the fact that the subjects being dealt with are quite literally different across the world. Cultural formations of Jamaican diaspora communities in New York are distinct from those in London because the regimes of power and the trajectories of solidarity under which such a collective sense (or absence) of ethnic identity becomes visible or causally significant are quite straightforwardly different in the two locations. Consequently international comparison must look for a 'toolkit of concepts for conducting inquiries into the contemporary world'[34] in understanding a history of the cosmopolitan present rather than assume it is possible to stand a rainbow comparison of migratory experiences one alongside another.

The configuration of the city consequently becomes a constitutive part of how we come to think of metropolitan multiculture. Chapters in the book consider how the street, the ghetto, the *banlieue* and the cultural quarter make visible very different sorts of urbanism and very different sorts of multiculturalism. Similarly, spaces of the city mediate demographic categorisation. Though rarely acknowledged, the demography of most of the major metropolises of the twenty-first century is in large part a product of migration. These migrations can come from the same country (like the migrant growth of the first industrial metropolises) or they may bring folk from across the globe to a New York or to a Hong Kong.

The categoric certainties of this demography may appear to offer an alternative register of a kind. The transnational movements are locked into patterns of urban residence and city labour markets, creating the classic patterning of jobs, homes and power marked by the mosaic of multiculturalism. But the city variously accommodates, assimilates or stigmatises these racialised patterns through its form. The multicultural city mosaic (of Shanghai or Karachi or Bombay as much as London or Chicago or Sydney) is classically subjected to the institutional logics of the melting pot and the reproduction of segregation and the ghetto. But both the exigencies of exogamy and the more prosaic realities of cultural flows that subvert ethnic boundary markers disrupt such narratives. The hybrid forms of multi-culture and the increasingly hyphenated forms of demographic mixing challenge a rubric that makes the city visible as a competing arena of ethnic cultures precisely because these cultures do not stand still to be photographed, analysed and measured.

So we search for a vocabulary that captures the changing cartography of the multicultural city. We are aware that the very act of description potentially ossifies, and so such a vocabulary needs to be careful about its categoric forms. And we are aware that we write in the shadow of all the other people that have written about cities and about multiculturalism and the processes of race making that has even created its own subdiscipline of studies of *race relations*:[35] so much in the shadows that the deep meanings that attach themselves to the shape of the city and the lexicon of urbanism form part of our cultural present. An urban sensibility structures the very act of writing about the city.

In this sense, in social policy terms we need to understand how multiculture is made problematic in urban policy and other social policy languages and the occasions and the reasons when it is not. Even in the official statistics that probably underenumerated migrant flows, London accommodated an increase in its population of almost a million between 1991 and 2001. This passed almost without comment in the decade in which it happened, but rapidly became a major topic of concern in the early twenty-first century.[36] How much was this due to the high proportions of Canadians, Americans, Australians and South Africans (re)settling in the city and who bore the markers of a certain kind of whiteness? But how much also was this caused by the sense in which many of the migrations of Lithuanians, Muscovites and refugees from international traumas in the Balkans and the Horn of Africa were rendered invisible by the spaces of the city?

What is undisputable is that we are confronted by a situation in which the certainties of academic disciplines, which take (often implicitly) the nation state as the principal building block of 'sociologies' or histories or politics or cultural anthropologies, are challenged by the messiness of the contemporary city. The social organisation of city resources may sit like a babushka doll within neat hierarchies of central, regional and local state power, but flows of culture, capital and population subvert such taxonomies. This leads to the second starting point of the volume. What is argued here is that the very vocabularies that are used to capture these new realities confront some very old problems within the loose array of writing and thought that we might call *urbanism*.

Starting point 2. The moralities, perspectives and implications of languages of urban studies

The diagnostic typologies and everyday maps through which we make sense of the city are culturally produced. The city phenomena under academic scrutiny therefore are subject to both cultural inflection and material empirical change. The ghetto and the street bear the traces of medieval Venice and Periclean Athens in their genesis, but they are also witness to specifically twenty-first-century forms of capitalist restructuring. A sophisticated understanding of the contemporary metropolis consequently demands both empirical awareness of its novelties and a self-consciousness about the historical traces and theoretical burdens that infest the vocabulary of urbanisms through which consideration of the city is rationalised. Such a reconciliation implies that any understanding of the city demands a process of continual perspectival movement. Straightforwardly, the economic and cultural logics of the dynamics of the urban are not reducible one to another. We need to consider the manner in which the city structures narratives of economic globalisation, ecological sustainability and structures of power.[37]

Such an approach demands a consideration of how the city itself is made visible as an object of academic research: through statistical deconstruction, cartographies of power and anthropological exploration. These different approaches (or *method-ologies*) tend to be identified with different subdisciplines in the human sciences, but more significantly draw on different technologies of measurement and observation to consider the metropolis. In some cultural theory the academic practice of leading urbanists is consequently criticised for its perspectival privileging of a particular view. Rosalyn Deutsche once famously critiqued the work of Ed Soja and David Harvey for the framing of the problem of the city that she suggested privileged critical distance. She suggested that a phallocentric objectification of the city could be traced to the notion of the all-powerful expert trying to explain the totality of the dynamics of metropolitan life by creating an analytical object of the urban that could be apprehended, rationalised and explained.[38] In a debate around urban poverty revisited later in this volume, Loïc Wacquant has similarly criticised both the putatively naively empirical perspective of the close-up ethno-graphers of city poverty and the beguiling certainties of statistical distance used to measure immiseration.

In this sense this volume argues that it is essential to consider the technologies through which city space itself is analysed, how both perspectives and narratives of the city are produced. Chapters consequently examine this phenomenon in terms of different technologies of representation: from the graffiti tag to the thick description to the state plan. This process does not privilege either the aerial view from the helicopter of objectivity that (metaphorically) flies above the city or the heroic everyday tactics or cramped spaces of the ethnographically particular cultures of the urban. Inspection up close in empirical engagement and then from a distance validates the multiplicity of perspectives through which cultural forms of the city are made visible. Speaking to the pressing concerns that surround the moral, social and economic organisation of the city demands an awareness of the vocabulary of social reproduction. The production of the spaces of the city involves both the transformation of forms of residence that draw on both the taxonomy and cultural history of dwelling.[39] Squat, hut, flat, tenement, housing estate, detached house, apartment, bungalow, brownstone, slum, *banlieue*, favela, suburb, loft. All these terms both describe a generalised form and invoke a cultural history that is normatively loaded and in some very specific senses inescapable.[40] In Chapter 2 of this volume, the manner in which the roots of thinking about both cultural difference and city life inflect our consideration of each is considered in slightly more detail to suggest an alternative way of conceptualising the multi-cultural city.

The volume attempts to argue throughout that the spaces of the city are in this sense commonly both plural in their realisation and at times invoked fallaciously to resolve particular kinds of academic debate that have immediate consequences for policy élites and political activists alike. The street, the ghetto and the cultural quarter can sometimes be the object of academic scrutiny, but at other times are invoked as self-evident empirical realities that as subjects verify particular debates about the changing nature of twenty-first-century urbanism. Understanding the nature of the cosmopolitan city (and hence the nature of contemporary urbanism) consequently demands a double act of academic scrutiny.

From one perspective the realities of everyday life demand an ever vigilant engagement from 'up close' with the empirical realities of city life. In the empirically substantive material drawn on for this volume such work most often implies an ethnographic engagement, and many sections of the book are derived from different research exercises based on ethnographies in the city over the last 20 years. But alongside a commitment to an empirical scrutiny of the present is a sense that the values of critical distance demand an understanding of both the histories of these forms of the present and an ability to stand back from these realities. This is not merely to make their familiarity strange (as in the best ethnographic practice). Alongside such ethnographic defamiliarisation it is imperative to contextualise such particularities against the broader settings of demographic, economic and global change. In this sense the book argues that the spaces of the city (as much as any other analytical form) warrant a consideration of their genesis. This implies that any consideration of the analytical settings of the city demand a genealogical understanding of what the volume regularly describes as the *lexicon of urbanism*. Such genealogies have become common to forms of humanities and social science research that are suspicious of the analytical tools that are used to make sense of the social world. In the context of this volume, the double act of scrutiny implies a reading of the interdisciplinary understanding of urbanism that always has a sense of what Charles Taylor has described as the perspicuous contrast at the heart of scholarly investigation.[41]

Social policy and the multicultural city

The volume is informed by a belief in the cross-fertilisation of academic and civil debate. It attempts to address the problems of living together in conditions of multicultural urbanism. Consequently, it is written from a position that sees the multiculturalism of the cities of the twenty-first century as both demographically inevitable and politically challenging.[42] Ethically we need to consider what it means to live in cities that are constituted by communities that may be the products of both different histories and histories of differences that bear the imprint of colonialism, slavery and domination. We need to recognise also that such communities may be constituted through globalised networks of sentiment and allegiance. Just as the economic drivers of contemporary capitalist globalisation challenge the sovereignty of the nation state, the flows of labour as well as capital creates transnational networks of culture and people.

Across the world the city provides a privileged arena in which such challenges are realised. Consequently, the volume is also written from a position which believes that an engagement with the structures of government is inevitable. There is a tendency in some literatures (from both the left and the right of the political spectrum) to romanticise the world beyond the boundaries of the state and to promote the virtues of civil society and community mobilisation. In Chapter 3 the book argues that it is important to understand that such civil society forms are framed within regimes of governmental power and that such romance might limit rather than progress our movement towards cosmopolis.[43]

In the allure of the contemporary global city, cosmopolitanism, diversity and difference shimmer for a moment. Racism, nationalism, ethnic cleansing and xenophobia return as urban nightmares. Indeed, the challenge of discussions that link urbanism to race, multiculture and forms and norms of intolerance is that both the subject (the city) and the object (multiculture) of debate keep on disappearing before our eyes, only to resurface in different forms.

The city appears so solid until we look for its boundaries. The streets appear to offer certainty until we find the beach beneath the cobblestones, the secret narratives of the hidden spaces of private lives and alternative public spheres of association and dissent. When history is the voice of the powerful, geography is the prerogative of both the explorer and the mapmaker. We do not always wish to take such voices and such cartographies for granted. The chronology of a Sydney or a London appears to offer the reassurance of a historical ordering of things. This happened and then that. Until you realise that, as Peter Ackroyd has described with the capital of the United Kingdom and Peter Carey with Sydney, the city has a biography that suffers always from the unreliable and imperfect flaws of the narrator.[44] In contrast the historiography of the city tells us how chronology has been used to make sense of the city and that *histories* are normally written by the winners, the voices of the dispossessed relegated to the marginalia.

Specifically, we need a new heuristic compass with which to navigate the contemporary city and inform social policy debates. Historically, we might place cities research and the interdisciplinary field of urban studies on a spectrum that crosses the west–east between what might be described as *conventional* and *critical* literatures. Conventional urban studies approaches tend to reify the social and economic order of the city (and strive to maximise its functionality and optimise its working form). Critical analysis, in contrast, seeks to undermine this naturalised ordering of buildings and people (and expose their patterned artifice as inscriptions of injustice and reified inequalities of power and capital).

The phenomenon of patterns of residential settlement and cognate debates around gentrification exemplify this contrast between the conventional and the critical. Critical struggles to reduce the processes of gentrification to the Ricardian rent curve vie with a boosterist urbanism that narrates the city as a site of consumption and measures successful growth precisely in terms of enhanced capital valorisation of residential preferences in the new districts of Jerusalem, Los

Angeles or Paris. But such a spectrum is necessarily two-dimensional in nature. It cannot adapt to the transnational challenge of globalisation and the ethical challenge of multiculture.

To do so demands insertion of a second spectrum into both urban studies academic debates and public concern with the future of the multiculture of globalising cities. It is fundamentally a product of moral philosophy and it challenges both economistic and cultural readings of the urban. It runs north–south between communitarian and liberal traces of moral philosophy but it is realised in the cities of multiculture in ferocious debates that our west–east spectrum cannot locate.

The spectrum creates a tension between the strange and the familiar and relates particularly to how we come to know the city and how we valorise either its *knowability* or its *anonymity*. The city has long been a site in which newness comes into the world. It has historically been the crucible of economic, political and cultural change precisely because old values and old orderings are disrupted by the tumult of city life. This produces the quintessentially urban horrors of populist fanaticism, as well as the metropolitan potential for Enlightenment critique. The city is consequently paradoxically or ambivalently located between these tensions. The sites of the city that display the most intense forms of intolerance are commonly also those that demonstrate the potential for the most intimate forms of cultural dialogue.

We need to recognise that the polar north and related points east, west and south provide a compass *for* but not a road map *towards* the good city. They identify a constitutive tension in the ordering of city life that sits agonistically within its frame. The additional ('north–south') dimension speaks to some of the fundamental tensions in moral philosophy, but it also resonates within cartographies of contemporary multiculturalism. Significantly, the choreography of the debates within contemporary moral philosophy and those in multiculture are homologous with longstanding arguments around how we consider the ethical markings of the spaces of the city.[45] Unless we understand how the city draws together, displaces and explodes these tensions, we will continue to misrepresent the challenges multiculturalism poses to an understanding of contemporary urbanism. Most significantly of all, such tensions speak directly both to the social policy questions that figure how we might organise the multicultural city and also to the academic questions that address how we might know it. These tensions are explored in much greater detail in the concluding chapter of the volume, which considers the degree to which it is possible to plan the future of the multicultural metropolis.

At one extreme the city has commonly welcomed *the strange* and the *unknowable*. The migrant, the refugee, the newly arrived or the post-contact indigenous cultures of the postcolonial metropolis potentially see the city differently. Seeing the niche market or the scope to innovate, as well as challenging the received wisdoms and ascendant hierarchies of power, the arrival of new people and migrant groups in the city potentially renews its lifeblood. The discursively ephemeral may suddenly become symbolically central. The hidden histories of colonialism and empire, slavery and suppression of native peoples, may resurface from their cells in the subconscious of the city. But they do not do so straightforwardly.

In contrast, the communitarian sense of the *familiar* unit of the ethically *knowable* and the moral legitimacy of the neighbourhood speak directly to debates that confuse the west–east typologies of what might conventionally be described as reactionary (coded as politically *right*) and progressive (coded as politically *left*) urbanisms. The sets of values that privilege the speaking positions of minoritarian voices may rapidly have to defend the ground on which their claims are being made. The right to police arrivals in such a (real or metaphoric) neighbourhood challenges such speaking authority. This speaks directly to urban policy concerns in terms of property rights, gender relations, schooling, visible sexualities, the control of subsidised rental residence (through state or social landlord provision) and the rights of cultural recognition in the market place of employment law and practice. It speaks indirectly to a debate about the relationships between rights discourses, state formations and transnational claims and enforcement.[46] The liberal indifference to the markers of identity likewise speaks directly to the rights to avoid discrimination, racial harassment and the symbolic and real violence of cultural intolerance. Crudely, our compass is complicated by this new spectrum. We can see both a right-wing and a left-wing communitarianism in the multi-cultural cities of the twenty-first century. The right of neighbourhoods to be turned into Business Improvement Districts and police themselves, and the right of local communities to take self-governing actions against the homeless, the anti-social and the badly behaved appeal to the traditional constituencies of the right. The sense of community grassroots organisation against property capital, protests against road extensions, building on green land and school closures speaks to the traditional agendas of the left. *Both* are communitarian in *both* their moral stance and their invoked urbanisms. They share ethical roots but differ significantly in their city visions and political routes.

But equally the right to be freed from state restrictions against wearing particular clothes or to exercise personal religious preference and the right to limit the state's power to arbitrary violence and to police the spaces of the city tend to be celebrated likewise on the left. Yet alternative strictures that limit state interference in the markets that structure the spatial realisations of Ricardian rent curves, the imperatives of global capitalism or government interference in market relations speak to a liberalism that few on the left would identify as their own. A strong suspicion of state action is at times shared by both left and the right of the political spectrum when defining *la droit de la ville*. Straightforwardly this cautions us to be more careful with our vocabulary. There is a liberalism of the left and of the right. Neo-conservatism is not necessarily best identified as neo-liberal, and cannot be subsumed in catch-all notions such as the revanchist city when we are identifying the enemies of progressive urbanism.

The extra dimension of this moral compass becomes more not less complicated by the realities of city multiculturalism across the twenty-first-century globe. Recognitions of the rights of indigenous and native peoples and migrant minorities sit squarely within the fourfold tensions of critical urbanism, functional city building, communitarian valorisation and stigma and the problem of liberal government. It does not always sit easily. The case in favour of migration for the benefits of the economy of the city plays against reactionary debates on the threats of migration to constructions of solidarity. They speak also to more complex debates about which cultural rights of migrant minorities should be recognised and which suppressed by the governance structures of the well-run city.

These are traced through the way that economic and social change are realised and managed in the city. But equally significantly the extra dimension of the north–south of our compass is complicated yet further by the dimensionalities of urban space and city temporalities. Can the rights of recognition of Islamic schools in twenty-first-century London, Paris or Brisbane be spoken about in the same register that gave church schools state recognition of Jesuit education in England or in the deep-rooted, Enlightenment-inspired anticlerical voice of nineteenth-century France? How does this anticlerical voice contextualise the francophone debate around the veil in contradistinction to models of education in the USA or England? Are the sites that are cherished as migratory zones of transition – metaphorical Ellis Islands of multiculture – to be naturalised for these processes of change or analysed for their contingency. The East End of London is sometimes spoken of in these terms. For some it has always (always is such a plastic adverb) been the site where migrant minorities arrive in London and then move on again. There is a sense of it as a space of *the changing same*.[47] Reassuring narratives of assimilatory tolerance follow each other in centuries-old succession and frame our understanding of the space itself and its setting within the city. But how does such fleeting transition sit with the aggressive gentrification of the same city spaces in the late twentieth century? Alternative narratives would render the spaces of today's East End visible as the logical frontier of capital appropriation, even as scholars such as Neil Smith have long taught us to be careful about the deployment of the metaphor of the frontier itself. Such questions are central to an interrogation of the multicultural metropolis of the twenty-first century.

Otherness, the urban and the language of the contact zone

In one sense all cities are reducible to their functions of governance and their economies of scale and scope. These two themes have one thing in common. They involve worlds and relations that exist beyond the boundaries of the city itself. The relations of territory that in part define relations of governance and forms of mercantile exchange, which by definition are related to market relations that cross time and space, both presume a relation between the city and something else. In this sense the city is always more than itself; there is a constitutive 'outside' to its definition that is present even in its absence.

Similarly, the language through which collective identities are identified is constitutively important in defining an ethnic or racial boundary, excluding what lies beyond the boundary of difference. Writing on issues of race, multiculture and ethnicity often struggles to avoid the injustices through which its categoric objects of study emerge. In the context of the contemporary city a major ethical dimension is quite properly unavoidable in discussion of the roots of multicultural diversity. However, such ethics are not always as straightforward as they might appear.

As we have seen, both the markers and the language of ethnic difference are subject to endless reinvention and redeployment in the realisation of such theoretical debate in contemporary social and political contexts. In short, a political debate about race and ethnicity is precisely about where and when markers of ethnic difference should be rendered invisible and when they should or should not be actively highlighted. Paradoxically, the struggle for visibility may in a moment rest either on an implicit call for invisibility or a specific cry for acknowledgement of particularism. Such a debate points to a questioning of the manner in which, in *specific* social and political contexts and through *specific* historical narratives, markers of race, ethnicity and cultural difference are rendered speakable, visible and recognisable as categories marked with *specific* ethical values.

Notions of 'race' and 'ethnicity' are themselves analytical categories that have been produced within the dominant strands of western thought. They are traced with the binary distinctions between private and public, individual and collective, community and citizenship, rationality and sentiment, that emanate from the roots of conventional political theory. More pointedly, as Barnor Hesse has regularly pointed out, the dominant strands of thinking through categories of race and ethnicity have been made visible as narratives of colonial encounters with subjugated peoples.[48] Consequently, particular strands of 'race thinking', or what Paul Gilroy has described as 'raciology', have become visible in specific imperial spaces and times. The historical specificity of analysis of ethnicity stresses that particular regimes of representation make visible ethnic difference in relation to broader structures of power. At its most prosaic, the 'race thinking' of colonial slavery is linked but distinct from the race thinking of nineteenth- and early twentieth-century imperialisms which is distinctive but connected to the racialised domination of late twentieth-century capitalisms.

As David Goldberg convincingly demonstrates, we need to consider the manner in which racial or ethnic difference is situated within specific power relations that validate some characteristics of particularity and denigrate others. Almost self-evidently the movement between slavery and citizenship in Imperial Rome was not identical in conferring rights on individuals or groups as the transition of the post-bellum nineteenth-century Deep South of the USA. Rights, recognition and discrimination are configured in patterns that are historically and geographically specific.[49] But, of equal significance, both history and geography provide standard narrative structures through which the reproduction of inequalities are naturalised. The inevitability of migrant arrivals 'catching up' with host majorities and the struggle for 'recognition' of specific community rights provide strong thematics in discussions of multicultural societies that privilege an almost evolutionary theory of change.

In short, if ethnic difference is significant (causally, politically, culturally) in this situation, but not at that time and place, if both temporality and spatiality are inscribed within the subject positions of race thinking, race ascription and 'raciology', then it suggests that it might be important to examine in a little more detail the manner in which context becomes a constitutive feature of the multicultural question. And the site in which such questions of context come so profoundly to the fore is the contemporary city. The city is represented as a site of cultural dialogue, fusion and hybridity in expressive cultures of syncretised contemporary music, arts, literature and sport, and also provides the arena through which such transformations are negotiated, staged and developed. It can be the crucible of conflict and also turn iniquities of racial injustice into the brick and stone of the Watts ghetto, the Khalija township, the racialised *banlieue* or the 15 'Peace Lines' that separate Protestant and Catholic in Belfast.

There is a twofold dimension to this. First, it is important to examine the manner in which the burden of historicity (after Touraine) and spatiality (after Lefèbvre) define the particularity of group difference, whilst simultaneously interrogating the manner in which history and geography provide organising tropes that narrate the processes by which such groupings are made visible and invisible. In London 'whiteness' emerges in the late twentieth century as a meaningful category displacing separations between generations of European settlers from Scandinavia, France and Germany; Catholic and Protestant, Jew and Christian in some parts of the city and at some times but not others. But at the start of the twenty-first century an ultra-right white nationalism that crosses northern Europe struggles with the particular resurgent English, Scots, Irish and Welsh nationalisms of a potentially fragmented United Kingdom.

Likewise, a contested political blackness that is popularised in London of the 1960s is informed by reflections on the civil rights movement and the long hot summers in the USA at the same time. The political category of blackness creates both an extended (geographical) debate about its boundaries and a *Zeitgeist*-laden (historical) debate about its explanatory power. And, equally, a serious debate about the inflections and meanings of white identities demands a commensurably serious debate about the constructions, identifications and representations of 'whiteness' in multicultural cities, where migrant flows may emerge from the proximity of old Iron Curtain countries as well as the postcolonial periphery. Such a debate needs to address the haunting of whiteness by the Celtic fringe, Jewishness, the Huguenot echo and the submerged and displaced senses of class. It cannot merely be a plaintive cry against the putative silencing of white voices in the debates around contemporary multiculture.[50]

The fluidity of the terminology is important because of the centrality of moving boundaries of racialised and ethnicised difference to this volume. In some important senses the common language of race, racisms, ethnicity and multiculture is significantly different on the two sides of the Atlantic. But even within the anglophone academy, where a shared language belies discrepant realities, these complexities multiply when considering the analytical concepts in the context of France or Pakistan.

Second, a focus on the processes of 'race making' or 'raciology' implies a constructionist understanding of the subjectivities that emerge in the cities of today.[51] But equally it is precisely a central argument of the book that the importance of the imprint of the spatialities and historicities of the city caution against a casual anti-essentialism when considering the profound nature of ethnic difference in the cities of the globe. When advocating the plausibility of the conceptual trope of 'the black Atlantic' Paul Gilroy helpfully drew on Clifford Geertz's sophisticated critique of the relegation of anthropological epistemologies to 'mere relativism'.[52] Geertz powerfully argued that the necessarily intersubjective nature of cultural change prompted him to advocate what he described as an *anti-anti-relativism*. In a similar vein, Gilroy argued that the historical traces that are inscribed constitutively through the black experience point him towards an *anti-anti-essentialism*. It is in this spirit that we need to consider the frequently incommensurable realities of processes of race making and practices of racism in the cities of today. Thus, the boundaries of the cosmopolitan are both fictional and real. Ethnicised boundaries that appear generally unbreakable, then momentarily invisible, need to be unpacked through their genealogy, their emergence in time and space, even whilst we simultaneously scrutinise the manner in which temporalities and spatialities are constitutive in their narration.

This contextualisation of markers of racial and cultural difference draws attention to the fact that their articulation is always simultaneously also an exercise of power. Chapter 3 of the book attempts to consider the sense in which such articulations are always within structures of power, and draws on the extensive literature around notions of governmentality.[53] In Hardt and Negri's terms 'there is no longer an outside to power'.[54] The sovereignty of both ethnic identities and people stigmatised and regulated by forces of racism is always set within structures of power. In this sense later chapters of the book attempt to suggest that the work of Achille Mbembe is useful in considering an understanding of the *banality* of the exercise of governmental power in regulating the multicultural city.[55] Although there may be no outside of power (in Hardt and Negri's terms) and there may be no world beyond regimes of governmentality (in Foucauldian terms), the ubiquity of state forms (frequently through their failure) structures the realisation of institutions of multicultural power and regimes of recognition and redistribution.[56]

Between the postcolonial and the cosmopolitan: towards a critical urbanism

There is a sense in which postcolonial theory has taken it as axiomatic that the modernity of the western Enlightenment privileges a particular form of historical narrative. Consequently, considerable scholarship has interrogated the manner in which the major part of the world has been constructed through a perspective that privileges a European and North American lens. The temporal is made problematic in both stories that illuminate the rest of the world in particular images (as in the landmark work of Edward Said's *Orientalism*[57]) and in plots that create a relationship between centre and margin through which the dynamic of whiggish progress privileges a particular cartography. In such intellectual labour, history becomes a site of contest and historiography a consequence of particular regimes of power in the telling of the temporal.

In part such a project draws its inspiration from the forms of twentieth-century intellectual debate that questioned the unthinking certainties of Enlightenment modernity. The postwar school of thought loosely considered as connected to the

Frankfurt School of social theory is one of the key sites for such discussion in the mid-twentieth century, Adorno and Horkheimer's *Dialectic of Enlightenment*, one of the canonical works through which the temporal became problematised in this way.[58]

Adorno in particular was recurrently concerned with the manner in which the histories of western modernity contained simultaneously both the seeds of politically progressive change and the genocidal logics of racial supremacy. His suspicion of the narratives of history was shared by his friend and correspondent Walter Benjamin. Benjamin's metaphor of the Angel of History disrupting the progressive story of historical change with the piling up of catastrophic wreckage as he is blasted into the future was based on a similarly jaundiced view of historical progress.[59]

The suspicion of the temporal ordering of things by the writers of such histories has become a received wisdom of contemporary postcolonial theory. For Dipesh Chakrabarty the notion of 'Provincialising Europe' consequently relates directly to a critique where

> this history challenges us to rethink two conceptual gifts of nineteenth-century Europe, concepts integral to the idea of modernity. One is historicism – the idea that to understand anything it has to be seen as both a unity and its historical development – and the other is the very idea of the political.[60]

Yet it is significant that in the context of this volume, which takes the city as its primary focus, there has been much less attention paid to applying the same sorts of logic to narratives of the spatial.

This volume returns in the final chapter to the manner in which the Adorno–Benjamin debates return us to a problematisation of the spatial in a manner that replicates the critical theoretical interrogation of the historical. It focuses on the manner in which the multicultural crystallises a moment in the tension between the analytical potential to *know the city* and the ethical imperative that privileges the position of the stranger, the newcomer or the refugee in the labyrinthine metropolis. There is a sense in which Adorno's rejection of Benjamin's Arcades Project was precisely about the manner in which Benjamin treated the spaces of the city seriously, and considered their curatorial power as suspiciously as he did the Scotland Yard certainties and detective credentials of the historian. Yet in hindsight, for all the occasional difficulties of Benjamin's opaque prose, both the pace of change of the contemporary city and its complexity seem now – 50 years on – to justify the methods of Benjamin's city studies that were never quite fully realised in the uncompleted work of the Arcades Project.

It is in this spirit that the chapters of this book argue for an extended engagement with both the temporal and the spatial simultaneously in urban scholarship. The landscapes of the city (of powerful and powerless) may be *read*, but they may also be lived, smelt, heard and haunted. In this sense the influential cultural geographies of the 1990s that were associated with the reading of landscapes[61] owed their lineage in part to an attempt to render plausible the cultural turn in social theory, and also in part to a recognition of the significance of the work of Henri Lefèbvre. This volume suggests that the important recognition of the processes through which city landscapes are produced that is the legacy of such work needs to be supplemented with a suspicion of the spatial narratives that is akin to the postcolonial suspicion of the historical. Metaphorically, this might be taken as suggesting that the city of Benjamin's Arcades Project must supplement the temporalities of the postcolonial in order to understand the multicultural metropolis of the present.

Space is central to the explanations of the metropolis but not merely as produced. The production of space central to the work of Lefèbvre is important, but at times underplays the manner in which space becomes the medium through which particular settlements of ethics, material interest and value are made to appear normal or inevitable. In the cities of twenty-first-century modernity space curates the social, the economic and the cultural. In this spirit the volume considers both the mapping of the city through the street, the cultural quarter and the ghetto, and also the technologies through which such practice becomes the subject of scholarly scrutiny (the tag, the city plan and the rhetorics of community safety).

In this sense the volume suggests that it is at the crossroads where a Foucauldian political analysis meets Benjamin's city that we begin to develop a critical urbanism that might be helpful in interrogating the configuration of the cosmopolitan future. For if the cosmopolitan is to represent a normative model of the future, the city is to be its empirical realisation. After the cosmopolitan the new city has to be refigured and narrated within a contextual understanding of the ethical challenge of the multicultural.

2   The mirage at the heart of the myth?

Thinking about the white city

In the early 1990s Birmingham, the second-largest city in the United Kingdom, reinvented itself. Formerly the metal-bashing heart of manufacturing Britain, and renowned for both its civic culture and brutal postwar redevelopment around a shopping market and traffic roundabouts, the city was traumatised by each of the postwar depressions. Like many another post-industrial metropolis across the globe, it attempted to foster the creation of a new site of mass consumption for the present and future, rationalised by a narrative of renaissance that was based on the tapestry of historical tales of the past. Mass consumption focused on new shopping malls, a theatre district, an international conference centre and associated hotels and new sports developments to host international events.[1] The storyline that stitched this tapestry together was in some ways more interesting.

The Council 'reimagineered' the marketing of the city by relocating it. A council promotion exercise, captured by the accidentally ironic strapline 'More then meets the eye',[2] drew on images of gondolas to boast that the city had more miles of canal than Venice; of Stratford on Avon and Coventry Cathedral to highlight the city's cultural heritage; empty shopping malls and (white) nuclear families walking through villages in Warwickshire to highlight lifestyle opportunities. Given that a 1988 quality-of-life report had placed Birmingham 38th out of 38 cities in the UK and that in 1988 Le Point had ranked the city 49th out of the 50 largest cities in Europe, it is perhaps not surprising that 'image' and reputation were central to the project to regenerate the city. But whilst the politics of the city clearly reflected the fact that over 25 per cent of the city's population were drawn from black and ethnic minority backgrounds,[3] the regeneration reconstructed a sense of the city that was profoundly white in its refusal to acknowledge the needs, presence or aspirations of such communities as Patrick Loftman has described in great detail.[4]

In stark contrast, on becoming millennial mayor of London in the year 2000, Ken Livingstone took dinner with the members of the City Corporation. Whilst flouting the dress code by refusing to wear the normal dinner jacket (tuxedo), he told the assembled audience representing the greatest concentration of wealth in Europe that:

> If London is to remain the financial centre of Europe, and to attract the inward investment and skilled labour for this, it cannot do so without internalising

and adopting the same international cultural norms and approach. Those who believe that London can survive as Europe's leading financial centre while adopting, explicitly or implicitly, a narrow racist or intolerant culture do not understand the challenges of globalisation.[5]

Across the city[6] the received wisdom of nostrums of globalisation has created for the twenty-first century a celebration of cultural diversity. The 'regeneration' of cultural quarters and 'ethnic' enclaves has become part of the mainstream rhetoric of projects promoting urban transformation. At first glance this may appear a welcome change from the whitening waves of gentrification in the 1970s and 1980s property booms on both sides of the Atlantic. But it was not for nothing that black civil rights groups in 1960s America proclaimed that 'urban renewal = nigger removal', and so it is perhaps important to greet the meeting of global capitalism with niche-marketed multiculturalism with a degree of caution, as this particular postcolonial encounter begins to reshape the cities of the twenty-first century.

Such stories are open to both easy derision and proper critique. On the one hand, in any particular city location it is imperative to subject the representations of a new urbanism to a realistic analysis. The political economy of the dual city and the political possibilities of the juxtaposition of the all too grim litany of socio-economic indicators of poverty and inequality are both generated by, and sit alongside, increasing concentrations of affluence.[7] But, on the other hand, it is also essential to question the hidden dreams and desires that shape future visions of the city that are at the heart of major changes in urban living characteristic of most of the cities of contemporary capitalism. And in descriptions of such city trans-formations the analytical salience of issues of race and racism is far too often either peripheral or silent. In part, this chapter suggests that such silence is not neces-sarily racially unmarked and that normality itself can be implicitly epidermal.

At the heart of this chapter is an assertion that it is not possible to disassociate the deep cultural roots of such narratives from the lived experiences of people in modern cities that are divided by imaginary but ever so powerful vectors of race thinking and racial categorisation. The simultaneously real and imaginary nature of the social life of cities demands that we think carefully about the manner in which the cultural traces of thinking about the cosmopolitan present owes much to techniques of governing, mapping and categorising populations that draw on ostensibly objective (but deeply value-loaded) lexicons of race and urbanism. If we take seriously the deep cultural roots of these structures of sensibility we might also think seriously about their impact, not so much to validate the polarities of opposition on which they hinge, but more to acknowledge the deeply implicated binary thinking that they invoke. For an understanding of the interplay between race thinking and contemporary urbanism cannot escape the seemingly contradictory observation that the abstract basis of both of these sociologically powerful terms is tendentious at best; race a perennially powerful mirage and the city a normative myth as much as an empirical locus of analysis. For these reasons an understanding of the interplay of race and the city is in part an articulation of the mirage within the myth.

The powerful mirage of race thinking

Race – with its uncertain relationship to 'ethnicity' – appears to be a term that captures one of the key fractures within both contemporary industrialised societies of affluent capitalism and also – after the end of history – increasingly structures thinking and writing about second- and third-world societies after the collapse of state socialism.[8] In their particular realisations race and ethnicity are historically and geographically produced forms of identification that acquire a self-referential analytical power. It is a prosaic paradox that the more that people *understand* their political systems and allocation mechanisms of power and resources in terms of race and ethnicity, the more the terms themselves acquire analytical *significance* in making sense of particular social moments. Across many of the metropolises of capitalism in all five continents a child's educational future may be determined by where they live, a settlement pattern structured by a racialised allocation of housing resources that reflects a historically determined ethnic migration of labour that still bears an imprint on the niched divisions of labour markets and racialised labour processes in a particular city. The conflicts that result from these histories in particular sites in the city may determine struggles for community rights, the party or movements that individuals are likely to campaign or vote for, and the processes of recognition and resource allocation that potentially reproduce social divisions of race and ethnicity as meaningful ways of understanding the social world.

Across the globe, narratives of empire, of slavery, of varying degrees of forced and unforced labour migration all articulate cultural differences in very real terms as differences in life chances that people from one racialised group may experience in relation to others. But also, as these differences in power, in rights and in wealth become entrenched through time in particular locations, the universality of humanity is potentially compromised by the legacies of history and geography.[9] Drawing attention to this academically may at times appear to cut against both a liberal tradition of thinking about relations between individuals and a communitarian sense that such patterns of racialisation create in some sense spurious forms of collective identity. Analytically, scholars of race and ethnicity are consequently caught between emphasising the often hidden significance of the imprint of racialisation,[10] and invoking another world beyond 'raciology'.[11] Put crudely, whilst the fundamental building blocks of race thinking are themselves ethically compromised, it does not make the edifice of racialised social divisions any less powerful a mirage.

The returning myth of the city

The city likewise is often offered up as an analytical centrepiece of social analysis. At the highpoint of urban social theory in the anglophone academy the tension between cities as ever more powerful *empirical descriptions* of places where the vast majority of humanity lived, and cities as *objects that might succumb to theoretical understanding*, foundered on the problem of the analytical unity of the urban. Effectively, by the early 1980s, scholars from diffuse ideological perspectives implicitly or explicitly agreed that the city could no longer be considered a basic building block of analysis or a coherent theoretical unit.[12] A chaotically conceptualised *object* of analysis ill served the task of an aspirant sociological rendering of contemporary life. And yet the *subject* of the city refused to disappear from the way in which academics, politicians and artists organised their ways of thinking about social and economic life. It has been argued elsewhere that it is consequently more productive to think about the manner in which the city comes to serve as an organising concept in writing and thinking about social and economic life than it is to attempt to 'theorise' the urban.[13] A focus on the relationship between observation of the city and the cities that are being observed problematises both subject and object. It disrupts any simplistic invocations of theorising the city, and concentrates on the manner in which an urban sensibility structures our narratives of the real. In this sense, the city has stubbornly refused to disappear as a category of social analysis. Liveable cities, networked cities, sustainable cities, global cities, dual cities, are all central to ways of thinking about the present and organising our ways of thinking about the possible and probable futures.[14]

Race and city. Both terms share an anchor at the heart of commonsense discussions about the way in which we live our lives. Both terms are the invisible centre of subdisciplinary studies in both social sciences and humanities. Both terms mean something, and yet when scrutinised more carefully they appear to expand to include everything or else melt into air as conceptually flawed caricatures of reality. More significantly still, there is a straightforward proposition from which this chapter flows. It is suggested here that the binary relationships that inform 'race thinking' and the uncertain values that are invoked through vocabularies of urbanism are mutually implicated in the history of descriptions that make the social life of cities comprehensible across a wide range of related sources, ranging through the imaginary world of novelists, the ideologically loaded paradigms of the academy, the seemingly mundane texts of governmental reform and the hyper-real excesses of Sim City and the virtual experience of the computer game. In this context we need to think carefully about the technologies through which representational practices create their own subjects and draw simultaneously upon 'race thinking' and 'city talk' if we are to understand the complex and recursively defined way in which people from different cultures live in the cities of today's globe.[15]

In an exemplary work in 1973 Raymond Williams used the couplet country and city as key organising themes in structuring the manner in which people thought – and wrote – about their lives. Drawing on the literary traditions from the seventeenth century onwards, but citing a tradition in which a 'contrast between country and city, as fundamental ways of life, reaches back into classical times',[16] he outlined the metaphoric and metonymic associations which allowed landscapes in general, and the city/country binary couplet in particular, to stand for a much wider structure of sensibility. This opposition invoked sets of social relations and power relations that were crystallised in specific buildings, aesthetics, characters and moralities. Williams suggests that the insinuation of the country and the city into a way of thinking about everyday life is always about something more than just a descriptive vocabulary, that 'whenever I consider the relations between country and city ... I find this history active and continuous: the relations are not only of ideas and experiences, but of rent and interest, of situation and power; *a wider system*'.[17]

Through a volume which focused on the English literary tradition, but which also touches on the work of Dostoievsky, Engels, Balzac and Baudelaire, Williams describes the manner in which urban life connoted a series of positive and negative values, the corollaries of which were logically identified with the rural way of life. He highlights notions of learning, of communication and of light as the positively signified aspects of city life in contrast to the peace, innocence and simple values of the country. Yet the stigmas of noise, worldliness and ambition that are associated with the city (and often the court as a metonym for the urban) are also juxtaposed against the backwardness, ignorance and limitations of the rural way of life.

If we take seriously the deep cultural roots of these structures of sensibility, then we might also think seriously about their import, not so much to verify or falsify the polarities and oppositions, but more to acknowledge the deeply implicated binarisms that are at the heart of ways of thinking about cities and the techniques of modernising, rebuilding, beautifying, regulating, regenerating and governing them.

If these values lie just beneath the ways in which cities are represented, they also condition changing attitudes towards the contemporary metropolis: the characteristics of an urbanism that is not straightforwardly (after Simmel or Wirth) a specific cultural form or a way of life, but can be understood as a tangle of ambivalent feelings, sentiments and commonsense 'knowledges' about the nature of city life. Moreover, if we take the spirit of Williams slightly further, it is possible through simplification (and a degree of caricature) to identify a *diagnostic cartography* of this urbanism. Crucially it is not just that there are particular positive and negative valorisations of city life but also that they resonate within the tensions between attraction and repulsion that echo in other structures of feeling. Space prevents a systematic reading of the canon of urban studies in this chapter through such a lens. But it is possible at least to suggest that a deconstructive reading of both the more dystopian and the more utopian analyses of contemporary city life across the social sciences draws at least occasionally from such implicit normative

Table 2.1 The country and the city for Raymond Williams (*The Country and the City*, London: Chatto and Windus, 1973).

The city	The country
Learning	Peace
Communication	Innocence
Light	Simple value
Noise	Backwardness
Worldliness	Ignorance
Ambition	Limitation

Table 2.2 Cultural cartographies and the urban imagination.

The city	The country
Disgust	
Debauchery	Propriety
Instability	Security
Danger	Stability
Transgression	Order
Desire	
Lust	Repression
Culture	Nature
Avant-gardeism	Tradition
Cosmopolitanism	Parochialism

and profoundly cultural understandings of the potential of the urban; whether even in recent times we consider texts as diverse as Peter Hall's study of the links between cities and civilisation,[18] Castells' networks of global economic change,[19] Sassen's treatises on the nature of globalisation[20] or the detective-like investigations of American capitalism scholars such as Mike Davis and Ed Soja.[21]

The psychoanalytic is important in this context and some authors have taken further its relevance to urban studies.[22] But in the world of symbolic values it is not necessary to resort to a full-scale psychoanalytic reading of the urban to identify both the tensions between attraction and repulsion implicit in the various representations of city life and the manner in which a reading of the city can provide a 'topos for the exploration of anxiety and paranoia'.[23] It is also the case that such a topos is both malleable and potentially pernicious in the manner in which the positive and negative valorisations of specific characteristics can become transcoded through particular processes that articulate representations of city spaces.[24] Iconic sites of disorder or indigence can invoke contradictory senses of celebration and condemnation. Historical description and metropolitan cartographies can naturalise, stigmatise, obscure and fictionalise the production of cultural landscapes. In novels, in cinema or in contemporary art[25] as much as in planning and in local economic development, the lexicon of the city provides both subjects that are analysed and a set of values and meanings that are not reducible to mere bricks and mortar.

Again space prohibits exhaustive categorisation here, but it is possible to point to a genre of writing that might be exemplified by Paul Rabinow's work *French Modern.* Rabinow identified the links between French urbanism in the early twentieth century and its colonial antecedents in the late nineteenth. Rabinow's work is important because it detailed the ties between the heroic technocrats who dreamed the future of the cities, the *image de la ville,* which provided the armature for the realisation of these dreams and the management of urban populations.[26] He demonstrates the link between the colonial imperative to administer in the built form of colonial cities and the subsequent translation of such rationalities to the cities of the French mainland. Regimes of *governmentality* emerge through the histories of design: 'Both in the garden cities and in the colonies, the symbolic central point of the city had been reserved for public administration. Administration was evolving from an organising symbol to a technical consideration.'[27] Similarly – though initially without the Foucauldian framing – a related project lay at the heart of Christine Boyer's landmark early work *Dreaming the Rational City* in its consideration of the relationship between ideologies of the built form and the development of Los Angeles.[28] In both cases the authors unpick the rationality that lies behind the organisation of city form and the technologies of power through which such rationality is realised in the built environment; put simply, to answer David Harvey's perennial question 'in whose image is the city built?' In each case and in similar work the city emerges as a sociological subject through specific regimes of power, both echoing and drawing on Michel Foucault's understanding of a notion of the conduct of conduct that lies at the heart of specific forms of governmentality.[29] For the purposes of this chapter it is necessary to link the Foucauldian genre of writing about the city, which takes the city as subject at its heart, to other investigations of the historical and cultural roots of city thinking in the spirit of Williams' conceptual framework.

There are three pieces to this analytical jigsaw. It is possible to imagine an intellectual project that takes both the vocabulary of the spaces of the city – (inter alia) the plan, the neighbourhood, the suburb, the inner city, the ghetto, the street, the tower block – and secondly the technologies of their representation – (inter alia) the map, the filmic, the visual, the virtual, the textual, the oral, the perspectival – and subjects both to a genealogical examination. It is not that the vocabulary is contaminated in some way. It is instead important to identify and to recognise the provenance of the representations that we deploy.[30] If we are to dig beneath the quintessentially urban celebrations of the 'neighbourhood' promoted by Tony Blair's Social Exclusion Unit in the early twenty-first century, or the suspect past, present and future rural spaces of the village of sociality espoused by Hilary Clinton[31] in the last years of the twentieth, then we need a sense of metropolitan provenance.

Such genealogies relate to popular culture and to economic rationale, to the rule of law and the etymological city roots of the nature of civilisation. It is precisely in this context that it is important to think about the manner in which the European Commission might suggest that 'the past decades have seen a rediscovery of the value of urban living and a growing appreciation of quality of life in the cities of Europe' and that '"urban areas" are a statistical concept. Cities are *projects for a new style of life and work*'.[32] It is also precisely in this context that alongside the spaces of the city and the technologies of their representation it becomes important to interrogate the third piece of the jigsaw: the characters that explicitly and implicitly, historically and geographically, inhabit these new spaces.

In this sense it has been argued elsewhere that the characters of the modern city have a similarly complex provenance.[33] They are invariably (explicitly or implicitly) gendered and classed, just as they are commonly racialised. In the imagined worlds of the government bureaucrat as much as in the anticipated urbanisms of the city architect a cast of citizens occupies the city stage. The nuclear family, the squatter, the single parent, the key worker, the cultural worker, the rioter, the single mother, the anarchist, the class-mobile entrepreneur, are just a few of the iconic subject positions that become reified in social policy and catered for in city plans. Such a cast list can be traced back to the characters of Henry Mayhew's nineteenth-century depiction of *London Labour and the London Poor* (published in 1851). They emerge from the Victorian explorations of the nineteenth-century city through which the social (and society) was first discovered, described and invented.[34] They too come loaded with their own histories of respectability and transgression, they too might logically form the subject matter of independent genealogical volumes. The inspiration for such an analysis might again be the work of Walter Benjamin – whose 'types' populated his work and served more than a merely analytical role.[35] Yet of central significance to this chapter is that whilst we can speak through a historically loaded vocabulary, it remains essential to understand that such spaces, such technologies and such characters are rarely racially unmarked.

The similarity between the structures of such sensibility that fascinated Raymond Williams and both the binarisms of gender and the structures of racial thinking is far from coincidental.[36] The fundamental premise of all racisms identifies a distinction between self and various others that are associated with particular characteristics. A casual glance at the attributes of urbanism detailed in Table 2.2 cannot fail to notice the resemblance to much 'commonsense' discussion of racial caricature. The sometimes crude boundaries of bigotry echo the crude binary oppositions of town and countryside, just as the more nuanced valor-isations of disgust and desire hide the more complex racisms of the contact zones between different cultures and the ambivalence of some writers about the possibilities of cultural fusion and hybridity.[37]

The burgeoning literature on 'whiteness' is significant here.[38] Absence can be as powerful a racialising force as presence. Racism at times works by a process of substitution, a coding of phrases and terms which conveys racist meaning without specific reference to explicitly racist beliefs. The urban renaissance currently promoted in the United Kingdom needs to look closely at its constituent parts as closely as the glibly multicultural globe celebrated by the new Mayor of London. Periclean Athens promoted an Enlightenment polis, yet simultaneously subsumed slavery. An architecturally rooted urbanism can at times produce streets and neighbourhoods purged of racial impurity.[39] Conversely, discussions of mugging, of faith, of sexuality can be racialised in a moment through the selective repre-sentation of the street, the mosque and the scene of domestic motherhood.

Such binarism has been subjected to a stringent criticism in much contemporary social theory. However, what is rarely contested is that at the heart of much thinking in the United Kingdom about a sociology of 'race relations' and in the USA about the centrality of racial thinking[40] is precisely such a phenomenology of self and other, transcoded through the epidermal, the governmental and the cultural into a model of normality and stranger, the latter potentially either 'assimilated' or rejected by a dominant – commonly implicitly white – social world.[41] And as always what is often most negatively stigmatised is at times most desired, a covetous tradition with scopophilic roots at the very heart of all social observation.

In the British historiography of writing about race, the barely postcolonial dark strangers that inhabited the writings of Richmond, Patterson and Banton through the Weberian constructions of John Rex and on to the more politically engaged models that focused on the problems of raciology that emerge in the crucibles of racism, the building blocks remain firmly binary in nature. Even the work in more recent cultural theory that has focused on issues of hybridity, syncretism and 'new ethnicities' is potentially open to the critique of synthesising alternative purities, or creating 'an essentialist opposite to the now denigrated cultural purity'.[42]

Likewise in the USA, for all the nuances of the Chicago School tradition and the occasional investigations of the construction process behind race thinking, the empirical horror of the racialised city measures itself for the academy.[43] It leads unerringly back to a dominant trend of investigation that begins with the categoric indictments of William Julius Wilson's mapping of socioeconomic disadvantage, moves through Mike Davis's cartographic certainties of Hispanic city life and on to Angela Davis's archaeology of the American prison industrial complex.[44] Loïc Wacquant's critique of the perils and politics of such measurement in understanding the racial complex of the ghetto is relevant here and is the subject of specific consideration in Chapter 4 of this volume. The point is not to underestimate the political power or the academic value of such work. It is important to discern the difference between empirical engagement with the world and empiricist theory. Just to stop and think for a second about some of the categories on which it relies – the racial subjects that inhabit such narratives – and the relationship of these categories to particular strands of thinking about the city. The apparent statistical solidity implicit in the demographics of migrant minorities needs to be set alongside the contingent nature of the creation of sociological and political subjects and the mediating force of cultural racialisation on which this contingency rests.

Even in a mainland European contemporary context that emerges from the phenomenon of migrant flows and the unspeakability of race thinking after the Holocaust, the categoric refusal of multiculture from writers as distinguished as Michel Wieviorka is in part reliant upon a distinction between the normal and the alien that fits precisely within both the longstanding traditions of French secularism and the categoric oppositions of Fanon's 'look a negro'.[45]

One possibility of moving beyond deconstructive critique of writing about cities is to reconsider the conventional relationship between empirical and rationalistic traditions of intellectual investigation. If the premise that racial categorisation seeps into writing and thinking about cities has a degree of validity, it may be worth developing the outlines of a synthesis of empirical and theoretical analyses of the contemporary city. Such a stance might take as its starting point the possibility of combining the rigorous empirical exploration of the forms of racialised newness that come into the world through the continuously mutating urban landscape, alongside a more rigorous scepticism about the plurality of representational practices that are used to capture such diversity in print and in film.

Towards some exemplary thinking: technology, landscape and character

It is possible to argue that the strength of urban studies is the logical corollary of its weakness. A predilection for interdisciplinarity both transgresses disciplinary boundaries and potentially neglects the logics on which conventional academic divisions of labour are based. To suggest that architecture, cultural studies, sociology, politics, history and geography might all be talking about a different city when they invoke notions of the urban is perhaps unsurprising. More significantly, in the contemporary academy, as disciplinary boundaries collapse, it becomes more important to examine the sorts of leakage that occur across previously sealed silos of knowledge production.

Social policy debates may be simultaneously structured by architectural concerns in the search for 'cities for a small planet',[46] a postnationalist political theory that attempts to develop an Athenian invocation of the urban as a basic building block,[47] or a social theory that attempts to relate trajectories of visual culture with regimes of urban design,[48] or a philosophy that celebrates the characters of the city as the bearers of the possibility of living with difference. The productive intellectual crossings of such debates do not render it any less significant to understand where different trajectories are emerging from.

In a similar fashion academic discourse draws upon particular representational technologies. The relationships between the plan and architecture, perspective and empirical observation, photography and anthropology, the map and geography, the archive and historical narrative, virtual space or spaces of governance and political theory, experience and ethnography, all demonstrate particularly diverse technological processes through which city life comes to be represented.

In this context the racialised nature of the contemporary city is likewise dependent on the processes through which the analytical world is made visible and rendered comprehensible as an object of study. For example, we need to think about the status of the film evidence that made it plausible that the police officers attacking Rodney King were innocent.[49] The case demonstrated that the field of vision is starkly racialised. As Martin Jay has demonstrated, it is possible to link particular regimes of the visible to alternative ways of thinking about the city.[50] Technologies of representation are constitutive of the subject. At a simple level it becomes important to ask why it is that in Sim City you can have a riot but never a revolution. It is also plausible – after Lefèbvre – to think of the city acting both as a product of representational technologies (a representation of space) and also as a theatre of representational practices (a space of representation).[51]

Similarly, through specific regimes of representation the city emerges as a political subject in relation to particular and specific configurations of the countryside, race and nationalism. Put crudely, studies of nationalism have long identified correspondent relations between the strength of nation states and the genesis and the artifice of national cultures.[52] In a sense the assimilatory uniformity of the nation state and its correspondent relationship with genocide identified by Bauman is inversely significant in relation to the power of city-based identities.[53] The weakening of the nation state and the strengthening of cities in the networks of global capitalism in North America and a potentially federal Europe need to be placed in the context in which the weakening of national ties is not without benefits. This is not to invoke a utopian urbanism characteristic of some of Iris Marion Young's work or the cherished urbanism promoted by architect Richard Rogers in his work heading the British Urban Task Force.[54] It is instead to subject the very notion of urbanism to critical inquiry both before and through its deployment in a progressive politics of becoming and a descriptive analysis of being.

The 'old new' racism of national rights and belonging in 1980s Europe is superseded by a debate about the racism of global capitalism tied to the German decision in 2000 to restart the *Gastarbeiter* system directed at South Asian IT skilled labour, an investigation by the British government into the possibility of further selective large-scale 'skilled' immigration, ongoing mass migration to the major American metropolises, an auction by the mainstream political parties in the UK to provide the most intolerant articulations of refugee asylum law, and the obscene deaths in June 2000 of 58 'illegal' Chinese migrants in the back of a refrigerated grocery van just down the road from the not so white cliffs of Dover.

Such weakenings of national ties are linked directly to the new flows of global migrant labour which both rely on cities as the reference points in which newly racialised populations coalesce and amplify the city as a representational site of refugee presence personified through beggars in streets and claimants in the town hall.[55] The three pieces of the jigsaw, landscape, technology and iconic characters, can be manipulated precisely because of the cultural depths of race thinking and city talk on which they draw.

In a complementary fashion, at times of national crisis the landscapes of nationalism can resonate through the countryside as much as the city.[56] The novelist Kazuo Ishiguro cleverly played with such a notion in tracing the seething growth of 1930s fascism to the bastion of Englishness in the country house at the centre of *The Remains of the Day*.[57] Likewise, it should be of no surprise at all that the British National Party in 2000 turned towards the countryside, with a Cambridge University-educated leadership based on a rural smallholding in Wales[58] to identify discontented nationalist sentiment, with its launch of a new journal, *The Countryman*.

At a different scale of analysis within the city theatre itself we might consider the relationship between spaces of representation and the characters that such spaces are inhabited by.[59] The nature of such an iconographic understanding of contemporary metropolitan life was touched on by Bourdieu in his final works, when developing his notion of 'site effects' where:

> These days referring to a 'problem suburb' or ghetto almost automatically brings to mind, not 'realities' – largely unknown in any case to the people who rush to talk about them – but phantasms, which feed on emotional experiences stimulated by more or less uncontrolled words and images.[60]

By definition, the structures of feeling that inform the languages through which we imagine the cities of the past, the present and the future are culturally specific. Just as the work of Raymond Williams was itself always subject to critiques of Eurocentricity, the way in which the city has been imagined in different national traditions generates related but different cultures of urbanism. The longstanding anti-urbanism of mainstream twentieth-century America that generated the twin totemic symbols of the city automobile and the free suburb, alongside the *fin de siècle* gentrifying reconquest of the city frontier documented in detail by Neil Smith, is self-evidently different from a mainland European sensibility that is most readily identified with Simmel, Benjamin and a cherished urbanism that lends itself so easily to the Parisian *grands projects* of the Mitterrand era in 1980s France and the millennial London of Blair's Britain.[61] As James Donald has noted, 'juxtaposing the category of the city with the concept of modernity is to ask about an experience, a repertoire of ways of acting and feeling that is culturally and historically bounded'.[62] Differences and similarities in the histories of articulation of cities structure the specificities of thinking about the racialised urban even as they reinforce the analytical power of the categories themselves.

But the purpose of this chapter is not, in the spirit of comparative sociology, to typologise geographies of city thinking and their cognate ideologies of city planning. It is rather to suggest that beginning to understand the genealogy of vocabularies of the urban alongside the spatially concrete forms of race formation provides an alternative perspective on ways of thinking about race and the city. Put simply, it is sometimes most productive to think about the invoked racial worlds of the urban social that are implicit when people talk of the ghetto and the community, the street and the projects, the problem estate and the regenerated neighbourhood, the 'burbs and the 'hood.

For most writing and thinking about cities shares at least some degree of cultural provenance which makes both imaginative similarities and the unique trajectories equally interesting. To take a case in point, it is precisely the historical and geographical specificities of the *banlieue* in contrast to the American suburb and the British new town that can make particular cartographies of racism comprehensible and the grim toll of racist murders meaningful in the white light that illuminates the social life of Thamesmead, Woolwich, Eltham and Welling in London and Howard Beach in New York.

Indeed such a call for the iteration between a continual questioning of the concepts and vocabulary that we use to investigate the social world and a sustained wonder at the possibilities of the empirical remains constant to the spirit of an investigative engagement with the nature of racialised city life across the globe. An acknowledgement that academic speech draws on language that is so deeply culturally embedded might prompt an acceptance that just as people make their social worlds in circumstances not of their own choosing, investigations of the racialised urban demands both a rigorous empirical openmindedness and simultaneously an acknowledgement of the genealogical cultural traces within which such investigation is generated. As one investigation of the American ghetto suggested:

> One must go against the flow of the dominant American tradition of research on the topic and break with the moralistic schemata and naturalistic reasoning

inherited from the early Chicago school to posit that the ghetto does not suffer from 'social disorganisation' but constitutes a dependent universe, finely differentiated and hierarchised, organised according to distinct principles generative of a *regular form of social entropy*.[63]

Conclusion: under the skin of the city?

So what does such an archaeology produce? It should in the very least make us consider carefully the historical problem of thinking about racialised city life. The gentrification of the ethnic enclave is causally related to the stigmatisation of the city ghetto and only a detailed examination of the interface of culture, political economy and social policy can explain to us how this comes to be the case. It is essential both to understand the progress that has been made in celebrations of cultural diversity that litter the policy arenas of today's mainland Europe and North America, whilst simultaneously understanding that they do not necessarily present us with either an 'end of racism' or even a significant improvement in the life chances of racialised minorities. And it is imperative to identify the manner in which racialised images inform city descriptions that may rationalise governmental intervention and then erase a racialised presence.

What is suggested here is not merely an iconography of the urban. Much productive work in recent cultural geography has pointed to both the possibilities and the limitations of taking forward the project of Walter Benjamin and Roland Barthes in reading the signs of the city.[64] Analytically we need to get under the skin of the city, to consider how the valorisation of racial subjects links to the institutional architecture of politics, economy and culture. Getting under the skin of the city is partly a task that demands an unpacking of the forms of collective memory and unruly mapping that structure our ways of thinking.[65] But it is also about a constant iteration between the concepts and vocabularies that are being used in academic analysis and the hidden racialised genealogies of precisely these same concepts. To accept the significance of technologies of representation of the urban is to point to a reconsideration of the valorisation of alternative forms of academic labour. The oral history and the graffiti tag generate an urbanism that is related to, but distinct from, the architectural plan and the urban futures envisioned by city hall. To investigate either is insufficient. The myth in the mirage of the racialised city comes into focus only when the two are triangulated through a sustained labour that does not return us to Chicago but does place gossip, interview and memory alongside the more rarefied theoretical considerations of commodification and governance.

The creation of the risk society potentially opens up particular cartographies of the underground and invisible worlds of the city where interrelated complexities of race, class and criminality are always rewriting new stories of symbolic spaces and places.[66] In terms of mainstream debate in the USA and Europe in the twenty-first century, it is essential to link a concern with notions of urban regeneration with a debate about pollution and displacement of the body politic. There is an ethical imperative to link a celebration of the urban public sphere with the racial subject positions of those included in it and excluded from it, to tie the street and the tower block to the images of the street robber and the racially marked victim, and to link the studies of 'risk' to the architecture of the racialised imaginary in the urban uncanny.

In subsequent chapters the three pieces of the cosmopolitan jigsaw (characters, landscape and technologies) are explored in slightly more detail through their realisation in the ethnic entrepreneur and the street rebel; the street, the ghetto and the cultural quarter; the graffiti tag, the spaces of danger and the city plan. But before doing so the next chapter develops the conceptual schema of the volume slightly further to consider the figuring of the cosmopolitan city within regimes of power and institutional architectures of contemporary politics.

3 After the cosmopolitan?

The limits of the multicultural city and the mutability of racism

On the road between the regimented Raj streetplans of postcolonial New Delhi and the shining beauty of another empire in Mughal Agra it is possible to stop at the extraordinary city of Fatehpur Sikri, built by the Emperor Akbar from 1571 to 1586.

This fort city has survived well, and though a virtual ghost town is notable for several buildings of extraordinary architectural effect. Among these is the particularly famous *diwan-i-khas*, or 'hall of private audience' which

> accurately reflects Akbar's character and idea of himself; from the outside the building appears to have two stories but within it consists of one high room, in the middle of which stands a sturdy swelling pillar, joined to the balconies half way up the hall by four delicate bridges. When Akbar was in conference, he would sit on the circular platform at the top of the pillar; those involved in the discussion would sit on the balconies on all four sides, and if they needed to bring anything to the emperor they would approach him along one of the bridges; those in attendance but not expected to participate could sit on the floor below, where they could easily hear what was said.[1]

Alongside assembling an extraordinary library, notwithstanding his illiteracy, Akbar designed the *diwan-i-khas* to facilitate the most cosmopolitan of discussions. Whilst the social structure was military in nature, with rank and status clearly built on an army model, he also created a 'civil service' of sorts, through which demonstrable social mobility occurred and the built form clearly aspired to promote a theatre of public and plural discussion.

In 1575 Akbar also built an *ibadat-khana* – or house of worship – whose function was to serve as a place of eclectic religious discussion and whose architecture was adapted to seat four different religious traditions along the four sides of the building. In both the *diwan-i-khas* and the *ibadat-khana* Akbar brought together different strands of Islamic thought juxtaposed – in open debate – with advice from Hindus, Jains, Zoroastrians and Jews alongside three Jesuit priests from the Portuguese colony of Goa.

But the city itself was barely occupied by the emperor. Although building at Fatehpur Sikri began only fifteen years earlier, the court was moved in 1585 to the

Punjab. The reasons for this are in part moot, but it is suggested that one of the main causes was that, for all its architectural grandeur and rational ordering, this particular Utopian city suffered major problems of water supply. The arena of ethical debate and the political economy of city power are sometimes connected in the strangest of ways.

Within the fields of social and political theory the nature of the cosmopolitan has come increasingly to occupy a central place in mainstream exchanges. In part such discussion represents a logical progression from the theorisation of the centrality of poststructural difference in fragmenting the unity of the subject. The recognition of the importance of cultural difference in patterns of social organisation prompted leading French sociologist Alain Touraine to suggest that the central question facing humanity is the ostensibly banal one of 'how do we live together?'[2] In a sense his work revolves around the sociological realisation of complex changes of social and economic subjectivity under condition of late modernity. But as earlier chapters of this book have suggested, a notion of 'living with difference' becomes increasingly not just a predilection of the politically correct but also simultaneously the rallying cry of globalising capitalism.[3]

Yet at times both the urban roots of debates about the cosmopolitan and the Kantian focus on the role of structures of governance in delivering the good life (perpetual peace) appear obscured in the linguistic complexity of some articulations of cultural theory. In this context this chapter attempts to reinscribe the centrality of both the city and the state to such debates, both for their theoretical salience and their empirical specificity. The chapter also develops the thinking of Chapter 2, to provide a framework for a reconfiguration of urban studies that would take multiculturalism as a central rather than a peripheral facet of city life.

What is particular to the contemporary urban condition is that the global reach of international labour markets and migrations and the localised identities of particular places are not mutually irreconcilable. Indeed processes of *glocalisation* are considered to be at the heart of most modern cities, where communities look to common identities and territorialised affinities within a particular city whilst simultaneously being part of family and kinship networks that cross the globe. Greeks in Melbourne, Haitians in New York, Chechens in Moscow, may look both to a part of the city and to *somewhere else* or another place for their roots and their routes, for a sense of identity and a network of social, economic and cultural relations.

Across the globe, citizens of the metropolis are asking themselves 'how do we live with difference?', as the problem of multiculturalism poses a challenge to the way in which people make sense of their own lives. It does so theoretically, as the 'cultural turn' across the social sciences invokes multiculturalism as a contested set of values that challenge the liberal democratic settlement after the end of history. But it also does so more prosaically through changing demography. A combination of declining birth rates and capitalist growth in the global north with the continued underdevelopment of the post-Cold War south will lead to steady migration flows from old and new colonies to the cities of affluence. In the areas of the south where economic change emerges, such as Manila or Shanghai, or in cities such as Lagos or Karachi, where political turbulence transforms historical form, labour migration concentrates people from very different cultural backgrounds into the focused arena of the urban. In such settings, cities themselves are being reinvented by the globalising mobility of labour and capital, and such changes will inevitably impact upon the manner in which the basic units of conventional social analysis – 'the social', 'the economic' and 'the political' – are themselves configured.

In this sense the sign of the cosmopolitan shelters many different shades of meaning. In its most banal articulation it speaks to the straightforward empirical diversity of routes of arrival and roots of origin of the populations of today's major cities. At another level of description it points towards a different way of seeing the city, an acknowledgement of the heterogeneity of contemporary social reality, a recognition of the uncertainties of identity and the uneven inscriptions of gender, sexuality, class and faith on the social body. Yet more normatively still, the cosmopolitan, both in its Kantian origins and in some contemporary invocations, can be seen to invoke a philosophical and moral stance. Less a descriptive vocabulary than an ethical project, cosmopolitanism in some of its most recent theoretical renditions in political and cultural theory becomes a way of resolving the moral questions that arise from the attempt to reconcile different kinds of difference.

Cosmopolitanism has always been in part about a debate between the fragile subject positions of state, city and nation: their relational articulation increasingly challenged over time and space in the search for putatively perpetual peace. So it is instead the argument of this chapter, first, that the processes of glocalisation help us to reconsider the relationship between the conventional units of social analysis when it is understood that the realities of ethnic difference and processes of 'race making' are central to this new configuration. Increased ethnic diversity consequently serves as a prism through which the ethical debates that currently focus on issues of cosmopolitanism can be cast. Again this is not simply to valorise an empirical specificity, but is more to acknowledge that the very grounding of a discussion of debates about the possibility of the cosmopolitan might serve as an antidote that qualifies celebrations of diversity, the optimistic promotion of hybridities and the more pessimistic conceptualisations of the inevitability of racialised city conflict. In short, it is imperative to disrupt some of the more crude globalising narratives of world cities with the progressively more pronounced processes of urban glocalisation in a manner that highlights the unstable relationship between city, region, state and nation.

Second, the chapter considers the significance of the fact that discrepant cosmopolitanisms and virulent racisms coexist simultaneously in a *conceptual* territory that is configured by the shifting boundaries between state and civil society and within the *empirically* heterogeneous spaces of representation of the contemporary city. This is an important – if straightforward – truth because, just as studies of race and racism have tended towards the erasure of the regimes of governmentality within which the processes of race formation occur, studies of city politics have tended to reify the boundary between state and civil society and consequently have commonly erased the relevance of racialised cultures to its definition.[4]

It is not that state structures and governmental powers are all-determining. It is rather that they are in a very specific sense inescapable. There is no world untouched by the multiple regimes of power that structure the regulation of domesticity, labour, public and private life and the rights of the citizen. This sort of power is in many ways quite banal. It structures the practices of everyday life; we might talk of *the banality of government* in a manner akin to Achille Mbembe's notion of the banality of power in the postcolony.[5] In this sense the chapter is arguing for the significance of regimes of governmentality within conventional studies of race and ethnicity, and equally for the significance of cultural processes in the structuring of the political subjects that are the necessary building blocks of urban social theory. In order to do this it is essential to consider the manner in which the temporalities and spatialities of the city are constitutive features of the cosmopolitan rather than merely empirical vehicles through which it is realised. Such a perspective places an analytic significance on *the staging of cosmopolitan* and *the contextualisation of theoretical debates* within the contemporary city.

Third, the chapter is arguing that the city provides a privileged arena in which cultures that are simultaneously local and global – that derive from precisely an iteration between these two positions – disrupt straightforward narratives of the global city, rendering visible the imperatives of western hegemonic capitalism.[6] This might be taken to suggest that the city is at the crossroads of a process that is increasingly being talked about as 'globalisation from below'.[7] However, it is perhaps more useful to use a phrase of Stuart Hall's to suggest that the global reach of today's multicultural city lies behind processes of 'glocalisation' that privilege a new localism that can be seen as 'globalisation's accompanying shadow'.[8] For precisely this reason the city provides the most dramatic arena in which the incommensurability of philosophical abstractions are realised in specific spatial and temporal contexts. The challenge of 'difference' is realised in the interplay between processes of cultural glocalisation that are always in part about 'somewhere else' and the sociological formations of metropolitan institutions that are embedded in specific urban settings. If we are to understand the manner in which cultural dynamics drive contemporary urbanism, we consequently need to consider the manner in which politics and cultural form mediate narratives of globalising economic change.

Governing the global city

Along with many others, Michael P. Smith has lucidly pointed out that the dominant narratives of globalisation and the founding texts that consider the problematic of global cities are unremittingly economistic in their logic.[9] He stresses how – particularly in the work of Sassen and Friedmann – globalisation is economically driven.[10] Capital mobility, concentrated in global terms on rapidly growing city regions, creates a new global urban hierarchy. The concentration of command and control functions in cities with global reach, the late twentieth-century shift from manufacturing to service and creative economies in the north, and the increased transgressions of national boundaries, produces a dominant narrative of global cities that became received wisdom both in some parts of the academy and in the town halls managing urban change.[11]

There are problems with such crude characterisations of globalisation and the role of the city within it. Longstanding critiques have challenged the degree to which the global reach of capital is novel,[12] the shortcomings of any erasure of the embedded nature of social and economic relations[13] and the political agendas that are potentially naturalised or normalised by taking globalisation as an inescapable and inevitable feature of today's cities.[14] Michael Smith's work is important because he attempts to draw together these strands of critique within a frame of reference that recognises the significance of cultural flows alongside the imperatives of capital. But for Smith there is a need to 'locate globalization' through three core principles of transnationalism, agency-oriented urban theory and a notion of globalisation from below.

In Chapter 7 of this volume the limited value of notions of 'globalisation from below' for either an understanding of contemporary urbanism or for progressive politics is explored in a little more detail. But for the purposes of this chapter Smith's notions of *transnationalism* and *agency-oriented theory* that he advocates as central to a rethinking of contemporary urban studies need to be considered in a little more detail. They exemplify in turn *a particular sense of power* and a specific *valorisation of the ethnographically real*. Both are problematic in a range of literatures that take as their subject a racialised narrative to make the city visible.

Smith develops his articulation of transnationalism against a contrast between forces of globalisation and forces of nationalisation. His sense of transnational urbanism provides a useful contrast to the 'paradigms' of global cities, postmodern cities and time-space compression that he critiques.[15] It is analytically helpful in framing cultural flows. However – beyond a paradoxically binary juxtaposition of grassroots and neo-liberal regimes of governance – it lacks a systemic framing of the *political* that structures the everyday lives and the momentous events of cities of today.

Similarly, an appeal to an ethnographically rooted counterweight to an understanding of contemporary globalisation is in many ways welcome. Smith's volume is important for highlighting the dense cultural networks in contemporary cities that mediate processes of globalisation. It in many ways echoes some of the appeals for multisite ethnography in anthropology and arguments in the planning literature of the last five years to acknowledge the cultural diversity that sits at the heart of the contemporary city.[16] Much of Smith's most recent work has been ethnographically informed. However, his appeal to reconstruct the paradigmatic city of Los Angeles from 'ground up' appeals to particular notions of the ethnographically real, for all its awareness of debates within reflexive anthropology.

The ethnographically real can privilege certain ways of reading the city and be notably naïve about the politics of the city. For all its notion of sympathy it can lead to a humanistic celebration of the subjects of difference. Hence, in a manner similar to Smith in Leonie Sandercock's influential, politically progressive but deeply flawed moves *Towards Cosmopolis* she successfully disrupts the notion of a singular public interest which informs the design of the urban.[17] However, her normative alternative model of the cosmopolitan city is based on a threefold 'expanding the language of planning' (p. 207), an epistemology of multiplicity (p. 216) and a transformative politics of difference (p. 217).[18] At times the work conflates modernism, (regressive) power, the aspiration to shape the social world of the city and the constitutive antagonisms of the multicultural. Again both the conceptualisation of the spaces of the political in the city and the very notions of temporality and spatiality of the *real* in Sandercock's city create their own problems. Her epistemology of multiplicity is useful, but resolves the tension between social engineering and community voices through an appeal to populism, making a moral equivalence between democratic planning and participatory democracy. The transformative politics of difference that looks more to process and becoming than achievement and being provides an interesting, if utopian, avenue for exploration. But the conceptual flaws are most starkly seen in the argument to create a new language of multicultural planning, focused on appeals to a city of memory, a city of spirit and a city of desire.

In the *city of spirit*,

> The tall chimneys that arose in the nineteenth century factory landscape (Mumford's Coketown) and the skyscrapers of the late twentieth century city perhaps symbolise the excessive dominance of the masculine yang force and its values . . . It is time to reintroduce into our thinking about cities and their regions the importance of the sacred spirit.[19]

The work foregrounds a *mystificatory humanism* that is amplified in the *city of memory* where

> modernist planners became thieves of memory. Faustian in their eagerness to erase all traces of the past in the interest of forward momentum, of growth in the name of progress, their 'drive by' windscreen surveys of neighbourhoods that they had already decided (on the basis of objective census and survey data) to condemn to the bulldozer, have been, in their own way, as deadly as the more recent drive by gang shootings in Los Angeles.

There is a sense of the power of ordinary urban landscapes to nurture memory but also a romantic attachment to a notion of historical sedimentation – a construction of an authentic past that awaits discovery in the meaning of the city beneath the cobblestones. And, most worryingly, in the *city of desire*: 'How does the city of desire translate into planning? Perhaps by giving more attention to places of encounter, specifically those which are not commercialised – the street, the square – and which are not placed under the gaze of surveillance technologies.'[20] This mythical space of the social that sits beyond government bedevils so much analytical concern with the grassroots realities of city life.

Such a rhetorical structure is even reproduced in more sophisticated understandings of the heterogeneity at the heart of today's urbanism. In another example of exactly this logic James Holston has suggested that:

If modernist planning relies on and builds up the state, then its necessary counteragent is a mode of planning that addresses the formations of insurgent citizenship. Planning theory needs to be grounded in these antagonistic complements, both based on an ethnographic and not utopian possibility: on one side the project of state directed futures which can be transformative but which is always a product of specific politics; and, on the other, the project of engaging planners with the insurgent forms of the social which often derive from and transform the first project but which are in important ways *heterogeneous and outside the state.*[21]

The *alternative city* (and a valorised urbanism) becomes a mythic space of a citizenship that is outside the state (and conventional models of politics) and awaits ethnographic discovery. Occasionally invoked through appropriating Foucauldian notions of the heterotopia, it is where the heroism of civil society can displace the gaze of the powerful. Unfortunately, such space exists principally in romanticised narratives of city life. Set against such thinking, this chapter attempts to qualify (yet still valorise) the privileging of ethnographic urbanism and to reframe the political thinking that can accommodate both culture and conventionally defined political institutions.

Politics in this sense does not refer only to the formal representative structures that may territorialise democratic (or non-democratic) rule of the urban. It refers to the whole manner of institutions, rules, protocols, norms, technologies and structures through which conduct is regulated in the city. Formal political structures are important, but they remain one facet of both the governance processes and the politicisation of urban life.

In this sense the political machine of the city needs to be understood as operating across newly configured spaces of government in which the notion of the *political* refers to sets of cultural values, sentiments and the moral organisation of the social world as much as to the allocation or resources, life chances and the regulation of practices of wealth creation. The manner in which the city configures structures of institutional government form is important. So also is the manner in which it makes visible the territorialised *objects of government* (such as the street, the tower block, the ghetto and the cultural quarter) and the *legitimate speaking subjects* of politics (such as the ethnic entrepreneur and the street rebel).[22] The political configuration of the city allows certain kinds of individual and group identity to become visible. The technological arrangements through which patterns of identification emerge and transform (ranging from the virtual spaces of the net to expressive culture to the graffiti tag to the policing of the polis, the production of surplus value and the planning of its form) become likewise implicated in the political constitution of urban cultures. As Andrew Barry has described, a contemporary democratic politics rests on the notion that anything can be made political that is the subject of contestation or dissensus. There is an imperative to understand how the production of technical skills, capacities and knowledge of the individual citizen are produced and 'technology offers a set of skills, techniques, practices and objects with which it is possible to evade and circumscribe politics'.[23]

Consequently, the argument of the chapter is advanced through five related propositions about the nature of contemporary urbanism:

1   Objects of government need to be considered in terms of their historicity and spatiality.
2   Racial subjects are fundamentally mutable and constructed rather than rooted in primordial or ethnic difference.[24]
3   Across the cities of late capitalism of the last ten years urban politics has been dominated by neo-liberal reforms that can best be understood in terms of the advent of the putatively minimal state. This deterritorialises and reterritorialises the boundaries between government and civil society; it does not create a heterotopic space beyond the state.
4   A crisis of bureaucratic rationality raises particular challenges at the heart of deliberative democracy in the city that have profound significance in multi-cultural settings.
5   The commodification process is invariably cultural, preys on cultural difference and creates a fundamental commodity fetishism at the heart of processes of racialisation through which the city is epidermalised.

Proposition 1: The historicity of objects of government

The city occupies a place in political theory and practice, but as with all objects of government must be considered in terms of its historicity. By this I mean that the very reasons why the urban becomes a problem of government configures structures of power within the city, but also provides a defining context through which new social formations emerge.

The relationship between *functions* of government and social phenomena is historically contingent. In the history of the city, sanitation, health, population, have all at different times and places become the central focus of governmental activity.[25] Likewise the degree to which political structures are considered responsible for processes of economic change, or thought able to influence economic growth, has varied at different times and places. Superficially, such an observation may appear mundane. At one level this may appear to be no more than pointing out that there is seldom a one-to-one relationship between state structures and city form; that city states are in many senses more an object of occasional nostalgia than legitimate theorisation. Likewise the social and economic nature of city life cannot be accounted for deterministically by the political configurations of state power.

However, in this chapter the attempt is made to argue that the creation of political subjects in the city is precisely about the simultaneous presence of regimes of governmentality alongside the cultural construction of forms of political subjectivity. Theories of urban politics at times ignore at their peril the complexities of problems of governmentality that complement the institutional structures of the state in the city. In a corollary fashion, representations of urban culture that ignore the power relations between state and civil society will inevitably fail to address the political nature of the dynamic urbanism at the heart of the contemporary metropolis.

To compare the United Kingdom and the United States. In the former many urban areas have, throughout the last 50 years, been dominated by housing tenure that is state-owned and run by the local authority as social landlord. The local governmental structure is a significant service provider of both education and social welfare support and through the planning process creates a regulatory framework that shapes the built environment.[26] In contrast, the United States is more often characterised by a less interventionist system of land use planning and a lower priority given to the provision of social housing – often residualised to 'projects'. However, the less centralised federal structure allows both a greater political intervention in the economic fortunes of specific cities and the more plausible development of 'growth coalitions' and particular city 'regimes'.[27] At times the binary caricature of differences between American and European models of city growth is captured by the iconic contrast of Boston and Berlin. More helpfully, the beginnings of a truly global understanding of city politics needs to begin with an analysis of the generation of city political systems in the context of national and global configurations of power and legislation.

Consequently, rather than focus on a straightforward contrast between putatively European and American models of city politics, it is suggested here instead that in both political analysis and conventional political practice there has been a shift from a vocabulary of 'government' to one of 'governance'.[28] In part this can be seen in the post-Cold War concern about the means by which the social and economic worlds are necessarily regulated or intrinsically 'self-regulating', a debate whose origins can be traced to the very roots of liberal political theory. In part this might be seen as a recognition of a Foucauldian debate about the plural-isation of the structures that we understand to be 'political'. In this genre it is possible to consider structures that define regimes of 'governmentality'. Defined by Foucault in terms of attempts to control 'the conduct of conduct', a focus on 'governance' draws attention as much to the manner in which the legal system imbeds and reproduces whole systems of normative values and power relations[29] as to the process through which the individual is constructed as an object of self-government.[30]

There are two consequences of such thinking. Analytically we might see the city as both a crucible of government imperatives and institutions and a geographically and historically determined *object of government*. In the former, the spaces of the city are criss-crossed by regimes of power that mediate the ways in which political subjects can become visible. In the latter, the city itself is a political subject with an identity, an economy, a set of interests and a degree of agency. A comparative understanding of city politics needs to be based upon the diversity of institutional forms of the former and a contextualisation of the latter against the alternative territorial *objects of government* such as the region, the nation, the trading block and the transnational alliance.[31]

In a different register, the recognition of multiple spheres of influence within a language of governance has changed both the manner in which structures of contemporary city democracy see themselves and the dominant paradigms through which they are theorised. In part also this change in emphasis is reflected in the resurgence of pluralism within urban political theory and the related attempts to legislate for city versions of a 'stakeholder' conception of democracy.[32]

Such changes in focus have particular consequences for the politics of the city. For the purposes of this chapter, it is significant to observe that in the study of cities a shift in theory and practice from the structures of 'government' to the problems of 'governance' has:

- emphasised the corporate relationship between public sector organisations;
- encouraged the development of 'partnership' relationships between public and private sectors in modern cities as mechanisms for both the regulation of the economy and the restructuring of the welfare state;
- naturalised a false understanding of a clear-cut boundary between state and civil society in the contemporary metropolis.

The first two of these generalisations are empirically demonstrable and are clearly demonstrated across the range of work in urban studies literature of the 1990s.[33] The emergence of both new public management arrangements in the public sector and private/public partnerships in processes of urban regeneration is common not only in Britain and the United States but across the globe. Special-purpose vehicles for city change that combine private finance with public sector representation are equally common in the Business Improvement District of Johannesburg as in the rail terminal construction at Lille in France. It is not my purpose to comment on the reasons for their genesis or their desirability here, only to acknowledge that their existence is particularly significant in understanding the political landscape of the contemporary city.

The third generalisation is both more interesting and more powerful in tracing the role that race plays in these new city landscapes. It is more interesting because of the contingent circumstances in which racial subjects emerge and the context in which the fiction of race is translated into the narratives of racial subjectivity. It is more powerful because the hidden configurations of power relations do not determine the future of particular racialised groupings, but they do define the governmental frames through which such subjects become visible.

At times, in a particular genre of political theory, there is a tendency to consider a territory that exists in some sense 'beyond the state'. This is precisely the sort of celebration of the territory of the social or the communal that we have already seen in the work of Sandercock and Holston. An urbanism that valorises civil society or that maps city communities as a *post-Chicago School* mosaic fashioned by their own autonomous dynamics might place the flux of urban life beyond the analytical reach of structures of government.[34] This may apply both to analyses of the social life of the contemporary metropolis and to the policy instruments that are developed to address it. Hence in some forms of social analysis the dynamics of community development or class formation are frequently understood as the realisation of generic national forces within a particular urban arena. In a related fashion, policy instruments that promote local empowerment may unproblematically valorise localised spaces of dissent and resistance or attempt to 'involve the local community'. Such a move both subsumes debates about the relative legitimacy of participatory and representative models of democracy and masks the imperfect boundaries of community formation within the city. Community formation is always set in a specific context, with its boundaries marking what community is set against and where its limits are demarcated.[35]

The contention here is that the positioning of particular residential communities or communities of interest is always relational to the structures of governance or regimes of governmentality within which they are set. In the literature on gentrification, the 'avant-garde' role of gay communities or artists in San Francisco, Jerusalem or Dublin has to be set against the institutional norms and forms that allow artists to subsist and the gay scene to become visible. Weberian housing classes emerge within specific regimes of collective consumption that are regulated just as the role of 'faith' communities in relation to education in Marseilles, Salt Lake City or Delhi depends on the state regulation of schooling. The reimagineering of particular city landscapes may share an architectural aesthetic in the building of palaces of consumption, but the consequent central developments of New York, London and Paris will depend on the role of communities of resistance to property-led redevelopment that depend in turn on the resources offered to them by differing regimes of land-use zoning.

In each of these cases, put simply, political subjects and social movements depend as much on what exists 'beyond themselves'[36] – their 'constitutive outside'– as they do on their internal coherence. In the context of today's city this accords closely with a much more permeable boundary between state and civil society than is normally theorised. Civic institutions, citizens' demands, populist protest, riots and political movements all take place within a city crucible that is configured by state/civil society relations. It is in this sense that Foucault preferred this relationship to be understood as a 'transactional' one. It is in this sense that this volume as a whole, and this chapter more specifically, is arguing that it is essential to understand both the institutional relationship of structures of city government alongside the way in which they are inhabited and reshaped by cultural dynamics of change and mobilisation.

In the context of the cosmopolitan metropolis this is important because there is a tendency either to privilege the autonomy of 'racialised' cultural and political subjects, or represent the political apparatus as to varying degrees 'penetrated' by demographic groupings that are variously successful in formal or informal systems of democratic representation. This leads significantly to the second proposition of the chapter: the importance of always considering the mutability of racial subjects.

Proposition 2: The mutability of cosmopolitan racial subjects

Demographic fractions of a city population do not constitute communities. Communities are built, imagined and fought for, frequently in struggles for justice and resources *against* the state. Commonly, such identities rest also on resistance to other forms of dominance in the city, ranging from the spatialisation of capital to the populist will of the people. In this context a striking feature in contemporary literature about multicultural cities is a tendency either to privilege culture (at the expense of institutional context) or to privilege demography (at the expense of the significance of meaning).

The interplay between the spaces of the city and identity politics has the capacity to generate arenas of cultural identification and ethical contest. Alexander Negt and Oscar Kluge argued that it was possible to describe such semi-autonomous arenas of debate and deliberation as a proletarian public sphere,[37] a concept that Paul Gilroy has developed productively to consider the routing of black diasporic cultures through the *alternative public spheres* of the city. Drawing on Gilroy, in this sense it is possible to conceptualise how community struggles have produced 'alternative public spheres', commonly in the cultural realm: in youth culture, in musical culture, in voluntary and religious associations. These arenas are political, though they are not always seen as such.[38] Their politics does not always fit readily within the conventional languages of academic political science. They are most readily seen as Goffmanesque framings of social and moral life. Erving Goffman's metaphor of the stage and the dramaturgical analysis of ethnographies of such worlds is an essential tool in rendering comprehensible the complexities of city life.[39] The transnational (including forms of transnational urbanism) challenges their constitution.[40] It is in the dance hall that gender politics is most clearly performed, in the church and the mosque where faith-based transnational identities are deliberated, and on the football field where forms and norms of masculinity may be contested.

Crucially, the demographic make-up of the alternative public sphere may be marked by specific fractions of ethnicity, but the key characteristic of the multicultural city is that it is in such spaces that new identities are generated and new solidarities are formed. In this sense the spaces themselves become constitutive features of the manner in which racial identity is defined. Both the (successful or unsuccessful) reproduction of social values or norms and the emergence of new ways of seeing and thinking through patterns of creolisation and hybridity are quite literally site-dependent. Chapters 8 and 9 of this volume explore in a little more detail both how the everyday landscapes of housing estates, clubs and schools generate such alternative public spheres and how a space as mundane as a small park or football pitch reproduces patterns of exchange and unruly debate.

Migration to cities of the capitalist north brings together cultures from across the globe. An analytical focus on the patterns of creolisation and hybridisation (examined in Chapter 7) of this volume has produced both important debates about the performative nature of intercultural dialogue and significant concerns about the terms and limits of such processes. Simultaneously, more conventional studies in political science and sociology have considered the degrees to which individual migrant minorities (and sometimes migrant majorities) have succeeded within the institutional networks of city politics, education, welfare, class formation or different economic sectors. In the former literature 'the cosmopolitan' assumes a sign of cultural transformation through mixing; in the latter the cosmopolitan stands as a valorised sign of reified diversity. Yet there are problems with both a decontextualised account of the powers of creolisation and with histories of migrant minorities that plot their relative successes and failures by privileging the temporalities of generational change and advance. Such problems can be addressed through a consideration of the spatialisation of both performativity and institutional form.

In this book the argument is that it is important to place the mutability of racial subjects within the spaces of the city on which such identities are staged. For example in the British context 'black' is both politically and analytically a significant sign of cultural difference at some times but not at others. The typology of Barbadian, Jamaican, Guyanese, Nevis and other small islands is likewise contingently significant. The term 'Asian' in a British context, used to capture demographic fractions from across the (sometimes twice) migrant diasporas of the Indian subcontinent, is similarly both contested and at times meaningful. The badge of Islam similarly simultaneously unites and divides. In the United States the Hispanicisation of cities at some times appears analytically meaningful, at others masks a cartography of 'new' and 'old' migrations that bear the imprint of different economic moments of the late twentieth century and very different political trajectories of homeland and settlement.

It is precisely the mutability of racial subjects that makes the urban arena simultaneously both exciting and dangerous: the scene of Les Back's metropolitan paradox on which both the most extreme moments of racial terror and intense forms of intercultural dialogue are staged.[41] The increasingly diverse nature of contemporary cities has to be understood as taking place through this process of staging and place making of the neighbourhoods of the city.

To take just one example, in the area of Deptford in South London the genesis of a black community can only be understood in terms of struggles that were simultaneously local and global. Communist Party black South African exiles from apartheid South Africa in the 1970s worked alongside West African migrants and African-Caribbean churches in the campaign against SUS, the police criminalisation of young black men under the Victorian common law of suspicion.[42] The next chapter of this volume touches on the events of 1980 when 13 people died in the New Cross fire and explores the contingent connections between mobilisation, identification and demography a little further. A wave of resentment spread out across the city over subsequent months, and in 1981 a national march from the inner suburbs to the central areas of the West End of London made the black spaces of the inner suburbs visible in the political heart of London. In this march some of these alliances were articulated in a mobilisation that performatively made visible a black community presence in London. Such micro-scale detail is linked to but not reducible to national debates. Across the United Kingdom a sense of struggle is historically linked to a debate about the nature of 'representation' whereby the penetration of the political apparatus of the state and representative politics is contested alongside the representation of black subjectivities in the expressive cultures of music, literature, clothing and sport.

Equally pointedly, in a mainstream European and American context the fragility of categories of whiteness becomes visible under closer empirical scrutiny. There is not a point in the history of London when cultural differences have not played a significant role in shaping the life of the city. Masked by a historical gaze that normally erases such conflicts, it is possible to narrate London's biography through the lens of ethnic difference. The struggles between Vikings and Danes resulted in a prefigured residential apartheid in the city, rural migrations from the Celtic fringe were embossed in place names and communal strife, and the religious moments of dissent and riot through centuries were invariably culturally inflected. Peter Ackroyd has even argued that for much of the eleventh to the thirteenth centuries the capital represented the heart of Saxon resistance (as city state) to Norman dominance of the fledgling nation.[43]

To the present day there is a beating of the bounds of Catholic Wapping that are marched on the Feast of the Virgin Mary, distinguishing the area from the Jewish territory north of the Highway. Throughout the early decades of the twentieth century violent conflict characterised relations between these two turfs.

It is against such histories that it is important to consider the particular development of the recent past. The acceleration of migrant flows and the global reach of migrant labour markets makes the current city different in degrees of multicultural complexity rather than different in kind. And against the setting of mainstream culture and conventional political participation migrant communities have historically created for themselves discursive sites through which newly localised versions of culture and politics develop.

Cultural production is marked by both homeplace and site of settlement. In comforting narratives of whiggish assimilationism, the Italian community in the United States creates pizza that is subsequently re-exported back to mainland Italy. Bangladeshi 'lascars' or seamen invent the curry in London that eventually becomes the national dish of the United Kingdom, displacing the quintessentially English fish and chips that historically owe their lineage to the combination of French *pommes frites* and Jewish traditions of frying fish that characterised the East End of the city in preceding decades.

In this sense this chapter is arguing that the multicultural city needs to be conceptualised in part through a cartography that links the conventionally defined political institutions of governance and the state to the arenas and spaces in which cultural politics regulates community life. Such spaces and places also become the sites in which collective identity, moral orders and the ethics of everyday life are contested. It is in this sense that in the interstices of state and civil society the city facilitates the genesis of 'alternative public spheres'. In the manner of Negt and Kluge's description of the proletarian public sphere, migrant minorities struggle to build their known sites of association and discussion.[44] These may provide the arenas in debating societies and working-class associations for the circulation of new Jewish international socialism that followed the work of Rudolph Rocker in early twentieth-century Whitechapel[45] or the exilic politics that runs from Marx and Lenin to the colonial struggles of migrant Africa and Asia in early twentieth-century London.

For the purposes of this chapter, two features remain important about such changes. First, the city itself becomes a *theatre* of many different – and sometimes irreconcilable – sets of cultural values, ideologies of the economic and the political, dynamics of social change. The nature of such cultural incommensurability provides a central organising principle of much postcolonial and poststructural social theory. In particular it informs the notion of a cosmopolitanism of hybridity and creolisation promoted in the work of Homi Bhabha that recurs in later chapters.[46] Similarly, Salman Rushdie has described the capacity to foster and subsume such incommensurable realities as the defining feature of the city and the central thematic of his own work.[47]

Second, the staging of such debates within the theatre of the city changes the very cultures that distinguish migrant minorities in the first place. Diasporic communities are changed by the very processes of cultural reproduction and cultural dialogue in which they are implicated. In France the everyday lives of the *banlieue*, so strikingly demonstrated in Kassiewitz's film *La Haine*, restructure the nature of Moroccan, West African and 'indigenous' French urban culture. In Birmingham, Manchester and London the communities of the former Commonwealth reclaim the nature of what it means to be black, Jamaican or West Indian; Sylheti, Bengali or South Asian emerge as 'new ethnicities' that are articulated through the *spatialisation of culture* within the city. The Hispanic takeover of the American metropolis makes sense within the categorising imperative of the narration of Mike Davis, but this very categorisation, contingently both false and valid, obscures both the demographic discontinuities between Mexico and El Salvador and the city habitus of specific communities of new migration.[48]

Proposition 3: The advent of the minimal state

The economic restructuring of city form across the globe has been accompanied by political restructuring of urban governance. Alongside the rapidly changing role of the nation state in an era of globalisation, the city has developed new features that both empower the political apparatus within regions of economic growth and also curb projects of social reform in an era of neo-liberal hegemony.[49]

Such change needs to be set against a broad historical canvas.[50] In urban sociology the notion associated with the early work of Manuel Castells that the urban was the site of social reproduction through processes of collective consumption, associated most closely with systems of housing class, education and welfare services, looks increasingly like a phenomenon that normalises the temporality of the Keynesian welfare state and flattens the diversity of 'objects of government' of the city alluded to throughout this chapter.

But what is common to complex regimes of city politics globally is the advent of what might be understood as the minimal state. Common to the city regimes of today are the national and global imperatives of the monetarist legacy that restricts public sector spending and the institutional reach of city welfarism. The regimes through which specific forms of conduct are regulated and specific claims are recognised are pluralised. Institutional forms of politics in the city consequently include the town hall and its affiliated agencies but also complex forms of partnership structures and instruments of self-government. In one sense this might be taken to represent an end of state theory,[51] but in another sense it can equally be understood as emphasising the need to contextualise the particular regimes of institutional power within the changing landscape of the city.

Whilst this book in no way supports such a trend, it most clearly fits into the model earlier described in which the 'objects' of government are historically and geographically contingent. As the city hall plays a diminishing role in the provision of welfare services, particularly around education and social housing, the territory on which the transactional boundary between state and civil society is mapped changes likewise.

In the United Kingdom and the United Sates the fiscal 'shrinking'[52] of the state at metropolitan level has been paralleled by a series of debates about the nature and organisation of civil society and the role of city communities in controlling their own structures of governance. Significantly such debates take many forms, whose political correlates are not necessarily straightforwardly translated onto conventional representations of left- and right-wing politics. For example, on both sides of the Atlantic a growing debate about the role of faith communities in the organisation of civil society has touched both left-wing and right-wing forms of social organisation.[53] In 2001 in the USA, which is characterised by high numbers of practising Christians, George W. Bush looked to faith communities as alternative providers of welfare support in the cities. In the United Kingdom, with social trends that demonstrate lower levels of participation in organised religion, government policy has similarly looked towards faith community participation in social policy interventions in the city, such as urban regeneration and neighbourhood renewal programmes. However, it is sometimes argued that the largest actively practised religion in city Britain is now Islam, with levels of attendance at all mainstream Christian denominations dropping significantly in white communities and with strong levels of religious Christian practice remaining characteristic of West African and some African-Caribbean areas of the big cities. The unproblematic invocation of 'faith' in the United Kingdom alone invokes ghosts of the urbanised Celtic fringe and the evangelical Christian colonial legacy; the transnational realities of the city globalise the plural worlds of religious observance in the metropolis.

Politically, the shrinking of municipal government opens up a new territory of social mobilisation that draws on sometimes distinctive political backgrounds. Analytically it focuses on the culturally defined nature of the boundary between state and civil society, as alternative projects of 'self-government' grow proportionately in significance to the older institutional forms of city governance. Drawing on left-libertarian and anarchist traditions, there is a longstanding history of activism in almost every capitalist city that has promoted the rights of local people. The trope that most commonly shapes such movements has tended to highlight the struggle of social groups with limited power against corporate structures and state imperatives for redevelopment, most commonly articulated in campaigns against property-led urban change, iniquitous forms of racial injustice, or within an ecologically informed protest movement. Whilst there has been a shift from thinking globally, acting locally in recent years towards a trend to think locally and act globally in the streets of Seattle and Genoa, the city remains a crucial arena for the expression of such protest mobilisation.

But there is an analytical accompaniment of the left take on social movements in civil society. Ranging from the analysis of actor network theories that study the linkages between players in mobilisation to the burgeoning literature that takes governmentality as its central focus, there remains in studies of both social policy and social theory a celebratory strand of analysis of putatively autonomous mobilisation that occurs beyond the boundaries of the state. The celebratory invocation of the politics of the grassroots in Sandercock and Holston, already considered in part, exemplifies this. In social policy terms this tends to focus on the empowering nature of localised self-organisation that develops through community-led initiatives, commonly focused at the neighbourhood level through the promotion of alternative structures of local governance such as development trusts or community land trusts in inner city areas. Theoretically, such a 'celebratory' nuance is most clearly articulated in literatures that promote a new associationalism. In this vein, in recognition of the mutability of the institutional structures of government, Paul Hirst has captured the ethical imperative at the heart of such associationalism as the recognition of the transactional boundary between state and civil society and the need to pluralise the former and the publicise the latter.[54]

Yet there is also a less progressive take on precisely the same changes in the cities of late capitalism. In the tradition of liberal thought, advocacy of lean government goes alongside the refusal of collective responsibility. Models of social responsibility that looked to the city poor as responsible for their own destiny date back as far as the process of urbanisation, and in its twenty-first century form the focus on self-help leads logically to a promotion of social entrepreneurs (and their ethnicised variant), self-government and a communitarianism most closely associated with the work of Amitai Etzioni.[55] If the state will not do it for you, then the individual (or the community) must do it for themselves.

But again – as Chapter 1 explained – there is no straightforward left/right split in studies of the new urban civil society. This is most clearly exemplified by the debate that surrounds the highly contentious notion of social capital that has become an increasingly significant metaphor in the vocabularies used in the analysis of such worlds. Space prohibits a more complex elucidation, but there is a clear sense in which the genealogy of this concept varies greatly in its political allegiance, from Bourdieu to Coleman to Putnam. At some times it may appear a mere sleight of hand for the development of an analytical tool that reinstates the significance of a 1960s argument about cultures of poverty.[56] Yet, as Mark Warren has demonstrated in an important book that focuses in particular on George W. Bush's home state of Texas, it is clearly the case that whilst the Alinsky-inspired model of the Industrial Areas Foundation is problematic, the notion of social capital can be actively taken up to inform and reflexively change social movements that are clearly progressive in their struggle to represent disadvantaged communities within the state apparatus.[57]

The advent of the city articulation of the fiscally minimal state is particularly important for a politics and a sociology of racialised diversity. Crudely, the politics of difference in the city can be simplified into a typology of two complementary forms of conflict, which exemplify the problems at the heart of the multiculturalism debates. One is a struggle not to be treated differently: a series of conflicts around equality of rights in the provision of or access to services, state provision and regulations of governance. From the policing of migrant minorities to the institutional racism of particular regimes of social housing or health provision, a central dynamic of migrant mobilisation has moved through implicit or explicit logics towards an erasure of the visibility of ethnic difference. But equally legitimately a second dynamic has struggled precisely to promote its visibility: in the recognition of cultural rights, religious particularity, dietary needs, medical predisposition or parental language. In the promotion of both visibility and invisibility the transactional boundary between state and civil society depends precisely on the changing cartography of objects of government. The extent to which welfare support is provided 'beyond the state' or through state bureaucracy, the degree to which social behaviour is regulated (in marketplace 'discrimination' and in social preferences of gender relations or sexuality) are just two examples where the minimalisation of state intervention has profound consequences for the multicultural city.

In the urban arena, consequently, we see the realisation in specific form of the intellectual challenges with which this chapter began and which build on the moral compass of multicultural urbanism developed in Chapter 1. Tensions at the heart of the philosophical definitions of multiculturalism are articulated through specific struggles around urban conflict and change. In the final chapter of this volume we return to the sustainability of such tensions in a global context of expanding multicultural metropolises across the world. In the final two sections of the chapter it is suggested that quite possibly the resolution of such abstracted incommensurability can only be considered in the spatialisation of its empirical specificity within the urban arena. In these circumstances we might be forced to ask ourselves slightly more seriously the degree to which we need to return to the limits of debates around the normative practice of liberal government in considering if it is possible to plan the cosmopolis.[58] This means considering both the basis through which the social, political and economic life of the city might be organised differently and also the manner in which the deliberative institutions of the state are shaped in the multicultural metropolis.

Proposition 4: The crisis of bureaucratic rationality

In one of the most misread works of the sociological canon, Max Weber states explicitly how the power and pitfalls of bureaucratic organisation must be considered dialectically in relationship with political power. These considerations become important both to an understanding of how multiculturalism works within the contemporary city, and in considering how we might wish it to be otherwise. They are consequently at the heart of any ethical engagement with the city. They are also at the heart of how urbanism might labour to understand the realities it confronts in a manner that avoids both excessive humanistic invocation of the subject and a privileging of either the proximity of the ethnographically real or the seductive objective distance of demographic certainty.

The power of bureaucracy for Weber lay in its ability to regularise. Repetition and quantitative and qualitative revolutions in administrative capacity were all delivered by the efficient bureaucratic machine. The technical advantages of bureaucratic organisation were akin to other revolutions in evolutionary change: 'The fully developed bureaucratic mechanism compares with other organisations exactly as does the machine with the non-mechanical modes of production.'[59]

In this context Weber's characterisation of bureaucracy is perhaps best known for his identification of the form with progress. In the Weberian vision the two defining characteristics of bureaucracy, causally linked, are efficiency and modernisation. Bureaucracy both produces a quantum 'industrial revolution' in the productivity of administrative labour and exemplifies a temporality. It is this couplet that is perhaps most identified with Weber's writing. It is this couplet that at times is taken to pass for bureaucratic rationality and that is most widely seen to be questioned by late twentieth-century critiques of bureaucracy. It is also through this couplet that urbanists such as Sandercock spatchcock modernism and the will to power: injustice critiqued through the surrogate figure of the city planner.

The teleological movement towards bureaucratisation is now widely questioned by alternative forms of administrative theory that introduce market-related models, *new managerialism* and/or notions of rational choice theory that develop explanations and reforms of administrative practice.[60] Yet Weber's analysis of the form is about so much more than this couplet alone. Weber linked bureaucracy to modernity, but also worked through bureaucratic organisation present in the very different temporalities of ancient China and the Roman and Prussian empires. Weber works with a notion of democracy as prevention of rule by closed status group and a minimalisation of the authority of officialdom. He consequently draws attention to what he sees as an inevitable conflict between democracy and the bureaucracy.[61]

The Weberian point is important in the context of the broader shift from theorisations of government and the state to a focus on notions of governance and regimes of governmentality.[62] Weber follows Kant in distinguishing between *justice* associated with reason and notions of *loyalty* that echo primordial ties of sentiment and kinship.[63] In the Weberian temporalities bureaucracy is in part important precisely because of the processes of *rationalisation* with which it is associated. It is consequently set against invocations of loyalty and sentiment, paralleling Tonnies' later distinction between *Gemeinschaft* and *Gesellschaft* forms of city organisation. The point that Weber makes about bureaucratic power within other historical moments is precisely that it subsumes a specific set of values and power relations and then reproduces them with the efficiency of an industrial machine. Bureaucracy is in this sense ethically neutral; it serves as well the Pope or the Chinese despot. By treating people as objects, systems as rules, an indifference to the nature of the particular privileges the systemic regularity which in one guise might appear to be the source of a known, regulated and transparent moral universe.

The tension between democracy and bureaucracy consequently arises for Weber because such regulation and repetition will inevitably be under pressure when the will of the people contradicts the regulation, reproduction and procedural repetition of the status quo. However, at the heart of debates about multicultural cities is the very knotty opposition between alternative perspectives on the arbitration between different forms of difference. Such debates find their abstract realisation in political theory consideration of the relationship between multiculturalism, citizenship and deliberative democracy.[64] But the city makes such debates even more complex because of the facility for its spaces both to subsume contradiction and to sustain incommensurable realities in a single place. A Kantian optimism that is most readily articulated in the work of authors such as Jürgen Habermas might presuppose that the urban condition of multiculture provides a test of the adaptability of the discursive arenas of the state to accommodate different cultures through overarching processes and generative sites of moral arbitration. In contrast, an ethnographic privileging of alternative moralities, loyalties and sentiments that are brought together in a Chicago-like mosaic of the urban suggests less reconcilable worlds.

These two (slightly caricatured) philosophical positions of abstraction are made both more simple and more complex when they are temporalised and spatialised in the contemporary city. The more universal notions of the Kantians and the more relativistic articulations of the multicultural are contextualised both by the changing nature of collective identity and the specific arenas in which moral claims are made on the urban stage. Through time, the nature of (collective or individual) identity, as we have already argued, depends as much on what is absent as what is present (the 'constitutive outside' of racialised or ethnic identity formation). Forms of cosmopolitan collective identity – in an older language, the production of racialised subjects – are inevitably mutable and mutating as the forces beyond them restructure. Migrant minorities subjected to the surveillance of state powers, but positioned largely outside the institutional apparatus of the state, are straightforwardly not the same *object* as the same demographic group twenty years on with a purchase on state power through the occupation of city hall and the successes of representative politics. And likewise the claims made in the city hall differ in kind from those in the police station. The polis of the city is itself in part premised on the spectrum between visibility and invisibility that we have already discussed.

Consequently there are two paradoxes that relate to the crisis of Weberian bureaucracy in both western common sense and the cities of the twenty-first century cosmopolis. The *first paradox* is that a series of debates around the construction of risk and uncertainty translate into debates around the construction of rationality that promote notions of self-government. There is a potential for the analytical insights of governmentality theory and analysis of risk to serve as an intellectual handmaiden for the minimalisation of state intervention[65] and an offloading of state arbitration onto the moral worlds of *self-governing* communities, local neighbourhoods and individuals.[66] Such self-government can appeal to strands of anarchistic and leftist thought as much as to the conventionally defined 'right' politically. But the notion that migrant minorities might therefore be responsible for their own welfare or that cultural conflict is beyond state jurisdiction is the logical consequence of a lack of faith in state institutions. A closer reading of Weber provides a useful corrective to such thinking.

The *second paradox* is that in an institutional realisation of Chantal Mouffe's Schmitt-inspired democratic paradox,[67] multicultural cities embody particular realisations of the tension between cultural change, democracy and systems of regulation. To the extent that bureaucratic power suppresses difference through indifference it will produce a dynamic tension at the heart of the urban arena. To the extent that the link between rationality and indifference is open to critique, the ability of bureaucratic structures to govern the cosmopolitan is contestable. But to the extent that sentiment and communal loyalty (or 'recognition' more generally) are themselves inadequate bases of redistribution of power (or wealth), then city bureaucracies will remain *both* a site of procedural contestation and one mechanism for effective redistribution.

The constant move between visibility and invisibility that is at the heart of racialised politics is consequently mirrored in a dialectical crisis of bureaucratic rationality. The picture implied by Weber is one where the procedural normalisation of the bureaucratic system is not innately opposed to democracy *per se*, but does sit in a constitutive tension with it. Bureaucratic imperatives normalise and reproduce a particular social order.

At its most powerfully effective bureaucracy erases normative change and elevates social reproduction. A corollary of this is that it has an innate tendency towards ethical stasis. It demands a valorised 'indifference' to the subject that is based on a classificatory system (any classificatory system) that is a constitutive feature of the bureaucracy itself.[68] Hence a bureaucracy can service a slave economy or the procedural mechanisms of racial genocide as much as it can serve the Keynesian welfare state or any specified institutionalisation of a cosmopolitan notion of social justice.[69] But in terms of a politics of contemporary cosmopolitanism what remains implicit rather than explicit in much contemporary theorisation is whether the ethical aim of organisational change is precisely based on the imperative of recognition and disinterest or on its moral corollary of 'indifference' and universalism.

For contemporary urban studies the implications of the crisis of bureaucratic rationality are straightforward. They stem from the relationship between cultural change and systems through which difference is regulated. Ethically, it is essential to consider the regulation of difference within a moral calculus that understands the tensions between transparent regulation and cultural pluralism. The cosmopolitan consequently territorialises the challenges to the politically normal within the city: in the schoolroom, the welfare system, the workplace, the canteen and the housing estate. The empirical realities of the cosmopolitan present, as much as the logical construction of its forms of subjectivity, are realised as ethical debates in specific social settings.

Analytically, the tensions in the dialectical relationship between cultural change and systems of regulation point to a different sort of focus for studies of contemporary city life that avoid *mystificatory humanism* and the unproblematic allure of the *ethnographically real*. Such a focus would need to adopt a multiple perspectivalism that understands both the view from up close and the virtues of critical distance. It would need to understand that the anti-humanism that treats people as objects has its logical and ethical appeal beyond Althusser. Most significantly it demands simultaneously empirical engagement with the flux of cultural form and state institutions alongside theoretical reflection on both the ethnographically everyday and the cartographies of subjectified power and injustice that demand to be supplemented by global and transnational points of view.

Proposition 5: The culture at the heart of the commodification process

In part there is nothing particularly new in acknowledging the cultural centrality of the labour process that structures the shape of the city. The gendering of the workforce, the social construction of the Fordist labour week and the generation of the labour forces of post-Fordism and the post-industrial metropolis have all been culturally mediated. This mediation has both accommodated and reproduced patterns of racial difference historically through the attribution of particular cultural forms to specific regimes of employment. From slavery, through the range of forms of unfree labour to the turbulence of migration,[70] cultural inscriptions of difference have at times been likewise marked. The genealogy that links colonial domestic labour to the survival of the British National Health Service through importing nurses from the Caribbean reveals as much about empire and identity as it does about the political economy of the postwar years.[71] Likewise the replacement labour streams of the railways, the transport networks and the decaying remnants of postwar British manufacturing tie explicitly to racialised patterns of migrant labour demand.[72]

In the post-1945 years in most of Europe and North America such patterns are easily discernible and conceptually straightforward in the first generation of migrant flows. But multiculturalism challenges its own reflexive reproduction as such patterns are reproduced or erased over time. In considering the artefacts of the city and patterns of urbanism it is essential to consider what kinds of objects are being scrutinised in academic analysis and become the subject of cultural movements. In part some of the most powerful dynamics of Paul Gilroy's explorations of 'the planetary traffic in the image of blackness'[73] relate to the manner in which the biopolitics of black identities either refute or succumb to such logics. In particular the commodification of life itself,[74] mediated through notions of cultural difference, challenges the extent to which the city serves as both crucible of life chances and the projection screen for the reproduction of racial difference.

For Gilroy both the category of diaspora and the condition of rootless cosmopolitanism elude the forces that conspire to fix ethnicised identity as pure sameness: '[T]he desire to fix identity in the body is inevitably frustrated by the body's refusal to disclose the required signs of absolute incompatibility people imagine to be located there.'[75] But whether through Gilroy's principled deconstruction of raciology or through Barnor Hesse's more explicitly spatialised metaphors of entanglements and transruptions the city provides the site through which racial difference is potentially erased (assimilated) or reproduced.[76]

In this sense it is important to distinguish between two legitimate but separate analytical tasks at the heart of contemporary urbanism. One stems from a notion of generalisation, the other from a sense of critical analysis. They provide alternative registers of voice. In the former the multicultural city is the product of a universally recognised phenomenon of contemporary capitalism. In the latter the subjectivities of race and ethnicity need to be mapped within the lexicon of contemporary urbanism. Context, time and space are constitutive rather than central to an understanding of multiculture. As Chapters 1 and 2 described, this volume argues that a critical urbanism can derive a sense of international comparison from an understanding of the differential realisation of similar tropes of representation. Migrant minorities are not just *found* in the contemporary metropolis. Instead the configuration of the metropolis mediates the realisation, visibility and (at times) disappearance of markers of cultural difference and collective identity.

The metaphor of the mosaic contrasts with that of the melting pot. The former potentially takes the hard boundaries of the epidermal or the kinship boundary to reify sameness. The latter potentially takes the contingencies of creolisation as the normative basis of twenty-first-century urbanism.

For the purposes of this chapter three points are essential. They set the scene for the remaining chapters of this volume. All demand empirical investigation in the cities of today, whether in the form of generalisation or analytical critique. First, in both registers of voice the material economy of work and worklessness provides a political economy out of which patterns of change emerge. It is not the primary but it is (in an Aristotelian sense) the material cause out of which contemporary multiculturalism emerges. Analytical urbanism needs to understand such material causality when considering the racialisation of Bradford alongside the myths and realities of contemporary London; when debating model minorities and the ghetto in the USA; or when configuring the disciplined cosmopolitanism of contemporary Singapore. In as much as ethnic identity is invariably in part about processes of commodification, then patterns of progressive cosmopolitanism and racist intolerance cannot be either reduced to or separable from economic systems of exploitation.

Second, the visibility of ethnic difference or sameness depends on the analytical tools that are used to scrutinise the city, as well as any straightforward understanding of the object itself. And these analytical tools are themselves implicated in processes of commodification. Seen through a lens of religious affiliation, the city looks very differently to cartographies of sexualised practices. Different regimes of representation render visible very different notions of multicultural subjects of the city. And through their territorialisations they open up specifically commodified relationships between place and the politics of identity. In this sense the interplay between demographic fractions of city citizens and regimes of cultural difference enter into a recursive play with one another. The common sense of multicultural London or ethnicised New York creates an iconography of racialised place names that structure land values that in turn structure the life chances of the people living in those parts, ghettos and cultural quarters of the city. Chapter 7 focuses on the nature of this process in the context of the cultural quarter of the city.

Third, new patterns of racism draw on such optics. As expanding economies in the north rode the long economic boom of the 1990s, consequent demand for migrant labour correlated directly with its concomitant migrant flows[77] and a new xeno-racism. A new assimilationism characterises contemporary European fears of the refugee in the cities confronted by the enhanced mobility of populations.[78] After 9/11 the translation of Islamophobia typologises the population of the city in ways that distinguish one migrant community from another in invidious patterns of intolerance.[79] At times intercultural conflict is naturalised in a rhetorical clash of civilisations.[80] The configurations of race, identity and nationalism in America in the wake of the invasion of Iraq or the rise of the (fascist) BNP in British cities, in the face of the Euro and other national insecurities, all figure the urban as a site of struggle.[81] The city is central to the regimes of representation of each of these new racisms but it mediates them differently.

Conclusion

For Seyla Benhabib 'democratic politics challenges, redefines and renegotiates the divisions between the good and the just, the moral and the legal, the private and the public'.[82] Such a notion accords well with most understandings of an 'agonistic' notion of political theory, the unsettled nature of hegemonic settlement and the ethically moving subaltern politics demand that the basic lexicon of political thought needs to be contextualised.

At one level this chapter is suggesting that this foundational lexicon of citizenship, justice and democracy needs to be figured through the spaces of the city as well as the historical epochs in which they are set. But, more significantly, it is arguing that the *time-spaces* of the city are actually constitutive of the very concepts themselves. The stages of the city – Hall's 'truly heterogeneous spaces' – are a narrative device through which such a lexicon is made comprehensible. Contemporary urbanism needs to consider the manner in which a fabricated nature of the spatial and the temporal creates mutable subjects and changing institutions at the heart of the dynamic cities of multiculturalism. Such a positioning demands ethnographic understanding of city cultures alongside alternative framings of the subjects and cartographies of the city itself. In subsequent chapters we draw on this framework to produce alternative explorations of the contemporary metropolis.

4   The ghetto

Knowing your place and the performative cartographies of racial subordination

Introduction

From before the origins of the ghetto in Renaissance Venice, the fabric of the city has repeatedly wrapped around spaces of poverty in a fashion that both displays and conceals the realities of contemporary immiseration. Such spaces are invariably the product of both political economies of residence and eschatologies of stigma. The combination of the empirical measurement of the former and the semiotics of the latter may at times confuse analysis. In any description it is possible to invoke sets of meanings that are *already known* about the ghetto, the banlieue, the township or the favela. Yet the strange realities of such places can also confound. Early in Matthieu Kassiewitz's 1995 film *La Haine*,[1] a pan shot across a Parisian banlieue blown by ganja smoke and the riotous soundtrack of 'Fuck the Police' intercut with Piaf's 'Je ne regrette rien' is suddenly interrupted by the presence of a cow on a derelict post-riot landscape. Likewise, the narrative through which the barrio is made visible in the film *Ciudad del Dios* is bookended by the sudden appearance of a chicken running through the street. The uncanny appearance of the strange animal in both cases disrupts the familiar and already known story of social immiseration in the ghettoes of the francophone and the Latin American city.

The ghetto debate

In the first years of the new century a row has rumbled through the American academy about the nature of the contemporary ghetto. In a classic debate of the sort that has long characterised disciplinary boundary making, Loïc Wacquant – a student and collaborator of Pierre Bourdieu and a former collaborator of William Julius Wilson – published in the *American Journal of Sociology* an excoriation of American scholarship of urban poverty. Wacquant drew on his earlier work in which he highlighted 'three pernicious premises' in the study of the American ghetto. Scholars had traditionally perpetuated three exemplary misunderstandings of the ghetto as, variously, an empiricist territory of the city, a container of the exoticised *others* of social research, and commonly reduced explanations to nostrums on the social disorganisation and cultural pathologies of the ghetto residents.[2]

For Wacquant the ghetto must be placed within a taxonomy of *peculiar institutions* of racialised suppression, developed through a rigorous analysis[3] of the macro-cosm of the social.[4] His 2002 critique alleged a failure properly to theorise the object of study and to contextualise the American ghetto internationally. More-over, it also suggested that this failure misconceived the relationship between empirical ethnographic observation and theoretical labour more generally. Notable scholars of urban poverty such as Mitchell Duneier, Elijah Anderson, and Katherine Newman[5] had consequently putatively privileged a naïve empiricism that produced neo-romantic tales of the ghetto that inadvertently became complicit in the neo-liberal politics of the American cities of the early twenty-first century.[6]

Wacquant's call for a theoretically sophisticated ethnography privileges the construction of the object of research (*the ghetto*) in contradistinction to the naïve presentation of facts about places and people that inhabit them.[7] He calls for a sophisticated analytical notion of the ghetto to contrast with the variations of alleged empirical naïveté in the works he cites. In line with his roots in Bourdieu's powerful anthropology, he argues that academics should focus on an analytical ordering of empirical reality rather than accept the *folk concepts* of either local people or powerful interests. Specifically, Wacquant sees the ghetto as a '*relation* of ethnoracial control and closure'[8] based on stigma, constraint, territorial confine-ment and institutional encasement.

Much of this debate has already generated the call and response antiphony of academic exchange. For this chapter, however, two facets of the controversy are significant. The first is Wacquant's notion that the analytical ordering of the spaces of the city can be separated from the folk concepts of the powerful and the powerless. I think the interplay between the representation of the ghetto, and the ghetto's invocation and mediation by both its residents and its oppressors, is slightly more complex than this might suggest. We might need to understand a little more about the manner in which this *distinct space* is made visible as an object of study, before denouncing either the perspectival distance of bureaucratic quantification of urban poverty or privileging the ostensibly heroic immersion in the proximate realities of ghetto life. If we are to scrutinise the street effectively, we might wish to consider carefully both the vocabulary and the lens through which the spatial is made visible.[9] The second matter of interest is Wacquant's contention that naïve empiricism begets neo-liberal orthodoxy. It is certainly the case that the fabrication of the ghetto[10] demands a complex notion of the political,[11] as well as an invocation of the repressive or revanchist state. Yet an omnibus notion of the oppressive state that is commonly invoked in some narratives of contemporary urbanism is not so much euphemistic about the exercise of state power in the cities of the present as simplistic about the banality of governmental practice.

In this chapter it is argued that the juxtapositions of empirical proximity and theoretical distance are not quite as straightforward as Wacquant suggests. The carceral figuring of the twenty-first-century city is marked by transience and terror. Its temporalities of workplace are those of the just-in-time production process that moves to abolish the career.[12] In temporality of settlement, residence displaces dwelling.[13] In such a setting the time horizons of the ghetto may be foreshortened.

The subjectivities of the protagonists of gun crime and itinerant migrant labour necessarily construct *the future* through the calculus of the ghetto and not the burbs. But likewise the stories they tell about the spaces in which they live are not isolated from the representations of the ghetto in the scripts of the bureaucrats, policy makers, politicians and academics whose temporalities may have more distant horizons. So this chapter also argues that a more iterative relationship between the folk-naming of city spaces and their official or analytical cartographies might aid and not detract from an understanding of the carceral imperatives of contemporary ghetto urbanism. This might foreground the sorts of political and policy questions that are properly raised in the study of the ghetto.[14]

Race, tenure and residential space in British cities

In the United Kingdom the use of the notion of the ghetto has a chequered history. In particular, the link between the ghetto and forms of residence has changed at different times, although the issue of tenure has not always been seen as analytically central. Famously, in the sociological traditions of the 1960s and 1970s, the Weberian consideration of housing classes in the early work of John Rex and Ray Pahl defined a cartography of the racialised city.[15] Though the term *ghetto* was occasionally used to denote the Jewish East End and the original Chinatown of Victorian London, some of its earliest British invocations focused on residential clustering of largely privately rented accommodation, commonly equated with Chicago-School-rooted zones of transition. The concentration of particular migrant communities around the neighbourhoods of the docks of the imperial cities of London, Liverpool, Bristol, Cardiff and Glasgow produced various 'coloured quarters', one of which, around Cable Street in London, was famously studied by Michael Banton in the 1950s.[16]

But it was a fear of the emergence of American levels of racial segregation that described one of the central characteristics of mainstream housing policy debate in the United Kingdom from the 1960s to the 1980s. In such work the *ghetto* was defined principally as an American phenomenon whose transatlantic translation should be resisted through a range of social policy instruments that capitalised on the distinctive and significant role of socially owned (predominantly local-government-owned) housing stock in the development of postwar urban Britain.[17] And whilst the tenure pattern of different migrant groups was not uniform, Susan Smith has demonstrated how even the most ostensibly equitable processes of residential allocation in the Keynesian welfare state decades that followed the war resulted in some entrenched patterns of racial segregation within British cities,[18] even if these were not quite on American levels of separation or dissimilarity of residential pattern.

But in the contemporary United Kingdom the future of social housing remains at the heart of debates about the changing boundaries of the twenty-first-century welfare state. A period of consensually acknowledged disinvestment in the last decades of the twentieth century has provoked a less consensual consideration about how future investment levels in deprived stock might be refurbished to a level that is habitable or might qualify for a government floor target of 'decent homes'. This target is one that defines basic conditions of reasonable residential amenity in some of the least affluent areas of British cities.[19]

Such a debate plays particularly prominently in parts of the city where the dominant form of housing provision has, in the postwar era, been rental tenure in homes built by the local state. Consequently, not quite coterminous with the contentiously defined inner cities – but closely correlated with it – the landscape of large tracts of urban Britain is testament to the most severe forms of this housing disinvestment. They are also sites in which the controversies around the future of social housing become most profoundly felt. The manner in which such tower blocks, estates, quarters and neighbourhoods are described consequently becomes central to a debate about their future.

In contrast to Wacquant's straightforward separation between folk and analytic concepts, this chapter argues that the interplay between representations of space and the spaces of representation generates a much more iterative relationship than academics might wish to acknowledge. The chapter draws on several pieces of longstanding ethnographic research on a number of estates in the inner south-eastern part of London.[20] These estates have at times, in the local vernacular of young people and also through policy debate, been referred to (both collectively and individually) as the *ghetto*. Two of these Deptford estates – Milton Court and Pepys – in particular exemplify some of the themes that characterise the tensions between community sentiment and bureaucratic rationality already explored in Chapter 3.

The estates have their very particular social histories. They have been marked by changing levels of racial segregation, but have both been characterised by significant concentrations of migrant minorities over the last thirty years. First- and second-generation African-Caribbean, West African, Vietnamese and, more recently, refugee minorities have settled locally. The right to residence rations a scarce commodity. The allocation of social housing in London patterns degrees of ethnic concentration. In such ostensibly banal everyday practices significantly different moral universes are normalised. Specifically, on these estates a bureau-cratically rational process that appeared to universalise the subject (and mask ethnic difference) and a community-empowered involvement programme (that appeals to popular sentiment) may both racialise allocation outcomes and segregation in ways that were not anticipated at the time but are no less significant for doing so.

The Pepys Estate was built by the Greater London Council in 1966. In the name of participatory democracy and community empowerment local residents were allowed, from the 1970s onwards, to become involved in the selection of residents who were eligible for rental properties as they became vacant. Unsurprisingly, the result was that the estate remained 'whiter' long after the surrounding area had become characterised by a strongly multicultural demography. Interestingly, when the estate was transferred to local authority control after the demise of the Greater London Council, the peak demand of Afro-Caribbean residents in this part of South London had been overtaken by the West African migrations of the

1980s. The subsequent 'colour blind' allocation of some of the less desirable housing in South London witnessed a significant increase in the numbers of African residents locally throughout the decade of the 1980s.[21]

The Milton Court Estate was built by the local authority in 1971.[22] It became marked by the sort of deck-access tower blocks that exemplify a certain visual repertoire of city living. It was no coincidence that the unpopularity of the stock coincided with the clustering of the allocations on the estate to the properties of migrant minorities in the 1970s. The estate witnessed the sort of racialised housing provision described in landmark works by Susan Smith and Deborah Phillips.[23] As Smith describes in detail, the perversely rational forms of bureaucratic logic can become the crucible of a very specific articulation of institutional racism, producing patterns of segregation as a product of systemic characteristics of the allocation process. As ever, the fabrication of the city provides a certain kind of cartography that is always in part a state artefact.

The estate became notorious in the 1980s for the increasing levels of confrontation between police and British black (mostly black Caribbean) residents. By the mid-1980s it was rated as one of the five estates in London most likely to witness a reproduction of the scale of racialised urban uprising seen on Broadwater Farm Estate in Tottenham in 1985: the riot that remains the most serious incident of racialised civil unrest on Britain's mainland. The decline of police–community relations spiralled in a manner that replicated processes explored in other parts of London.[24] In the early 1990s many characterised the area as 'no go', with cab drivers, postal services and at times even emergency ambulances refusing to service the area. In the 1980s and early 1990s local narratives of police oppression sat alongside accounts of the discovery of Ouzi machine guns in police raids on the estate.

A combination of a major social renewal programme (through youth work, community safety and welfare programmes, the Safer Cities programme and the Deptford Task Force), a physical renewal project ('Estate Action') and massive community effort has transformed the estate in the last decade. It is moot how much the balance between population dispersal, architectural solutions and new forms of solidarity have changed the quality of life for those who now live there. Several of the tower blocks were torn down and tenure was *diversified* through the addition of housing association and privately owned stock to the estate. It is also the case that it remains an area with a particular reputation, though perhaps one of diminishing notoriety. But in this particular part of South London it remains at the imaginative heart of the *ghetto*.[25]

Clearly, the levels of intense segregation witnessed in the United States and mapped conscientiously by William Julius Wilson, his collaborators (including Wacquant), and the generations of empirically oriented American sociology have never yet been replicated in the United Kingdom (or in the French *banlieues*).[26] Clearly, it is also important to recognise structural processes by which the ghetto is made and remade. In South London the future of both Pepys and Milton Court is the subject of considerable controversy. Central government policy is premised on generating housing investment through the transfer of such stock to registered social landlords (principally housing associations), which can borrow money on the open market, securitised against rental returns (unlike local government that is bound by tight fiscal regimes that restrict borrowing). Some support such transfers, others do not. Ironically, in some parts of London the extent to which sentiment supports such transfers tends to be inversely correlated against the degree to which people trust the institutions of the local state that currently manage the property.[27]

These factors produce specific relations between tenure, residence, citizenship and regimes of governance in the creation of residential space and the fabrication of the ghetto. Significantly, the manner in which forces of devalorised property tracts produce similar results to state-controlled residential allocations plays differently in Britain, mainland Europe and the USA. Consequently, the institutional structures of such differences, the interaction between state and market place, the transactional boundary between state and civil society, underscores the production of the ghetto and needs to inform transnational comparison. However, it is not such processes alone that shape the future and the past of the area. The locality is constantly the subject of iterations between place and identity. People make their own cartographies of the city – if not in circumstances of their own choosing. The vernacular ghetto in Deptford retained its power in the narratives of young people describing the gangs of twenty-first-century London in work that explored the imagined geographies of urban territorialisation.[28]

In part such processes are about the relationships of surveillance and control that play out in debates around community safety examined in Chapter 9 of this volume. So on the Milton Court Estate the right to walk the street cannot be disassociated from the campaign against the SUS laws[29] in the 1970s which confined British black communities to the ghetto and a generation later to the baptismal creation of self-ascribed *ghetto boys* who reappropriated these residential spaces as badges of pride in the articulation of gang identities on the estate.[30] In part such processes are also about the struggle to imagine communities locally. Communities of West African diasporas in the 1980s and of refugee settlement (Vietnamese in the 1980s, multinational in the 2000s) shape themselves from the vernacular representations of the ghetto. But in part also such processes are about the emergence of the ghetto as an *in-between space* – not a romantically invoked heterotopia but a frame of reference through which the mimesis of place and the politics of identity emerge in the multicultural metropolis: structured by racism but reconfigured through resistance. To understand such mimesis demands an acknowledgment that the spaces of the city are produced by different frames of representation. Understanding the ghetto demands more than a juxtaposition of the perspectival distance of bureaucratic quantification of urban poverty with a privileging of the heroic immersion in the ethnographic realities of ghetto life. It also demands that we move beyond the chimeric romance of the exclusively *real* description of the ghetto spaces of the city. Two examples serve to illustrate this point: one drawn from the even more iconic heart of Brixton in South London; the other returning us again to the streets of Deptford.

1980s Brixton: the ghetto and the romance of the real

In the juxtaposition between folk and analytical concepts advocated by Wacquant there is a danger that the iterative structuring of each by the other will be finessed through a common *romance of the real*. There is an element of the mirage that is present in such a romance. It is because meaning is unstable throughout its genesis, at the level of the social (ended or just begun), the author (dead or alive), and the audience (visible or invisible), that appeals to a spatial grounding of the metaphoric excesses of social theory will be necessarily fruitless. The reason is simple in one sense, complicated in another. In the simple sense, as Laclau and Mouffe have suggested: 'all discourse of fixation becomes metaphorical: literality is, in actual fact, the first of metaphors'.[31] This assertion explicitly does not imply a slide into epistemological relativism.[32] At a more complex level, boutique cosmopolitanism's occasionally naïve celebration of 'difference' is paralleled in the epistemological crises of representation of the multicultural city that are best examined through the spatial metaphor of the cultural quarter in Chapter 8. But, consequently, in this way the issue of closure is similarly central to the contingency of the truth claims we make, to the bounding of political interventions and to the abolition of any opposition between the metaphoric and the real in the spatialisation of social theory.

Representations of 'the ghetto'

Prefiguring more contemporary invocations of the postcolony,[33] the seminal work on the social construction of black criminality in Britain written in the 1970s – *Policing the Crisis* – was in part based on the deployment of the ghetto as a central analytical concept. Stuart Hall and his associates, when deconstructing the ghetto in this work, regularly resorted to the metaphor of the *black colony* as both victim of racist practices of criminalisation *and* (apparently) social reality.[34] The authors point out the way in which racist classification of mugging can be connoted by place, by highlighting black areas of settlement. A case in which a white youth assaults a black bus conductor could still (in 1970s Britain) reproduce the racialised imagery of mugging because 'The specification of certain *venues* reactivates earlier and subsequent associations : Brixton and Clapham.'[35]

Crime, race and the ghetto could be conflated as social problems after incidents such as the clashes with police in Brockwell Park because they '*located and situated* black crime, geographically and ethnically, as peculiar to black youth in the inner city ghettos'.[36]

However, in the Britain of the last thirty years the broader social context against which processes should be set is less readily identifiable. Taking up many of the themes of *Policing the Crisis*, Hall developed the notion of authoritarian populism in his landmark Cobden Lecture of 1979, which traced out a political project which uses the 'forging of a disciplinary common sense'[37] to undermine welfare rights, notions of citizenship, and the freedoms of organised labour. At its formative stages Hall's analysis took as its driving force the realisation of *urban crisis*[38] with 'the use of police powers to contain and constrain, and in effect to help to criminalise, parts of the black population in our urban colonies',[39] defining the black community again as the *victim* of these changes.

This analysis led logically into Hall's pioneering explanation of Thatcherism as an ideological project, neatly summarised by Gamble:

> Within the working class the groups that stood to lose most were women and blacks and particular regional communities. The costs of restructuring the economy, however, could be loaded much more easily onto such groups if the political credibility of their case for equal rights had first been destroyed. Conversely, if social democratic arguments retained their dominant place in public debate on welfare provision, it would be less easy to ignore the claims of blacks and women and other disadvantaged groups to assistance and subsidy from the state.[40]

Alternatively, Paul Gilroy questioned the notion of a 'drift' into a law and order society,[41] preferring to explain criminalisation more in terms of the construction of nationalism: 'The ability of law and the ideology of legality to express and represent the nation state and national unity precedes the identification of racially distinct crimes and criminals';[42] 'black law breaking supplies the historic proof that blacks are incompatible with the standards of decency and civilisation which the nation requires of its citizenry'; 'It is precisely this unified national culture articulated around the theme of legality and constitution which black criminality is alleged to violate, thus jeopardising both state and civilisation.'[43]

It is not necessary to arbitrate between the different emphases here. The point is more simple. Both analyses contain a tension which is not clearly resolved between the empirical reality of epidermal demographics victimised by racist processes of criminalisation and the invention of cultural significations (and scopic regimes) of race as criminality. The tension is not so much a flaw of the analyses as the point at which the processes of criminalisation and racialisation become one.[44]

In *Policing the Crisis* in particular, there seems to be a repeated elision of the ghetto as metaphor and the ghetto as reality: a fictional black colony that signifies criminality in racist discourse and a factual black colony of subordinated communities. In one sense this is one of the most analytically powerful elements of the work, distinguishing it from most descriptions of criminalisation. An analytical tradition which consciously echoes and expands the theories of labelling and social deviancy[45] tends to describe the manner in which a group is picked out of society and victimised. Yet in a sense the failure to clarify the metaphoric/real distinction that the text itself draws upon weakens the argument in *Policing the Crisis* because, in the absence of such specification, the *black colony* remains needlessly more a rhetorical than an analytic term.

There is an echo of this ambivalence in the late Edward Said's brilliant (and masterful) deconstruction of Orientalism.[46] It is a common criticism of his most famous work that Said in a sense wanted to have his cake and eat it. Simplifying the critique considerably, Said makes the point that the discourse of Orientalism creates a place, invents an imagined geography, and yet is simultaneously a misrepresentation of a place that he himself refers to as the Orient. Said wants to be both inside the political context of colonialism and outside the discourse through which colonialism is reproduced, an acrobatic that Robert Young has described as the 'significant lacuna of the book',[47] leaving Said in a position where 'Said's account will be no truer to Orientalism than Orientalism is to the actual Orient, assuming that there could ever be such a thing'.[48]

What emerges here is an *apparent* tension between the *imagined* and the *real* that renders the spatiality of both Stuart Hall's ghetto and Edward Said's Orient equally problematic. Yet if we understand that such confusions arise in part from a conflation of the abstract and the empirical, it becomes clear that space is no more (or less) material than it is ideological. Places too, such as the ghetto and the Orient, are moments of arbitrary closure. Representations may be material, but are never reducible to the material; signification rarely guarantees its own reception. In this way social differentiation is played out across terrains that are ever shifting; racism in part subsists and in part is challenged in and through metaphoric and metonymic appropriations of landscape. The landscape is simultaneously duplicitous and cogent, metric and dramaturgical, real and imagined. Analytically, I want to highlight just three aspects of these forms of spatiality, neither as exhaustive typology nor as distinct productions of space. The analysis moves towards an end which rejects any opposition between the real and the metaphoric, disrupts the easy separation of folk and analytical concepts in mapping the ghetto deployed by Wacquant. Such disruption might make us think differently about naming the diagnostic cartographies of the multicultural cities of the twenty-first century.

Representations of space and spaces of representation[49]

Lived space and the dangers of literalism

There are several senses in which a literal interpretation of spatiality can cause only problems for theoretical analysis. Most obviously it is possible through a focus on the spatiality of social relations to attribute to space autonomous ontological status and concomitant sets of mysterious causal powers. This process of mystification has long been rejected in the Marxist literature with a critique of the *spatial fetish*, a phenomenon most commonly seen in those state policies that attribute to particular places or areas immanent properties and characteristics (e.g. certain expressions of regional policy, inner city policy).[50]

A second trap that has bedevilled analysis is the naturalisation of the inevitably territorial nature of human organisation, an analytical step that tends always towards, if not always as far as, behaviourism and an Ardrey-like rendition of *The Territorial Imperative*.[51] Third, and perhaps most importantly here, there is a seductive danger of creating a false duality between a world of metaphors, on the one hand, and a world of reality, on the other. David Harvey's suggestion that 'there are *real* geographies of social action, real as well as metaphorical territories and spaces of power that become vital as organising forces in the geopolitics of capitalism' (emphasis added),[52] is very stirring and sets up an implicit opposition between the comfort of the abstract and the relevance of the empirical, the seduction of the ivory tower and the romance of the street.[53] It is this latter set of oppositions that involves a misapprehension of the manner in which metaphor and metonymy work in the representation of places.

Staged space

The metaphors we live by are not escapes from reality as much as a means through which reality is rendered comprehensible. The easiest way to understand this is through a by now unexceptional rendition of dramaturgical analysis in city life. It is in this sense that when Sennett suggests that '"(t)o go out in publick" is a phrase based on society conceived in terms of this geography',[54] there can be no clearer invocation of the *social* as spatialised urbanism.

There is no notion here of a literal space; we are instead in a Goffmanesque world where spaces are signifying, placed in a semiotic chain. It is in this world where we can see that the ambiguity in Hall and Said's work is nothing to do with fundamental analytical flaws; it is instead a constitutive element of the manner in which the relationship between language and meaning is always ruptured by the tension between socially produced and individually defined understandings (effectively the tension between *langue* and *parole*). This tension slips into racist discourse and mediates the reproduction of racism, a phenomenon best illustrated by example.

One of the minor, but significant, debates that ran through the public hearings of the Scarman Inquiry into the 'riots' in Brixton in the spring of 1981 concerned what the term 'Front Line' actually meant. Courtney Laws (of Brixton Neighbourhood Community Association) suggested that 'The historical fact of the Front Line, as I understand it – because I helped to name it – is where people from the Caribbean normally gather, meet and talk and often start up socialising groups and functions. It is very peaceful and quiet.'[55] District Detective Chief Superintendent Plowman flatly contradicted this image:

> the words 'Front Line', as far as most people understand it, came about from . . . a film that was done by the BBC in 1965 when they said that Railton Road was the front line of confrontation between black and white in the Brixton area and . . . that is why it is called the Front Line.

> [T]here is only about 200 of that black community that collect in the Front Line or Railton Road area. They are mostly black people that are unemployed or Rastafarian types who display an anti-authority attitude.

He also suggested that the Front Line was used to 'dispose stolen property'. Plowman was candid, the '*place*' was stigmatised, explicitly labelled as a 'criminal area'. In stark comparison, in 1976 the radical black newspaper *Race Today* had claimed that, 'Railton Road is a heavily policed area. The Brixton end of the road is referred to among blacks in military terms as "the Front Line". It is the front line of defence against the police.'[56] In the political campaign for 'black resistance', *Race Today* in the mid-1970s was explicitly characterising the Front Line as a source of potential black political solidarity. From this perspective the '*riots*' were the logical outcome of this local mobilisation.[57]

Similarly, although everybody accepted that the Front Line covered some part of the Railton Road, several different definitions of its precise boundaries were offered at the Inquiry, some confining it to a very small stretch of the road between Atlantic Road and Leeson Road, others including a larger section of Railton Road, yet others using the term more generally to describe a whole area.

The point Scarman missed in his search for the meaning of the term was that Front Line may have been clearly defined for some individuals but on closer inspection there are many different understandings of this '*sense of place*'. There is no one meaning of Front Line: a social centre, the epicentre of black resistance, a location for trading stolen goods, a home, a drugs market place – a variety of competing, frequently contradictory, perceptions held by individuals and institutions. At one time or another the Front Line has been, in part, most of these things. The choice between these meanings is, quite properly, as much a question of politics as of accuracy (realism). In a strictly geographical sense it is a term that serves in 'the naming of parts', spatial parts. As meaning, shorthand definitions of places, based on subjectively defined salient characteristics of those places, are near universal features of the way in which the lived world (*Umwelt*) is internally reconstructed in comprehensible form. A name denotes a place and connotes a history. As ever, assorted histories are woven together, sieved by experience. Front Line did not mean the same for old and young, black and white, police and policed. Yet, through all these histories, a common theme was always the conflict between black people and the police. But the vernacular (or folk) concept of the front line infests both policy-oriented response to a policing of the ghetto and an analytical conceptualisation of its genesis. What the tension between the Front Line as an empirical location and the Front Line as a symbolic place masks is the situation of the term itself as an organising theme of completely contradictory rationalisations of this conflict.

The manner in which places evoke racist connotations was integral to the *naturalisation* of policing strategies of racial subordination.[58] The process of signification by which places are constituted is a necessary element of this but it is essential to see the communicative uncertainty of the dramaturgical process as central rather than incidental to the apprehension of the real world, apprehension that is simultaneously metaphoric and metonymic. In each reading of produced space, what is going on is a *slippage* across the dimensions of the Saussurean field of meaning (as in Figure 4.1). This ambivalent quality of spatial signification becomes even more pronounced when the central metaphor of the stage, dramaturgical analysis as the generator of signification, is itself taken as problematic.

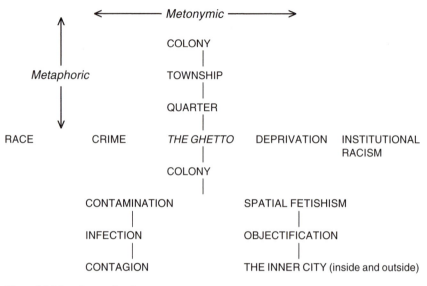

Figure 4.1 Metaphors of racism.

The imaginary city: ghetto urbanism, ambivalence and alterity

Ultimately the notion of places signifying meanings is always going to be unsatisfactory because it ignores the sense in which they too are representations. Places themselves are constituted in our apprehension of them by the broader social patterns of communication. If the metaphor of landscape as text is to mean more than the privileged translations of the cultural élite, then not only do the corollaries of the metaphor need examining,[59] but the political constitution of authorship and audience of the text needs to be considered. It is by returning the text to its production and reception that it is possible to avoid a distinction between some false dichotomies that at times characterise analysis of ghetto urbanism: between the metaphoric and the real, between the abstract and the concrete, between absolute space and abstract space.

As Chapter 2 argued, it is possible to suggest that a series of attempts to define the nature of the city have created both a lexicon and a series of discourses of the *urban* and its constituent parts (such as the ghetto) that leave us with the city as a central organising theme in the imagined geographies that we use to make sense of the social world. As such, the ghetto is neither reducible to ideology nor constituted as a coherent analytical unit (in Bourdieu/Wacquant's terms), but is instead an exemplary case of the inseparability of the abstract and the empirical. Racist meanings are closely connected to the notions of the urban that permeate European and North American culture, but they are not connoted in any straightforward or consistent manner. It is instead the case that urban representations of race draw on a repertoire of effects that are characterised by:

- ambiguity and ambivalence
- contradictions
- slippage.

These properties destabilise the racialised meanings of the *urban*, rendering them context-dependent.

AMBIGUITY AND AMBIVALENCE

As the dramaturgical examples of the Front Line demonstrate, places signify different meanings to different people. Fanon, in *Wretched of the Earth*, made precisely this point about the symbolic order of the colonial city:

> The symbols of social order – the police, the bugle calls in the barracks, the military parades and the waving flags – are at one and the same time inhibitory and stimulating; for they do not convey the message 'Don't dare to budge'; rather they cry out 'Get ready to attack'.[60]

CONTRADICTIONS

The racist discourses of the imaginary are riddled with contradictions – desire is conflated with disgust, identification clashes with scopophilia, analytical clarity looks for gestalt synthesis. Ghetto urbanism may be simultaneously the object of a conceptual gaze and an imagined autobiography, the self-positioned as both insider and outsider. There is a racist discourse of depravity that draws its provenance from a racialised construction of a black urban Babylon but there is also a Renaissance evocation of whiteness in the urban etymological roots of the term 'civilisation'. 'Race' can be used contextually to signify both utopian and dystopian visions of the urban in precisely the manner explored in Chapter 2 of this volume.

SLIPPAGE

Numerous authors have demonstrated how the parallel vocabularies of disgust can draw on each other through a process of metaphoric and metonymic slippage between one another. Racist discourse has characteristically picked up themes of sanitation, bestiality and the primitive. Such discursive intertextuality is not necessarily racist, but it is a path through which racist meaning may be coded. Stallybrass and White developed an analytical framework for understanding these processes of *transcoding*, exemplified in their contention that:

> Like most of the sanitary reformers, Chadwick traces the metonymic associations between filth and disease: and the metonymic associations (between the poor and animals, between the slum dweller and sewage) are read at first as the signs of an imposed social condition for which the State is responsible. But

the metonymic associations (which trace the 'social' articulation of 'depravity') are constantly elided with and displaced by a metaphoric language in which filth stands in for the slum-dweller: the poor *are* pigs.[61]

Spaces of the urban such as the ghetto, the inner city, or the *banlieue* may consequently occupy territories that are spatially and politically marginal but symbolically central to the psyche of the metropolis. It was also in this way that for Haussman the unholy trinity of disease, crime and revolution slipped one into another and rationalised particular forms of reconfiguration of the city. Similarly, Elizabeth Wilson has made the point that:

> Prostitutes and prostitution recur continually in the discussion of urban life, until it almost seems as though to be a woman – an individual, not part of a family or kin group – in the city, is to become a prostitute – a public woman.[62]

The slippage of meaning is at the heart of both ethnographic inspection of the ghetto and analytical deployment of the term. Slippage provides a central theme because it is at the moment that the continual elision of different discourses stops that a place is produced as a site of meaning, the Saussurean position is closed.

On closure

Closure is the moment at which the generalities of language are cemented into the specificities of the individual speech act. Ghetto urbanism is a product of both specific carceral processes and particular contexts of social stigma. For the purposes of this chapter, this social context of knowledge production can be framed by drawing selectively on four of the proposals that have characterised Ernesto Laclau's considerations of the dimensions of the antithetical relationship between subject and structure:

- Any subject is a mythical subject.
- The subject is constitutively metaphoric.
- The subject forms of identification function as surfaces of inscription.
- The incomplete character of the mythical surface of inscription is the condition of possibility for the constitution of social imaginaries.[63]

Taken together these statements can form the basis of a renewed consideration of how urbanism might come to terms with the sort of metaphoric spatialisation of social theory that Anglo-American cultural understandings of the ghetto exemplify. In such analysis materialism need not be sacrificed, the Lefèbvrian stress on space as produced remains, but the identities of specific places become much more complex. Such analysis does not understate the social injustices of the ghetto or traduce attempts to describe it. It does contextualise the will to describe displayed in all accounts; from those of the academics to the city managers and organic intellectuals who might challenge or reproduce its carceral form.

Places as moments of arbitrary closure

The characteristic of metaphoric and metonymic slippage is considered normal in most contemporary cultural theory. In this context Gayatri Chakravorty Spivak developed her contested notion of strategic essentialism, and in this sense Stuart Hall employed the concept of arbitrary closure in some of the late 1980s/early 1990s debates in postcolonial theory:

> All the social movements which have tried to transform society and have required the constitution of new subjectivities, have had to accept the necessary fictional, but also the fictional necessity, of the arbitrary closure which is not the end, but which makes both politics and identity possible.[64]

> For if signification depends on the endless re-positioning of its differential terms, meaning, in any specific instance, depends on the contingent and arbitrary stop – the necessary and temporary 'break' in the infinite semiosis of language. This does not detract from the original insight. It only threatens to do so if we mistake this 'cut' of identity – this positioning, which makes meaning possible – as a natural and permanent rather than an arbitrary and contingent 'ending' . . . Meaning continues to unfold, so to speak, beyond the arbitrary closure which makes it, at any moment, possible.[65]

It has been less usual to consider the relevance of spatial metaphors in this context. Consequently there is at times a tendency to resort to a spatial sense of the concrete. Hence even for Stuart Hall, 'young black people in London today are marginalised, fragmented, unenfranchised, disadvantaged and dispersed. And yet, they look as if they own the territory. Somehow, they too, in spite of everything, are centred in place.'[66] There is almost a sense of *déjà vu* here. Once again the trap of Said: framed within a dialectic of insiders and outsiders there is a false duality of the mythic and the real. It is the iconic power of places that ties together a moment of arbitrary closure and their moment of recognition in the world of the real. It is surely though, at this point, that an understanding of spaces as produced and contingent undermines such appeals to the spatial real.

It is instead the case that places themselves are no more and no less than moments of arbitrary closure. Materially produced and multiply signified, 'a place' in precise terms can have only a meaning of a particular moment, just as any word has only the meaning of a single usage and yet as parole or unique utterance this does not prevent the realisation of a communicative language.

So there is no a straightforward dichotomy between the imagined and the real or the folk and the analytical ghetto. It is more complex than this. The material nature of literal space guarantees closure in a signifying chain that has no other necessary beginning and no other necessary ending. This can be taken both optimistically and pessimistically. On the one hand, space is a realm of privileged metaphor. On the other, spatialised vocabularies may betray a misleading equivalence between the empirical and the real. The semiotics of the ghetto confuse a dichotomy between analytical and folk concepts.

Figure 4.1 explores just how such slippage can frame the spatial vocabularies of social theory. The ghetto is a term much used in progressive and reactionary analysis, but it would be wrong to limit the term to a single referent ('valorised' or 'stigmatised'; analytical or folk concept). The example drawn from *Policing the Crisis* effectively draws on the richness of the imagined geographies associated with the term to great rhetorical effect. It begins to fall down (as does Said's *Orientalism*) when the term stands as metaphor for racism and simultaneously with a set of metonymic associations with social deprivation. The former is the geography of what Laclau might describe as a 'frontier effect', an imagined geographical ground of mobilisation, the latter the parameters of an entity whose empirical definition can lead to a reification of problems of residential segregation. Neither one is more 'real' than the other; both are potentially dangerous if overendowed with some sort of essentialist ontological status. It is not that metaphor *per se* misrepresents; it is instead the case that in any particular usage the slippage across the diagram is frozen, because meaningful communication is only possible if the production of space is arbitrarily closed.

1990s Deptford: ghetto urbanism and cartographies of deterritorialisation and reterritorialisation

Making the ghetto invisible

It is appropriate to ask 'what kind of object is the social?' In many different strands of critical inquiry a term which on many levels seems so self-evident has been subjected to a scrutiny that questions the origins and the development of the concept of the *social* in academic writing. It has been variously suggested that the social is invented, promoted, found, imagined or even ended.

I do not want to examine these different questionings of the social in this chapter. However, I do want to think momentarily about how the particular social universe of ghetto urbanism is *spatialised* through particular geographical practices. If the social is a conceptual territory that is made visible in academic analysis through particular forms of investigation, then it is important to consider the narrative structures that are privileged in describing this particular field of vision. More specifically, I want to question the manner in which various mappings of 'race' at some times territorialise the social and at other times are rendered invisible by alternative stories of the social that are ostensibly unmarked by any trace of racial difference.

One brief example may be taken to illustrate this point from an urban regeneration initiative in inner South London – in Deptford once again. In 1991 Michael Heseltine, fresh from precipitating the resignation of Margaret Thatcher from her position as leader of the Conservative Party and Prime Minister, returned to the Department of the Environment as Secretary of State. Heseltine had for a long time had a personal interest in the processes and the grandeur of city regeneration programmes, and in the early 1980s he had fronted the introduction of Urban Development Corporations in the old waterfront areas of Merseyside and

London's Docklands. The City Challenge initiative was to be a creature of Heseltine's second coming, a new policy device to deliver urban regeneration programmes through a partnership between central government, the private sector, local government and local communities.[67]

Local authorities were obliged to bid to central government to win the £37.5 million that went along with the City Challenge initiatives. In South London the borough of Lewisham chose to focus its bid for resources on the northern wards of the borough in the area of Deptford. To impress Heseltine, as part of the bidding process, they brought the minister down to the massive Canary Wharf development on the Isle of Dogs, a potent symbol of Heseltine's earlier experiment in inner city revival. Heseltine was taken to a pier at the foot of the landmark Canary Wharf tower (1 Canada Place) and brought by boat the few hundred yards to the south of the river to the shores of old Deptford where Francis Drake, having circumnavigated the globe, returned in 1581 in the *Golden Hind* to be greeted by the queen and receive his knighthood.[68] This moment of discovery of an urban territory of a dark space of the city interior is common to many narratives of the inner city and resonant of the discovery of the social by the urban explorers of the late nineteenth and early twentieth centuries. Indeed, in his famous novel, *The Heart of Darkness*, Joseph Conrad's protagonist Marlow sets sail from Deptford towards the dark continent of Africa. But looking back he is reminded of the territories of the dangerous city he has left behind.

> The sun set; the dusk fell on the stream and the lights began to appear along the shore. The Chapman lighthouse, a three legged thing erect on a mud-flat, shone strongly. Lights of ships moved in the fairway – a great stir of lights going up and going down. And farther west on the upper reaches the place of the monstrous town was still marked ominously on the sky, a brooding gloom in the sunshine, a lurid glare under the stars.
>
> 'And this also,' said Marlow suddenly 'has been one of the dark places of the earth.'[69]

So, for Heseltine, the landing at Deptford Creek was in many ways a profoundly symbolic moment, captured on television cameras. But it was trumped by the next stage of his journey when he was shown around precisely the area known as the ghetto described earlier in this chapter. He was taken up into the sky over Deptford's mass of derelict social housing – including the Pepys and Milton Court Estates – and he toured the run-down industrial estates by helicopter. The landscape below him was almost literally turned into a map that was subsequently recognised as a space of governmental intervention, the territory that defined the borders of the urban regeneration initiative of Deptford City Challenge.

A governmental landscape was laid down beneath the helicopter. In one sense the ghetto could never be more clearly defined as a site of governmental intervention, a site for a particular form of experiment in governance. But, more significantly, this optic defined the area conceptually in terms of a naïve geography and rendered the languages of race peripheral to a problem of space. Made visible as a set of social housing problems and marginality adjacent to some major sites of renewed East London, the Deptford City Challenge initiative was defined in official documentation through the 'vision' of a 'gateway' that would link up the poverty of Deptford to the affluence of the capital. This metaphor of proximity, of a flow or diffusion of affluence, created a space of the social world defined through a governmental imagination.

It was a metaphor that did not lend itself easily to the notions of racial difference, to the suggestion that the forms of exclusion and indigence that characterised the area might have something to do with the fact that the profoundly multiracial nature of the local population might be locked into systems of resource allocation and life chances that were deeply racialised, inscribed with the processes of racist exclusion as well as geographical liminality. It also does not quite fit with a separation of empiricist naïveté and theoretical sophistication in the critiques of ghetto ethnographies by Wacquant.

The promotion of the ghetto (making the ghetto visible)

As vocabulary maps the city, it creates cartographies of the social. The manner in which such cartographies become analytically central to the manner in which we explain the workings of city life consequently depend in part on how they make multicultural forms of life visible. The wish to go the top of a hill and look down on the body of the social in all its glory may be indictable at some times as a moment of masculinist desire, but at other times it becomes an analytic point of view with a politics that defends its scopophilia.

In many ways the postwar history of the black presence in British cities can be characterised as an ongoing struggle around the terms on which the presence of blackness in the body of the social was to be made visible in late twentieth-century Britain. In his work, Barnor Hesse has consistently made this point through an analysis of both the temporalities and the spatialities of the black presence in the United Kingdom.[70] The New Cross Fire in 1981 illustrates the political ambivalence that surrounds a visibility that is generated by the technologies of representation by which social life is rendered (in)visible.

In the 1960s and 1970s one of the principal themes around which this debate raged was the relationship between Afro-Caribbean communities and the police. This had many specifically spatialised facets. Places of black settlement became both the iconic focus of racialised meaning and the particular site of techniques of police operations. In the sense we have already explored, the *ghetto* was both a metaphor of a presence and a metonym for particular forms and norms of rumoured behaviour. A black presence in some parts of the inner city at some times of the day was tolerated, but for black people – particularly young black men – to step outside these routines was to risk arrest, incarceration and criminalisation.[71]

In the 1970s and 1980s fears and moral panics associated with various forms of street crime were identified with a black presence through the complex interweaving of stories of race and space that carved out a place for sites of black settlement in the popular white imagination. The very visibility of black people in the social world of the high street, the estate and the journey home late at night came to represent a 'threat' in national press coverage and political debate. This was nowhere more clearly the case than in South London, and Deptford was just one of several locales where clashes between police and local black people became identified with particular geographies of everyday life, sites of ill repute and symbolic moments of resistance.

However, on 18 January 1981, 13 young people were killed when an arson attack on an Afro-Caribbean party burnt down a house in the New Cross Road in Deptford. Public reaction was remarkable. National press coverage was minimal and, as local black histories have recorded,[72] particularly insulting was the absence of any message of sympathy to the families of the bereaved from either Downing Street or Buckingham Palace. It appeared that for the prime minister of the time (Margaret Thatcher) and the British royal family the grief and the horror of the tragedy were unseen. By metaphoric extension, the black presence in British society was rendered invisible. The rallying call of the time, 'thirteen dead, nothing said', was an indictment of a failure of recognition as much as it was a condemnation of the obscenity of the fire itself.

The community reaction was straightforward and dramatic. A massive march was organised to start at the site of the 'New Cross Massacre' and walk via the Houses of Parliament and Fleet Street to Hyde Park. The numbers marching grew as people joined from across the country and traced a route from the margins of the inner city to the centre of London, bringing the capital to a standstill. In both a mundane and a profoundly moving sense this was the politics of visibility: a defiant moment of presence which, however it was subsequently misrepresented by the national press as a disorderly event, made a categoric statement that the territory of the social world of 1980s London could not be mapped in a single colour. The tale is exemplary. Black presence in the social was in many fields of representation framed by a narrative of criminality. Afro-Caribbean victimisation, tragedy and communal grief could only be made visible as the outcome of direct political intervention: quite literally the movement of what was socially marginal into a territory that was so politically central.

Conclusion

In this sense, then, spatialisation of the social in ghetto practices should be seen as different in degree rather than different in kind from the spatialisations of the social at other moments and through other techniques of representation. The term itself (like the whole lexicon of urbanism) has a genealogy which is clearly tied to the early origins of European capitalism, the invention of the nation state and a form of technocratic rationality that is commonly identified with secular modernity. The implication of vernacular forms in analytical conceptualisations of the ghetto arises precisely from such genealogy.

Likewise its geography has a history that is umbilically linked to the moments in which the social has been mapped by the city explorers of the nineteenth century and the bearers of the Chicago School tradition. The social is invoked in juxtaposition to the world of production (in oppositions of homeplace and work-place) and traced through the bibliographies of individual academics. As such, the configuration of this analytical terrain and the visibility of its landmarks are as much an outcome of these hidden institutional processes and varied techniques of mapping as they are a reflection of any set of visual ideologies *per se*.

In short, we perhaps need to consider *the way we look* and *the way we tell*, to privilege neither but to reveal the artifice of both. This might make us reconsider some of the more casual narratives of the social that either render the social world visible, unmarked by traces of racial difference in a moment of curious denial, or foreground particular facets of racialised landscapes as unduly significant in an analytical moment of metonymic abuse.

Either way, scopophilia itself – the (frequently ethnographic) act of empirical observation of ghetto urbanism – is perhaps less the villain of the piece than the twin conceits of some totalising rhetorical moves of generalisation and a blinkered institutional refusal to valorise the empirical moment in the search for the *cutting edge*. In such circumstances, an understanding of the ghetto rests on an iteration between different perspectival frames of reference. The objectification of statistical artefacts of poverty and the ethnographic milieu are not mutually exclusive. However, they are not necessarily commensurable one with the other. More significantly, the interplay between place and the politics of identity creates tensions that infect both the conceptual naming of the parts of the city and its reappropriation by its citizens. This we will explore in the next three chapters of this volume.

5 Ethnic entrepreneurs and street rebels

Looking inside the inner city[1]

A friend of mine once wanted to be a parliamentary candidate in a constituency in the East End of London where from the 1980s until the rude shock of the second Iraq war about 60 per cent of Labour voters in national elections regularly came from the local Bangladeshi community. The community originates mostly from the region of Sylhet and has been present in the area of East London near to the docks for many decades. It can be most easily understood as largely the product of the last wave of postwar boom British Fordist migrant labour in the late 1960s that gave rise to the taxonomic shorthand BME to stand for the black and minority ethnic demographic that is most commonly used to describe the more visibly multicultural nature of twentieth-century Britain. Or perhaps not. Given that this particular fraction of New Commonwealth settlement was deployed principally in the rag trade and in the restaurant and catering business – case studies in the flexible labour process – Sylheti settlement in the East End is perhaps better understood as the first British case of post-Fordist labour migration. Either way, the vagaries of both trades have contributed to an instability in the racialised labour market which paradoxically parallels the East End's history of casualised labour and almost normalises the 'exceptional' case of Bengali settlement.

My friend comes from a particular subdistrict within Sylhet but grew up principally in the London borough of Tower Hamlets and has made a reputation fighting the racism for which the area is so notorious, rendering the term East Ender itself at times a metonym of white English working-class identity. Another acquaintance, articulate, middle-class, in Tower Hamlets for a shorter time but likewise with a track record of support for progressive left politics, also wanted the same parliamentary seat. Commonly, representations of him, instrumentally choosing to exceptionalise his identity, often pointed out that whilst he comes from Bangladesh he is from Dacca and a more affluent background than most Sylheti people locally. I ask my first friend why he should be preferred in the parliamentary selection process, expecting a similar line. But instead of restating this categoric form of the global local, the subdivision of Sylheti/non-Sylheti in London, he says to me: 'Michael, this is a poor working-class inner city area. We need an Eastender to be the MP here. That is why I should be chosen.'

For a moment the whiteness of the East End itself is not only challenged but also rhetorically colonised. The moment, though on one level insignificant, stays with me. It is an exemplary case of the manner in which, for all the sometime fluidity of a politics of cultural difference that takes race, class and gender as mutable, the much celebrated hybridised identities that result, defining themselves as speaking subjects, invariably come to rest in a moment of closure that creates, however temporarily, an *inside* that lends meaning to 'community', that defines a structure of sensibility without which transcultural communication cannot begin. It is an inside invoking complex notions of spatiality that is subject to endless reinvention, (mis)appropriation and (mis)representation. It is also quite clearly an inside that cannot be measured within a straightforward metric of correspondent truth. More specifically, the incident, though anecdotal, highlights the manner in which a particular set of places – in this case the East End, Bangladesh, 'Asia', and most of all the 'inner city' – do not so much bracket identities as become constitutive features of them. In this sense the mapping of subjects is constituted by the invocation of place as much as by the genealogy of placing.

On one level there is something quite unproblematic here. We make sense of the world by the stories we tell ourselves, by the urban narratives and tales of the inner city through which characters come to life – sometimes exemplary, other times exceptional; sometimes didactic, other times mundane; sometimes reassuring, other times horrifying, though as always this horror itself rests on the sublime conflation of disgust and desire.

Such characters owe their life to the narrative forms through which they are allowed to emerge. The racialised city has a full cast list, the process of 'mapping the subject' is about how such subject positions or 'subjectifications' are made politically, epistemologically and aesthetically visible. In this chapter I want to look briefly at the manner in which two subject positions of racialised otherness draw on the historical genealogies of representations of 'blackness' to define the parameters of policy thinking and urban policy practice that may on the surface appear to be free of such culturally specific traces.

The two characters are those of the *ethnic entrepreneur* and the *street rebel*. These two figures share a historical provenance that is far too complex to outline in great detail here, though both become organising themes through which race, gender, class and sexuality are invoked to make sense of the inner city. Thus read, they become sublime personalities with iconic status. The ethnic entrepreneur is the assimilationist hero, the street rebel the bourgeois nightmare. They are characters who have made sporadic appearances throughout industrial history but whose realisation is always historically and geographically specific – in the British experience from the Huguenot weavers of the seventeenth century to the Asian shopkeepers of the twentieth; from the hooligans of the nineteenth century to the black rioters of the 1980s and the mill town rioters in Oldham, Bradford and Burnley in the early twenty-first century, almost a hundred years later.

Across the globe one of the ways in which the multicultural city is known is through the comparative gaze that attempts to measure the putative 'success' or 'failure' of specific migrant minorities within a particular national context. A language of 'model minorities' demonstrating 'high social capital' characterised by high levels of 'ethnic enterprise' is commonly used to capture the experiences of the former. At other times a putatively contrasting low level of social capital or other sets of cultural predispositions are used not just to differentiate but also to explain the experiences of the latter.[2]

Though not directly relevant either to this volume or this chapter, the very act of 'reifying' ethnicity, and consequently translating ethnic boundaries into objects of the multicultural mosaic, focuses analytic attention on the pieces of the mosaic itself. This will lead logically to a search for properties that are attributable to these constitutive pieces, such as quantifications of predisposition or social capital. Looking at 'cultural groups' as objects, divorced from time and space, prompts a search for a causality that resides within the ethnic organisation or cultural propensity of migrant groups themselves. This can lead to a debate about whether ethnic diversity mitigates or promotes putatively 'high' or 'low' measures of social capital, or 'trust' or the general good. It is not the purpose here to suggest that such quantification is necessarily flawed or that there is never a value in 'generalising' at times about culture, but it is the case that such a generalisation needs to be treated with extreme caution and based on sustained analytical engagement rather than positivist caricature.

This chapter attempts to suggest that, in contrast to such perspectives, at the interface between community struggles and the racialised imagination social policy instruments may create an institutional recognition of ethnic difference. Such recognition is not particularly measurable by its degree of correspondent truth. It is instead the outcome of the setting of localised city struggles for acknowledgement of racialised difference against social policy interventions that have an apparent aim of addressing inequalities and promoting economic wellbeing. In this context the city becomes a governmental landscape of intervention.

Notions of 'the social' and 'the economic' are bound up in the founding principles and funding practices of organisations and agencies that structure the lives of multicultural localities. Although the institutional forest that is referenced in this chapter focuses on the British experience, similar processes characterise every city that is traced with the imperatives of governance networks that are sometimes controlled democratically (by central or city government), and are sometimes the institutional outcome of regulatory or funding regimes that create new organisations that structure processes of government within the city.[3] In each city across the globe the governance landscape draws in institutions as small as the hygiene inspectors and as large the land-use zoning and planning functions. In this sense the governance landscape involves obvious functions of 'police' and fire prevention, but also includes the regulatory and monitoring frameworks of food provision, leisure time, behaviour in public and sometimes in private. Invariably designed to structure what Michel Foucault described as the 'conduct of conduct', such institutions form dense webs of 'governmentality'. Such networks are historically and geographically specific but are universally implicated in both the generation of identity and the figuring of the city both as governmental territory and as an institutional assemblage.[4]

In their rules and regulations, as well as in their power to allocate resources and to arbitrate between interests in the city, governmental institutions shape the way different social worlds are recognised. In this context – depending on time and place across the globe – they may or may not recognise the legitimacy of cultural or ethnic difference in shaping their own working practices. Consequently, it is at this interface between the cultural and the institutional that the changing shape of acknowledged racial difference is often most pronounced. In this chapter this interface is examined through the cases of two specific iconic characters. The intention is to demonstrate the manner in which processes that are common to all cities of migration find specific articulation through the interplay between structures of urban government and the cultures of social and political mobilisation.

Iconic characters, urban policy and urban regeneration

For the ethnic entrepreneur the inner city market is a mysterious place that generates its own protocols of institutional behaviour and generates their 'placed' forms of expertise; for the rebel the city provides a stage for transgression, a place where the 'shouts in the street' can be heard. 'Race' echoes through both characters, though creating quite distinctively racialised subject positions. Both are quite clearly absent presences in the imagined cities that inform contemporary urban policy.

We know that the inner city is not the straightforward product of a uniform set of processes working through the production of spaces in a sovereign political economy to manufacture identifiable tracts of urban decline. It is, among many other things, the product of the political imagination which generated popular understandings of an inner city problem, a mythical space that is at once both inside and outside our own society, that owes its own genealogy to the very cultural roots of a fascination and fear of the city itself.[5]

In such a context I take it as unexceptionable that, inter alia, policy initiatives in the inner city rest on narratives of urban decline and salvation, replete with aestheticised and deeply politicised representations of contemporary urbanism. These stories of the inner city require and define their moral cast list: an array of exemplary characters who can serve as both the suitable objects and subjects for techniques of state intervention that are sometimes characterised as urban policy. This chapter is about how such characters are imagined, written and enacted. For the purposes of this volume I am interested in teasing out the forms and techniques of government in the inner city which render racialised subjects visible at some times but not at others.

In small-area urban policy the very act of mapping at once both erases and reinvents, and sometimes creates and defines 'a place' from a disparate set of census tracts. Political spaces are transformed into natural objects. This involves a process of erasure and a process of reinvention. The vagaries of cartographic boundary lines confer upon an area of the inner city a unity that is entirely governmental. It may be rationalised in terms of an array of pathological or material indices of deprivation that maps 'a population', or it may be marked by a particular potential for economic growth, but it defines a 'suitable case for treatment', a proper place for inner city government. It is not the case that by making visible the fabricated governmental root of this inner city geography there is an implicit alternative natural or organic geography of authentic urban areas. It is instead the case that implementing agencies create a space of governmental practice which, thus legitimised, becomes the natural object of regulatory practice.

In this chapter I want to draw on two such mapping exercises in London, one in the East End, the other in Deptford. Both are cases of governmental mapping of the official inner city through the City Challenge initiative, launched in 1991 by Michael Heseltine when Secretary of State at the Department of the Environment. It was an initiative characterised by an auction of victimhood: local authorities had to compete one against another to prove both that their 'inner city' was more deserving of additional resources and that their techniques of urban renewal were the most impressive. Two London boroughs, Lewisham and Tower Hamlets, were among the eleven local authorities, out of seventeen invited to bid, that won City Challenge initiatives for their locality in the first generation of the exercise.[6]

Some basic features of this creation need to be restated. In the 1990s people in the northern wards of the London borough of Lewisham were generally poorer than most other people in the capital city; they had worse housing conditions, poorer health, less chance of being in employment, and greater chance of being poorly, or seriously ill or dead by tomorrow morning than people living in other parts of London.[7] It was an area dominated by social ownership of frequently poor-quality housing stock and a de-industrialised economic base. The clichéd litany of socioeconomic deprivation indices that identify the area itself as an area of lack may be the product of particular techniques of quantification, and may be the potential source of tales of urban pathology, but they are no less grim for being so. It was in this area, which receives most attention in this chapter, that Deptford City Challenge (DCC) was established in 1991 and began operation April 1992.

In the Spitalfields area of the East End a similar list of socioeconomic characteristics, coupled with a number of derelict land sites with clear development potential near to the City of London, prompted the government to invite the London borough of Tower Hamlets to locate its City Challenge bid in the Spitalfields area rather than in any other part of the borough.

Attenuating in one place, emerging in the other, our two racialised characters appear quite differently in the two sites, generating quite different forms of political action. In one case the character is progressively erased: the ethnic entrepreneur so favoured in the free market world of the Thatcherite 1980s began to look progressively out of place in the corporatist 1990s. In the other case the spectre of inner city uprisings offers the Faustian bargain of political salience and state criminalisation to the previously unheard and unseen mobilisations of young Bengali men, prefiguring wider disturbances in the settlements of South Asian communities in the northern cities of England in the summer of 2001. The purpose of this chapter is neither to valorise nor to denigrate the agency involved in either form of action, only to make visible the manner in which such political manoeuvring depends on, however momentarily, inhabiting such subject positions: occupying the inside of characters generated by an institutional landscape that defines the inner city.

Ethnic entrepreneurs in the inner city market

In the wake of the uprisings of the early and mid-1980s, and Margaret Thatcher's election-night pledge to 'do something about those inner cities', British urban policy went through one of its periodic changes of direction, this time closely steered by the libertarian right's invocation of the natural social relations that emerge from the free market place, that utopian site of social order. Old and new policies were bundled together and presented in the form of the 'Action for Cities' programme.[8] One element of this new portfolio was the prominence given to the potential for enterprise to resolve the crisis of the inner city. There had long been a fascination with the sometime remarkable success of migrant minorities in the economies of metropolitan receiving countries on both sides of the Atlantic, an interest occasionally endorsed and reified by academic study of a phenomenon of *ethnic minority enterprise*.[9] For the designers of urban policy, the technocratic engineers of the imagined city, the ideological power of such a subject was considerable.

As a 1980s character the ethnic entrepreneur was given prominence through an unholy alliance between political expediency and academic fashion. Institutionally recognised and defined agencies were created to seek out these racialised saviours of the inner city. Specifically, the government created enterprise agencies with a brief to enhance the potential of black and ethnic minority businesses in the inner city and charities such as the Prince's Trust were quick to follow suit with similar initiatives, whilst the newly created Training and Enterprise Councils (TECs) were also allocated old Section 11 monies in the form of an Ethnic Minority Grant, part of which was to be directed at 'enterprise services'. In the recognised 'inner city' area of the London borough of Lewisham the Deptford Enterprise Agency (DEA) was established in 1988, funded by the DTI and by Section 11 monies, whilst the local authority also created its own STEP Business Club with a brief to support 'ethnic enterprise'. In part strategically linked to such developments, many different ethnic minority groups have formed their own associations across the country, though rarely working across areas that match exactly the imagined geographies of 'inner city government'. In the case of South London the Afro-Caribbean Business Association worked across a broad swathe of the area, not just within the Deptford City Challenge boundary, and were a powerful political lobby locally.

Deptford City Challenge was obliged to present to central government a 'face' of the private sector to represent capital in the governance structure of the 'partnership'. Through a logic of 'forums' created to represent fractions of the partnership, the local authority – in establishing the implementing agency that was to become City Challenge – created a 'business forum' to 'represent' the private sector interests within the partnership. In its early form the body attracted little interest once it became known that the monies of the new agency – some £7.5 million annually – were not to be hypothecated to each forum. The intention instead was that these representative bodies would elect members of the board who would, in a non-executive fashion, steer the strategic direction of urban regeneration. In short, the business forum did not control resource allocation, although it did create a rubric through which 'business' in all its forms, from major corporate players to stall holders in the local street market, was to be made institutionally visible. Significantly, it homogenised fractions of capital through a democratic structure that defined the very different elements that constitute the 'private sector' in terms of what they had in common, mediated through a mandate that awarded each properly acknowledged 'member' of the business forum a single vote. Thus the 'local' private sector was institutionally defined within the overarching corporate framework.

The case for developing a support framework for local business, an element of the programme that the DoE had already pointed to as weak in the first-year review of the DCC, was strengthened by an external consultant's report which made the case for the development of an independent local business association. From late 1993 onwards, once it became known that the 'business forum' would be transformed into a long-term Deptford Business Development Association (DBDA), the representation of the private sector developed into a controversy that split the board and threatened the working of the new regeneration agency. At one point a senior officer of the company, when asked how serious they thought the crisis could become, responded:

> It could become extremely serious. I think it could fracture the board at one level. The local business sector could be even more split than it is. And we might not be able to function in this area. It would be very difficult to know how we were going to go anywhere.[10]

At the heart of the issue was the fact that though time-limited themselves to five years, the new City Challenge companies were intended to create a permanent 'impact' on their area, leaving behind sustainable institutions. In the case of the Business Forum/DBDA transformation, sustainability of the new organisation was linked to a £0.5 million 'soft loans' (reduced rate loans) package for inner city enterprise floated by the Midland Bank and a possible future as a 'one-stop shop' or 'business link' supplying 'enterprise services' for the South Thames TEC. An uncontentious consultative arena had been transformed into a site of political contest and perceived potential financial power.

Although the Midland Bank was to administer the soft loans scheme it was mooted to be linked to the DBDA, who would administer business 'health checks' to those receiving funds, for which they would be paid. This tied the initiative to funding and resources. The governmental landscape of the city is invariably labyrinthine, the cartographers of the maze and the gatekeepers of finance always politically powerful. Although the link with Midland was subsequently broken – the soft loans scheme, it transpired, could proceed without the link to the Midland Bank – the DBDA remained closely linked with the possibility of attracting a 'Business Link' into the area, another policy instrument for mediating government relations with nascent new businesses, another possible funnel for regeneration monies.

The process of urban regeneration is shaped by the political agenda at ministerial level and the manner in which this translates into an institutional environment is established in the inner cities by the various departments of government. This was true historically as much as it is the case in contemporary times and it is frequently the case that political fashion changes more quickly than the institutional forms that it creates. The city landscape is characterised by an institutional archaeology. Various initiatives, all the product of their own times, litter an area, all bearing testament to yesterday's vogue notions of urban regeneration. Hence, within a few miles of Deptford, it was possible in 1994 to find Urban Programme initiatives, reflecting the urban policy agenda of the 1970s, an Urban Development Corporation, reflecting the government agenda of the early 80s, a Task Force, reflecting the responses to the inner city riots of the mid-1980s, various enterprise initiatives reflecting the 1987 election-night promise of the Prime Minister and the development of Greenwich Waterfront, reflecting the preferred left local authority perspective of the same time. And, of course, a City Challenge company.

These initiatives, in their different ways, were created as different solutions to the single, politically defined problem, the decline of the 'inner cities'. Moreover, whilst it would be overstating the case to suggest that there is no lesson learning process, they cannot be considered to evolve one from another in Enlightenment fashion, passing on 'good practice' and building on the accumulated wisdom of their predecessors, at least not in any straightforward sense. They are instead at least as much the product of changing political thinking and definition of the 'inner city problem', mixed with the perennial need of government at ministerial level to launch new initiatives invested with maximum symbolic impact. Consequently, they inevitably involve some level of duplication – in funding revenue posts for the voluntary sector, in financing capital improvements to the environment, in training initiatives and in grants and loans packages for small businesses.

All places have their appropriate codes of behaviour of subjects – the notion of 'good practice' in urban regeneration creates a realm of technocratic, value-free government of the value-laden social world of the inner city. In this sense the encouragement of ethnic enterprise had by 1994 been routinised within this world and the institutional players had been endorsed by several years of central and local state funding. These practices set funding precedents, inventing a whole new vocabulary and set of administrative protocols that defined the black business community as a political entity as well as one aspect of the local economy.

However, with the apparent absence of uprisings within the black community in the 1990s, the central government will to address explicitly issues of racial deprivation in the inner cities, never particularly strong at the best of times, was not what it was ten or even five years earlier. Partly in consequence, in the market place of institutional fashions the notion of 'ethnic enterprise' was in the government circles of the mid-1990s in the United Kingdom about as avant-garde as yesterday's breakfast.

This left the institutional legacies of the 1980s competing to survive in an era when Section 11 funding, one of the major resources for ethnic minority support in the inner city, had been largely abolished, where the Ethnic Minority Grant in the TECs has also been abandoned, and where the calculation of the Standard

Spending Assessments for local authorities has been changed to exclude ethnic minority presence as indicative of social need, and thus cut central government support for local authorities with a large ethnic minority presence.

At the same time, across the country the newly empowered Training and Enterprise Councils[11] were looking to establish 'one-stop shops' for business advice and support, a concept that in its early life was known as the 'business link'. TECs were relatively well supported, and South Thames TEC even ran into some controversy when in the 1992–3 financial year a seven-figure underspend was represented in their annual report as a 'profit'. The apparent affluence of the TEC, and their increasingly significant role in disbursing enterprise monies, contrasted vividly with the ostentatiously empty coffers of the local authority. In the arcane world of 1990s urban politics and inner city policy, the sustainability of some organisations depended in part in shifting their support (financial and political) from the latter to the former, where necessary reinventing themselves in the eyes, rules and protocols of new funding regimes. It was in this context that the new mediation of City Challenge regeneration ran into difficulties, caught up amidst unsubstantiated but publicly aired accusations of disingenuous manoeuvring, personal and corporate corruption and institutional racism involved in its development. All developments were framed by alternative invocations of 'race' in the inner city and all were underscored by competing and contradictory representations of who were to be the proper subjects of urban regeneration.

At one City Challenge board meeting in late 1993 the DBDA issue erupted into controversy. Objections were raised about the implications of the DBDA in terms of the possible duplication of existing services, and it was alleged that the ethnic minority business sector were being excluded from the new package. Two members commented: 'we should treat this report with all the contempt it deserves . . . This is a load of baloney. I have never been so insulted in my life' and 'This is nothing but a feather in somebody's cap.' Other members disagreed and expressed concern that any uncertainty around the association might jeopardise the Midland Bank's commitment to a scheme welcomed by all.

BOARD MEMBER: '[without DBDA] would we lose the Midland £500,000?'
DCC OFFICER: 'I think we might. They have said that they are very keen on the
    Business Development Association to act as a referral agency.'

It was also suggested that by another board member that because of the weakness of the company's commitment to the business sector 'the reputation of City Challenge within the local business community is already at a low ebb'.

The issue went to the vote, with the majority in favour of delaying approval of the DBDA pending further investigation by the chief executive. Controversy continued over subsequent months. The business forum, which had approved their own transformation into DBDA at an earlier meeting that was not well attended, reconvened in January 1994, in a well-attended and rancorous event that eventually supported DBDA but, in the terms of one DCC officer, 'split down the middle on race grounds', voting 15 to 6 in favour of supporting the transformation, with several present deemed controversially ineligible to vote. By March 1994 disagreements were still not settled, and for the chief executive the issue had become 'a corporate embarrassment'. A resolution appeared to be imminent in June when a reconciliation launch of DBDA took place facilitated by an external consultant. However, controversy engulfed the appointment of a manager of the organisation, again focused around the race issue. This prompted the suspension of City Challenge funding of the new business association, pending the resolution of alleged equal opportunities irregularities, casting further doubt over the future of the DBDA.[12]

At board level the struggle took form rhetorically through the allegation that the new association excluded 'black business', a collective entity whose very existence was disputed by other members of the nascent organisation.

In this context it is useful to distinguish unsubstantiated charges of corruption from the rhetorical structuring of these changes. Both those vigorously opposed to the new DBDA and the officers of DCC concerned with promoting it spoke a new language through an old tongue. Agencies that had subsisted on the support for ethnic minority enterprise owed their funding to Section 11 monies that were rapidly disappearing, and were forced to rationalise their behaviour in terms which echoed the protocols, vocabulary and political realities that reflected the normalisation of something called ethnic minority enterprise.

For one board member the DBDA development was a case of racial 'divide and rule'. A representative of one enterprise agency locally remarked:

> Well, I mean, we're not talking about political democracy or a plebiscite or whatever it is. I mean, what is democracy – 2 per cent, 3 per cent, 4 per cent? I don't know. But I mean, it certainly wasn't . . . and it didn't have, or it does not have, as far as I'm aware – even as it stands – the confidence or the support of the black and ethnic businesses in any significant degree . . . it will fail because it will not be the only representation in the area. I'm confident that it's not going to have the confidence of the ethnic minority and community businesses in any significant fashion.

Not dissimilarly, one senior DCC officer suggested that the original feasibility study for the association was not as 'inclusive as it should have been' and that 'the community of Deptford is a diverse one and you ignore diversity at your peril'. The suggestion was that there was a genuine problem, even though it was not premeditated: 'I don't know that they were cut out [black businesses] – that is to suggest that it was deliberate – I think there was a flaw in the process.' Crudely, for some the contest was all about the new agency as a source of potential finance:

> Then we decided that we know very little about the DBDA and it was coming into the Deptford area and regenerating the whole area, going to get money from the Midland Bank and from the Prudential Insurance, and they were going to bring investment into the area and all the rest of it and to me it was just a wild idea and it was pie in the sky as far as I was concerned. So we said

how can people sit back and say they are going to do that because the local community don't know nothing at all about the DBDA. If you walk round Deptford and say to anyone: 'Have you heard about the DBDA?' they would probably think it was an illegal organisation and that nobody had heard at all about it! So we try as far our best to try and find out what the DBDA was and what they are going to do.

It was in similar terms that at one time a board member suggested that there was no legitimacy in going ahead with the transformation from Business Forum to DBDA, and in reference to the controversial vote in favour of this move suggested that 'There has been a lot of mistrust for whatever reasons in the community. I don't call it a mandate, I call it a . . . stitch up.'

Yet the terms of those involved directly with the new DBDA contested this challenge by disputing the legitimacy of the terms in which it was set. At the heart of the race issue within this debate is whether or not 'the black business community' is a meaningful term and a collective that defines a real 'player' in this equation that can take part in the new 'partnerships' through which the inner city of the 1990s was to be governed. In the terms of one influential figure in the history of the Business Forum:

> I don't know why people like xxx are insisting on – well I don't know what they really want. I mean the kind of logical corollary of what they are saying is they want some kind of black section of the business forum. They want a constitutional guarantee to a certain number of seats . . . I will stand against it because I believe in democracy in a way. I mean I do agree with Edmund Burke in that it is sort of rule by the swinish multitude but nonetheless we have to work with it . . . I don't believe there is this kind of racial tension within the business community that maybe xxx or xxx or xxx worries about, certainly like xxx. It is a convenience or whipping post I think to whip us with, and when I say us I mean sort of white business people, in order to get a disproportionate share of resources, time, energy, you know that kind of thing. When you look at the business forum, when you go and talk to some of these people, there is not this sort of racial worry that I am trying to be persuaded exists.

Once the DBDA became a contested issue, various interests clearly began to perceive, rightly or wrongly, that rival interest groups were trying to seize control of an initiative that some construed as a potential source of future revenue, and legitimacy was to be contested in every way, from who was to define the geographical extent of the local business community – should governmental boundaries, corporate entities or racialised business associations define this territory? – to a game controlling the membership of the new entity. Though in some respects parochial, this struggle was significant, though not because there was clearly signalled right or wrong on either side. Conventional understandings of racist exclusion are of little help in making sense of the processes at work here. It instead reveals the changing visibility of racial difference within the institutional frameworks that define the city as a political field.

Politically, some truths become unspeakable. In slightly simplistic terms, the visibility of racial deprivation in the 1980s was only rendered acceptable through the nostrums of the free market. Left to choose between working within this frame of reference and receiving no money at all, it was understandable that whilst some would take such notions at face value others would subscribe more pragmatically to the maxims of 'ethnic enterprise'. Alternative paradigms of labour marginal-isation that might have diagnosed racialised poverty in different terms and prescribed alternative remedies to such inequality were denied mainstream political currency in the formulation of 1980s urban policy. The 'black business community' could thus never be divorced from the political symbolism with which it was endowed, or the institutional regimes which variously either reified it and recognised and legitimised the very essence of ethnic enterprise, or in the colour blindness of the 1990s deemed the very notion a chaotic conceptualisation of the market process.

Analytically this is significant for a broader understanding of urban studies. The value of the case is not to denigrate the historical significance of migrant minorities in innovation and niche marketing within metropolitan economies, only to contextualise the legitimation of inner city subjects. Both an understanding of racist practice and an analysis of empirical realities depend on holding on to the true lies of race thinking: its realities in the practices of specific institutions, the recognition in some places and not others of a vocabulary of ethnic difference, and the inevitably mimetic manner in which groups and individuals position and reinvent themselves in relation to the governmentalities of the city that are invariably a constitutive part of urbanism.

At the heart of the new private–public partnerships through which so much of government policy across the globe has been mediated since the 1990s is a notion that there is such a 'thing' as an identifiable 'business community'. Private sector interests are institutionalised through novel structures of government which deter-mine the 'players' at the table in this contemporary form of urban corporatism. It is easy in hindsight to suggest that the history of the DBDA illustrates that there is a complexity to the nature of private enterprise. This belies the imagery of a singular 'business community' which at times almost implies a sense of common purpose, which does not fit well with the multiplicity of interest groups and institutional maze that defines the contemporary business environment. Moreover, the affair illustrates how innovations in urban regeneration must negotiate this institutional maze, exemplifying the sort of pragmatic power brokering that has long been characteristic of city government.

More significantly, at another level, the example reveals the whiteness of the urban policy-implementing agencies through which 1990s techniques of city government were mediated. The new partnerships were at least in part about key 'players' in the inner city coming together, a form of government that is unmarked by racial difference. Ironically, normalised institutional roles for public and private sectors endow the ethnic entrepreneur with far less symbolic power than was the case in the free market rhetoric of the 1980s. Yet it is equally the case that such changes are not readily framed within the mainstream left paradigms of the same era. Debates that owe their provenance to 1980s equal opportunities notions of hypothecated resources for minorities, and a focus on the position of ethnic minorities among the personnel of local government, cannot readily come to terms with this new vision of the city as a set of institutional relationships. With the 'community' reified as a singular player at the bargaining table of partnership, it too can be constructed in singularly deracialised terms.

In this new landscape the shibboleth of the ethnic entrepreneur is discarded even as the reality of ethnic minority businesses continues to struggle against the odds in impoverished urban areas. The racialised subject position of the mythical ethnic entrepreneur was not consonant with the consensually colour blind and implicitly white form of the new urban corporatism of the 1990s.

Street rebels

In the summer of 1992 in the London borough of Tower Hamlets a series of disturbances loosely connected to fights between 'gangs' of young people culminated in clashes between young people in Brick Lane, the symbolic heart of the local Bengali community. Luridly reported in the local press, the events were one of several key passages whose representation has created a constitutively racialised link between Bengali masculinity and the streets of the East End in the last few years. The cultural construction of masculinities of otherness on the streets of London is explored in more detail in the following chapter, but the governance cartographies which map such a presence are relevant here.

The demographic structure of the Tower Hamlets Bengali population is largely a product of the timing of Bengali migration. Male-dominated first-wave migration, with family reunification often taking place in the mid-1970s, produced a baby-boom generation that came to adolescence and maturity in the late 1980s and early 1990s. This generation of frequently British-born Bengalis has been ill-served by all the agencies of collective consumption. The borough has long been demonstrated to be one of the poorest in Britain, with housing conditions reflecting extraordinarily high levels of overcrowding and health figures poor for any and every index of deprivation that could be chosen.[13] Moreover, the same generation came to maturity at a time when education locally was also badly hit by the teaching disputes of the mid-1980s, and Bengali 'underachievement' in schools has long been a fascination of education academics. These trends were compounded by a political culture set by the particular racialised coding of the Tower Hamlets Liberal Democratic Party[14] who controlled the borough from 1986 to 1994 and for whom the problems of 'young people' readily translated into a bigoted imagery reflecting the asymmetrical age distributions of white and Bengali communities. Youth services were frequently cut back to allow for alternative uses for local government revenue. One study revealed that in the neighbourhood of Stepney, which covered a large area of Bengali settlement focusing in particular on the Ocean Estate, grants to the voluntary sector were reduced from £426,065 in

1990–1 to £44,215 in 1991–2, a cut of almost 90 per cent.[15] In the same 'neighbourhood' the Community Education Service, which was the principal funder of youth support services, regularly underspent its budget in the early 1990s.

It is only in this context that it is possible to understand the progressive emergence of a series of representations of the social problem of putative Bengali criminality.[16] The evidence of growing antagonism between police and young British Bengalis was incontrovertible, the creation of new inner city subjects the result of both collective action and the manner in which such actions were framed in the mass media. In 1992 in London there were marches protesting at police tactics, campaigns about specific incidents and arrests and appeals for calm from senior police officers. One national newspaper[17] went so far as to suggest that the East End Bengali community was a likely focus of an imminent incident of serious public disorder. Significantly, the story was told through the image of young Bengali men occupying the streets of the East End, challenging police order – the organising trope of narratives of street crime – with the Ocean Estate linked directly to the sites of black uprisings in the mid-1980s. The politics of such representational practices are the subject of the next chapter of this book but of central importance for this chapter is the manner in which the street becomes a site through which slippages occur in racist discourse.

It has also been argued elsewhere that through racist constructions of criminality the criminal justice system has become a locus of racialisation, manufacturing a criminalised classification of 'race' that coexists with alternative, often contradictory, invocations of 'race' that derive from other racialising discourses. A theoretical analysis of criminalisation helps to understand the manner in which 'blackness' is produced as a sign of criminal otherness.[18] Geographical references perform organising roles within these common forms of criminalising rhetoric. The racialised other is constructed as dangerous, defined through presence in the public sphere. Hence, in the seminal work on the social construction of black criminality in Britain – as we have seen in Chapter 4 of this book – Stuart Hall and his associates, when deconstructing the *ghetto*, regularly resort to the metaphor of the 'black colony' as both victim of these racist practices of criminalisation and (apparently) social reality.[19] The lawless black ghetto is a place that is both a racist myth and a site of criminalisation.

This racialised subject position of criminality can envelop British 'Asian' communities as well, most commonly through discourses of gang violence, as experience in Southall and Birmingham in the 1990s and the northern 'mill towns' of the UK such as Bradford, Burnley and Oldham in the last three years demonstrates. There is a barely hidden genealogy of place and identity here, normatively construed. The interpellation of the black body through the street and its relationship to languages of aesthetics, politics and knowledge production is an important one examined in Chapter 7.

More straightforwardly the street is also constructed as the site of insurrection, and when in autumn 1993 Quddus Ali was savagely beaten outside the Dean Swift pub in Stepney, the demonstration of respect that gathered outside the London Hospital in Whitechapel and developed into serious clashes with the police was rapidly classified in the national media as the riot that the *Independent* had been predicting over a year earlier. This was a moment of confrontation rapidly endowed with extraordinary political symbolism when Derek Beackon became the first successful BNP (fascist) candidate in a local by-election a few days later. The position of racialised street criminal was found to be, once again, one step away from the arrival of the racialised street rebel. And in terms of the central focus of this chapter this racialised character (much more than the complex social dynamics of the lifestyles of young men of Bengali origin) was seen to traumatise the governmental imaginary.

The events of 1993 resonated and the problem of 'Bengali youth' became a problem of inner city government, as the local City Challenge demonstrated in microcosm. In early 1991, when the degree of socioeconomic deprivation was just about as bad, when the demographics were known, and when the realities of everyday life for young Bengali men were not so different from three years later, the original Bethnal Green City Challenge Action Plan barely mentioned the 'problem' of 'youth' at all.[20] By late 1993, one riot and one fascist later, 'promoting youth empowerment and access to opportunities' had rapidly become a key strategic aim of Bethnal Green City Challenge, and a year after that there was already a focus on a youth forum and even a 'youth representative' on the board of the company, something that could not be reduced to the vocabulary of co-optation.[21] But such a change is a product of a particular diagnosis of the problem of government in the contemporary East End, a diagnosis that must bring the street to the state. In order to understand it we must understand simultaneously from up close the manner in which the ethnographic realities of street disturbances are related to the cultural production of a street sensibility (as Chapter 7 explores) and link this back to the construction of regimes of governmentality and institutions of governance. The street rebel's access to the institutions of power is mediated through both these institutions' political imagination and its haunting by the narratives of violence and disorder that form part of the very roots of city life.

Conclusion: race power and cartographic subjectification

Colin Gordon has suggested that in defining the nature of governmental rationality Michel Foucault talks about the problems of contemporary government in terms of 'the deamonic coupling of "city-game" and "shepherd-game": the invention of a form of secular pastorate which couples "individualization" and "totalization"'.[22] The conduct of conduct at the heart of governmental practice is the move towards simultaneous invention of the social and complete knowledge of the individual. Just one aspect of such trends within the contemporary inner city is the definition of racialised subject positions divorced from ethical self-evidence, something that at one level might appear to deny the possibility of transformative politics. Yet, seen differently, the characters that emerge in this way raise new questions that disrupt some of the old certainties of political action and that reframe old problems of authenticity, of aesthetics and of the nature of institutional racism.

They demand a contextualisation of the processes of rendering visible particular subjects and the manner in which a variety of discursive practices, including techniques of city government, shape speaking positions, and map the grounds from within which political subjects might speak and trap themselves in their own parochialism. It is only in so doing that the vagaries of cultural theory can be brought to bear on the concrete realities of institutionalised political practice. It is at such points that there is some sense to the claim that 'the non-synchronous temporality of global and national cultures opens up a cultural space – a third space – where the negotiation of incommensurable differences creates a tension peculiar to borderline experiences'.[23] It is through this imperative to move consciously between positionalities that such a language opens up the vocabulary of inside and outside to a progressive politics, returns us again to the selective appropriation of 'the East End' with which this chapter started, and disrupts the race power cartographies through which subjects are mapped.

The institutional rationalities of the agencies through which urban policy is mediated are structured by the definition of the inner city as a problem of government. But the subjects that both inform and are defined by their techniques and practices both reflect and challenge the characters such agencies script; the ethnic entrepreneur and the street rebel are contingently both the products of hegemonic power the and the cast list of political change. In this sense comprehending the changing face of the cosmopolitan metropolis is partially about coming to terms with the manner in which institutions at the heart of regimes of governmentality figure the racial imagination. This is not straightforwardly about the conventionally understood politics of recognition which does or does not acknowledge group rights or collective entities. It is just as much about the manner in which the traces of the racial imagination come to haunt the working of the micro-structures of the state. Although the focus of this chapter has been on the manner in which this has been the case for ethnic enterprise and disorder in contemporary Britain the same principles apply equally to the manner in which alternative forms of racial imaginary might inhabit the town halls, class rooms, licensing committees or sites in which the conduct of conduct bear the imprint of normal behaviour and is challenged by the presence in the city of 'other' forms of action, value and caricature.

In short the institutional landscape of the inner city creates a cultural reality that in part defines the frames through which mapped subjects are rendered legitimately visible; 'the relation between government and the governed passes, to a perhaps ever-increasing extent, through the manner in which governed individuals are willing to exist as subjects'.[24] It is through the interstices of this structural complex that communities of resistance can emerge as political subjects. Living the true lie of racialised subject positions is at least in part about both colonising the normalising whiteness of British government and re-appropriating the racialised subject positions such techniques and practices generate.

6   The street

Street sensibility?[1]

Edward (businessman, played by Richard Gere): 'Vivienne, It would take you off
the streets.'
Vivienne (prostitute played by Julia Roberts): 'That's just geography.'

Pretty Woman (1990)

The street has for a long time occupied a cherished place in the lexicon of
urbanism. Romanticised as the site of authentic political action, celebrated and
reviled as the font of 'low' culture, or feared as a signifier of dangerous
territorialisation the *street* can be gazed at, walked through and appropriated time
and again in representations of the city.

This chapter takes as its empirical focus the racialised and racist mobilisations
that occurred in the East End of London in the late summer of 1993. It was a
summer of extreme-right political success, racist violence and public disorder
which resulted in confrontations between the forces of law and order and young
British Bengalis. Disorder arose firstly from confrontations between the police and
the crowd gathered in a vigil for Quddus Ali, the victim of a horrific racist attack,
outside the London Hospital. There was also further violence when attacks on the
shops and restaurants of Brick Lane by far-right activists culminated in serious
clashes between police and local Bengalis and a petrol bomb attack on the local
police station. It was in the week following these clashes that, a mile or so away in
the east of the borough, Derek Beackon became the first successful local authority
candidate from the British National Party (BNP) in a by-election in the Millwall
ward on the Isle of Dogs.

This chapter looks at some of the tensions in the notions of spatiality that are
both masked and naturalised in our common understanding of 'the street'. It is a
term that invokes a range of spatialities that are a constitutive feature in understanding not only the parochial specificities of Spitalfields and Stepney, Wapping
and Whitechapel, but also the very nature of racist and anti-racist mobilisation. At
times the vocabulary of resistance may appear similar or even identical to the
language of the carceral and territorial imperatives that codify and institutionalise
racist practices. On closer inspection subtle distinctions arise from particular
articulations of street sensibilities, raising questions that are essential for a plausible

and politically progressive reading of violent disorder and indispensable to an understanding of the constellation of contemporary debates around public space and the perennial discussion about 'insiders' and 'outsiders' in anti-racist mobilisations.

There is a sense in which claims of authority rest on their spatialisation. At some times this may be masked by the normalisation of a particular place in the name of universality. The well-documented tendency for mainstream social science to subsume the existence of the social within the nation state is one example of this; the manner in which social theory may glibly naturalise 'the west' and multifarious forms of Eurocentrism is another. At other times this problem is rehearsed through problematics of position: the privileging of either the aerial view or the everyday, the one linked to the sometime masculinist and totalising metanarrative certainties of the plan, the other tied to a softer, more ambivalent, sometime feminised world of the quotidian. There are many subtexts to such juxtapositions, not all of which are reducible to a contrast between paradigms of explanation. It is the contention here that this framing of the problematic of the view is frequently unhelpful, not least because it frequently rests on particular invocations of authenticity that may themselves be geographically naïve. In short, if we begin to unravel the problematic of authenticity we can begin to address the manner in which the grand scheme is linked to the multiple realities of the everyday, the global revealed in the local, even as the metonymic powers of the local can never alone render visible the nature of the whole.

Politics in the East End of London

At various times over the last two decades, living, working and carrying out research (and politics) in the London borough of Tower Hamlets, I have sometimes thought that all politics in the East End of London is about authenticity. Veering between wanting none of the sectarian spectacle this creates and standing back in respect at the sincerity with which such claims are made, the garrulous rush to stake bids in the auction of authenticity can surely only be understood by reference to both outstanding expressions of communal solidarity and singularly frightening manifestations of mutual intolerance that the area is famous for.

Quite clearly, on some levels this is nothing particular to one part of one city in the decaying metropolitan heartland of old capitalism. The right to make claims on behalf of one of many imagined communities, the right to articulate demands for jobs, for welfare and for houses, in short the representation of genuine political subjects, is the very stuff of social theory and political action. More often than not, such claims to be heard contain within them, either explicitly or implicitly, reference to a place. Literal or metaphoric locations draw on the full vocabulary of urbanism to authenticate claims of knowledge, of aesthetics and of ethical judgement: from the Clapham omnibus to the Bonaventure Hotel. And among these spatial reference points 'the street' has historically occupied a privileged position in the cities of modernity.

There is a narrative structure through which the street itself may signify authenticity. Immersion in the street generates its own way of knowing the city and the politics of the street can connote both populism and transgression, whilst as the site of a celebrated vernacular aesthetic, street culture readily stands for the contemporary – truly 'where it's at'.

In this chapter I want to work through three instances in which the street has been used as an organising trope in the fields of art, knowledge production and popular protest, to make sense of the multiracial and multiracist place that is the contemporary East End of London.[2]

In 1993 Tower Hamlets witnessed the first election of a British National Party (fascist) councillor in Britain, an upsurge in popular protest, a mass mobilisation of young people, drawn in the main from second-generation Bengali households, clashes between young people and the police, and a savage 300 per cent increase in racial attacks exemplified in the beating of Quddus Ali, which was so severe that it left him in a coma and near death for three months.

In part this chapter is written from a strong personal belief that it is as obscene to divorce this grim and steady rise in brutal racist violence and populist racist culture from the mutating political economies which have produced the economic space of the East End as it is to reduce such racist cultural forms to the status of mere effects of these sea changes. I am trying to argue in this chapter that it is through a sophisticated vocabulary of urbanism that we can link the contemporary cultural studies invocations of spatiality with political economies of the production of space in order to take apart some of the most horrific forms of racism in the 1990s, something that is the object of endless popular interest and the subject of appalling institutional indifference and complicit political inaction. It is precisely this process of the production of urban spaces, which informed a generation of Marxian geographers of city life throughout the 1990s, that lay at the heart of David Harvey's *Social Justice and the City*, and clearly tied his own work to that of Lefèbvre. But it is also through a sophisticated understanding of these processes of production that it is possible to reconnect economy and culture, in part through the return to spatiality so salient to contemporary social theory but also through a rejection of any simplistic opposition between 'real' and imagined or metaphoric spaces of identity.

Street aesthetics and street identity

The first case is that of an exhibition that took place at the Whitechapel Gallery from 14 February to 29 March 1992.[3] The exhibition was of the work of the New York-based, Chilean photographer, Alfredo Jaar: part of his broader project of 'a new cartography' examining the relationships 'between the developed and developing world'.[4] As part of the exhibition, Jaar had worked with Gayàtri Chakravorty Spivak to produce a site-specific multimedia installation 'inspired by the Bangladeshi community living in east London'.[5]

Just before the exhibition Jaar and Spivak talked about their work at the ICA. Jaar's work has for a long time fascinatingly focused on the interplay of place, naming and the politics of identity, using 'a spare honed aesthetic practice to provide visibility and space to sites and people in crisis'.[6] Together they wanted to make of the grand institution of the Whitechapel Gallery a truly public space that is open to all, a site-specific installation that in the words of John Bird, the author of the exhibition guide, 'raises the possibility of an aesthetic dimension that can contribute to change across the terrain of the social formation'.[7] Somebody asks them at the ICA: 'Why do you want to come to London to do this work?' They reply that they do not find the question either interesting or relevant; it is just not an issue.

The installation is titled 'Two or three things I imagine about them', consciously drawing on Godard's *Deux ou trois choses que je sais d'elle* ('Two or three things I know about her'). It has three main elements and an introductory 'framing' of video and water.

The first element consists of two neon lights, legible only in their reflection that is read in the mirrors placed alongside them. One says 'What is it to make the street visible', the other 'What is it to make the visible visible'. The second element involves some images of young girls skipping, whilst on the floor nearby about 20 speakers make a hubbub of street noise, talking and shouting, many voices, mostly speaking Sylheti, Bengali and English. Third, a series of light boxes, with cropped fragmentary images of glamorous young Bengali women, diagonally traverses the space of the gallery at ceiling level, with selective quotes from a sweat shop manager placed across them. The quotes include comments such as 'They are all unskilled and illiterate'; 'The £20 a week they earn just helps the family'; and 'We are all a big family here.'

All of this is introduced by a large video screen with a looped film which partly features Spivak talking to 'local people' but consists mainly of an image of her in a soliloquy addressed to the camera. The Delphic image of the latter appears on screen as a talking head that is upside down. To see it the right way up it is necessary to look in the pool of water in front of the screen. Spivak intones:

> How to make the street visible. How to learn to see differently. To learn to see differently is to see with the back, to learn to see differently is to see well in front. To learn to see differently is to see broader . . .
>
> To learn to see differently. You are innocent, they are not? They are innocent, you are not? To see is to see differently. To learn to see differently. Seeing differently. Is it to make the street visible? To see and to make visible. What is it to see? What then is to make visible? Who are they? Who makes visible? Who sees? How do we see? How do we make the street visible?
>
> (IN A LOUDER VOICE) *How to make the street visible?*

The installation was clearly very clever, highlighting the practices of representation, the aesthetics of the gaze, the fragile play between representation and (in)visibility. It was exciting in the manner in which the standard conventions and protocols of the art gallery exhibition were transgressed. Deliberately enigmatic, the installation simultaneously tried to highlight the exploitation of the local rag trade,[8] the absences and silences of practices of representation, and also a more optimistic invocation of the possibility of the public spaces that find their exemplary form in the streets of the modern city. In the terms of John Bird:

> On the street is where we negotiate the complexities of cultural differences made deceptively familiar through the repetitive encounters of daily life, at one moment made to feel our singularity, at another to sense our otherness fragmenting in the fleeting connections of community and dependency expressed in the glance or gesture that bridges a gap, dissolves a boundary, initiates a dialogue.[9]

But the exhibition itself prompted a considerable furore. A group of young women from a local school objected both to the way their images were cropped in the light boxes and the matching of them with the quotes from the sweat shop owner, prompting protests at the gallery itself. They suggested that as successful sixth-formers in the educationally most successful school in Tower Hamlets they were ill-served by the portrayals of themselves as victims of the exploitation of the rag trade. The installation had failed to capture the dynamics of the contemporary lives of young Bengali women, reproducing the stereotypes of victimhood. The length of time Spivak had dedicated to putting the piece together and finding out about the local streets was criticised in public, an exchange took place in the British press, and a well-known black artist withdrew from a public talk about the exhibition at the gallery.

In one sense such a minor controversy might seem unremarkable. Yet even in its marginality the installation is in some important ways almost paradigmatic. Challenging the exoticisation of ethnicity in an informed manner, problematising the gaze of the urban spectator, the installation surely contained precisely the sort of street aesthetic that must lie at the heart of a radical multiculturalism in its appeal to a contingent and ambivalent invocation of public space. But ultimately the representational space of the gallery was transgressed more symbolically than practically, failing to take along with it the audiences who came to see the installation, not to mention those whose images constituted it.[10]

Ultimately the weakest link was the framing of the installation, the immediate presentation of Spivak herself at the very foreground of the exhibition space. It is surely part of the ambivalence around which the whole installation was structured that whilst we were expected to gain knowledge by looking into the pool of water and seeing Spivak the right way up, the narcissistic conceit produced an effect where cursory observation suggested that most spectators looked at the inverted image on the screen whilst Spivak appeared to be looking at her own reflection in the water. And if the Narcissus myth teaches us anything, it is surely that this is not always the best way to look at things.[11]

Street walkers

The second case I want to reference is a particular instance of the spatial practice of walking and knowing the street, a specific invocation of the claims to knowledge

that are made when 'botanising the asphalt'.[12] On 10 September 1993, shortly after
the attack on Quddus Ali and after clashes between police and the crowd that was
mostly young, male and Bengali had broken out around a vigil outside the London
Hospital, Brick Lane was attacked by a group of fascist sympathisers who ran
down the street throwing bricks through the windows of restaurants, daubing
racist graffiti and assaulting people on the street.[13] This occurred in spite of the fact
that the area was saturated with police patrolling the area at the time. One van in
particular had been on a small circuit that included Brick Lane itself for many
hours and several young Bengali men had been picked up by the police. Into the
early hours of the morning an impromptu march took place of between 50 and 200
which went straight to another main area of Bangladeshi settlement around Canon
Street Road, protesting at the outrage.[14] The following night several gatherings
took place of local people, still furious at the previous night's events.

On Brick Lane groups of people, black and white, milled around in a scene
palpably expectant and fractious. One meeting in a community hall I witnessed
was particularly tense, with a large crowd of extremely angry local people, mostly
young, disgusted by the incursion that had been made on the symbolic heart of the
Bengali community of Tower Hamlets, mad at the police for their perceived
complicity. After the meeting I went with friends into one of the pubs just off Brick
Lane, which had itself had its windows bricked as a result of the revenge actions on
more than 15 public houses that had followed the Quddus Ali attack. And into the
pub walked a man in deer-stalker and overcoat, his pipe making up the full
Sherlock Holmes set, the simulacrum of an English eccentric: a walking guide with
20 American tourists in tow giving one of the many Ripper tours of Whitechapel;
revealing the inscribed knowledges of the Victorian East End through the street
walk; a performative *flânerie* that re-enacted the serial murders and assaults.

On one level this appeared surreal, on another obscene. The place itself was
staged as Jack's East End and the tour proceeded, blithely unaware that there was
anything beyond the ordinary going on. The American tourists were more
concerned that they might be ripped off by the rogue taxi drivers that arrived at the
pub to pick them up than they were by the hidden possibility that they could be
caught in the middle of an urban uprising. And the authority of the guide
remained, unquestioned and unquestionable, resting on identification with the
street: an insider position that cast him as the font of local knowledge.

Seemingly only a single bizarre event, the incident is more typical than it might
appear. The rich history of the Whitechapel area leads to a cluster of different tour
guides working the area: Ripper tours, Jewish tours, Kray tours, Huguenot tours.
The street walk on each occasion renders visible particular genres of spatialised
knowledges. The tour itself becomes the medium through which the identity of the
place is revealed, the knowledge production process replicated through the
individuals making the tour. In this way the knowledge production process of the
flâneur is mimed for the benefit of the contemporary tourist; but is it rendered
inauthentic in doing so?

Paradoxically, it has always been the unknowability and the illegibility of the
urban that privileges the episteme of the street.[15] Knowing that nobody knows, or

ever can know completely, putatively places the spatial practice of the walk above the metanarrative certainties of the plan, the scheme, the totalisation of the panoramic view.[16] But such a valorisation can become the guarantee of parochialism – both a licence to stroll and to gaze and a limit to the scientific value of botanised asphalt. It is also a privilege that is not open to all equally. As Liz Heron has pointed out, the very act of walking prefigures seeing, which prefigures viewing, which may prefigure a particular form of knowledge production, which was gendered as a dominantly male preserve, the classic modern public, but was also contested by women in the spaces of modernity.[17]

It is in such representational spaces that poststructuralist critiques of the totalising narratives of social justice derive from the epistemological violence that works through logics of identity that harden soft borders – inside–outside, me–you, black–white, self–other: the clichéd binaries of the Enlightenment imagination.

Yet the street is dangerous and desirable simultaneously, the site and material cause of intercommunity violence and the condition of possibility of intercultural identification. The street is not a space which is necessarily signified, but it is a medium through which particular cultural forms are expressed.

I think there is a point here where the project of Harvey's *Social Justice* meets the Sennett of *The Fall of Public Man*. A positively understood invocation of urbanism has to be about opening oneself up to difference.[18] The creation of a political space, a social space and a cultural space where the boundary stalking logics of identification are overturned, where uncertainty and unpredictability provide the conditions of possibility for the mutations, hybridity and combinations that define how newness comes into the world, are all definitive features of the lived city, just as the roots of democracy and citizenship are part of the city's history.[19] But such spaces can never be assumed. We have always to answer Harvey's question 'In whose image is the city made?' We have always to map the political economies of the production of city spaces whose cartography may exceed and escape the desires of their designers. The contingencies of such spaces demand that a naïvely rendered 'public sphere' cannot and must not be normalised by casual reference to a street that may be scored with eighteenth-century roots and twentieth-century taboos. The 'public' is always, almost self-evidently, marked by traces of its historicity and spatiality.

In this context the relationship between *flânerie* and epistemology is neither straightforward nor consistent. In most representations of the *flâneur* the individual walks through the urban environment finding themselves as they read and tell their way through the great city. The frequently implicit masculinity of this subject position has prompted criticisms of the failure to acknowledge the gendering of both the right of the gaze and the practices of visual pleasure itself.[20] Modernist cities were in part structured by gendering processes that in part defined the public/private distinction, whilst at times both the city generally, and the streets specifically, represented as feminine, were frequently eroticised through the processes of exploration and capture of the soft city.[21] More recently the nuances of these gendering processes have been disputed in the assertion that the *flâneur* might be seen as androgynous,[22] or else that a more historically inflected study reveals that spaces of the city were contested terrains open to selective appropriation by women.[23] At other times it is the process of immersion that is celebrated as axiomatic of the constraints of knowledge production, the poets of the street contrasted to the will to power implicit in the aerial view of the urban plan.

It is against this background that it is interesting to think again about the will to know implicit in the practice of walking and the performative knowledge of the tour guide. The guide claims an insider status, a privileged position to narrate the secrets of the everyday. Yet even in its celebration, the episteme of the street is surely at its most powerful at the moment of recognition of its own limits; the act of making the streets legible reinforces and reproduces the illegibility of the urban.[24]

Certainly the process of knowing the city through becoming lost in its streets, espoused by Walter Benjamin, is far more complicated than some celebrants of *flânerie* have subsequently implied,[25] but we can still suggest that the links between walking, seeing, knowing and writing do create their own epistemic genealogy. It is a commonplace to note Benjamin's own notion of the *flâneur* prefiguring the popular fictional detective, a curio personified by the tour guide as Holmes: the timely anachronisms of 1990s detective fiction as *film noir* navigation of the streets of Whitechapel.

Central to Benjamin's work was the politics of the manner in which reassuring narratives of historical progress are disrupted by alternative modes of temporality, the interruption of the normal and the taken-for-granted. Spatially, the order of things is likewise never more clearly revealed than through disruption; the striking juxtapositions of the street walk become pedestrian equivalents to the photographic montages of John Heartfield that so inspired him.

From Benjamin, for the purposes of this chapter, it is necessary only to stress that there is a misreading of his work that is increasingly common in some forms of urban studies in which the ambivalence of his positioning becomes apparent. Whilst keen to stress the value of losing himself in the city, the process of street walking was always a process of doubling. On the one hand, the precariousness of the *flâneur*'s losing himself (sic) in the crowd always led to an immersion in the street but also through immersion in the crowd, to an identification with and fetishisation of the commodity – so that the *flâneur*, once confronted with the department store, finds that 'he roamed through the labyrinth of merchandise as he had once roamed through the labyrinth of the city'.[26] Making contradictory sense of oneself in the street is about locating the body in the possibly incommensurable matrices of economy and culture.[27]

What Benjamin clearly never accepts is that the walk involves the sovereign subject moving through space. His is no situationist dérive through the unknown city. To understand the episteme of the *flâneur* it is first essential to reject the notion of the individual body penetrating the spaces of the city. Mapping and walking instead prefigures, and is prefigured by, the process of identity formation. As an interior the street is a constitutive feature of the walker, be it the *flâneur* as tour guide, detective, rebel or even white male academic.

What I want to reject is the dualism that is so central to Lewis Mumford's great work *The City in History*,[28] through which he contrasts the urban as container with the urban as movement. The corporeal walker through urban space is always rhizomatically linked to the streets through which that body inscribes their route.[29] If we return to the scene just off Brick Lane, the relationship between the character who returns again and again to the Ripper and the resident who walks the same streets is one of degree rather than one of kind. The privileged 'inside' of the local is always contingent.

So there are two points to be made here. One is that the street is not the point at which immersion detaches the body from the matrices of political economy. It is, certainly for Benjamin, a point at which the *flâneur* and the commodity become subjects created by geography. Second, street knowledge is not hermetically sealed: in fact, quite the opposite, it is always part of the collapse of inside and outside.[30] Acknowledged as such, heterotopic public space is defined by and defines a street where it is possible to go out in 'publick'[31] and meet strangers.

In this way the hermetically sealed inside of community politics is unlocked, whilst at the same time the spatial practices through which particular places are inscribed differently by different spatialities and historicities are preserved. This sort of cognitive mapping is in part about the prioritisation of 'routes over roots',[32] partly about placing all people on the net of humanity, but it is also valorising some claims to place over others: not a strategically essential moment of identification as much as a topography of authority claims which says in a moment that this person's claim to this place at this time for these reasons is superior to that other person's. Such valorisation has to be of the moment, in a context. It is always precarious, invariably open to questioning: in short, a form of synchronic authenticity.

In part we answer Harvey's own rhetorical question 'In whose image is the city made?' with a call to focus on the process of making which is about the inscriptions of both commodity flows and personal and collective agency. The street is just one modality through which these inscriptions are made visible. In such circumstances the bizarre spectacle of the guided tour has a place in the East End alongside the symbolic marches of protest that have been the first resort for communities besieged by the violent spectre of racism. We always have to map out where they are coming from and where they are going to.

Bluntly, it is on the street where it is possible to 'come to see with eyes of those who come from a special place', where emotional relations are based on actions shared rather than states of being, and where public life can disrupt and transgress destructive *Gemeinschaft*.[33] But it is never easy, never innocent of the inscriptions of time and space which the street itself represents and realises in the body of the individual *flâneur*.

Street politics: heroes and villains

Articulated as politics, the street is 'where it's at'; it is everything the ivory tower is not[34] – which is why it is perhaps so much loved by academics. Here we find a generic narrative form that is not so much about making the street visible as about making the barricades visible: the intoxicating rush of ethical certainty, social justice in a spatially corporeal form.

But what kind of a vicarious experience is this? And who is to man these barricades? Manning is the operative term here. The third case I want briefly to examine relates to the proliferation of political mobilisations that developed in Tower Hamlets from late 1993 onwards. These were both national and local. Whilst the national anti-racist organisations, once again, looked to make Tower Hamlets a battlefield for the fights against Nazism, there was also a mushroom growth of movements amongst local people, both men and women, to combat the growth of racism. In particular, there was the clear politicisation and large-scale mobilisation of local young Bengalis, demonstrated in vigils to show respect to victims of racist attacks, in marches through and laying symbolic claim to the area, in benefits to raise money, and in the defence campaigns to protect those arrested in the struggle. Such mobilisations became the subject of intense press and media attention, featuring in several documentary programmes, in detailed journalistic essays and on the cover of a variety of journals: 'the youth' heralded as new political subjects of the East End.

I want to distinguish between two strands in this revolutionary story. The first is judgemental. There is no way in this chapter that I am attempting to evaluate, undermine or underestimate the remarkable patterns of politicisation that were taking place among second- (and third-) generation Bengalis in London. This is no ethnographic analysis of the experiences of young Bengali men and women. That is only one element of the mosaic that is East End life. I am, however, trying to comment on the racialised configuration of the whole mosaic. It is a configuration that reveals the East End as both lived and signified, an exemplary urbanism in which places are both the conditions of possibility and the expressive modality of identities.

But how are such identifications represented? I think it is important to understand the narrative tropes which make such stories comprehensible. There is a barely hidden genealogy here of place and identity, normatively construed. The black body interpellated through the street. It was after all Lord Scarman who so egregiously talked about 'West Indian' people as a people of the street. Here we have the corollary of Fanon's 'look a Negro':[35] a successful racist placing of the body of the other in the field of vision.

A couple of British press stories illustrate this.[36] The first image appeared in the *Independent* newspaper in 1993. The second was from the *Sunday Times* in 1982, more than ten years earlier. In the latter, young black Rastafarian men occupied the streets of Liverpool (L8) in the wake of the 1980s uprisings, the defiant pose invoking a proprietorial sense of placed masculinity that confronts the gaze of the lens defiantly. In the former, young Bengali men posed in almost identical fashion on the streets of Stepney. Set side by side I believe there is a very real sense in which the two images merge one into the other. Set apart in time, they are linked in a more complicit fashion, the earlier image not only prefiguring the later, but also caught up in the intricate and complex processes of criminalisation[37] that render the *Independent* photograph comprehensible.

We know these stories. They appeal to a knowledge that predates the moment when the camera shutter closed. They place race in the field of vision in a way in which sense becomes self-evident. Two young men, aggressively looking into the camera, evoke a host of not only histories of black looks[38] but also commonsense geographies of racism. These images work because we, the viewers, know what they mean: two or three things we know about the racialised masculinity of the dangerous street.[39]

But the carceral gaze that fixes the dangerous young men on the street in a placing of criminal otherness is not so easily confined to the invocations of delinquency that they may conjure up. In the wake of the events of late 1993, a series of anti-racist stories appeared, with 'the youth' of the East End cast as the heroes of the struggles against the forces of oppression. Again there is no intention here to demean the mobilisations that did occur. But it is worth examining some of the images of these journals.

Across the front covers of a range of progressive left publications in the wake of the 1993 incidents that generated national publicity, some of the Bengali youth organisations appeared in celebratory images: technicolour forms of dissent captured by the iconic image of young male bodies occupying the streets of the East End. When we look at such examples on the covers of *Socialist Review*, *Searchlight* and *Campaign against Racism and Fascism*, and the imagery of the *Independent* and the *Sunday Times*, can we really say they are unrelated? Is it really coincidence that the lineaments of racist culture share so much in common with the rhetorics of revolutionary action?

Now this is undoubtedly a complex story. The subject positions of oppression are regularly taken on board as the vessels that secure movements of resistance – from pejorative black to politically black, from pejorative queer to queer politics. The categories are taken on board to be mocked and subverted in the mimesis of the mirror dance.[40]

But there is also a sense in which the liberal white left themselves, in a desperate search for the transformative political subject, will cast young Bengali men as the teleological delivery boys; and, as Stuart Hall[41] pointed out, in a not dissimilar context after the uprisings of 1981, the streets will not only stage glorious insurrection, they will also witness the fact that it is upon young male Bengali heads that the fully armed apparatus of the state will fall; it is they who will be attacked on the streets at the vigil for Quddus Ali outside the London Hospital, and they who will be confronted by and confront the BNP gangs who increasingly conspire to roam the streets of Tower Hamlets to go Paki bashing. Street politics is easy for the absent.

Three-way street

I think what these three examples share is the foregrounding of place and authenticity, which misleadingly conveys the authentic aesthetic, the authentic episteme, the authentic political subject. Place, specifically the street itself, serves as rhetorical backbone rather than as a medium of articulation through which beauty, truth and politics are mixed together and hybridised. It is possible to take the three examples in turn to see how this 'cross-dressing' takes place.

In the Whitechapel Gallery, accidentally orientalist fragments of eroticised glamour, boxed up and packaged, together with the disembodied murmuring of the chaotic public, are all framed by the arcane image of wisdom and insiderdom reflected in the pool of water. Narcissus lives.

In the pastiche detective figure of Sherlock Holmes, the walker who desires the otherness of difference, eroticising street life, is seduced by the aesthetically captivating nature of experience that allows them to read themselves into the illegibility of the great city and then rationalises this triumph of being over becoming by writing the street, by transforming the gaze into the script through a claim to knowledge – 'to have been there'.

And in the media coverage of 'youth movements' the subjectification of the transformative agent valorises street politics as ethical action and revels in the connotative dreams of St Petersburg, Paris and the barricades. Through such connotative slippage a project is validated – the political is defined as the moment of contestation[42] and action validates the epistemological frame through which such contestation is known. And, more than anything else, there is the spectacle consumed – mass insurrection on the TV screens, heroes framed in the photographers' lenses nourishing the utopian romance in the eroticised imaginary.

In each case 'the street' is more than a stage on which authority claims are made; it is a constitutive feature of the authority itself: something that I want to go on to argue can only be addressed by unpacking the spatialities that such claims invariably invoke. These spatialities are themselves conditions of possibility which demand a more sophisticated and contingent notion of both politics and social justice than we are normally ready to develop: something that I believe can be addressed by a project of radical contextualisation.

Radical contextualisation

Is beauty truth, truth beauty? Are fact and value so distinct? The questions that are no more easily resolved now than two thousand years ago in part reveal the artifice of the moments of identity production, knowledge production and political judgement that I have just described. But they do share some important features. In each case the spatiality of the street is both the condition of possibility through which claims of authenticity are staked and a sign of empirical specificity that is silenced as soon as it is voiced because geographical traces play to the audience as the stigmata of relativism.

Yet it is surely the case that in each example the claims – mediated as they are by this silenced spatiality – are all contingently valid, just as they are contingently fraudulent. As Martin Luther King said, 'the riot is the voice of the unheard', but equally, when 'shouts in the street' turn into the brutal vocabulary of racial battering and ethnic cleansing, we find the moment when Rousseau turns into Robespierre.[43] Likewise, identifying with otherness must surely depend upon both the representational spaces through which it occurs and also the mapping of such spaces into the political economy of the city, whilst the eroticisation of the street is surely on its own, free of necessary morality.

In part this is no more than saying – *pace* Habermas – that the classic notions of public space filled by universals and individuals must be replaced with a more nuanced version that acknowledges both individual rights of humanity and communal or collective rights that reflect inscribed structures of power, a proposition outlined in Iris Marion Young's demands for an understanding of heterotopic public space. However, it is also a way of suggesting that an understanding of social justice and *fin de siècle* urbanism must always revolve around a politics of articulation, contingent epistemologies and situated aesthetics: a set of practices that has elsewhere been described as radical contextualisation.[44]

The project of radical contextualisation is at one and the same time straightforward and arcane. Straightforwardly, many of the old binaries are subverted because neither abstraction nor empiricism (in knowledge production), neither theory nor practice (in political action), neither universalism nor relativism (in aesthetic judgements) can resolve any of Kant's three fundamental questions of philosophy – what do I know?, what should I do? and what do I want? The answers to all such questions depend on abolishing the a priori. They demand a spelling-out of the terms on which they are made, accepting that the traces of historicity and spatiality are always a constitutive feature of the processes of subject and object formation.

But the confusion between ethics, epistemology and identity is not just one of plurality. At one level I think it important to find a vocabulary that indicts the Jaar/Spivak installation as fascinating but fraudulent, that ties revolutionary plaudits to their prefiguring of racism, and renders the walker as always problematic.

Through radical contextualisation it is possible to foreground both the dead ends of standpoint epistemology and the false promises of universalism. It is possible to cherish the public spaces of modernity without romanticising them. Third space, liminal space, the privileged margin – all open up the moment of identification as a moment of uncertainty. Reassuring narratives of time are dislocated by the uncertainties of the spatial. Acknowledged as such, heterotopic public space is defined by and defines a street where it is possible to go out in publick and meet strangers.

But the project of radical contextualisation is also about acknowledging the contingency of all identities, affirming that the traces of historicity and spatiality are inscribed not just by presence but also by absence: by a lack as much as a plenitude. Within this heterotopic public space claims of authenticity and redress are not just grounded, they are also constituted by their historicity and spatiality in what Homi Bhabha, drawing on Benjamin, describes as 'a dialectic of cultural negation as negotiation' in that:

> Community is the antagonist supplement of modernity: in the metropolitan space it is the territory of the minority, threatening the claims of civility; in the transnational world it becomes the border-problem of the diasporic, the migrant, the refugee. Binary divisions of social space neglect the profound

temporal disjunction – the translational time and space – through which minority communities negotiate their collective identifications. For what is at issue in the discourse of minorities is the creation of agency through incommensurable (not simply multiple) positions. Is there a poetics of the interstitial community? How does it name itself, author its agency?[45]

It is this incommensurability that arises from and constitutes the spatialities of subjectification that work through and on 'the street'. It is out of the incommensurability of different spatialities that both the spaces of resistance emerge as social practice and the moments of utopianism can insert themselves as political projects of discursive closure.

The spaces of the street are, in other words and a familiar language, contradictory.[46] And a language of contradiction usefully returns us to the agenda of Harvey's *Social Justice and the City*, not in search of Hegelian resolution but for bearings. For if, as Paul Gilroy has repeatedly argued forcefully, 'the problem with the cultural left' is that they have never been cultural enough, it is worth echoing this with the comment that cultural politics without political economy will be equally rudderless.

The power of a focus on the practices and processes of production of both culture and class, of moralities, identities and knowledges, is to place the stress on becoming rather than being, is to open up politics without reducing it to either economistic caricature or cultural self-indulgence. Invariably this must involve foregrounding the influences of time and space through either radical contextualisation or something that would look much like it. Moments of productive cultural syncretism, fusion and hybridity take place not just in any place, nor in some rarefied, abstract liminal space or third space or marginal space. They are realised through particular articulations of spatiality, just as those spatialities are a constitutive feature of their formation. The street is frequently one such articulation and it is as such that we can celebrate the 'shouts of the street'.[47] For where is the place at which 'communality is not based on a transcendent becoming'[48] if it is not the street, if it is not a celebration of the places where one can go out in publick and meet strangers.

The street is an organising frame through which the social is rendered visible, neither authentically real nor merely metaphoric, a moment of placing and a *mise en scène*. In this sense the street is both a state of consciousness and a locus of meaning, a way of thinking about the world and a semiotic source of dramaturgical keys and cues. As such it is an exemplary case of the sites of the urban. If, as Harvey said in the opening sentence of *Social Justice and the City*, 'The City is a manifestly complicated thing',[49] the complexity in part arises from the multiple spatialities that it is constituted by.

In one sense we clearly have to do away with authenticity, to understand the lie that is at the heart of the term. But in another it is equally the case that the rights of local people to speak out against property capital valorise a particular understanding of authenticity; the rights of minority communities to represent themselves in the anti-racist movement valorise a particular understanding of authenticity; the right of the Bengali community to defend themselves against racist attacks acknowledges a territorial authenticity; and the political moment at which the democratic act is legitimated with a vote valorises a particular understanding of the authenticity of the 'real me'.

It is from such articulated speaking positions, in such explicit spaces of representation, and at particular historically contingent moments, that a politics of authenticity will continue to find a place in progressive left politics. Diachronically, we know that authenticity has no place, but if we freeze the moving film momentarily, in particular places at particular times, the authentic can be voiced synchronically, an appeal that is of the moment, directed to particular audiences and justified by specific ends. This is not so much an instance of the strategic essentialism favoured by Spivak and others as much as the 'true lies' described by Fanon.[50]

Authenticity is a true lie of political action, a strategy but not a goal. What we saw in the East End of London in the 1990s, and continue to see in so many other places where authenticity underscores the very vocabulary of popular politics, is what happens when such a strategy becomes mistaken for a goal in and of itself. In such situations the message is clear for both contemporary politics and cosmopolitan urbanism, in the words of the Tower Hamlets 9 campaign.[51]

'No justice, no peace'. This is a slogan in which the concerns of the local consciously and deliberately draw on a vocabulary of the global. The slogan popularised in the Los Angeles campaigns that followed the uprisings inspired by miscarriages of social justice that defined the Rodney King beating echoes in London and resonates in a vocabulary of resistance. In so doing the street may be a reference point that crosses the globe and transcends localism, just as it may be frighteningly parochial. To ignore both the possibilities and the dangers of either inflection is to deny geography.

7 The cultural quarter

Globalisation, hybridity and curating exotica

'A skyscraper recognises by virtue of its height that it has acquired civic responsibilities.'

César Pelli, architect of Battery Park City in New York and
1 Canada Square in Canary Wharf, London

'The continuous growth of cultural institutions and the increase in ethnic diversity have reduced the sense of an unbridgeable gap between monumental spaces and slums. Moreover the anointing of various cities as culture capitals has occurred along with greater tolerance for different kinds of cultural activities. Today there are more playful exhibits, more public art and more recognition of the cultural value of ethnic communities.'

Sharon Zukin[1]

'The interest of the panorama is in seeing the true city – the city indoors. What stands within the windowless house is the true. Moreover the arcade, too, is a windowless house. The windows that look down on it are like loges from which one gazes into its interior, but one cannot see out these windows to anything outside. (What is true has no windows; nowhere does the true look out to the universe.)'

Walter Benjamin[2]

Bill Clinton comes to Harlem

Just what was Bill Clinton doing in Harlem? In 2001 the man described by Toni Morrison as the first black president of the United States[3] ensconced himself in the iconically black heartland of New York to build his business, wipe out his legal debts and support his wife Hilary, the newly elected senator. Clinton's base in Harlem received mixed reviews.[4] For some he demonstrated the redemptive potential of the commitment to multiracial democracy of an individual that came out of a particular kind of poor white communion with the civil rights movement. For others he represented an alien presence of white power in the heartland of black New York. Malik Zulu Shabazz of the new Black Panther Party of New York suggested Clinton's professed affiliation with Harlem lacked authenticity. For others again – as brownstone properties had begun to top $800,000 a piece locally –

Clinton's presence merely gave the final twist to the difficult process of rebranding Harlem land values that gave a green light to processes of ethnic gentrification.[5]

Shortly after his move, in April 2002, Michael Jackson – the clinically deracinated minstrel figure personified – performed in a benefit event for the former president at the Apollo Theatre, itself another iconic site in the history of African-American culture. At the event Clinton spoke passionately about the need for the performing arts to provide an arena for the sort of transcultural dialogue so essential for New York and the nation in the wake of 9/11. It is the ambivalence of Clinton's position that – as ever – speaks volumes about the racialised politics of the USA. But it also speaks volumes about the choreography of a cultural dance that took place simultaneously both within the parochial cartography of the quarters of New York and on the stage of the global city.

Clinton's story captures in miniature a problem recurrent across the cultural contact zones of the multicultural cities of the twenty-first-century world. The story can be read in (at least) two ways. For some, inauthentic performative cultural dialogue commodifies ethnic difference to the benefit of a minority of cultural producers, and consequently serves as the handmaiden to capital in the shifting of Manhattan's gentrification frontier a few blocks northwards. To others, a more optimistic scenario is generated by the belated appeals to universal humanity that Clinton personifies. The poor white from the country recognises and confronts the black ghetto and transcends the hard boundaries of race through the medium of culture. Music, performing arts, literature, figurative and abstract representations know no synthetic boundaries; they realise an actually existing globalisation. They are also putatively the vehicles for the precious creolisation, hybridity and mixing of cultures that challenges the conventional in aesthetics and the hegemonic in politics.

The spaces of the city are particularly important in these processes of cultural dialogue. They constitute both the stages of communication and one medium of separation: the nodal points of cultural flows and the commodified arenas of residence and performance. Consequently, contemporary urbanism can curate the presentation of ethnic difference and new forms of hybridity whilst simultaneously displacing appeals to community through processes of city transformation. Indeed an examination of the growing power of culture (and the *cultural industries*) to shape city form might lend important insights into the manner in which we conceptualise not only contemporary patterns of race and multiculture but also the more casually invoked notions of globalisation itself.

However, the notion of the cultural quarter of the city can imply a moral geography of the metropolis, a seductive place of cultural dialogue and a particular regime of city knowledge. In this chapter it is suggested that the relationship between global flows and city realisations of processes of cultural production sometimes engender a confusion between the registers of the ethical, the aesthetic and the epistemological in narratives of the city. In noting the growing significance of culture (and the cultural industries) to the dynamics of city change it might be helpful if we consider a little more closely the perspectives that are deployed in framing the cultural quarter. If we look at city life simultaneously from up close and from a distance it might be possible to rethink some of the dynamics of globalisation, displacing misleading juxtapositions of *globalisation from above* and *globalisation from below*. It might also be possible to draw on this perspectival dance to develop a notion of the spatial sublime that helps to develop a sense of the ambivalence of city life. Neither naïvely celebrating creolisation for its own sake nor reifying the boundary markers of race and ethnicity will do justice to what Les Back has described as the metropolitan paradox of city multiculture. Back has suggested that those sites where intercultural dialogue is most profound are paradoxically also the sites of some of the most extreme articulations of intolerance.

There is a burgeoning interest in the manner in which the cultural industries shape the future metropolis. How significant such a force might be is moot. In this chapter, two sources of suspicion about the power of the cultural industries to reshape the city are followed by an alternative take on these debates. *One source of suspicion* is the categoric cannibalism of the very notion of the cultural industries. The elements of design, creativity and culture in the high-added-value end of a range of economic activity, including such manufacturing staples as IT-driven high-tech engineering, might suggest that there is a possible category error creeping into the analytical system. The generation of value-added design-related profit across the full range of standard industrial classifications from car manufacture to food products might suggest potential for conceptual inflation. When Rupert Murdoch's News International multinational corporation and a squatting artist are lumped together as part of the cultural industries, it might be time to think about whether there is a degree of chaotic conceptualisation behind the term itself.

The second suspicion arises from the derivation of academic concern with the cultural industries. It is at least in part true to suggest that the cultural drivers of the division of labour (particularly around gender and race) and the labour process have long been overlooked in mainstream urban studies. *In part* the putative rise in cultural industries and the study of creativity might just be symptomatic of a degree to which the study of culture has been valorised in the academy in recent decades, and culture is recognised within the frame of reference which scrutinises the city economy. The extent to which cultural significations marked the division of capital and labour in the naturalisation of gendered and racialised work was true in both the mills of Bradford in the 1960s and the Mac world of the burger flippers in the 1990s. The role of cultural innovation was central to the tenets of Fordism as well as to the just-in-time world of post-Fordism. The 'cultural turn' in economic sociology, political science and political economy both acknowledges this, as well as at times advocating the increasing significance of the power of culture in the economy.

Neither caveat is advanced here to erase the significance of the rise of cultural industries in the cities of today, only to qualify the claims made on their behalf. But if the term *cultural industries* is potentially chaotically conceived, and the cultural turn in the academy significant in refocusing the lens through which the city is read, then it might be worth turning this problem on its head. It might just be worth asking how rhetorics of cultural industries and the practices of their promotion render comprehensible the social and the economic spaces of the city. In so doing this chapter argues that the manner in which cultural quarters make visible understandings of multiculture and privilege certain forms of culturally driven economic activity is not insignificant in reshaping the way in which we think about the multicultural metropolis of the twenty-first century. However, this is true in ways that relate as much to issues of commodification, gentrification and globalisation as to straightforward changes in categories of metropolitan economic growth. In this context we might wish to think differently about how the city curates multiculture and the emergence of newly hybridised identities and products within its boundaries. In passing, such a perspective disrupts the sometimes simplistic juxtapositions of a *globalisation from above* with an alternatively heroic *globalisation from below*.

Cultural industries

There is now clear evidence of the development, in post-industrial cities in general, and London in particular, of the new 'cultural industries' sector as a significant force in the restructuring of the urban economy. There is also, on both sides of the Atlantic, clear and pressing evidence of an increasingly complex pattern of both social and economic exclusion and inclusion of ethnic minority communities. In Britain this is particularly true of those descended from the generations of New Commonwealth migrants that arrived in the United Kingdom in the postwar years.

Sharon Zukin has defined the cultural industries as a 'symbolic economy' which 'unifies material practices of labour, art, performance and design'.[6] Although not always recognised as an industrial sector in some conventional literatures, the cultural industries have over the last decade belatedly achieved a collective identity in the imagination of government officials and city planners in Britain and elsewhere. Zukin's notion of a symbolic economy helps to consider the cultural industries in terms of a series of economic activities that have provided some of the most significant increases in the London labour market in recent years. Evidence from the USA suggests that cultural industries represented the largest source of employment growth throughout the 1990s, generating more jobs than the health-linked services and six times more jobs than the automobile industry.[7]

For some, creativity and culture become the heart of new economies of advanced capitalism. Intellectual labour, knowledge economies, information and design putatively form the post-industrial dynamics behind the notion of living on thin air in the creative city.[8] In his best-selling work, Richard Florida has argued that the cultural industries generate and are generated by the drivers of change in *the creative class*: 'The rise of the Creative Economy is drawing the spheres of innovation (technological creativity), business (economic creativity) and culture (artistic and cultural creativity) into one another, in more intimate and more powerful combinations than ever.'[9]

The extent of growth of the cultural industries has belatedly received the level of academic attention the phenomenon warrants, bringing with it a commensurately significant bloating of the related academic research.[10] In work around the spatial development of cultural industries and the urban realisation of their form this tends to focus on how the clustering of cultural industries growth is both facilitated by and realised through specific clustering within *the cultural quarters* of the city. The manner in which the producer networks at the heart of the cultural industries are structured, locational preferences decided, marketing strategies developed and employment practices defined suggests an autonomous development of the quarters of the city.[11] But such spaces are also set within land use regimes that may facilitate or prohibit the translation of (old industrial) workspace to residential (lofted or gated) development. An understanding of locational preference or residential value may also be inflected by informal repute (the buzz)[12] and official promotion in strategies of urban regeneration. In this context, this chapter considers the manner in which the multicultural mediates both the symbolic economies of the city and the representation of social life in the cultural quarters of the urban. The chapter is routed through London before returning to Harlem. The chapter argues that notions of perspective and global scale may help to explain the spatialisation of the cultural quarter. In this sense Clinton may take us from the ridiculous back to the sublime.

Cultural quarters and skinning the city

Foregrounding the cultural basis of parts of the city has long been a contested feature of urbanism. Notions of sexuality – most prominently gay *villages* – and taste (jewellery quarters, artists' networks, night-time economies) have at times provided the organising principle for the notion of the cultural quarter.[13] Yet, commonly, ethnicity has provided a focus for debates around both forms of consumption and the reproduction of processes of identity and identification that the spaces of the city facilitate. The emergence of Chinatowns and other *ethnic enclaves* as sites of cultural consumption has provoked important debates that have considered the changing cartographies of cultural quarters within the rubric of contemporary urbanism.[14] The interplay between colonial desire, exoticism and gentrification has been explored in Jane M. Jacobs' landmark work *Edge of Empire*.[15] In part of her work Jacobs examined the changing shape of East London, exploring both the gentrifying potential of the exotic and the authentic and the manner in which identity politics was generated by the specificity of configurations of culture and economy.

In cities across the world new geographies are emerging of patterns of cultural production that are often the focus of local and central government attempts to generate employment and economic growth.[16] In London alone, attempts to refashion the urban spaces of the old Vauxhall Pleasure Gardens and the Elizabethan entertainment centre of London at Bankside in Southwark have become the focus of major investment plans by significant private sector players as well as by local and central government. The City Fringe (covering parts of Camden, Hackney, Tower Hamlets and Islington), Brixton (through the 'Action Plans' and 'Vision' of the local City Challenge) and the 'Pool of London' partnership have all in recent years identified 'cultural industries' as the central economic force behind the encouragement of a new geography of cultural quarters, and the London Development Agency has recognized the cultural industries as a key driver of economic development within contemporary London.[17]

Jacobs cleverly explores the manner in which the notion of identity politics is overtaken by cultural flows and economic change. The paternal local left expected the Bengali community to resist the manner in which their culture was commodified. Yet, for Jacobs, the predominantly white mainstream left locally were disappointed when many in the Bengali community rejected such vicarious heroism and preferred instead to become implicated in the rendering attractive of their home area to the displacing forces of capital. Instead the marketing of the area within the rubric of *Banglatown* was developed by local Bengali entrepreneurs, inverting the abusive notion of the term deployed by far-right racist populism in the 1980s and promoting ethnicised patterns of consumption and gentrification in the area.[18]

What is to be made of this sort of interface between epidermal commodification, gentrification and authenticity politics that Jacobs explores and that has become a diagnostic feature of contemporary cities across the world? What kind of economies of desire do the cultural quarters of today's metropolis represent? Do such sites or contact zones between different cultures generate cultural mixing, intercultural dialogue and the hybridity much prized by some, or do they reinforce ossified notions of cultural form, drained of political charge and freighted with conservative forms of ostensibly discrete ethnicities?

The ethnic enclave, the gay quarter, the entertainment district, the conservation (heritage) area. Like the ghetto and the street, the cultural quarter is in a sense *overdetermined*. It is simultaneously both a *generalised label* to describe emergent social and economic spatial formations and a narrative trope that makes one part of the city analytically visible. And, as Chapter 4 explored in the context of the ghetto, it would be misconceived to consider the former more *real* than the latter. They link one with the other, frequently in two-way relations of causality. And the vocabulary of racialised difference frequently mediates between the two. Narratives of cultural difference structure place-based identities that influence property values in New York's East Village and Williamsburg as much as in London's Whitechapel and Deptford.[19]

Across the globe, strategies for urban regeneration have increasingly looked to the notion of the cultural quarter to provide a central element in the transformation of the post-industrial metropolis. Culture – once seen within mainstream studies of city development as superstructural effect – has in the last decade come to feature as a significant driver of city change in its own right.

There are at least three influences that structured such change: the commodification of culture, the interplay of residential preference and cultural urbanism and a globalised sensibility. The cultural quarter consequently features as a significant analytical framing of city economies, debates around contemporary gentrification and the cultural facets of globalisation. In each of these related fields of inquiry the cultural quarter frames and makes visible a particular metropolitan landscape and city multiculturalism occupies a privileged position.

The commodification of culture

Ash Amin has suggested that 'the aestheticisation of commodities and the commodification of aesthetics are two aspects of the emerging age which serve to blur the traditional distinction between economic and cultural activity'.[20] As Paul Gilroy has explored, in powerful contributions throughout both *The Black Atlantic* and *Between Camps*,[21] nowhere is this process more pervasive or ethically problematic than in the commodification of multiculture in general and black Atlantic culture in particular.[22] In this context the configuration of multicultural quarters within post-industrial cities raises important questions about:

- What impact will major sectoral expansion in the new cultural industries have on the employment patterns of ethnic minority communities?
- What is the emergent ethnic and gender composition of the cultural industries labour force?
- What are the processes by which characteristics of ethnic diversity, cultural difference and 'multiculture' become commodities in the new cultural industries to be marketed?
- What is the institutional form taken by expanding firms in this sector of the economy in terms of labour processes, recruitment practices and supply chains?
- What is the relationship between one particular industrial sector and the attempts to develop redundant capital fixed in land assets through new forms of state intervention to produce new 'cultural quarters' in the contemporary city?

The relationship between multicultural urban settlement and the development of the cultural industries is curious and is also potentially a causally interesting one. Although the focus here is on the United Kingdom, the lessons may be more international. The demand for labour created migrant flows to the late twentieth-century metropolises of the global north. Like a photographic negative, patterns of settlement tended to reflect the carious ecologies of white flight or declining residential demand. Residential concentrations of migrant minorities tended to be concentrated on the least wanted or most remote parts of the city. The transformation of the city may reconfigure such spatial patterns: what was once least desirable in Tompkins Square or Whitechapel or Brixton might change as property values reflect the reconfiguration of demography and economy.

Much research established that the dominant sectors of employment amongst first-generation New Commonwealth migrants closely reflected specific patterns of Fordist labour demand in the growth years of the 1950s and 1960s.[23] Migration was seen as largely producing 'substitute' or 'replacement' labour, both within the sectors of the economy that domestic labour shunned throughout a period of near full employment, and geographically through settlement of parts of the city that had witnessed the most intense forms of industrial restructuring and residential suburbanisation. The familiar and well-established pattern of ethnic minority settlement that resulted was characterised by high concentrations of ethnic minority communities in a few specific cities in the UK and migrant labour in a few specific sections of the economy. In London these trends were also demonstrably ethnically specific, with high levels of distinctive settlement patterns that were even characterised by significant differences in settlement and employment concentrations between different island groups migrating from the Caribbean.[24]

In the capital the ethnically specific nature of these patterns was exemplified by cases such as Sikh migration that clustered around the expansion of Heathrow Airport and the residential areas of Southall and Ealing, Jamaican migration to South London with a focus on the low-paid public sector service posts (most notably in transport and health services), and Bengali (Sylheti) migration to the East End of London with notable concentration in the clothing and restaurant trades. Similar stories of specific forms of labour demand, informal chains of residential concentration and the consequent changing nature of large areas of British cities characterise the roots of the complex geographies of today's London. The Horn of Africa, Nigeria, Brazil and Vietnam each provided a particular motor of neighbourhood change in the 1990s, even whilst the increasingly complex second and third generations of British-born communities of Caribbean, South Asian, Irish and Cypriot descent came to define neighbourhoods of the increasingly mosaic-like structure of the city.

It was in this context that the major restructuring of the British economy in the 1980s left the first-generation workforce of minority communities doubly exposed. It has been demonstrated that both the industrial sectors characterised by minority labour market concentration and the geographical areas characterised by migrant settlement – notably in zones of inner city de-industrialisation – were those likely to see the most marked reductions in labour demand throughout the late 1970s and 1980s.[25] Moreover, the labour process has been mediated by specific notions of gendered cultural difference for many decades. Colonial and slave economies translate into visions of black masculinity. Genealogies of racism underscore caricatures of black femininity. Imperial histories traced through the Raj roots informed representations of the Sikh faith and of the lascar recruitment of merchant seamen from Sylhet. The culturally freighted recruitment of nurses and Caribbean labourers on the railways in the 1950s, Punjabi links to Heathrow, and the roots and routes of the Indian (truly Bangladeshi) takeaway are all sculptured from these genealogies. Across the globe the homogenising force of capitalism has always been able to draw on the ostensibly contradictory cultural fictions of gender and ethnic difference to produce specifically racialised divisions of labour. Discussions of boutique multiculture need to be placed within the histories of such epidermal commodification. The exotic has always had a price. Perhaps only the valorisation of cosmopolitan multiculture has changed, not its constitutive role in the labour process.

Both the significant patterns of racialised exclusion and the major expressions of social unrest that have been linked to such exclusion have been well documented in the social science literature in the last three decades. There is now a commonsense acknowledgement that the degree of 'racialised' exclusion in both social and economic life is a major concern not only in the cities of Britain but also in all the European cities that have become, if only by default, crucibles of 'multiculturalism' through labour migration in the postwar years.[26] However, conventionally the academic focus in the race relations literature has tended to be on forms of labour market segmentation,[27] equal opportunity practices[28] or trans-generational ethnic mobility.[29]

From the 1990s onwards, however, two trends have emerged in sites of urban multiculture relating to the experience of descendants of migrant communities and the fate of areas of postwar migrant settlement. There has been relatively little research focus on the labour market experiences of second and third generations of New Commonwealth migrants or consideration of the broader geographical and sectoral relationships between forms of economic growth and ethnic diversity.[30] This is of particular significance because there are a few clearly identifiable signs that some of the strongest forms of economic growth seen in growth sectors in post-industrial cities across the world are both conceptually and geographically related to concentrations of ethnic minority settlement. Certainly across London there is some a priori evidence to suggest that concentrations of ethnic minorities correlate closely with the clustering activity in a sector of growth loosely linked by the omnibus term 'cultural industries' as well as with poverty.[31]

This in turn raises questions about the future relationships between the creative city and the multicultural futures of urbanism. These relate to the market advantages of diversity, the potential of the multicultural promotional strategies of ethnic exoticism and city change, and the coincidental correlations between segregated settlement and gentrification potential.

Conceptually, new cultural industries emphasise diversity as a key strength of urban locales, and there is a tendency for cities such as London and Birmingham in the United Kingdom to market the economic advantages of culturally specific 'quarters' that commonly market ethnic specificity through both consumption and 'ethnic' products. Cultural quarters commonly coincide geographically with historic patterns of migrant settlement, with parts of London as diverse as Brixton, Deptford, Notting Hill and the East End all marketing their ethnic diversity as a key locational strength. Cultural industries frequently exemplify characteristics of the post-Fordist labour process, such as 'just-in-time' production and the blurring of boundaries between conception and production in employment sectors as diverse as the furniture trade and the design professions.

In this context the apparent hopes vested in the new cultural industries has prompted some urban regeneration programmes to make an explicit link between the promotion of this particular form of economic growth and the promotion of multiracial economic inclusion to combat problems of social exclusion. In 1990s London cultural quarters were actively promoted by urban regeneration programmes around the fringes of the four London boroughs surrounding the financial district (the City 'square mile'), the London borough of Lewisham's Creative Lewisham Programme, the marketing of Banglatown and through the efforts of Brixton City Challenge to promote the cultural economy of South London. These are just a few of many examples of this nationwide trend.[32]

It is commonly the case that in the promotion of parts of the city in contemporary urban regeneration programmes places are created as sites of consumption. In part this 'place marketing' is not so much an innovation as a standard element of the commodification of space.[33] Cultural industries do produce 'goods'; they are not simply an extension of a variety of service industries. They thus display all the characteristics of the commodification process. But equally significantly, in sectoral growth, where the boundaries between conception and manufacture, consumption and production are increasingly blurred, the locations through which clustering is developed and economic multiplier effects are maximised is itself in part about the manner in which these new geographies are narrated as integral to the economic development process.[34] Such questions are of economic relevance. In a consideration of the material impacts of the growth of cultural industries, David Harvey's question 'In whose image is the city made?' was rephrased by Zukin as 'Whose culture, whose cities?' It is in the answer to such questions that the interplay between gentrification and multiculture will be revealed.

Through the creation of such place-based identities a new cosmopolitanism in most post-industrial cities tends to rely on specific narratives of race, place and nation.[35] In such contexts, areas of ethnic minority settlement are at times cast as potentially *innovative milieux* for the development of new industrial forms. Cosmopolitanism itself becomes marketable: at carnival in Notting Hill, in Brixton after hours and in Brick Lane on a Sunday morning. The possible relationship between such innovative milieux and the racialisation of forms of economic change clearly has the potential to valorise local property markets and promote both increased residential desirability and the displacement effects of gentrification.[36]

Residential preference and gentrification: the geographies of urban governance, planning and equity

This is particularly the case where gentrification is seen to have developed in the affluent metropolises of the north. The concept of gentrification has evolved and expanded from its 1960s coinage as a product of accumulated idiosyncratic locational preference that first defined the term to cover more coordinated interventions from property capital. Neil Smith has argued that the term is 'no longer about a quixotic oddity in the housing market, but has become the leading residential edge of a much larger endeavour: the class remake of the central urban landscape'.[37] Culture mediates the representations of the sites for such intervention both through dynamics of repute and regimes of place marketing. In this sense the cultural quarter is analytically a site in the city that potentially conflates issues of place promotion, governmental intervention and the locational preferences of both residence and the new industries.

Cultural quarters are not only the product of place-based promotion. Within contemporary practice and the new economic sociology,[38] it is generally acknowledged that economic activity and clustering takes place and thrives within both producer networks and 'man-made' politically determined institutional governance structures. In this context the development of new strategies of socioeconomic governance in an urban context has been in part based on the changing spatial character of economic processes, particularly in relation to new patterns of economic localism and regionalism. This 'new localism' generates two connected research themes in relation to the role of public and semi-public agencies in promoting and steering economic development in the cultural sector. The first of these concerns the function of governance agencies as 'facilitators' of private economic activity. The second concerns the relationship of planning and development strategies to issues of social equity.

In the spatial context of development given by new forms of economic localism, urban economic success is closely tied to strong institutional networks and conducive locational factors.[39] A primary concern for governance agencies operating in such a development context is to facilitate the locational and institutional conditions for local economic growth. These agencies have a crucial role to play in the creation of desirable supply-side conditions for development through a range of measures: integrating corporate networks; supporting innovation; the provision and enhancement of public infrastructure; environmental improvements and planning strategies; site acquisition, development and marketing; and through the 'soft-site' functions of place marketing. The potential for new agencies to promote growth in these areas provides a potential theme of research. This 'facilitative' function of urban governance itself rests on a rejection of a straightforwardly free market understanding of the territories of the contemporary city.

A second sub-theme concerned with urban governance analyses the incorporation of issues of equity and difference into a planning and development framework. As the city concentrates diversity, so it produces spatial fragmentation. In a context where 'diversity' or 'difference' may more frequently signify unwanted proximity, sequestration and withdrawal, the 'new cosmopolitanism' of cultural developments indicates a distinctive response to urban fragmentation. Cultural policy and urban planning in this sense seek to harmonise economic development with social and aesthetic improvements based on the valorisation of 'difference'.[40] Such programmes are consonant with shifts both to market-led planning,[41] and to small-scale local planning which emphasises equity concerns.[42] A planning context which seeks to 'manage diversity' through the arrangement and enhancement of urban spaces questions the will, the ability and the ethical basis on which the cosmopolitan city will be planned, a topic that is addressed in Chapter 10 of this volume.

But of significance here is the coincidental proximity of areas of migrant settlement with zones of employment de-industrialisation. In London alone, the inner ring of postwar settlement in iconic sites such as Hounslow, Southall, Brixton, Deptford, Spitalfields, Whitechapel, Stratford, Stoke Newington, Tottenham, Notting Hill, Wembley and Harlesden occurred in areas proximate to concentrations of post-industrial warehouses and redundant employment space. Twenty-first-century urbanism concentrates the densities of employment, and even in the upturns of the early 1980s and late 1990s property booms these areas were frequently still zoned for employment uses for which there was relatively little employment demand. Moreover, the price of land with residential zoning constantly dwarfed the acreage values of land zoned for employment uses. Their increasing cultural cachet, mediated through the allure of (sometimes exoticised) place-based identities of commodified ethnic consumption was commonly instrumental in a hidden process. In all of these areas, numbers of redundant industrial spaces were de-zoned from employment use and re-zoned for upmarket residential development. The language of gentrification *displacing* existing communities is consequently supplemented by processes by which new zoning laws enhance residential density through the *addition* of residential gentrifiers with the sites of change mediated through the marketing of their ethnic identities. The functional land-use zoning of the city is complicated by rhetorics and governmental practices that promote *mixed use*. A mosaic of land uses displaces the cartographic certainties of postwar convention that divided the city more categorically between functional differentiation of not only workplace and homeplace but also an explicit taxonomy of economic activity.

So the cultural quarter might be the accumulation of slightly different spatial economies. It is an *object of marketing promotion*, a(n) (object-human) formal and informal *producer network* that might stretch beyond the boundaries of the city and a *governance territory (or territories)* of both state forms of local government and alternative regimes of governance that address capital and finance availability and sector-based support. So even in their most prosaic economic guise the narrative spaces that make the cultural quarter visible might be plural and incommensurable.

Multiculture, consumption and the global city

The shrinking of the globe by flows of cultures, goods and peoples poses challenges to even the most monocultural urban setting. Any contemporary metropolis realises its consumption patterns within such a context of time-space compression. However, the simultaneous presence of multiethnic patterns of consumption alongside culturally diverse demographics challenges the manner in which patterns of globalisation are considered in the multicultural city. In particular, they reconfigure the conventional hierarchies of city, region and nation state. Cultural quarters of the city provide spaces through which such new inflections of globalising practice might be realised.

The relationship between globalisation and urban cultures exemplifies the need for both a more nuanced spatial vocabulary and a more sophisticated understanding of the temporalities and spatialities that mediate social change. An analysis of the cultural quarters of the twenty-first-century city may provide a helpful critique of some of the more clumsy invocations of patterns of globalisation. In particular, *the elsewhere of place* and the ambivalence that surrounds the commodification of the particular within transnational circuits of information, taste and belief might help us to understand that the cultural quarter represents an alternative lens through which to observe the theoretical apparatus of globalisation.[43] In this chapter it is instead suggested that if we are to understand the manner in which urban cultures de-territorialise and re-territorialise then we must understand simultaneously the iterative relationship between the activity that takes place in the spaces of the city and the narratives through which such spaces are made visible. On a theoretical level such work would interrogate the relationship between culture and commodification that is at the heart of many of the most significant forms of economic change in post-industrial global cities.[44]

The cultural quarter is consequently one of the spatial forms through which the twenty-first-century city reconfigures the conventional hierarchical relationship between city, region and nation state. It is invoked to attract consumption that is both national and international in origin. It is also the site where the contact zones of cultural flows of politics, food, music, film and faith become both visible and contested, crossing international boundary lines and making a claim for the privileged international spaces of twenty-first-century urbanism. As medium of city regeneration it potentially both reifies and ossifies notions of cultural difference, but as a site of new cultural practices of production it is simultaneously the arena in which both new products and new identifications link explicitly to notions of creolisation and exchange. Consequently, it is an ambivalent space. It is characterised simultaneously by both the fixity of the boundaries of ethnic difference and the flux of cultural hybridisation. These alternative readings of such spaces create a tension between the metaphor of the city mosaic and that of the melting pot. They demand a closer sociological inspection that is careful about the privileging of the view in the curation of the cultural quarters of the city.

In this context the distinction between globalisation *from above* and globalisation *from below* is not a particularly helpful one. Globalisation from below has been invoked by scholars such as Appadurai to make the case for alternative framings of the sociological.[45] The two-dimensionality of the vocabulary potentially prefigures an equally two-dimensional Manichean morality. Especially for those that espouse the latter as a politically heroic positionality, this binary opposition may hide as much as it reveals. The model of causality implicit in this opposition also demands some justification. The notion that all that comes from above is bad and all that comes from below is good would in other analytical contexts barely warrant plausibility. Internationalised environmental controls and regimes of justice and human rights might appeal to a notion of cosmopolitan democracy in the postnational constellation that is not exclusively the moral prerogative of defenders of Enlightenment reason.[46] Likewise, the commodity fetish, xenophobic intolerance of the stranger and cultural imperialism might at worst emerge from the stygian depths of the human condition, and at the very least are the product of an iterative relationship between structures of power and behavioural predisposition.

Mosaic and melting pot: recognition, curation and creolisation

In this sense the manner in which the cultural quarter makes comprehensible specific narratives of urban change is centrally important to the dynamic realisation of capital and culture in spatial form. In part this relates to the manner in which aestheticised production – and arts practice in particular – is simultaneously increasingly part of the economic fabric of the city, a harbinger of change and a frame for corporate intervention in the metropolis.[47] But in part this also points to a consideration of the manner in which the city itself is curated.

The cultural quarter plays an important role in the lexicon of contemporary urbanism because it illustrates the manner in which space mediates narrative. Certain kinds of cultural industries can flourish and certain kinds of multiculture can become visible because of the visual ordering of the spatial. This argument is illustrated here through the exemplification of contemporary artistic practice, but could be considered diagnostically for other cultural industries: popular music and web design as much as any rarefied aesthetic. If certain kinds of multiculture are allowed to become visible, then perhaps other kinds are not. If we accept this, then an implicit rejection of certain kinds of (commodified) multiculture and privileging of alternative forms of hybrid culture becomes slightly more problematic. The chapter concludes that the organisation of the visual order of the city curates *permissible multiculture* in this way. Rather than decry what is at times labelled as boutique cosmopolitanism through a rhetoric of authenticity, it is perhaps more useful to interrogate this process through a consideration of the nature of the sublime (and its politics) that underscores most notions of the aesthetic.

This points us towards an interrogation of the manner in which the cultural quarters, and cities of modernity more generally, exhibit their diagnostic parts. There is an echo of this in Walter Benjamin's Arcades Project. At one point in the *Panorama Convolut* Benjamin discusses 'Le tour de monde', a panorama of world travel at the World Exhibition of 1900. The architecture had already caused a sensation because of its cultural bricolage through which 'An Indian gallery crowns the wall of the edifice, while rising at the corners are the tower of a pagoda, a Chinese tower, and an old Portuguese tower . . . The similarity of this architecture to that in zoological gardens is worth noting.'[48]

In a sense Benjamin reminds us that the city has always been a curatorial edifice whose properties could be registered by the curious visitor and whose self-representations draw their most potent force from the metaphor of the exhibition or world fair. In various polyphonous registers of voice such a process of curation speaks to an understanding of the cultural quarter. In the most straightforwardly economic reading of the locational preferences of clustering, the narrative spatialisations of producer networks, marketing promotion and governance may be distinctive or invite generalisation. In the cartographies of land value, Ricardian rent curves on the one hand and cultural identity on the other do not (*contra* first-wave gentrification debates of the 1980s) provide rival or alternative paradigms of analysis. And in this sense the promotion of the sites of the city as arenas of commodification dovetails closely with the celebration of the creativity of the city. But these different registers of voice cannot always be separated so easily. As ever with the dirty reality of the contemporary city it is the manner in which one narrative bleeds into another that is at once so problematic and so interesting.

This can be illustrated by the economic and ethical realities of the aestheticised practices that have marketed cities themselves as sites to be consumed through the mediating influence of niche-marketed tourism. In figurative arts practice the postcolonial disruption of the curatorial privileging of western art is both exciting and important. Yet at times its most prominent achievement is manifested in displays of cultural capital that reinscribe the networked metropolis within a place of displaying privilege. Thus in two of the most prestigious of the global exhibitions both Documenta 11 (in 2002) in Kassel and the Venice Biennale (in 2003) took the cosmopolitan as a central thematic, reconfiguring the normative geographical territorialisation of aesthetic judgement through an appeal to distinctive transnationalisms and globalisms, articulated through major international patterns of the glocal. But in doing so the metropolitan basis of taste is routed through the exhibiting city. In Documenta a series of platforms attempted to overcome this problem by preceding the final exhibition with 'platforms' in Vienna, New Delhi Berlin, St Lucia and Lagos.[49] Yet the culmination of the most prestigious festival of the global circuit of contemporary art practice in the parent German city of Kassel leaves this global peregrination open to charges of spatial teleology. Deference, difference and the reproduction of cultural capital are reinforced by global reach as it all comes together in the curatorial city. Venice, meanwhile, takes its extraordinary *biennales* in art, architecture, film and dance to exhibit itself as a certain kind of cultural capital that in recognising western humility in the face of the postcolonial global reinscribes the cosmopolitan urbanism of European hegemony on which its entire history is based. Just as Venetian mercantilism was humbled by the navigation round of the southern cape of Africa in the fifteenth century, its reassertion as the capital of transculture depends upon the specific routing and terms of trade of new forms of cultural traffic.

Such commentary is not novel. The place of the metropolis within it might be. Homi Bhabha has long ago pointed out that:

> All this may make global culture more readily available to the embrace of multicultural aesthetics or a meticulous archival study. But the angle of visibility will not change. What was once exotic or archaic, tribal or folkloristic, inspired by strange gods, is now given a secular national present and an international future. Sites of cultural difference too easily become part of the globalising West's thirst for its own ethnicity; for citation and simulacral echoes from Elsewhere.[50]

Bhabha's long-established celebration of the properties of creolisation and hybridity are clearly significant here. He has long been associated with a political project that takes the thematics of Deleuzian minorisation and the hybrid as axiomatic of the contemporary human condition. At times this has pointed to a progressive attempt to intervene in a project that rethinks the nature of the national. Both Bhabha and Stuart Hall were jointly closely associated with a British Council project that took as a central theme 'reinventing Britain' in 1998.[51] It was a progressive project of major political significance that Hall in particular has been honourably associated with in the translation of similar tropes into the more directly policy-related world of the Runnymede-Trust-funded inquiry into multiethnic Britain, commonly known as the Parekh Report.[52] Importantly Parekh was both most progressive – and most controversial – when committing itself to rethinking British national identity under the sign of multiculturalism. But how plausible is the attempt to rescue the nation in this way? Is it possible that the nation is beyond rescue – what Ulrich Beck has chosen to describe as zombie category?[53]

Rather than proffer a straightforward answer to such a question, it might be more sensible to consider how far the city (and the cultural quarters within it) might extend both the potential for an alternative way of thinking about the territorialisation and de-territorialisation of global flow and an alternative normative horizon of the political imaginary. In doing so, it is essential to consider what the project to reinvent the nation might displace or subsume. It is suggested here that the attempt to rescue an idea of multicultural Britishness speaks to an ethical agenda of the first order. However, there is also a concern that it might displace a consideration of notions of geographical scale and has a potential to conflate the racialised injustices of institutional funding with the politics of recognition.[54]

A problem of metropolitan scale and a problem of recognition

Again there is an echo of Benjamin's Arcades here: 'the wax museum (Panoptikum) a manifestation of the total work of art. The universalism of the 19th Century has its monument in the waxworks. Panopticon: not only does one see everything, but one sees it in all ways.'[55] We know the hubris of the panopticon as well as its less attractive relationship to a Foucauldian rendition of disciplinary power. In a world after Foucault we might ask how Bhabha's 'angle of visibility' translates into different curations of the urbanism of the cultural quarter.

Crucially, within Stuart Hall's approach is an important take on the cultural politics of globalisation that he describes as 'the nub of the argument'. For Hall, Globalisation disturbs the notion that people come from originary whole cultures, that they can negotiate their work and artistic practices with other whole cultures and that what each person does is to speak from within, to be responsive and to represent only those cultures of origin from which they come.[56]

In the vocabulary of classical sociology the cultural quarter might be seen as part of an urban mosaic of ethnicised fragments or part of a melting pot. These are very different sorts of city space. The former might point to harder interethnic boundaries than the latter. The former speaks to stories of 'race relations', the latter to an assimilatory dream that was in part shattered by Glazer and Moynihan's 1960s rediscovery of ethnicity.[57] Both raise the challenges of the academic's ability to narrate reality or map the city. Either articulation – mosaic or melting pot – raises what Kobena Mercer described as the burden of representation that is placed on the creative face of the cultural producers of literature, art or even cuisine in such locations.[58] When considering how we read the multicultural quarter of the city, the cultural politics of globalisation invoked by Hall might question the manner in which the forms of new sentiment and new commodities that emerge in the new economies are reconcilable with the imagined communities of the (old) nation state. The scale of the city articulates global economies of commodity circulation, transnational sentiment and localised production of novelty. The issue of scale speaks to the debates of the cosmopolitan but is less easily reconciled with the spaces of the actually existing city.

In disrupting the horizon of the nation Homi Bhabha in particular develops a notion of the cosmopolitan based on affiliative hybridisation that appeals to very different politics of location. This is for Bhabha explicitly an appeal to a moral calculus that unproblematically celebrates a metric of human scale (after the work of Anthony Appiah), the unknowable nature of the city habitus (after the work of Richard Sennett), and the ecological certainties of a finite globe (after the environmental feminism of Vandana Shiva). In each site 'a radical cosmopolitan concern can only articulate itself by conceiving the rapidly accelerating and expanding world as somehow "incomplete", narrower than the horizon of human totality, in contention with the modernist myth of linear progress elsewhere'.[59]

The perspectival nature of the globalisation invoked is important (particularly in contradistinction to a globalisation from below), but so too is the lack of register of the metropolitan basis of its curation. In reframing the problem of the cosmopolitan through a language of geographical scale, Bhabha poetically appeals to the dark cloud in his own anthem but frames his multiple perspectives within an uncertain register of the spatial. Linear time is juxtaposed with multiple perspectivalism within an ethical measurability that provides little defence against charges of a routed ethnographic relativism. The tension between the unknowable ethics of the stranger that he looks to Sennett to provide, and the circles narrower than the human horizon that for Anthony Appiah[60] are the appropriate spheres of moral concern, are perhaps not straightforwardly lined up alongside one another. In a sense Bhabha's sophisticated aesthetics betray a contradictory politics. Such alignment demands a more specifically spatial reading of the tensions between the strange and the familiar (and the liberal and the communitarian) that are not only subdued through the conceptual deployment of the uncanny, but are also narrated through the tales of the city that return us to the political and ethical tensions between sentiment and the rights of the stranger, the newcomer, the migrant, the refugee or the alien.[61]

Understanding glocalisation: politics, aesthetics and narrating the commodification of the cultural quarter

This confusion of the registers of ethics, aesthetics and commodification appears to be particularly common to the romance of multicultural urbanism. This confusion questions exactly what sort of space the cultural quarter is and what sort of hopes we might invest in both its political and economic future. This can be clarified if we think momentarily about the manner in which the cultural quarter is read metonymically as part of a much larger city. What sort of space is the cultural quarter? What sort of place might it become? The cultural quarter is an object of government (in planning language). It is a moment of innovation in cultural industries, a moment of authenticity in some versions of commodification and at times in the scopic regime of the tourist gaze. Yet it is also a moment of creolisation or hybridity in the production of aesthetic transformation. So though it may be all of these things, they are not necessarily commensurable with each other. Each articulation in turn frames a relation between the global flows of culture and the local realisations of urbanism. In this sense the cultural quarter may embody different spatialities, akin to, but not necessarily reducible to, a Lefèbvrian taxonomy of lived, perceived and conceived spatiality and the dichotomy of his juxtaposition of spaces of representation and representations of spaces.

Each of the articulations of the cultural quarter foreground different registers of scale through which the global is made visible constitutively as part of the local through a process of *glocalisation*. In this sense the metonymic readings of the spaces of the city inform a way of coming to terms with contemporary urbanism that invokes a genre of writing that takes the found cultural (re)configurations of the city as the source of a broader diagnostic reading of ethical and cultural change. The links between the writings of Benjamin, Barthes and Raban's iconic 'soft city', which in a more literary genre are witnessed in the work of Iain Sinclair and Patrick Wright, are just some of the more poetic examples of such texts.[62] Similarly the organisations of ethnic difference in the cities of the twenty-first century invite readings of the deeper meaning of the curation of cultural festivals, creolised cultural expressions and vernacular multicultures.

Yet in an important sense the city also curates itself. In a manner that an artist such as Hans Haacke would be proud of, we need to think about both the stories of development that urban space articulates and the cartographies that render comprehensible the city's *true* identity – and be equally suspicious of both. There is a timeless architectural conceit that appeals to the visual ordering of city form to evoke sentiment. Awe, timelessness, a sense of reassuring place and a sense of disconcerting modernity may all be the products of architectural affect. A notion of grandeur and a sense of social order, a degree of legibility and the capacity for becoming beguilingly lost may be properties of a city quarter that can be more than incidental products of design.[63] In this sense it is possible – but dangerous – to try to read the cultural quarter metonymically: to derive from its identification a wider pattern of meaning attributed to *the city as a whole*, to the nature of contemporary urbanism. The act of curation of the city, as much as the act of consumption of its exhibited form, points us towards a different cultural politics of the built environment.

As Haacke himself has suggested, 'Inscribed in every collection, like the rings of a tree, is the history of an institution [and] its relation to donors.'[64] Haacke's ethic is to 'act as a social secretary who puts together a guest list and a seating order hoping that a sly arrangement of unexpected encounters will bear fruit'.[65] In this spirit we might want to adopt a genealogical scepticism about the stories that the individual building or the collection of the street or the city quarter presents to us. Our guide to the cultural quarter – the academic explorer, the city planner, the ethnic entrepreneur – all curate very different spaces of the city that speak both to what lies inside this space and what the quarter is a part of.

The very notion of cultural quarter suggests something that is part of a larger whole. It implies a relationship between fragment and totality without necessitating the naming of the totality as such.[66] This may seem unnecessarily arcane until the identity of the cultural quarter itself is interrogated. The gay village or the ethnic enclave may speak to very different notions of the manner in which the quarter fits into the wider metropolitan cultural and social fabric. The very mapping of the urban through a lens of race might be taken to imply some very different cultural processes.

In this sense the cultural quarter speaks analytically to an understanding of cultural production in the city, refiguring our language of globalisation. In this sense the cultural quarter is both analytically productive in rethinking global-isation and rhetorically problematic in generating *shibboleths of the cultural.*

The culture of cities necessarily bears the toppling weight of the genealogies that lie behind an understanding of the *cultural.*[67] At times, through category inflation, creativity expands to include the generic notion of wealth generation as well as an aestheticised (post-)avant-gardeism. Culture may likewise expand to cannibalise or is restricted to predisposition. When Richard Florida expands his definition of creativity to the point where all forms of wealth generation are part of the creative economy, then the foundations of the cultural industries begin to look slightly unstable and we might reconsider the claims made within his work.[68] In contrast, when Peter Hall looks to the cultural basis of the civilisation of cities, his invo-cation of cultural capital in Renaissance practice, Enlightenment scholarship, Memphis music and grand art appeals more to Matthew Arnold's conservative version of the highbrow than to contemporary anthropology. It might fit less easily with forms of creativity that are less readily domesticated or commodified.[69]

What we begin to find is a number of category errors that arise from the manner in which the spatial ordering of the city facilitates an analytical slippage between the political, the economic and the aesthetic. As we have seen in previous chapters, space mediates analytical conflation and displacement. Consequently, there are series of conceptual pitfalls that potentially occur in the slippages between culture and economy that are translated through the sign of race. The first concerns the notion of wealth creation and relates to the manner in which market niche depends on difference. The second concerns the manner in which the commodification in the cultural quarter can be taken to privilege either a reified fixed authentic cultural form or a sense of the eternally novel forms of cultural hybridity. Both are problematic. This leads us to the third conceptual danger: the worry of making the cultural quarter visible through a single descriptive register.

The first pitfall (the first shibboleth of cultures of urbanism) is an ambivalence about the ethical nature of ethnic commodification commonly translated through a language of authenticity. In this framing, a series of appeals to novel cultural forms might attempt to displace economic exploitation through rhetorics of cultural exchange. Picasso's appropriation of the African mask in reconfiguring the perspectival innovations of *Les Demoiselles d'Avignon* may have generated a certain kind of cultural capital, Madonna's assimilation of South Asian cool a more naked form of money capital and personal reinvention.[70] The cultural politics of bricolage – hybrid forms of expression that beg, borrow and steal from elsewhere – raises major questions about the significance and power relations of so doing. It is less clear that the financial success of such initiatives, from multimedia design to niche-marketed catering economy, correlates in any way whatsoever with any ethical register. If translating difference into market value works, then both the valoris-ation and the denigration of the processes of epidermal commodification might be of questionable value.

But this applies to the commodification of ethnic difference by both 'outsiders' and by 'insiders'. The proliferation of global links – in clothes, fashion and restaurant identity as much as in multimedia and web design[71] – implies both geographical reach and a mutating sense of novelty that potentially instils market advantage on the diaspora links of multicultural minorities. They appeal both to the curated authenticities of the tourist gaze that rests on the mosaic-like spaces of the multicultural city[72] and the boutique cosmopolitanism of Stanley Fish that has been so widely condemned.[73] Significantly, both the mosaic of authentic identity and the melting pot of hybridity are equally subject to the whims of commodity fetishism.

Whilst tracing the routes of cultural appropriation of the zoot suit or the sound system may provide fascinating insights into the nature of cultural travel, it is perhaps inadvisable to moralise too strongly about the impurities of commodifi-cation. In some senses commodification *just is*. The object, the thought, the increasingly ephemeral nature of the commodity and the simultaneously all-embracing nature of the commodification of life itself[74] provide survival strategies for communities in the metropolises of the global economy as well as transfor-mations of cultural form.

The second pitfall is a confusion between the successful nature of commodifying practices (economy) and a politics of recognition (ethics). Ethical practice needs to be distinguished from the mere celebration of diversity talk and the recognition of difference that plays to the hard boundaries of the cultural mosaic. In an optimistic reading, the mediating role of the spaces of the city in describing arts practice in the cultural quarters of today's metropolis can almost echo Benjamin's invocation of the zoological gardens. Sharon Zukin exemplified this sort of optimism in a piece written for London's celebration of cities, spectacle and global culture, the millennial opening of Tate Modern in 2001.

> The continuous growth of cultural institutions and the increase in ethnic diversity have reduced the sense of an unbridgeable gap between monu-mental spaces and slums. Moreover the anointing of various cities as culture capitals has occurred along with greater tolerance for different kinds of cultural activities. Today there are more playful exhibits, more public art and more recognition of the cultural value of ethnic communities.[75]

In the United Kingdom a recognition of diverse arts practice is likewise a laudable phenomenon of the early twenty-first century. In formal processes, major arts funding agencies have recognised (at least rhetorically) the institutional racism that has failed to support minority-led (normally invoked as black and minority ethnic or BME) organisations. Steve McQueen and Chris Offili have been awarded the Turner Prize and the hyphenated British work of Anish Kapoor, Anya Gallacio and Mona Hatoum dominates many major gallery spaces across the country.

But this sort of institutional recognition alone is not the point. The spatialisation of the cultural quarter has the potential to play to a language of the synchronic snapshot. At times space fixes meaning unhelpfully. Either mosaic or melting pot. Authentic ethnic culture or genuine hybrid novelty. Fixture or flux. Whether we are thinking about new forms of cultural industries production or the processes of creolisation themselves, the identity of the cultural quarter mediates ethics and aesthetics simultaneously. Identity recognition points to an identity politics that is complicated in its minoritarian and majoritarian forms. The spectacle of the city can lead to the conceptual overexploitation of the notion of the hybrid as simultaneously commodity, ethical stance and measurable aesthetic.

In such a context recognition and celebration are not enough. We have instead to understand how the very reading of the spaces of the city demands a cartographic sensibility that can understand simultaneously proximity and distance: the neighbourhood or quarter a realisation of novel processes of *glocalisation*.

This leads to the third conceptual pitfall. This links to the silences, simplifications and narrative abuses that arise from the boundaries of the multicultural container that defines the cultural quarter. The parts of the city have long been the subject of the scopophilic gaze of the orientalist at home. The pitfalls of describing in an unfortunate register the exoticism of the sites of difference within the contemporary city replays many of the debates of colonial anthropology and potentially privileges the sites of multiculture's reified objects. In this vein, in the twentieth-century mainstream, social science witnessed the dangers of Chicago School ethnography falling prey either to menagerie culture collection or *post hoc* ecological functionalism. The resolution of such dilemmas in the positivist hegemony that infects the American received wisdom, but sorely traduces Park's legacy, is merely one symptom of this pathology.[76] But to what extent is the privileged *inside* of the lived spaces of the cultural quarter properly the object of academic investigation and the subject of the *representational space* of the scholarly text?

The answer to such questions is to be found precisely in both a more up-front consideration of the ethical dilemmas of description and a more sophisticated understanding of the plurality of the spatialities of contemporary urbanism. The former problematic speaks to the ethical dilemmas of all social research.[77] The latter speaks to a more explicit rendering of the perspectival nature of sociological observation. The 'inside' of the cultural quarter is in part a rhetorical artefact.[78] What are striking about the cultural quarters of the contemporary city are both the contact zones between different cultural forms and the manner in which distinctive places are invariably globally networked. Both *contact* and *networks* are inscribed with relations of power, intolerance and bigotry alongside the potential for communication, resistance and reconfiguration. The *elsewhere of place* is an empirical phenomenon; it describes the links between these diasporic spaces and global circuits of culture, capital, objects and information.[79] It is observed in the spaces of the cultural quarter. The act of description (however thick that description might be) is consequently inevitably partial, quite properly in the spirit of Samuel Beckett's injunction to 'fail again, fail better'. In such circumstances the academic appeal must properly be to the sort of Geertzian anti-anti-relativism discussed in Chapter 1,[80] in which both the ethical obligation and the epistemological imperative demand a form of academic research and writing that is qualitative, ambivalent and explicitly humble in some of its conclusions.

From curating the city to a spatialised notion of the sublime

A notion of the sublime may be helpful in navigating our way between the shibboleths and the category errors. To understand that ghettos are *not good* and that rainbow cosmopolitanism is not dawning we may need a vocabulary that acknowledges the simultaneous presence of hope and despair in the new configurations of the cultural quarter in the global city. The sublime captures a note of the ambivalence that is at the heart of contemporary urbanism's embrace of multiculture.[81] In both Addison's notion of self-transcendence and Burke's understanding of the sublime as delightful horror, the sublime moment has the ability to disrupt our placing in the city.[82] In Romantic art this is normally described in terms of the notion of awe, commonly in the face of particular landscapes (for example, in Friedrich or Turner). But the manner in which today's city realises the sublime in translating global influences through specific tropes of localisation also offers insight into the unintended effects of some processes of *glocalisation*. This returns us to a reading of the relationship between the cultural quarter (fragment) and the sovereign city (totality).

The most influential writing on the sublime generally either emanates from Immanuel Kant himself or engages in a dialogue with Kant's legacy.[83] And for Kant the sublime was a quality that was precisely about the moment where the measurable failed. It explicitly contrasted with a notion of measurable beauty. The sublime was to be considered as the experience of magnitude without limit that involved 'an oscillation between fragmentary detail and a notional totality' ('the creation of the autonomous eye').[84] Like all Kantian taxonomies it is infused with an explicitly theorised understanding of the relationship between the temporal and the spatial that is perhaps less helpful in coming to terms with modernity's metropolis and the simulacra cities of today's multiculturalisms.

Poststructuralist thinkers such as Blanchot, Kristeva and Agamben have tried to engage with the Kantian sublime through the translating category of absence. Such a register is persuasive and important, but for the purposes of the argument here it is perhaps helpful to consider the manner in which the *Critiques* of Kant are taken on in the work of Jean-François Lyotard.[85] For Lyotard, in his work *Discours, figure*, the politics of the sublime are generated by 'a movement out of the notional "we" that governs most things in social life and establishes "the event" as outside any formulation of the normal'. In this sense 'normal implies a real perspective, a real place and a real history. The forgetfulness required by the event on the other hand, for good or ill, must sublate all three.'[86]

The cosmopolitan is in this sense most powerful when it demonstrates the

capacity to disrupt the common sense of the measurable aesthetic and the calcul-
able ethical register. Lyotard's work is useful precisely because it engages in a
dialogue with the Kantian understanding of the spatial and the temporal that help
us to reconsider the narratives that make visible the cultural quarter or the
cosmopolitan aesthetic behind the rebranding of Benetton Britain.

The lived space of the multicultural cities of today confront theoretical excess
with empirical awe. In Brick Lane, East London, an old brewery provides a base
for the transnational movement of clothing from China to Africa and the old Iron
Curtain East of Europe. The global coordinates bear testament to the global reach
of an old empire, the Jewish migrant routes of the family that still runs the company – Ely and Sydney – and the abiding cosmopolitan nature of the commodity.
The front of the same brewery provides a hub for the new cultural industries
growth of East London: web design, high-tech fashion, multicultural arts. The
façade displays a coffee bar and club through which, in Sharon Zukin's memorable
phrase, the pacification by cappuccino of the inner city proceeds apace. It is a
planner's nightmare. Locally, the site is both vilified as the promoter of white
hegemonic ethnic exotica and celebrated as the crucible of hybridisation of the
already impure cultures of the East End. The processes, the personnel and the life
of such venues demand a more nuanced description. As empirical objects such
sites are properly the subject of the sociological imagination as well as critical
research. And empirical exploration finds behind the façade the accidental
urbanism of installations such as Caresky's 'Ghost Train' that in 2004 used the
metaphors of the haunting of the city in an art show crossed with theatrical event
to provide a ride that foregrounded the migrant experience of the past and the
present. Such presence can be read symbolically in many different ways, but its
practice can only be understood through something that approaches ethnographic
engagement.

In this context, the sublime disrupts the normalised narrative of the city. It
appeals to the wanderlust of the situationist dérive and the surreal sense of the
shock. In thinking about how we narrativise the spaces of the city, a notion of the
spatial sublime might draw on Lyotard to emphasise a sense of giddying oscillation
between the heroic immersion of the view from up close and the academic rigour
of objective distance. A notion of the spatial sublime might be helpful in valorising
the manner in which the spaces of the city confront complacency with the global
reach of contemporary capitalism. The everyday city provides the sites in which
the irreconcilable anti-anti-essentialisms of the particularities of place sit side by
side with the incommensurable appeal of the global universal. If this is the force
that informs the curators of major exhibitors of the city in Documenta 11 (2002)
and the Venice Biennale (2003) it is surely also the more prosaic but equally
powerful force behind the glocalising nature of contemporary urbanism.

Urbanism is central to the narrative through which the configurations of
sovereignty reconvene. Forms of cultural expression shape both the political
horizons of such thinking and the political imaginaries through which these
changes are articulated. A spatialised sublime is germane to an understanding of
the multicultural urban precisely because it has the ability to shock, to shake and to

reconstitute this imaginary. In the cartographies of the contemporary city a dialectical interplay of universal and particular create, if not a third space, then at least an alternative framing of the global and the local. Urban multiculture figures these new forms of representation. The contact zones of multicultural cities might consequently be understood in the words of the curator of Documenta 11, Okwui Enwezor, to:

> signify journeys and experience and methods for thinking the global at the height of its own reconstitution. Within their individual formats, there is no need to make a polemic of globalisation, multiculturalism and difference; the wider scope of the project assumes them as already part of the complex weave of tongues, the tide of voices that will activate the final meaning of its dramatization.[87]

In recognising the sites and politics of a city that is less than homely this is in part an acknowledgement of the place of the uncanny in the mapping of the metropolis.[88] But only a part. The spatial sublime of the contemporary city might imply a moment of re-territorialisation simultaneously alongside a process of de-territorialisation.

In this spirit, an appropriate *ambivalence* about either the marketing of China-towns or Banglatowns, or the presence of Clinton in Harlem, is neither an ethical cop-out nor an epistemological caveat. It is more an acknowledgement of the figuring of the city within the calculus of political and aesthetic judgement: economic and social organisation. A notion of the sublime captures the incalculable events through which these incommensurable ways of theorising the world are made visible in the city.

8 Tagging the city
Graffiti practice and transcultural communication[1]

In a metonymic flash the graffiti tag frames the contemporary city. It signals a particular moment of contemporary urbanism even as that moment is as much reviled in some quarters as it is celebrated in others. Particularly since the rise of the graffiti art of the 1970s and the gang wars of the late decades of twentieth-century Los Angeles, the iconography of graffiti has drawn its inspiration principally from the USA but has been translated across the globe. Its roots in the ghetto appeal to, draw on and reconfigure forms of racialised sensibility generally and particular genres of African-American black expressive culture. Hence, as a technology of representation, the tag makes multiculture visible through a loosely conceived but transnationally generic language whose familial similarities at times transcends the linguistic specificity of the words that are commonly deployed. It both appropriates space and draws on conventions that are spatially globalised. It expresses a claim but appeals to an audience. And if the tag is hailing somebody, it might even assume that the audience will recognise itself.

Graffiti is perhaps the exemplary mode of outlaw communication. By definition it is intrusive, emblematic and opportunistic. Derived from the Italian *graffiare*, meaning to scratch, graffiti has been understood variously as a form of popular protest and a people's art, and it has also been implicated in brutal forms of symbolic violence, genocide and racism.[2] Much of the concern about the proliferation of subway graffiti in the United States was a reaction to the unwanted infringement into the public imagination of the anonymous face of inner city racial otherness. In a very different fashion, in recent years the spraying of racist and neo-fascist graffiti over the premises of minority shopkeepers in France, or Jewish graveyards in Britain, provided a haunting reminder of the endurance of a proactive and expressive white power politics. Yet, graffiti is more than just a haunting emblem of public fears and anxieties. It is crucially implicated in cultures of urban expression, both as means to inscribe a 'decentralised and decentred insubordination',[3] and because it challenges the very status of language, dialogue and discourse within the public sphere.

The debate about graffiti, in both the United States and Europe, has tended to focus on viewing wall writing as a form of 'visual pollution'. This was compounded by the indecipherability of the esoteric hip-hop signatures tags or more elaborate cartoon-like paintings on subway cars. Equally, racist forms of graffiti have deployed mysterious stylistic elements alongside crass forms of racial rhetoric and abuse. Common to all types of graffiti is that it is written on what is taken publicly to be an illegitimate canvas. Graffiti is always an intrusion and in this sense it is premeditatedly – but purposefully – *out of place*. So, understanding urban writing is ultimately about appreciating the symbolism of the surface on which it is inscribed as much as the ostensible message of the tag or the script. The way in which graffiti is interpreted, is then, in a literal sense, semantically dependent on the space which precedes the text. As Patrick Hagopian points out:

> The question of whether graffiti constitutes an 'enhancement' or 'defacement' seems . . . to depend on whose property is being written on, and who is doing the writing and who judges the results . . . Thus, the question of whose world will be 'written over' and whose writing will prevail, is never a pure aesthetic question.[4]

This chapter suggests that there is a complex interplay between the surface and the inscription. The planes of the metropolis do not determine the writing, but equally the inscription cannot completely govern the meaning of the abraded concrete or metal canvas. Rather, what is at stake in these forms of urban graphology is an emergent struggle over inclusion, citizenship, entitlement and belonging.

The chapter considers whether there is any ground between the naïve celebration of transgression and the fear of the populist inscription. It is possible to find such a ground if we begin to think about:

- graffiti as a technology of expression;
- writing as invariably aimed at an audience;
- articulation as invariably and simultaneously both aesthetic and political, crystallising complex desires, dreams and claims;
- inscribing as a moment of articulation that is not necessarily discursive but always narrative in its power.

Anthropologists and other commentators have stressed the importance of the seemingly banal character of wall writing with regard to the way it reveals the hidden codes of a particular culture.[5] The chapter is particularly concerned to look at how graffiti is implicated in the sphere of the urban politics of difference, identity and racism. In particular, how is the practice of urban wall writing connected with the expressive cultural mechanisms of racism and anti-racism?

Wall writing has a long history which dates back to ancient times.[6] What makes it interesting in the context of this book is the diverse ways it has been interpreted. Some epigraphologists have connected the emergence of graffiti with the expansion of literacy and popular protests.[7] Others have viewed wall writing as personal expression and spontaneous acts of symbolic subversion in the tradition of *détournement*.[8] Equally, there is a literature which argues that in repressive societies graffiti is an underground means of communication for those who are excluded from the public sphere and makes claims for the subcultures graffiti promotes and draws upon.[9] It is the very ambiguous nature of this archaic mode of communication that makes it interesting in the informational age. Why should this most basic communicative technology have survived amid the throng of multimedia late modernity? Is graffiti an alternative discourse, or is it an example of the end of discourse itself? Before coming back to these questions the chapter first looks at how graffiti has entered the wider debate over urban culture and the nature of the public sphere within cities.

Signs of danger: graffiti, urban culture and the public sphere

Public space is variously the terrain in which civil society is performed, the social space over which 'proper' political regulation is deployed, and the arena in which particular kinds of sociality are developed. If the first two uses of the term imply a consensual set of values, the third most certainly does not, and this chapter consequently examines the manner in which one form of intrusion into the public spaces of the city might make us think about the relationship between society and space.

In a celebrated article, the right-wing American criminologist James Q. Wilson famously identified graffiti as the defining moment of incipient community breakdown.[10] The inscriptions of those who deface the received order of the spaces of the city challenge and disrupt order and the neighbourhood as the spatial realisation of pure *Gemeinschaft*. Left unchallenged, graffiti is both symptomatic of threat and a signal that prompts further moral decline. Out of such environmentally deterministic rhetoric and a particular concern with graffiti the notion of 'zero tolerance' was born. Similarly, Nathan Glazer has written on the fear engendered by the graffiti as a subway rider in New York: 'While I do not find myself consciously making the connection between the graffiti-markers and the criminals who occasionally rob, rape, assault, and murder passengers, the sense that all are part of one world of uncontrollable predators seems inescapable.'[11] Glazer, the champion of the passenger – who seems implicitly coded as white – presents the other side of James Q. Wilson's vision of attrition and social breakdown. Glazer's discussion might also be read as liberal democracy itself struggling to come to terms with the unknowable and the seemingly uncontrollable. Glazer wrestles over and over again with his question: 'Why can't graffiti be controlled?' But it is clear that graffiti simply cannot be tamed by his version of sociological pragmatism, because the logics and impulses that compel people to write are outside a liberal democratic imagination. While never really speaking the language of race, such frustration seems to invoke metaphorically the gap between the democratic ideals of American citizenship and the fact of social exclusion and racial inequities within the public sphere.

The issue of reconciliation within the public sphere is one of the central themes of the work of the urbanist Richard Sennett, for whom graffiti also signifies an important symptom of urban life. Over a wide range of important works Sennett has developed a series of theses on the relationship between particular forms of social life and the spaces of the cities in which they are realised. Drawing heavily on many of the themes from Wirth and Simmel, Sennett – in the *Uses of Disorder*

(1973), *The Hidden Injuries of Class* (1972), *The Fall of Public Man* (1976), *The Conscience of the Eye* (1991) and the collection of essays *Flesh and Stone* (1994) – has developed a sustained engagement with notions of city life that addresses a massive agenda that is not readily simplified. However, at the heart of all of his work he has developed a construction of urbanism that attempts to cherish the city as the privileged medium for the reconciliation of *difference* and *strangeness* so essential to the construction of both a realised polity and an imagined sociality.

In Richard Sennett's vision of the city, particularly that expressed in his most behaviourist text, *The Conscience of the Eye*, there is something about the design of cities that structures social life. At times, with debts to Skinner barely hidden, we are told that some spaces 'work', by facilitating the sociality of the public sphere through ways in which others do not. The Rockefeller Center, Battery Park City and the artefacts of the Miesian legacy create anomie, but the coffee house and the piazza open the individual up through 'streets full of time' in which fragmentation of self and encounters with difference can coexist. Drawing on the work of the Chicago School, he suggests that this is not the result of the city permitting difference, but rather a product of the concentration of difference: 'urban differences seemed to [Robert] Park and Louis Wirth provocations of otherness, surprise and stimulation. Yet these sociologists had a brilliant, counter-intuitive insight; provocation occurs in the very loosening of strong connections between people in a city.'[12] He continues:

> Thus Park in his later writings, like his younger colleague Wirth, moved away from the conceiving of the city as a place that permits differences, and towards understanding the city as a place that encourages the concentration of difference. Its moral order is the lack of moral order that exercises hegemony over the city as a whole.[13]

The sense of modern fragmentation of the self is understood as positive, a celebratory facet of self-regulating urbanism, because the fragmented self is more responsive. Enlightenment unity, metropolitan order and coherence are thus not the means to self-development, rather fragmented urban experience which opens itself and collides with differences of both flesh and stone offers new possibilities for personhood and public life.

There is much in Sennett's argument to commend it, not least the ethos that celebrates the meeting of difference at the expense of the *destructive Gemeinschaft*. Nevertheless, his suspicion of the planning imperative to sanitise space is surely overstated. Indeed the tensions between knowability, order, power and multi-culture in the metropolis return when we consider the potential to organise or plan the cosmopolitan city, a problematic that is the focus of the final chapter of this volume. But in Sennett's cosmology graffiti is necessarily symptomatic of a failure to reconcile social life and urban design, in some ways inadvertently echoing the reactionary sociology of James Q. Wilson. For Sennett, who cites Glazer's essay on graffiti, New York graffiti is little more than an announcement of the unified subject. The impasto of painted IDs fails to communicate 'any message save one:

feci, "I made this," this mark is me . . . An "I" declared'. It is the very concreteness of graffiti, both literally and as sign of identity, which Sennett opposes.[14]

Yet Sennett is wrong to reduce the technology of the sign writer and the tagger to the single message. In marked contrast, alternative historians of graffiti have traced the redemptive force of this transgressive moment: the power of graffiti to accrete far greater symbolic power through its presence in particular places. A range of sociologists, linguists and photographers have suggested that Chicano and Afro-American young people have used subway graffiti as a mechanism for self-expression and resistance in the context of their social marginalisation and disenfranchisement.[15] The nuances of these forms of expression and allusion constitute a hidden semiological realm and a kind of alternative public sphere which operates beyond the understanding of both liberal and radical commentators. This is summed up by Wicked Gary, a Brooklyn writer:

> If you needed to know anything that happened on the subway, you could ask a graffiti artist . . . That was our playground, that was our work and . . . we were involved. Schedules of trains, schedules of tunnels, we had information on everything. It was a whole other system of communication and interaction from the normal system that we deal with like the English language and money and stuff like that. We had our own language, our own technology, terminology. The words we had meant things to us that nobody else could identify.[16]

This amounts to much more than Sennett's view of graffiti as a throng of identity marks; indeed there may well be things at stake in the process of naming that transcend a narrow declarative individualism.

In a sense, the focus here is a degree of uneasiness about both of two very different takes on behaviour in the public sphere. Certain forms of reactionary contemporary populism see the public sphere primarily in terms of risk minimisation and the rights of individual security. Writers such as Glazer and Wilson may be influential, but they are principally symptomatic of such positions. In contrast, Sennett's intellectual project is far distant from such conservative ideology. Whatever else the book is, *The Conscience of the Eye* and other work self-consciously celebrates a certain form of urbanism, in the attempt to create a city ideal tied to an imagery of the proper behaviour of strangers, one to another in a public realm of the present day. One flaw that is common to both of these slightly caricatured positions is that they underestimate the degree to which the spaces of the public sphere are malleable surfaces rather than passive containers of forms of sociality. The forms of communication invoked through graffiti writers' transformation of such spaces is just one dimension through which this malleability is illustrated. The chapter suggests that graffiti writing invokes a technology of communication which is neither entirely logocentric nor merely symbolic, but instead challenges the practices of representational theory and creates a regime of communication that refigures the public sphere just as it is defined by the surfaces of inscription on which this and other forms of wall writing occur.

In this context it is interesting to think back to the early 1980s, when the aesthetics of the writers on the wall were momentarily the subject of great artistic acclaim, and to think more about the relationship between allusion and aesthetics. In particular, it is interesting to look with the wisdom of hindsight at the work of Keith Haring and Jean-Michel Basquiat, the most famous of this time, neither authentically street writers, both graffiti artists. Popularised by poet and commentator René Ricard,[17] Basquiat and Haring were celebrated as the most innovative artists of their generation. In Haring's work 'the installation could compete with the urban environment, the space and content from which the drawings were evolving. And because these drawings were also appearing in subways, they became urban guerrilla art, like that of the graffitists.'[18]

In New York, the graffiti painters, the East Village artists and the political coalition groups were brought together in major exhibitions including the 1980 Times Square Show in which *Village Voice* commentator Richard Goldstein described 'a concordance of styles . . . often referred to as visual punk'. Urbanist juxtapositions of high and low culture resonate through such work. It was the appropriation of city spaces as alternative 'spaces of representation' that was as much a part of the populism as the aesthetic of graffiti art itself. In this sense it appears apposite that it should be in Times Square, an invocation of the dissolute that such a transgressive moment should initiate the 1980s, just as much as the newly disciplined and sanitised Times Square sets a marker for the public spaces of the Business Improvement Districts of Giuliani's New York of the late 1990s in which there was to be zero tolerance of any deviant presence.

As Hebdige has persuasively argued, it is as misleading to seek in the inscriptions of the graffiti artist the authentic voice of the street as it is to understate the possibilities of an alternative aesthetic that is based on a set of expressive practices that do not render themselves easily mapped by conventional calculus of aesthetic value. It is clearly the case that:

> The idea that Jean Michel Basquiat was an 'idiot savant' who merely poured out his heart in the white heat of his genius and put it on display for all and sundry is palpably misguided. It is as ludicrous and patronising as the implication that he didn't speak with the authentic 'voice of the street' because his daddy lived in a three story brownstone in Boerum Hill.[19]

But equally the debates that rage around the 'value' of aesthetics illustrate just one of the key problems with the easy relegation of the writing on the wall. Basquiat's frame of reference was expressed through the visual ideology of the graffiti writer; the crown, the constant erasures of tags, the allusion to alternative expressive cultures of music, body and comic magazine are all testament to their own aesthetic which in Basquiat's case 'did us all a service by uncovering and recapitulating the history of his own construction as a black American male'.[20] It is not that such a repertoire, so acutely deployed, diminishes Basquiat or renders him commensurable with the taggers of the everyday, but neither does his genius disconnect him from them. The commensurability of the repertoire that Basquiat draws on instead confirms that the writing on the walls always subsumes an aesthetic of its own, a desire, a beauty an ugliness, an eroticism but never just an expression of a particular 'I' or a function of a specific space.

More recently, the streets and walls in urban America have provided a canvas for memorial graffiti. These often elaborate and colourful murals often have at their centre a name, usually of a young person who has died, often violently. This form is a hybrid and updated version of the simple roadside crosses often erected at the site of an automobile accident in predominantly Catholic countries, where it is believed that sudden death before receipt of last rites means that the spirit of the victim is caught in purgatory. The marker serves as a reminder to passers-by to pray for the person's soul and thus enable passage to heaven. Similarly, spray-can memorials in urban America serve as a communal remembrance of the premature loss of life engendered by 'the systematic poverty and pervasive racism that promote the rampant flow of drugs and guns into inner city communities'.[21] Painted crosses are combined with hip-hop calligraphy, producing very moving murals which remember young lives cut short by the epidemic black on black and brown on brown violence. Their genealogy is thus complex. It draws on the basic repertoire of wall writing – the technology of the means of communication – and makes an appeal that is profane in its ritual of aestheticised transgression of space. It also speaks to a public, constructs an audience of strangers, in a sacred appeal that has much deeper antecedents. The graffito itself becomes a rallying point, a new place that lies behind the name, where people return to face pain, loss and suffering in public.

Marshall Berman long ago drew attention to the redemptive nature of such association. For him public space becomes a site for reconciliation where modern men and women have to work to put their split, fragmented and alienated selves together. Drawing on the work of Michael Walzer, Berman argues for a radical-ised notion of open-minded space in which city dwellers can confront and integrate their divided selves. He goes on:

> It would be open, above all, to encounters between people of different classes, races, ages, religions, ideologies, cultures, and stances towards life. It would be planned to attract all these different populations, to enable them to look each other in the face, to listen, maybe to talk . . . Open public space is a place where people can actively engage the suffering of this world together, and, as they do it, transform themselves into a public.[22]

Memorial graffiti offers a moment in which these processes of transformation can occur, but this is nevertheless momentary and incomplete. They are perhaps best represented as sutures over the divisions that Berman so articulately described.[23] Perhaps, as Sennett argues so powerfully, it is the very nature of fragmentation of self that offers the potential for the confrontation with the stranger to be settled in less violent terms. What is interesting is that both of these figures seek a more polyphonous and ethnically plural public culture, but they also both share a kind of latent environmental determinism, in that particular places can offer or foster such outcomes. The graffiti writers – including those like Basquiat and Haring who operated in and out of the gallery – demonstrate that this process is always emergent, the product of an indeterminate relationship between particular urban arenas and surfaces and the spaces of identity.

Perhaps neither a reactionary nor a naïvely celebratory understanding of wall writing and graffiti is particularly helpful in reaching an understanding of life in the multicultural cities of late modernity. In particular, as part of an attempt to think about the modalities of expression through which various forms of intolerance are communicated, racist and nationalist graffiti and wall writing highlight both the paradoxes of the communicative rationalities that they invoke and the necessity to develop a more nuanced understanding of the relationship between places and identities than most representations of the public spaces of contemporary urbanism would imply.

'Spaces of identity and the identity of spaces': an iterative understanding of graffiti, community and conflict

It is not just the case that the inner cities provide surfaces of inscription through which identity is itself mediated. Graffiti is reducible neither to articulations of a priori natural areas nor to *projections* of territorial claims. It has to be placed within a narrative structure, a process of telling the identity of places. In this sense graffiti marks an emergent and phantasmal territory. Paradoxically, in the contest to control the spaces of the urban, a shared reality creates a contested but nevertheless shared territory. The status and stakes of communication, be it by conventional or outlaw means, become crucial. As Borja and Castells argue: 'Without a system for social and cultural integration that respects the differences while also establishing codes for communication between the various cultures, local tribalism will be the other side of the coin of global universalism.'[24] An extended project developed this argument in the English inner city and the suburban contexts respectively.[25] From the research it seemed clear that it is in the outer city suburban context where openly racist graffiti is most commonly expressed, while the profoundly multicultural metropolitan interiors exhibit more complexly inflected moments of hate writing. In this chapter the focus is on the relationship between the communicative technologies of graffiti and the emergence of local tribalisms.

The chapter focuses initially on the graffiti of the East End of London, a place which has historically been the reception area for new migrations into the capital. French Huguenots settled here fleeing religious persecution, along with East European Jews. Latterly, West Indian and South Asian migrants – most notably Bengalis – have made East London their home. This area has equally been a centre for right-wing political organising. In the 1930s a march by Oswald Mosley's fascist Blackshirts prompted the famous battle of Cable Street in which Mosley's men clashed violently with anti-fascist opponents. More recently, in 1993, a British National Party candidate was successfully elected on a 'Rights for Whites' platform as a local councillor in the district of Millwall. The chapter draws on a series of examples of graffiti writing in this district by way of bringing into focus the emergent and complex struggles over entitlement, exclusion and belonging that are taking place within present-day London. The first are sited in a park where a young Bengali man was racially attacked and killed.

Graffiti, memory and erasure: Altab Ali Park

In 1978, Altab Ali was murdered in one of the more extreme of the grim catalogue of racist assaults that characterised East London at the time.[26] Altab Ali was attacked in St Mary's Gardens, the site of the church of St Mary Matfelon, known locally at the time as one of the 'Itchy' Parks after the tramps and vagrants that so often slept there, a coinage celebrated in the Small Faces' 1960s record 'Itchacoo Park'. Altab Ali's murder provoked a mass mobilisation of the Bengali community locally. It came to represent a watershed in the self-organisation of the community, as the protests against the murder, initially fronted by anti-racist activists and worthies from outside the area, politicised a generation of young Bengali activists. Demonstrations and sit-ins on Brick Lane, just a few hundred yards from the site of the murder, were aimed at purifying the area of far-right National Front activists who at that time used Brick Lane as both a point of congregation and a focus of fascist activity, not least against the stallholders and restaurateurs from ethnic minorities that were common in the street.

Partly in commemoration of his death and partly in respect to the mobilisation, St Mary's Gardens were officially renamed by the local council as Altab Ali Park in 1979. A memorial gate was erected in the churchyard and a sign displayed the new name of the park. The sign was immediately subjected to defacement. This is perhaps less than surprising. However, more significantly, the name continues to be erased. In 1997, almost twenty years after the murder, the sign that confirms the name of the park continued to be painted over with a black spray can of paint. On no fewer than seven occasions in that single year the municipal authorities would paint in the name of the park only for the black paint to cover it up. No attempt was made to inscribe alternative names or ostensibly to reclaim the park in the name of particular political groupings. Moreover, the repeated processes of defacement have rarely been accompanied by specific political graffiti. Instead, a slightly surreal choreography has developed between the local state and perhaps a very small number of individuals. In each case the 'graffiti' – if it can be called such – involves only the erasure of presence.

Characteristically, in some analytical treatments, such actions are cast as territorial statements of an ethnologically threatened individual or group.[27] Yet the repetitive nature of the process over such a long period of time might be taken to imply something slightly different. There are many histories here, all with a validity of their own, many of them almost forgotten. From an open-air pulpit in the former church preachers famously once harangued passing pedestrians. An old water fountain has left a hole in the wall of the park which is said to be a sight line for one of the psycho-geographical ley lines of London, and at one end of the park, directly on this line, an imam held theological discussions each summer from 1999 to 2001. It is also the site of the burial of Richard Brandon, the executioner of Charles I who was paid £30 for his regicide. But Altab Ali's death was equally violent and took place on his way home from shift work in a nearby sweatshop. The event lives on popular memory with a resonance that municipal renaming acknowledged as much as bestowed.

But attempts to exclude this particular set of memories continue. Arguably, the erasure is as much a refusal of recognition as an assertion of territorial primacy. It *renders invisible* a particular telling of the story of the park, subtly different from merely asserting alternative ownership. This is a narrative moment that is not discursive, or even emblematic; it is a matter of overwriting and suppressing the polyphonous traces and chronologies that are latent within this public space.

The stories through which the landscapes of the city are rendered legible are commonly contested, and in Altab Ali Park this contest in 1998 coalesced around proposals to site a Bangladeshi martyrs' memorial in the park. The original Shahid Minar was a memorial erected by medical students of Dacca Medical College in 1952 to commemorate their peers who had died the preceding year in the effort to establish Bengali as a recognised language. In the years after independence in 1947, the Pakistani state attempted to impose Urdu universally across both West and East Pakistan, as part of the 'nation building' process, and was concerned at the perceived *corruption* of the Bengali language by Sanskrit words and phrases. The contest over the putative Arabisation of the Bengali language contained within it the microcosm of confrontation between contrasting essences of identity: between a shared Islam that was the *raison d'être* for the state of Pakistan West and East in 1947 and the secular nationalism that emerged as a Bangladeshi independence movement. Replicas of the original Shahid Minar have been constructed globally as commemorative marks by the Bengali diaspora, including one in the northern British town of Oldham, and 21 February is observed in Bengali communities across the world as National Language Day.

The choice of Altab Ali Park for the East London copy of the Shahid Minar was not insignificant. In this sense the martyrs' memorial in East London consciously linked Altab Ali to the nationalist struggle and reinforced one particular telling of this space. Consequently, opposition came from *both* those Bengali voices that reject secular nationalism as opposed to Islamic universalism as the basis of British-based diasporic politics, and also from expressions of white racist populism that resent this appropriation of the history of the park. Such disputes exist within a frame of reference that approximates to the notion of an alternative public sphere.

This is precisely what is meant in stressing an iterative understanding of both graffiti and the relations of conflict. It is not a simple matter of graffiti constituting the *effect* of conflict. Much more is at stake here. It is rather that the iterative cycles, the to and fro of naming and erasure, shape an emergent and contested landscape in which the geography of identity and the identity of particular places is manifest, if continually in flux.

Allusion and semiotic integration: Chicksand Street

The next site described is the Spitalfields area in the west of Tower Hamlets, immediately adjacent to the financial district of the City of London. Coterminous with some of the most intense forms of concentrated poverty in the country, in this area were found some of the highest levels of residential segregation in 1990s Britain, with several estates and blocks by the end of the decade being over 90 per cent Bengali. It is one of the oldest sites of Bengali settlement, and over the last 30 years it has witnessed many clashes between racist groups and local communities, as well as between far-right activists and the predominantly white articulations of the anti-racist movement. However, it is now also popularly thought of as an area that in terms of racial danger is much 'safer' than other parts of the East End, precisely because of the generations of self-defence activism. In particular, the analysis moves to describe briefly one part of Spitalfields.

The area between Chicksand Street and Brick Lane is dominated by a sunken five-a-side football pitch and an area of piazza-like open space in which people can watch the football, meet people, 'hang out' or just engage in the deepest routines of 'doing nothing'.[28] The cluttered array of wall writings tell many stories. Dozens of individuals have tagged the walls. A constant writing and overwriting of the names of the local gangs are sometimes superimposed, sometimes juxtaposed alongside such marks: the 'we' alongside the more specific 'I'. In the early 1990s a local street sign was covered in white paint and the street name replaced with the word 'Banglatown'. London districts are given postcodes, which are the British equivalent of the 'zip code', and these signal whether they are in the north, south, east or west of the city: they are also given a number, e.g. SE23 or N4. The postcode for this part of London is E1, and so the horizontals of the letter have been joined in several cases to read B1, Bangla 1 or Bengali 1. Thus the metropolitan way of designating this territory is fused with a diasporic reference, so that Banglatown enters London and through its insertion playfully disrupts the established grammar of locality.

But most interestingly of all, in the period from the early 1990s until 2002, when it was demolished, one wall alongside the football pitch was covered with highly decorative, carefully wrought, invocations of an Islamic order. A stylised tag 'Islam', painted over six feet in height in 1996, was characterised by a calligraphy that resembled adjacent tags which owed their origins to the New York subway graffiti discussed earlier. The decoration was captioned by the term 'Enjoin the Good and Forbid The Evil'; also in hip-hop style and alongside it for a couple of years was another massive inscription proclaiming 'Jihad Those who fight for the cause of Allah'. But these inscriptions are – like so many other graffiti – challenged locally, not so much by open patterns of racist abuse as by alternative notions of narrative space. Above the 'Islam' tracing it is possible to make out the cautiously ironic inscription of another hand, 'The Neutral Zone Woz Here', whilst the Jihad graffiti was erased from the wall in late 1997. Likewise in 1997, a series of posters in support of the Islamic group Hiz b'T Taheer (HT) prompted much controversy locally when they made declarations such as 'Peace With Israel Is Haram' and carried pictures of the Middle East Peace Process and characters active in it with captions such as 'Whoever gives away a handspan of Muslim land, Allah will grant them an equal handspan of hellfire.'

Posters and flyers, as well as graffiti, were left principally across the Bengali areas of the borough, with characteristically assertive messages, along with messages of support for the group Al Muhajiroun, listing their world wide web page.[29] Yet such inscriptions were frequently challenged. The Bangladesh struggle for independence was a civil war fought against a theocratic state, and the messages of graffiti and posters were commonly challenged. In particular, whilst the tags and the gang graffiti near Chicksand Street were left untouched, somebody erased with whitewash the 'Jihad' from the wall and many of the HT posters were also defaced. Ironically the anti-Semitic tone of many of these messages was echoed in the winter of 1997–8 with a resurgence of far-right activity in almost exactly the same area. On Cable Street, a site that witnessed clashes between the far right and the anti-fascist movement in the 1930s, the mural commemorating the confrontation was defaced in a manner that, whilst not ostensibly directed at the majority Bengali population in the immediate vicinity, was directed again at a mythical Jewish presence which in demographic terms is now almost a historical memory and a residue of some of the older generation.

But what is to be made of this Babel-like set of messages, this admixture of words and symbols? Such writings repay a sustained analysis, precisely because of what they reveal about the contestation and construction of imperfect and unruly forms of public debate. The forms of expression are not consciously discursive or straightforwardly representational, precisely because the concatenation of inter-textuality defies any meaningful 'fields' of discourse. The depth of the provenance of some of the semiotics is undoubtedly commonly unknown. But also the breadth of the fields of reference on which the systems draw is quite consciously equally commonly sophisticated, drawing on cultural reference points that are simultaneously local and global. For both of these reasons cultural forms that wall writing and graffiti represent are frequently much more complex and warrant far closer scrutiny than is normally the case.

Graffiti has been long associated with the articulation of race, territory and youth groups and subcultures in urban contexts.[30] Particularly important is the work by the psychologists Lomas and Weltman on Los Angeles and the social geographers Ley and Cybriwsky's research in Philadelphia. Contained within this work are some clues as to how one might conceptualise the relationship between graffiti, identity and racism. Lomas and Weltman found in their research that the graffiti of youth groups was connected to claiming territory and that gang graffiti became more frequent the closer it got to the home range of a particular group.[31] Beyond this they noted that graffiti was a key way of expressing class and ethnic markers:

> By considering the cultural milieu in which the wall writer operates we find messages reflect shared attitudes and values as well as ethnocentric variations on main cultural themes. Thus a comparative study of contemporary graffiti is to a great extent a cross-cultural investigation of class and ethnic differences.[32]

The problem with this way of thinking about graffiti is that it ultimately reduces it to the expressive effect of geographically defined social and cultural groups and identities. In this sense visual ideologies draw on an iterative relationship between places and identities and the viewer and the viewed. Such a relationship disrupts and conflates Lefèbvre's distinction between spaces of representation and representation of spaces.[33] The graffiti is instead rendered visible through the particular nature of the modality of expression. Specifically, there are characteristics that warrant attention here, namely:

- the breadth of allusion;
- the aesthetic appeal and symbolisation of the wall writing;
- the integration of the reader within a community of signs.

Paradoxically, the imperative to communicate demands as much as assumes a shared set of cultural references: the will to distance and to purify is undermined by precisely this shared field of allusion. This returns us to the issue of communication that was raised earlier: the communication of hatred or opposition in and of itself involves the integration of the hate object into a community of allusion and symbolisation. Otherwise, there would simply be no point to these communicative acts at all. In order to harass or challenge the presence of the other the writer needs to share a communicative technology with him or her. This involves the exchange of a de-centred and promiscuous field of allusion, a symbolic language and, as we shall see later, even the mutual crossing of particular emblems.

Who are you talking to? 'Fragments shored against the ruins'

It is not simply that graffiti constitutes a secret language tied semantically to specific messages that need to be decoded. Any notion that implicitly or explicitly suggests that its meaning is to be found in the pathologies of the producers and the topographies of the spaces in which they are realised is at best simplistic. In contrast, a focus on the audience for the messages of the wall writing undermines such caricature. Put straightforwardly, the scribe invariably has an audience.

What difference does it make if we think of wall writing as a narrative genre that invokes the ethics and aesthetics of a particular scopic regime?[34] First it makes us think about the precise form of visualisation that is at work in such scripting. Graffiti is rarely an attempt to produce a realistic or naturalistic representation of a social or political reality; it neither replicates nor describes. Instead it tells by visualising; the I that is here, the we that tagged this place, the presences that must be erased and the erasure that must be overwritten. Second, it makes it clearer that the spaces are rendered visible in an iterative relationship with the scribes. This displays the link between space and identity in a different register from some of the more ethologically deterministic understandings of *public spaces that work* and those that do not. Even the bleakest spaces of desolate inner city estates are humanised by particular moments of expressive culture. Third, it problematises the easy taxonomies of racist and anti-racist forms of wall writing. The point returns later, but put simply, politically opposed groups may share a communicative repertoire that constitutes little more than the mimetic mirror opposite of the opponent. Fourth, it places a focus on the nature of allusion deployed in the process of graffiti writing. As has already been argued, the allusions of the graffiti of intolerance in some ways undermine themselves through their own imperative to communicate. In this sense the field of reference may not be discursive, but is almost invariably intertextual. Tagging, writing, bombing all share the need to develop a particular moment of communicative rationality at a time when the city declares war on itself.[35]

If the notion that people 'putting themselves together in public' through the modalities of graffiti writing is implicitly overoptimistic, it is not to underestimate the power of the forms of intolerance that are so often mobilised, but instead to foreground process over outcome. This foregrounding of function over form highlights the construction of self and the articulation of place that is at the heart of the inscription of graffiti on the racialised walls of the city.

In the case of openly and explicitly racist graffiti the ethnographic project on which this chapter is based also considered examples of racist graffiti in a suburban district of Birmingham, UK, in order to examine the sometimes complex ways in which graffiti is used to communicate intolerance and harassment.[36]

A recurrent theme highlighted the plural mode of address of the hate writing. Scripts directed sometimes towards victims were overwritten. Racist tags that could be read by the residents or shopkeepers looking out from a shop were sometimes succeeded by further graffiti that inverted the address by 180 degrees and was directed towards other residents or passers-by in the locality. Local reaction to this appeal for 'white solidarity' was revealing. Most local residents resented the opportunistic tactics of the right-wing graffiti writers and poured scorn on them. This was in large part a resistance to the entryism from right-wing political groupings because they were from outside the neighbourhood. Yet within the performance of community the tactics of the far right could be condemned while local styles of racism continued to be expressed against an Indian shopkeeper. This example shows clearly that one needs to be cautious about reading the territorial claims made through graffiti as merely a reflection or organic expression of the aspirations of particular geographically distributed communities. The 'England for whites' graffiti was the projection of a particular claim to this locality as a 'white space'.

Some people within the local community subscribed to this view but resented its being imposed by a group of politically motivated outsiders. Other anti-racist white residents rejected both the political agenda of the National Front graffiti writers and the definition of the neighbourhood as an exclusively white territory. Racist graffiti tried to mask or conceal the diversity of interests that existed within this predominantly white neighbourhood. It attempted to stylise the community in a particular way, which both undermined the status of local ethnic minority residents and sent a clear message to black citizens from other areas to 'keep out'. In this sense it narrates the imagination of community through a process of systematic erasure. Consequently it is necessary to view graffiti as a signifying system that is not only inscribed *onto* the social and physical fabric of the city but is also part of the process by which the social objects of *community* and *identity* shape the reconstruction of the city itself in a different image.

Although graffiti writers might be placed in an antagonistic relationship, they constitute a linguistic community united in its opposition to a wider normative community. Graffiti writing itself constitutes a kind of unruly alternative public sphere in which political argument and verbal debate is substituted with a kind of non-discursive battle between opposing groups armed with spray cans and marker pens. British racist and anti-racist graffiti writers monitor each other in an intense fashion, learning the other's symbolic language. Graffiti politics is as much a semiotic/interpretative process as it is a struggle for a public presence through the quantity of inscription. As a result, racist and anti-racist writing often entails over-writing, or erasing, the opponent's graffiti. Where the canvas is the property of black or ethnic minority residents, their walls may be written over time and time again by both right-wing and left-wing graffiti.

Examples like this one suggest there is a dependent and reciprocal relationship between racist movements and anti-racist organisations. One might ask, to what extent do these avowedly antagonistic groups need each other in order to sustain themselves over time? There is no space to answer this question here, but what is interesting is that graffiti politics brings this question into focus. It seems clear that within the writing wars being waged in British cities and elsewhere in Europe each side of the political divide is locked into an antagonistic but reciprocal relationship. The effectiveness of challenging racism through these means is limited, because of the mutually reinforcing nature of graffiti politics. This also raises some important questions about the quality of communication or dialogue that is being performed within graffiti. There is no discursive argument that is exchanged through these means; rather what is traded is a series of slogans and emblems.

The relevance of these issues needs to be evaluated in view of the rise in neo-fascist activity in Europe and the growing intensity of popular racism. If these movements are to be effectively countered, it is essential to develop a sophisticated appraisal of the protean nature of racist cultures and their networks of circulation. George Mosse, perhaps the pre-eminent scholar of fascist culture, has commented that a key part of the power of racism is the way in which it helps to account for specific social relations in a simple manner through a visual ideology.[37] Viewed from this perspective, graffiti can be seen as one of the key ocular mechanisms of racist expression.

It is necessary to be able to decode graffiti not only to interpret contemporary forms of racism but also to evaluate the political strategies that have been mobilised against them. There is a real danger that anti-racist politics is fast becoming little more than the mirror opposite of its professed foe, whose very existence is locked into an ever more functional dependency on the activities of the opponent. One of the most alarming things emerging from the graffiti project was that graffiti politics appeared almost divorced from the experience of the victims of racism. No wonder, then, that the victims themselves are sometimes reticent to remove racist graffiti. One shopkeeper stated:

> I stopped taking it off at one time, I left it there. In the daytime when the shutters are up, there's nothing you can see, it's at night when you're closing

[that you see the graffiti] . . . I think to myself 'let the people who live here see what their children are doing,' let them have to look at it. I have been here too long to be shocked anymore.

Here the homes and shops of the victims have been reduced to little more than a canvas for the expression of competing slogans and political desires. But, powerfully, this sentiment inverts the narrative force of the graffiti; the tale of ethnic erasure becomes a testament of shame as the putative victim refocuses the writing to address a different audience.

Conclusion

The forms of wall writing examined are clearly driven by contrasting political impulses. It is not our aim, or even desire, to suggest that these modes of urban expression can be tamed within a totalising model of graffiti writing. Yet, while stressing variety and the importance of context and situatedness in reading graffiti, it is also necessary to identify the key elements contained within this form as a mode of expression. Throughout the chapter the notion of a communicative technology referred to the elementary apparatus of wall writing. In concluding it is necessary to draw together these ideas with regard to how they relate to the issues of public life, communication and dialogue.

The only thing that unites the New York tagger with the neo-Nazi propagandist is that their inscriptions are outlawed equally. But the prohibitions on each of these forms of graffiti are articulated through very different moral imperatives. Graffiti is also a symptom of a failure of the public sphere, or at least the limits of permissible or legitimate communication within it. Yet what is interesting about graffiti in all its diverse forms is that it challenges us to think about the relationship between people and places. We have stressed throughout this chapter that graffiti is a profoundly iterative form of urban expression. The types of social identity which emerge are produced by the people in a particular place as much as the place in them. More than this, graffiti is not merely the sign or the effect of an underlying ethological community; rather it *is* the embodied social landscape. As a result, graffiti draws attention to how communities are manifested and articulated in a necessarily incomplete, uneven and contingent fashion.

The unruly spaces of the city disrupt the cartography of the neatly mapped and segregated ethnic mosaic. Space simultaneously mediates creolisation and marks difference. Thus graffiti as a communicative technology is crucially implicated in an emergent spatial politics of entitlement and belonging within the city.

One of the key features of graffiti is that it combines multiple modes of signification. So, in a Sassurean sense, graffiti is more *parole* than *langue*. It includes a visual repertoire of emblems and symbols with an often syncretic linguistic structure that deploys standard forms of language in order to articulate slogans and snatches of discourse. These forms of communication deploy encryption to encode the intended meaning. This can take a lexigraphic form in which letters symbolise whole words, e.g. NF for National Front, or where numerals denote letters which in turn symbolise words, e.g. 88 for Heil Hitler. Seemingly opposed groups of writers may in this situation share symbolic resources. This traffic between graffiti writers may be opaque and unselfconscious. Bengali taggers known as the Danger Zone Posse (DZP) from the Whitechapel district of East London have in recent times assimilated elements from racist graffiti. Apart from the three-letter acronym style which is evocative of BNP graffiti, this group has also assimilated the target-like symbol of the Celtic cross and the crown commonly deployed both by racist writers and in the iconography of Basquiat. The point here is that graffiti writing is a polysemic and open linguistic form both at the level of lexicon and genre.

Graffiti works through allusion rather than the explicit discourse of the mainstream. Allusion operates in one sense both *externally* and *internally* here. Internal allusion means a coded communication which is interpreted by a distinct community of writers and readers. For example, New York hip-hop graffiti, which, it was argued, is read in very different ways depending on whether it is viewed from the inside by the writers themselves and their constituency or from outside liberal or radical commentators such as Wilson, Glazer and even Sennett. In this sense these outlaw forms of communication are precious because they transform the mainstream through writing over it, yet at the same time exclude the mainstream from their – the graffiti writers' – discourse. External forms of allusion refer to the strategic use of signs to provoke a particular audience, be it an individual or a social group. A good example of this is the way in which Palestinian Intifada graffiti uses the swastika alongside the Star of David, often connected with an equals sign. The swastika invokes the experience of the Jewish Holocaust both to implicate Zionism in fascism and simply to offend through the sheer symbolic weight of its presence.[38] Oliver and Steinberg describe a young Palestinian who 'grabbing our notebook, scrawled a swastika across a page and exclaimed, "See this? It drives the Jews crazy"'.[39] This distinction is to some degree artificial because many forms of graffiti combine to different degrees internal and external elements of allusion depending on the nature of the audiences.

All graffiti is narrative in that it attempts to tell alternative stories about places. These stories at their most basic signal the failure of the public sphere to incorporate them. In this respect graffiti creates and communicates through an unruly alternative public sphere which, while allowing forbidden inscription, contains contradictions of its own. The patrolled and circumscribed nature of graffiti culture militates against it being open and inclusive. So the self-regulating endogenous nature of graffiti expression limits its own potential to spawn a true alternative. It may well be a mistake to yearn for a utopian and inclusive public sphere which engenders authentic communication. The achievement of such an inclusive urban culture seems inevitably tenuous. Perhaps this is why graffiti has endured as one of the most archaic forms of written communication. In this sense, we need to be able to read the writing on the wall, for in these opaque and arcane inscriptions we can find both the limits of public discourse and outlaw voices that threaten to be heard.

9 The cartographies of community safety

Mapping danger and rumours of risk

In the often melancholic subtext of urban social theory, a nostalgia for the permissive public spaces of old persists alongside critiques of the putatively inauthentic or repressive public spaces of the contemporary shopping mall, the themed urban experience, or the dystopian streets of our surveillance society. Following the pioneering but immensely influential work of Ulrich Beck the spaces of the city become a plane of variable risk.[1] The mapping of this world by the institutions and agencies of the state and its proxies becomes the subject (and rapidly a technocratic language in its own right) of something that increasingly is referred to as *community safety*. Community safety consequently mediates specific cartographies of the urban. Its maps are themselves technologies through which some cosmopolitan subjects are made visible and others are not. The city itself both conspires with such technologies and simultaneously resists their will to map and to know.

This chapter is consequently interested in thinking about how the nature of government and of urban space is changing in the context of various moral concerns over racial tension, community safety and the behaviour of young people. And in that context the trouble with the melancholic narratives of urban social theory about the world we have lost is that they fail to address two major forces transforming the cities of everyday life. First, both the city and the communities inhabiting it are now becoming the objects of new governmental regimes designed to regulate the conduct of conduct through localised and participatory mappings of urban space and the objects within it on planes of risk. Second, the institution of these new regimes of governmentality is locally mediated by story-telling and other forms of behaviour that reinvent the nature of everyday places in the city and transform the parameters of acceptable conduct. These popular reimaginings are sometimes progressive, but at other times reiterate racialised conflict and violence, thus confounding the populist instinct in urban social theory to lionise (progressive) civil society against the (repressive) state.

Drawing on interviews and other material collected as part of a study of social policy initiatives in the Isle of Dogs and Deptford in inner London, the chapter advances five related arguments:[2] first, that a new policy agenda in the over-developed 'north' – loosely associated with third way politics on both sides of the Atlantic – demands a specific *localisation* of governmental practices that implicitly reinvents a particularly communitarian notion of public space. Second, it suggests that the localities of the city might be considered in terms of the specific *spaces of governmentality* through which the myriad of policy professionals and social policy organisations focus on and attempt to affect particular forms of social behaviour. The third proposition is that it is helpful to think about the landscapes of the city in terms of the *micro-public spheres* of specific buildings, sites, and places associated with routinised forms of behaviour structuring the temporality of social processes. At times in a mundane fashion, and at others more profoundly, they symbolise the lived, remembered, and forgotten *histories* of particular places. They are also often the subjects of 'institutional rumour and gossip' that invoke variations on these local histories as a narrative frame to render the geographical present comprehensible. Fourth, it is argued that the stories woven around specific sites and places in the Isle of Dogs and Deptford exemplify broader processes by which the local disrupts the localising practices at the heart of the new regimes of government. Finally, a specific discussion of these two areas on either side of the River Thames in London highlights for us the importance of thinking carefully about the sorts of times and places that both provoke racial antagonism and promote intercultural dialogue.

The localising spaces and subjects of governmentality

Taking as its starting points the imperative to regulate capitalism and the failure of state socialism, Anthony Giddens' (1998) influential *The Third Way* provides an influential diagnosis of the liberal democratic project that was closely associated with the governments of Bill Clinton and Tony Blair[3] in the late 1990s. Giddens suggested that across the world of late capitalism we are witnessing the emergence of a new democratic state without enemies.[4] Though looking increasingly implausible in the wake of the Iraq war, Giddens' vision for a state without enemies echoed Fukayama's 1990s nostrums of the end of history, in which liberal democracy was to become the global norm. It promised to renew the public sphere and produce a double democratisation (of both state and civil society institutions) through the mechanisms of direct democracy and devolution coupled with greater transparency, administrative efficiency, and a new role for the state as manager of risk rather than provider of security. As Giddens explains:

> An open public sphere is as important at local as at national level, and is one way in which democratisation connects directly with community development. Without it, schemes of community renewal risk separating the community from the wider society. 'Public' here includes physical public space. The degeneration of local communities is usually marked not only by general dilapidation, but by the disappearance of safe public space – streets, squares, parks and other areas where people can feel secure.[5]

Giddens' recipe for democratic renewal appeals, in particular, to the notion of 'self-government'.[6] The operative term here is the *self* in self-government. What kind of *self* is to govern itself as the state reinvents the public sphere as an arena of self-regulation? This language of self-government demands careful scrutiny. Self-regulating forms of subjectivity have a particular history that cannot be reduced to a simple movement of something called 'power' away from the state and towards 'the people'. Many critics identify their emergence across the globe with new forms of economic government. In response to the perils of globalisation, the state is divesting itself of the responsibility for 'progress' through an increasing stress on the responsibility of self-governing economic actors, whose actions must take as a first principle the rudiments of economic competence.[7]

One major context in which these new, self-regulating approaches to governance are crystallising is in the contemporary state's approach to 'community safety'. It seeks to regulate 'anti-social behaviour' through curfews, individualised legal injunctions (such as anti-social behaviour orders in the United Kingdom) and the criminalisation of marginal forms of social interaction, such as begging and sleeping or drinking in public. Critics have seized on these reforms as hallmarks of a new 'revanchist city'.[8] But both conventional and politically radical urban social theorists have paid less attention to the manner in which such approaches to crime reconfigure the relationship between state and civil society through the localisation of governmental scrutiny of the 'dangerous' parts of the social. In the rhetoric of self-government exemplified by Giddens, cities are imagined as landscapes of risk. Within these imagined worlds the term community, sometimes with attendant communitarian imperatives, mediates the relationship between state and civil society.

In the United Kingdom, the ongoing transformation of 'public service' delivery institutionalises this governmental focus on self-regulating forms of community.[9] For instance, local authorities are now required to work in partnership with other agencies, including the police, to develop crime-reduction strategies, youth justice audits, Youth Offender Teams, and Youth Justice Boards. Through these collaborative processes, each local authority is expected to inscribe the spaces of their jurisdiction in terms of a cartography of risk that marks out urban hot spots, risky spaces, and places of crime and disorder.[10] Within this officially sanctioned geography of social policy, young people are often taken to personify the risks of the city, and local authorities are given powers to issue Child Safety Orders and Parenting Orders to restrain their activity.

The project of community safety and crime reduction through self-government contains within it both a moralising reinvention of individual selves and some straightforward disciplinary measures, such as youth curfews, to create time-spaces in the public sphere where young people will not be allowed. This criminalisation of various forms and norms of behaviour in the United Kingdom both speaks to and draws on similar experiences in the American city in the past decade.[11] But something more than criminality is at stake here. We are witnessing some major changes in the institutions involved in the socialisation of young people. In this context the simple division between what is and what is not the state is perhaps not very helpful when the legislative changes relate much more to a transactional relationship between forms and norms of behaviour and of official sanction. Official sanction is now seeking to produce well-behaved young people as much through the activities of particular arms of welfare support as through the punitive institutions of criminal justice. Thus current social policy reforms are as much about what it means to be a young person and what are the rights and responsibilities of such *subjects* as they are about the straightforward relationship between authority and community.

These reforms of government reinvent a notion of public space as a site of civility and possibly even of civilisation. Arguably, they are localising a particular communitarian project.[12] Such a vision of localised self-government rests on an appeal to community that sits uneasily with the cultural complexities of most British multicultural cities, and certainly with the sites of the research on which this chapter is based. What legislative changes mean for the rights of people who are coming of age, or for people whose access to public space has been shaped by racism, poverty and fear, may be moot in its detail but is certain to be profound in its substance. According to most analyses, intercultural dialogue is deeply dependent on the stages on which it takes place. If the public spaces of the city have conventionally been the sites of what Les Back has described as the metropolitan paradox, in which they are simultaneously sites of intercultural dialogue and racist intolerance, then the freedom of the city in a multiracial context is currently being redefined through the reinvention of its public spaces.[13]

Maps and narratives of the micro-public sphere

The Isle of Dogs and Deptford – where twelve months of ethnographic research was based in two secondary schools – are old riverside areas of London on the north and south sides of the River Thames. Both have seen successive waves of neighbourhood change and transnational migration, as well as a succession of policy instruments and initiatives aimed at reducing inner city poverty and de-industrialisation. In turn these initiatives have created a specific form of institutional landscape in the name of 'urban regeneration'. This is precisely the sort of institutional stage examined earlier in this volume. It allows certain iconic characters to emerge, bestowing legitimacy on some for a while then others: the ethnic entrepreneur, the street rebel, the single mother, the youth gang and the neighbourhood manager.

The argument made here is that this institutional landscape shapes the definition of inner city subjects. Funding agencies legitimise the existence of some groups and not others; some forms of social provision receive revenue support and others disappear. Accordingly the boundaries between what is and what is not 'the state' are being renegotiated as funding agencies make visible what is and what is not sanctioned and funded within what is conventionally understood as 'civil society'. Specifically, in the late 1990s, the activity of welfare professionals responded to 'the risk agenda' prioritising funding around 'community safety' and 'social exclusion'. In the words of one youth worker:

> the rush for everyone to describe everything they're doing in terms of social exclusion and the combating of it . . . [is] the same . . . as a couple of years ago,

[when] everyone suddenly had spent their whole life ensuring the safety of the community. And before that everything you did was about skilling and training and access to employment . . . The professionals . . . refilter the debates on the ground through whatever lens we're using at any given moment.

Such comments point to an alternative history of community safety initiatives in which the national interest in 'community safety' as an object of governmental concern is translated into local initiatives and reshaped at the local level. It is not the principal function of this chapter to explore such a history. But it is important to remember that when 'policy élites' are imagining landscapes of safety and danger they are influenced in part by the regimes of inner city government, which are the institutional realisation of the boundary between city government and a remoulded civil society.

The formal territorialisation of safety through regimes of localising governmentality and regulation of conduct translates into both officially sanctioned maps of localising state intervention and informal narratives of racial fear and danger. Particular sites become emblematic of more substantive issues. On the Isle of Dogs certain estates were seen locally as 'Bengali estates',[14] characteristic of a racialised distinction between Bengali and non-Bengali housing that itself reveals much about ways of thinking about and representing social housing provision. By contrast, in Deptford particular places were referred to as 'beyond the state' and the rumoured site of particular forms of criminal activity. The 'ghetto' in the young people's vernacular in South London was used to describe graphically a particular set of estates. In both areas the racialisation of space did not correspond exactly to the demographics of settlement, but instead conflated reputation and residential presence. The narrativisation of space by local youth considered in this chapter disrupts a transparent sense of the spatial and undermines static cultural geographies of urbanism.

Of particular significance, the professionals of the localising states are no less subject to the informal storytelling practice of what we are calling the micro-public sphere. The way some places feature in the narratives of policy élites suggests that their formal location on the officially sanctioned cartographies of risk and danger is influenced, in part, by their reputation within the more informal circuits of rumour and gossip within the respective public sector organisations. In interviews informants would not only use a particular estate to exemplify either racial antagonism or problems of racial harassment, they would also refer to the reputation (past and present) of such an estate for particular forms of behaviour. Some youth clubs are identified as the sites of criminal activity, gang behaviour or drug dealing. Others have a reputation of cross-cultural working. Particular events are said to have precipitated changes in the thinking of the local authority, the police service or community activists. The dictates of space prevent a full analysis, but it might be possible to imagine how a gradual accretion of these stories would produce an iconography of the micro-scale public spheres of the city, a spatial semiotics of the everyday knowledges of welfare professionals.

Significantly, this chapter is not suggesting anything about the empirical accuracy of these accounts of community safety and danger in the two case study areas. However, it is suggested that such informal anecdotes about particular clubs, streets and occasions serve, in part, as nuclei around which official cartographies of much wider areas coalesce. At this micro-scale policy actions are shaped by this narrative web. Such storytelling literally constructs the local through processes of narration. It is in this sense that there is a 'micro-public sphere' of debate that links actions to reputations around the specific times and spaces of the city.

In this way what we might work towards is a rethinking of how *the local* is constituted. Such narrative constructions of the local do not sit easily with the sorts of localising practices of governmentality emerging from the contemporary political agenda of social reform. Such narrative constructions render space and place as plural, opaque, contested and frequently contradictory. In contrast, the localising practices of governmental imperatives render the spaces of the city as translucent, uniform, communicatively consistent and ethically purified. Nor do they accord with Richard Sennett's more recent typology of reflections on the public realm, in which he juxtaposes the abstracted notions of Arendt and Habermas with the more dramaturgical conceptualisation of public space identified within his own work and that of Geertz.[15] They do not do so because the narrativisation of place and space becomes performatively constitutive of the places themselves.

It is possible to identify a set of relationships operating at the interface of government and civil society that collectively generate racialised landscapes of safety and danger in the governed territories of urban Britain. Crudely this might be summarised as follows. At a banal demographic level, specific socioeconomic conditions and levels of historical provision generate particular concentrations of young people in specific localities. However, the *wider youth question* only emerges from the manner in which problems associated with young people are interpreted through local networks and translated into the policy sphere through particular regimes of governmental knowledge, power and practice.[16] This is mediated by specifically local moral panics and representations in debates around community safety and public danger.

At the heart of this process is a communication of generalised perceptions through rumour, gossip and repute. The place on the political agenda of the youth question is shaped by local fears of the behaviours of young people as much as by the recognition of any 'real' social need. The form of youth-oriented provision is shaped by regimes of funding that reflect the positioning of troubled urban areas as spaces of governmentality. The sites and the projects that are funded reflect the *unsaid* as much as the *said* that emerges from a politicised landscape of institutions and people competing for scarce resources. This becomes even more pronounced in the context of the actions of young people operating within the city spaces territorialised by these governmental regimes.

Repetition, repute and disruption

Although the officially authorised discourse of racial danger and community safety rendered local history in rather similar ways in the Isle of Dogs and Deptford, these concerns were articulated very differently in the geographies of risk shaping local youth and community relations in each place. On the Isle of Dogs, the language of 'rights' and 'fairness' used by young white people and their parents articulated a strong sense of outrage around new housing allocations to Bengali families, whilst their territorialised fears were focused on the presence of Bengali boys. These themes were taken up and reworked , often in a displaced form, in stories of 'Bengali on Bengali' violence foregrounded by the press and police locally and communicated through dense social networks.

By contrast, in Deptford the official rhetoric of race bore a much closer relationship to the neighbourhood nationalism identified by Les Back in an earlier study of the area, which held out the possibility of intercultural identification linked to a strong, officially sanctioned problematic of neighbourhood harmony.[17] In this context the embedding of 'good vibe' stories in a critical mass of positive urban imagery enabled them to travel across racial divides, although there were important instances of discrepancy between these 'authorised' story lines and the plotting of racial encounter on the streets.

The subject of 'youth gangs' was also interpreted differently in the two areas. In Deptford, there was a strong sense that youth gangs, which were predominantly male but sometimes also with small numbers of female members, were distributed as distinct territorial units throughout South London. Gangs had emblematic territorial names like 'Ghetto boys', 'Deptford men', and 'Brixton youth', and at one level they bore the marks of a 'baptismal naming' linked to the popular iconography of black street crime.[18] Talk about gangs was pervasive, but fewer younger people in the ethnography had any direct connection to these gangs. The sense of Bourdieu's city phantasms that haunt the city considered in the introductory chapter of the volume returns. In some of the accounts by young white people, these gangs were viewed as a diffuse source of anxiety and threat. At the same time, however, there was a reluctance to racialise these feelings or focus them in some concrete embodiment of the other, for example by invoking the figure of 'the black mugger'. At the end of one interview in which a young white girl had talked extensively and quite fearfully about the threat of gangs, she was asked if there was anything else she would like to say. After a short pause she replied, 'Yeah, about the gangs and that. It is true that they are mostly black boys involved but it's not because they're black.'

For the black boys in particular the symbolic nature of gang labels was often in evidence; much of this had to do with claiming male pride of place that might otherwise (for example, in the domestic sphere) be heavily contested. To proclaim 'Ghetto boy' status brought with it both a space of preferred identity and a claim to exclusive entitlement. For instance, the area around the Milton Court Estate in New Cross was referred to as 'Ghetto', and as one boy pointed out 'To me now to be from Ghetto is an honour'. Such claims often project the terms of masculine dominion into wider domains of 'imagined community'. For example, young men would give the numbers of the local telephone boxes as if they were their own public/private home from home. The talk about gangs became a means through which these young people positioned themselves in an alternative map of belonging.

The ludic dimensions of the process could be limiting as well as empowering, particularly for young women. A black girl complained of being labelled by her male peers:

> Just because you know certain people doesn't automatically make you a part of a gang. Like saying I am like a Peckham Girl. I don't think so! I live in Ghetto and the Peckham Boys think I am a Ghetto Girl but because I was born in Peckham the Ghetto Boys think I am a Peckham Girl.

Because baptismal naming is such a powerful rhetorical device for inscribing myths of origin and destiny in local prides of place, it is very difficult to detach these labels from positional attributions once they have initially been made to stick. Nevertheless, while gang territories were acknowledged to be dangerous places, it was generally agreed that the risk from gang violence was low unless you were involved directly in that world.

The situation on the Isle of Dogs differed considerably. There was a pervasive sense that 'Asian Gangs' constituted the main threat. Here issues of crime, violence and risk were strongly racialised and associated with a specific ethnic category: young Bengali men. What became clear in discussing youth violence in the area was the split between black and white youth on the one side and Bengalis on the other. This distinction was kept very much alive in local circuits of rumour and gossip; this, in turn, authorised young people to appeal to adult authority and 'common sense' in validating their iterative statements. This is clear in the following account by a young white woman:

> Like even black and whites fight and things like that, but you don't hear of many white people fighting with weapons and things like that, that is the thing. They couldn't just fight with their fist or anything; they have to have their knives and things like that and that is the worst bit. Like my Dad said years ago there wouldn't be weapons, that it would be like getting in a ring and that, and my Dad says they should put them all in a ring and let them just beat each other up, using nothing. But these days they have to use weapons all the time . . . It's just the Asians, the boys act 'flash', sit in their cars as if they own the place.

Here it is the Asians who constitute the threat, who use weapons, fight unfairly and act 'flash'. This was also present in the accounts of young white boys. Video walkabouts were developed with young people in the two locations so that they could make their own films to narrate the spaces of their neighbourhood. One case involved three white boys. As they were walking through Mudchute Farm on the Isle of Dogs the conversation turned to Bengali youth and their lack of mixing with white peers:

DAVID: They all hang out together they never hang out on their own.
STEVEN: Like us. We never hang out on our own.

RUSSELL: [referring to Asian youth] The Bangles!

DAVID: The Mukhtas!

STEVEN: They re-named Brick Lane. They named it Banglatown – that takes the piss. I wanna go down there and blow 'em all up.

DAVID: We're in England, not fuckin' Bangladesh for fuck's sake. Fair enough if we were in Bangladesh like, they wouldn't name a town . . . – fucking London!

STEVEN: I'd get killed, mate, if I went down Banglatown. I'd get killed.

This extract illustrates the way in which the walkabout provided the context for a dialogic, yet highly racialised engagement with processes of baptismal naming: 'Bangles' and 'Mukhtas' are immediately associated with the renaming of Brick Lane, which is then seen to remove the area from both local and national jurisdiction. The boys continue:

STEVEN: They're all racist down there; they are, they stare at you cos they think it's theirs, their town.

DAVID: You see them bowling along (he starts to rock shoulders, strutting holding his head and looking around mimicking 'the bowl').

STEVEN: I guarantee you'd find a blade [knife] on every single one of them.

In the course of the walk, the Isle of Dogs is defined, performatively, as a safe place for whites. It can be prone to the incursion of 'outsiders', but it is the areas outside that are understood as comprising an alien ethnoscape inhabited by violent Bengali boys. The Bengali young men are accused of mirroring the exact forms of masculine embodiment associated with white working-class male street culture. A curious cultural amnesia masks the links between African-American expressive culture, the zoot suit, the pimp roll and the classically English working-class boy's bowl down the streets of East London and its reappropriation by the second-generation British Sylheti boys of the new East End of the twenty-first century. Yet these forms (i.e. acting 'flash' or 'the bowl') are also seen as threatening because they either challenge 'normal' (coded white) territories, or establish exclusionary zones into which whites cannot seemingly venture. In this context the function of the precautionary tale is precisely to map out a potential space of adventure, which is at the same time closed off to empirical exploration by the operation of exclusionary rules and rituals of territoriality.

This imagined geography becomes narrativised around specific incidents. This was particularly true on the Isle of Dogs in the aftermath of one particular case of inter-racial violence where a young man had his head split open by a series of blows to the head with knives and machetes. Here the full potency of the construction of Asian gang violence was brought to effect. As a local youth worker put it, a 'fear zone' was created. The articulations of race and racism in this case have been explored elsewhere.[19] But in summary it was suggested that this violent incident, along with others, signals an important local shift in both the focus and the forms through which racist constructs are made, narratively, into common sense.

'Asian' (or Bengali) gangs in the contemporary East End and some other urban sites in contemporary Britain are now regarded as the prime sources of risk of urban violence.[20] This has developed to such an extent that at times it supersedes previous concerns over black male criminality associated with motifs of mugging or civil unrest. It was particularly telling that even local activists from the British National Party claimed 'black and white youth' were equally the victims of police 'double standards' about urban violence, while Asian youth were seen to be getting away with attacks on whites and with violent crime. This shift is not complete and echoes of the 'black mugging' discourse are still registered, but locally these formulations are increasingly faint.

At the same time the communicative genres through which these incidents are plotted, remembered, relayed and given a racial twist seem to be shifting. In these boys' accounts, rumour and precautionary storytelling have increasingly come to predominate over the more verbally elaborated and socially embedded forms of gossip associated with the full-blooded (in every sense of the word) cautionary tale. Scare stories about what would be likely to happen if you did venture into Bangla-town are now, increasingly, the gist of the white peer group conversation about race, place and identity, not atrocity stories about what happened to so and so.

Of importance theoretically is that some of these stories are organised spatially and others are organised historically. Time and space are both resources through which particular versions of reality are made visible. This is not ignoring the grim confrontation that accompanies such brute violence. Nor are we here making claims about the accuracy of such generalisations, only about their power to shape the official understandings of the racialised landscapes on which policy initiatives will take place.

Historicity and spatiality

Some progressive genres of urban social theory have appealed to a language of the vernacular urban to displace dominant histories and geographies of the local with alternative senses of the past and cartographies of the present.[21] In both the areas of research dominant narratives of inner urban poverty exist in spaces of the city made rich by traces of alternative histories and geographies. It was in Deptford that Francis Drake landed after circumnavigating the globe, and Walter Raleigh laid down his cloak for his queen. Such local histories also hint at the contested stories of Empire: Drake's landing presaged the Middle Passage, the return of Empire to the homeland in the migrations of the postwar years, the notorious confrontations with the National Front in the late 1970s, the conflicts between local black communities and the police in the 1970s, and the deaths in the New Cross Fire in 1981. Geographically, the Isle of Dogs is often imagined as the heartland of British racism through the iconic first victory of a fascist councillor in a British local election in 1993. Yet, in our research, young Bengali women at a local school spoke of the potential freedoms of the Island in contrast to a different kind of surveillance in the more segregated area of Brick Lane and Banglatown.

Progressive appeals to vernacular narratives by urban theorists seek to reinscribe history in place by making visible the stories that have been lost to the landscape of the inner city.[22] This fundamentally redemptive project is similar to work carried out in the UK by groups such as Common Ground[23] who attempt to trace the local histories of particular sites.[24] In such work there is a particular valorisation of the *local* through an invocation of the imbedded meanings of *place*. While this may at times be critiqued for romanticising the local, it also serves as an interesting contrast to other stories that are woven around the same landscapes and landmarks.

It is not simply an observation of ethnographic relativism to point out that such historicities and spatialities are contested and evolving. As Doreen Massey has commented, this is in part about tracing the global networks that foreground the global connections of *place* as much as the immanent sense of 'presence' in *space* of particular landscapes, networks and communities.[25] But only in part. Of equal significance, the telling of the temporal and the spatial configure the subject. In this sense narratives of time and space become expressive resources, performed through acts of memory and place making, which policy élites and young people alike use both to make sense of acting subjects and to set the stage for further social interaction. Predictably, the research highlighted patterns that were much more nuanced and ambivalent than such a simplistic opposition would suggest. Other work from this research has explored how narratives of 'harmony discourse' and 'conflict discourse' are drawn on strategically by young people in making sense of their everyday lives. However, it is interesting how the dominant notions of Deptford as harmonious and the Isle of Dogs as a racist landscape of conflict echo in the rationalisations and explanations of some of the policy élites.

Most celebrations of public space focus on the manner in which forms of sociability are facilitated by particular kinds of space. In one of his more behaviourist texts, Richard Sennett even goes so far as to suggest that in this fashion it would be possible almost to design streets full of life and places full of time.[26] In policy discussions, racism or cosmopolitanism are often imputed to places, as almost essential attributes of certain sites of the inner city landscape. Racism and racialised antagonism are rendered comprehensible through folk geographies that inform and structure the local definition of the *youth question*.

Such attribution replicates in form the manner in which particular sites become known as racist places, with identities with characteristics of their own. In part the chapter argues against such behaviourist renditions of the essentialising identity of places and in favour of a much closer focus on the processes of narrativisation of 'local culture' in the stories that are told by young people, policy élites, community activists and others. Here it is important to highlight the predictable simplifications that underscore the deployment of 'harmony' discourse in Deptford and 'racial conflict' discourse in the Isle of Dogs. This is more than just saying that patterns on the ground are complex. Racialised landscapes are places that are constructed as subjects through the techniques of governmental practice that emerge as a cumulative effect of national initiatives: their local realisations and the processes of rumour and gossip through which specific sites are made visible. These cartographies are simultaneously reappropriated in both the alternative stories and what Bourdieu might have described as the *bodily hexis* through which spaces are occupied by a corporeal presence.[27] What our work with policy élites demonstrates is the manner in which places are invoked and reinvented through the interface of practice, regulation, and rumour.

Conclusions

> 'How do men learn to accept painful surprises and disorder? In that acceptance lies the secret of how purification myths come to seem unreal.'[28]

It is important neither to glorify nor demonise what is going on at a local level. An analysis that indiscriminately valorises the actions of young people potentially celebrates the reproduction of racism and intolerance that assumes ever more complex vectors and creates a diversity of victims. But equally an analysis that allows for the potential of narrative practices to create theatres for dialogue between cultures will run the risk of naturalising social divisions between genders, ethnicities and age groups in a sanitised built environment.

Whilst having many reservations about the authoritarian thrust of contemporary social policy, we cannot ignore the grim realities of the racialised violence it seeks to address. The experience of young people in cities is still dominated by the anonymity of irrational and brutal racist attacks, both white on black and also increasingly nuanced by more complex patterns of racialised confrontation. Social policy norms with a behaviourist focus that assume that we can discipline the subjectivities of young people through the creation of new rites of passage, communitarian understandings of social responsibility, and an ever stronger labour market focus on the educational process, may not be a particularly effective way to address issues of racialised differences. A process of socialisation that emphasises the need to accept parental norms and the ethics of labour market competition can play out in some perverse ways when mediated by rhetorics of lineage and white unemployment both north and south of the River Thames.

If this is the case, there is a sense in which an understanding of the public sphere which thinks more contextually about the arenas in which the citizenship of young people is both given and restricted might form a more coherent way forward for thinking about issues of community safety and racial danger in some of the more troubled urban contexts of contemporary Britain. In an important work written over 30 years ago, Richard Sennett drew on Max Weber's distinction between an ethic of responsibility and an ethic of ultimate moral ends. As he put it, 'a responsible act, Weber said, is always impure, always painfully mixed because of diverse motives and desires; an absolute act on the other hand, is a struggle towards purity of desire and act as well as toward a "pure" end'.[29]

There is something anomalous about a political project that normalises a national agenda at a local level through a set of institutional reforms that we would equate with a set of governmental localising practices. Such a project has the potential to contradict itself as it attempts to purify the public sphere, suppressing local autonomy in the name of self-government. Potentially it anaesthetises precisely the sort of surprising settings that Phil Cohen has characterised elsewhere as 'the urban uncanny'.[30]

Intercultural dialogue is premised upon transcending particular kinds of subjectivity. It is about escaping, however momentarily, particular forms of disciplined selves and sharing something with a stranger, communicating across boundaries that might only be the product of time and space but are no less powerful for being so. A crude caricature might be that in a Habermasian invocation of the city the exigencies of time and space become obstructions to effective communication. Transcultural dialogue is merely obscured by contingency. Yet perhaps there is something extraordinarily naïve about the manner in which such optimism draws on an implicitly behaviourist understanding of both temporality and spatiality. Just as there has been a postcolonial critique that is founded on the ambiguities of *authoritative history* that disabuses this notion of transparent time,[31] we might look to an urbanism that rescues Simmel's sensory overload through an acknowledgement of the plural (and at times incommensurable) worlds of the city. As we described in Chapter 1, this is not a moment of relativism as much as a moment of anti-anti-relativism.

There is a sense in which we are created as racialised and gendered subjects, in part through the regimes of spatiality and temporality in which we are recognised. This might point to an understanding of both temporality and spatiality as constitutive of subjectivity rather than just as arenas in which subjectivity is performed and hailed. It might also suggest that we need to pay closer attention to the times and places at which sublime moments of identification occur which challenge the taken-for-granted self and look to both an aesthetic *and* an ethics of the production of public space.

10 The plan

Knowing urbanism: between the allure of the cosmopolitan and the horror of the postcolony[1]

In the autumn of 2001 a report published by Bradford City Council, authored by Herman Ouseley – one-time head of the Commission for Racial Equality – diagnosed the causes of the disturbances of that year principally in terms of the segregated geographies of 'white' and 'Asian' communities. Echoing an earlier equivalence made by Robert Park between social distance and geographical space, the extreme forms of social segregation witnessed in the city were blamed for promoting civil collapse. Social malaise was written as spatial configuration.

At almost the same time Ken Livingstone – looking down from the thirtieth floor of César Pelli's 1 Canada Square – stood in Canary Wharf Group's board-room and gave a diagnosis of why he believed that London had not witnessed similar disorders to those seen in northern cities of the United Kingdom earlier in the summer. London had had its riots in 1981 – he said – and had learnt from them and so history would not repeat itself, not even apparently as farce. In a narrative that figures the city as increasingly comfortable with its own ethnic diversity, postcolonial London was apparently framed by a Whiggishly progressive history. London – or so it appeared – knew better. This was an interesting way to historicise London's present.

In contrast, for Theodor Adorno 'history had no meaning in itself, but only in reference to the present, and then only as a critical concept which demystified the present'.[2] Similarly, Walter Benjamin expressed an allied suspicion of the chronological ordering of things. Benjamin's work has commonly been taken as a cautionary tale, urging the academy to be suspicious of narratives of the temporal, a warning to the reader of the fabricated nature of the historiographic artefact.

What would it mean to have a similarly cautious take on the postcolonial city? If we were to be as suspicious about the spatial ordering of things as Benjamin and Adorno were about the nature of the historical narrative, how might we come to terms with the ambivalent stew of cosmopolitan hope and racist intolerance of global cities such as London? How do we map the increasingly multicultural condition that defines contemporary urbanism? These are the diagnostic characteristics that are simultaneously sources of hope and despair in the city that claims to be capital of the twenty-first century. Both the colonial legacies of the population and the imperial imprimatur of the global networks of the London economy have left their mark on the city. They point to the possibility of a metropolis that not only predates the existence of the nation state but may also survive it. But what sort of analytical frame is most helpful in making sense of this place that is always both visible and invisible – a city where the past is always present and the here always subsumes a frequently colonial elsewhere? How is it possible to name the parts of rhizomatic multiculture that constitute contemporary postcolonial London?

In this context it is instructive to remember that the spirit of collaboration between Adorno and Benjamin was displaced at times by the attempt to translate shared insights into the maelstrom of the contemporary urbanism of their time. Adorno became increasingly impatient, not only with Benjamin's inability to complete his work on Paris – what has become known as the Arcades Project – but also with his perennial obsessions with the empirical found objects of the city at the expense of theoretical synthesis. Their correspondence provides an interesting reflection on the relative merits of intellectual labour (or 'theory') and ('empirical') engagement with the tumult of the city. By 1938 Adorno was increasingly suspicious of the constellatory methods of allusion so central to Benjamin's prose. He reprimanded him for his recourse to surrealist juxtaposition and refusal to reconstruct social reality 'through an immanent dialectical analysis'.[3] Adorno comments:

> One might express it this way: the theological motif of calling things by their names has a tendency to reverse into the astonished presentation of simple facts. If one wished to speak very drastically, one could say that the study has settled at the crossroads of magic and positivism. That spot is bewitched. Only theory could break the spell – your own determined, good speculative theory.[4]

The *convolutes* of the Arcades Project are evidence of Benjamin's refusal to privilege particular representational regimes in articulating the meaning of the city. When younger, Benjamin attended the lectures of Georg Simmel, whose influence is readily seen in his work. In Simmel's seminal essay on 'that synthesis of nearness and remoteness which constitutes the formal position of the stranger', he addresses some of the core concepts that link the concerns of moral philosophy to the spatialisation of the urban that are central to this chapter. For Simmel, the stranger organises the unity of remoteness and distance that defines all human relations, so that 'distance means that he who is close by is far, and strangeness means that he who also is far is actually near'.[5] This interplay of perspectival movements between closeness and distance[6] correlates directly with the privileging of different kinds of city view – central to earlier chapters of this volume – and different genres of urban knowledge that later become central to Benjamin's own essays on photography and the work of art in the age of mechanical reproduction.[7]

It is perhaps an exploration of this double interplay between closeness and distance, strange and familiar that might help us to understand not only Benjamin's unfinished work but also the particular incommensurabilities of the postcolonial present and its valorised urbanistic cognate, the cosmopolitan.[8] As such, this chapter attempts to explore the uncertain cartographies of the post-colonial city in a way that avoids both instant empirical anachronism and the sort of privileged speculative theoretical exegesis Adorno advocated.

In this sense this chapter considers the manner in which spatial ordering of the urban returns us to the notion of the plan. In concluding this volume we might wish to consider how the temporalities of globalisation challenge the spatialised political imaginaries of the cosmopolitan city. This is not an attempt to reassert a singular rationality of the metropolis. In twenty-first-century urbanism the utopian will to power is confounded by the pluralisation of the spaces of the city that has already been explored in earlier chapters. In this limited sense architectural theorists and practitioners such as Boeri, Koolhaas and Kwinter[9] celebrate the existing multiplicities of city life. Through both the exponential growth of the third world megalopolis in Africa and Asia and the hyper-accelerations of global capitalism in Europe and North America, the governance of the metropolis cannot identify a *singular rationality* or *plausible urban theory*, and so some architectural writing in particular searches instead for understandings of the generic conditions of urbanism and the intensities of the vital city.[10] In contrast, this chapter inverts such a problematic, questioning the ways in which spatial and chronological ordering is used to make narrative sense of the urban.

Through such a route we might reconsider both the politics and the technology of the plan. This is, first, because the attempt to rationalise the city may not succeed, but the (frequently failing) attempts to govern the city through ordering its spatial form (and addressing its challenging ecology) remain. Consequently, architectural urbanism sometime loses a sense of the *politics of the plan* even whilst architectural practice simultaneously becomes increasingly implicated in envision-ing the future of urbanism through more limited interventions in the built form in acts of site-specific master-planning. So the second reason for reconsidering the technologies of the plan is that the cosmopolitan challenges the relations between time and space in the city, and questions the temporality that defines the *public interest* in a rapidly changing demographic in a manner which returns us to an older literature about the interplay between closeness, distance and the politics of the stranger in the city.

In particular there is a threefold metaphoric equivalence between some of the key longstanding debates in moral philosophy, contemporary urbanism and race thinking (or raciology). In these seemingly distinct rhetorical worlds there is a homology in the replicated tension between the liberal and the communitarian, the tension between the city of strangers and the regulated metropolis, and the tension between the recognition of difference and notions of racial equality.[11] And whilst both multiculture and the city can be narrated through frames of the temporal and the spatial they cannot be reduced to their histories or geographies. In mapping the interests of the individual, the collective or the culture we speak directly to the ethical basis of regulation and governance in the city. So if we are to understand the manner in which the spatial configuration of the multicultural repeats the homologous tensions of moral philosophy and raciology, then we might need to think differently about both the need to regulate and plan the cosmopolitan city and the unstable and contingent foundations on which such interventions will be set.

Yet, in the wake of a burgeoning fascination with diaspora populations across the humanities and social sciences, it has become a commonplace to invoke the cosmopolitan as both an ethically progressive way of being and an aspirational goal of becoming.[12] As Aihwa Ong pointedly comments in her critique of the term's popularity in the academy:

> The new interest in diasporas and cosmopolitanism registers a special moment in interdisciplinary studies that seeks to invoke political significance in cultural phenomena that can be theorised as resisting the pillaging of global capitalism as well as the provincialism of metropolitan centers.[13]

As ever at the heart of debates a linguistic uncertainty surrounds the term itself. Though it is not germane to explore such inconsistencies and contradictions here, these range from a common erasure of governance that was so central to Kant's original coinage of the term, through to a tension between the cosmopolitan as mere descriptor of a mosaic of 'perpetual peace' and a more kaleidoscopic invocation of the term that privileges the contact zones and mixing that is frequently implied.[14]

The city invoked as the crucible of difference

In particular, when the ethical allure of the cultural mixing of the hybrid is translated into practical realisation it is to the city that cultural analysts look. From diverse positions in contemporary cultural theory, Appadurai, Bhabha, Clifford, Hall all invoke the privileged space of the city within the realisation of the cosmopolitan. In the case of Britain, '"cosmopolitan communities" – marked by extensive transculturation [are said to be] transforming many British cities into multicultural metropolises'.[15] In part this might be seen as no more than an empiricist demographic. Yet perhaps this is not the case. In a world after September 11, where in London the kids coming home from the war may have fought on either side and the urban myths of returning Taliban heroes abound, there is an urgency in asking if the narrative role of the city in these structures of logic is of more than peripheral significance. Indeed there is some reason to ask if the city can bear the weight of this burden of the expectations of cultural theorists. Are the spaces that remain marked by everyday racisms of racial attacks, institutionalised disadvantage and systemic discrimination worthy of being the repositories of such hope?

It is imperative to consider carefully the dynamics of the contemporary city that might help to qualify both the more utopian claims of the cosmopolitical and the more casual invocations of contemporary urbanism within political and social theory.[16] This foregrounding of the city contrasts with the increasingly implausible organising force of the nation state that is analytically implicit in much traditional political theory.

It is also essential to consider the extent to which such ethical positions might be realised in civic action. The manner in which the city becomes an analytical or theoretical object is a theme that has run throughout this book. This concluding chapter attempts to reframe questions that interrogate the manner in which it might be possible to plan the cosmopolitan. The homology between race thinking, moral philosophy and the languages of urbanism might point to a reconfiguration of the politics of city change and the notion of the city planner.[17]

Studies of nationalism have commonly identified the historical and geographical production of imagining and tradition that identifies rhetorically at the heart of the liberal nation states a combination of civic allegiance and citizenship rights, along-side a kinship or imagined bloodline and national allegiance.[18] But both the notion of civic association based on national citizenship rights and the unifying force of cultural sentiment look increasingly less plausible in the contemporary metropolis. The contemporary city shatters such – albeit somewhat hypothetical – couplings of nation and state in liberal democracy in two ways. It does so because through new globalised networks of affiliation and sentiment the citizens of the city may identify with causes and imagined communities that transcend national boundaries. This may apply to causes that link on a global basis – movements of NGOs, struggles against capitalism or social movements based on ecological or environmental concerns.[19]

In corollary fashion identification with the consciously transnational is mirrored in the emergence of narratives of universally localising identification. The city commonly witnesses the paradoxical emergence of a *global familiar*. In the contemporary metropolis the strategic neighbourhood-based principles of mobilisation developed by the sociologist Saul Alinsky – aligned with the value-based commitment to knowable artefacts of 'home', 'community' and 'family' – can be identified as the source of a new form of democratic participation that foregrounds the familiar 'local' but stretches transnationally.[20] In just one example, faith-based neighbourhood mobilisations have been transported to East London through the foundation of TELCO (The East London Community Organisation). TELCO is directly inspired by the work of Alinsky and the events in Texas where the Industrial Areas Foundation provided influential forebears within the political landscape that generated George W. Bush.[21] They link back to Texas in training programmes and information exchanges that attempt to share the Alinsky-style model of direct action and participatory democracy. Both draw on an appeal to a global universalism that privileges a politics of identification with the familiar causes of neighbourhood concern and the *known local*: mobilising school governing bodies and youth groups around construction jobs for local communities and the planning rights of religious buildings.

But the city also breaks the rhetoric of the liberal nation state in a second way, more prosaically. It does so empirically because the very demography of the city is increasingly able to sustain contacts with family, diasporic and other transnational sentiments of identification. Robin Reid, father of the shoe bomber, describes himself as a cockney born within the sound of Bow Bells.[22] His son found disillusionment with the broken promises of British belonging in the prison cells of the state's jails and the newly emblematic networks that link to Brixton mosque, the site that ties Reid to Zacarias Moussaui, the twentieth hijacker.

Diasporic communities have an increasingly straightforward ability to sustain transnational affiliations; configurations of closeness and distance are subverted by cheap flights, the telephone, the internet, the cable television and the video link. Transport networks make it possible to confound conventional models of chain migration culminating in family reunification. A young Bengali man in East London in the 1990s described to Phil Cohen the affiliation with familiar relatives and friends in Sylhet and Toronto as more powerful and more imaginatively proximate than those with his neighbours on the uncanny landscape of the Isle of Dogs.[23]

This tension between the strange and the familiar is a longstanding one throughout social and political theory. At its most stark, in the work of Kant the hard boundaries between rationality and sentiment distinguish the obligations of justice from the imperatives of loyalty. Such tensions become central organising themes of debates in moral philosophy that, either with Habermas return to Kantian typologies as the foundation of liberal democratic organising principles, or prefer instead to provide various formulations for the accommodation of difference within the political imaginary.[24]

Strange and familiar, close and distant, cultural particularity and universal rights. These mark out not so much boundary parameters as poles of iteration. The terrain of debate differs, but the choreography in respectively moral philosophy, theoretical urbanism and race thinking is remarkably similar. And when they come together in debates around the cosmopolitan future of the metropolis it is important to understand the dynamic tension between these poles.

This agonism at the heart of the tension between the liberal and the communitarian readings of justice and loyalty that resonates at the heart of debates about the nature of contemporary multiculture finds a homology in debates within contemporary urbanism. Conventionally, axiomatic resolution of the tensions between abstracted justice and family-rooted loyalty rests in the liberal tradition on a strict separation of private and public spheres. Feminist theory, and the weight of work around studies of the empirical realisation of such distinctions, have repeatedly revealed the tendentious and ethically contentious basis for such typologies. Invariably, both history and geography have the potential to provide narrative accounts of such agonism that naturalises the contingent and inserts generalising explanation in the place of empirical caution. At times the city provides a ready catch-all conceptual residuum: either the *stage* of resolution of such dynamics through the inevitability of mixing or the *site* through which such tensions are contained in what Rushdie describes as the *locus classicus* of impossible realities of the urban or Bhabha prefers to cite as the incommensurabilities of city experience.[25]

In their urban form these processes are also not free of the economic bases of cities. In one of the most powerful foundational descriptions of the city as a metaphoric extension of the factory – suppressing difference through homogenisation – Engels compellingly described the power of the capitalist city to anonymise corporeally, to make the familiar appear strange.

The manufacturer is capital, the operative labour. And if the operative will not be forced into this abstraction, if he insists that he is not labour but a man, who possesses, among other things, the attribute of labour-force, if he takes it into his head that he need not allow himself to be sold and bought in the market, as the commodity 'labour', the bourgeois reason comes to a standstill. He cannot comprehend that he holds any other relation to the operative than that of purchase and sale; he sees in them not human beings, but *hands* as he constantly calls them to their *faces* (emphasis added).[26]

It is possible to unpack some of this conceptual residuum by thinking through the realisation of the racialised tensions between the strange and the familiar in the fabric of the city and the languages of urbanism.[27] In doing so it is necessary to ask what sort of imagery can portray such contradiction and incommensurability in the landscapes of the metropolis.

How the postcolonial city disrupts racial narratives: the limits of the mutlticultural

In political rejections of racism and ethnocentrism the tension between recognition of particularity and difference, on the one hand, and demands for civic equality, on the other, reproduce the binary logics of debates between the liberal and the communitarian. In an important article, Stuart Hall[28] – drawing on the psychoanalytic resolutions of such work and the work of Butler and Laclau – has argued that it is important to go beyond such stale alternatives, through the reconceptualisation of the incomplete nature of both the universal and the particular, defined in terms of their constitutive lack.

Suggesting that what can no longer be sustained is the binary contrast of 'their' claims for particularity and recognition of difference versus 'our' claims of universal civic value (in juxtapositions of 'the west and the rest'), he speaks to the need for a new political logic that unsettles culture and identity. But the contradictions and incommensurabilities of the communitarian/liberal debate are not so much resolved as subsumed within a spatiality: 'the moment of difference is essential to defining democracy as a genuinely heterogeneous space'.[29] Incommensurability and an agonistic notion of the democratic is conflated within the heterogeneity of space.[30] Like 'the ghetto' earlier in this volume, the spaces of the city reconcile the seemingly irreconcilable in social theory.

At the logical conclusion of his argument Hall echoes Paul Gilroy's imprecations to go beyond 'raciology' in calls for both 'a deepening expansion and radicalisation of democratic practices in our social life; and the unrelenting contestation of every form of racialised and ethnicised exclusionary closure'.[31] However, it is less clear how such a theoretical closure translates into the mass of social movements that occur under the sign of race, precisely because it almost works within an implicit model of the state that places racial thinking and categorisation as disconnected from the mimetic processes through which the conduct of conduct emerges, as explored in the consideration, in earlier chapters, of the relation between governmental form and racialised 'subjects'. The former is perhaps a tautologous good. The latter appears to contradict Hall's own workings of the notion of arbitrary closure in a politics of race. In what follows I want to explore some of these uncertainties through the specificities of the multicultural urban.

City spaces: do we dare to plan the postcolonial city?

Thinking about the spaces of political settlement and ethical contest in the city refigures the way in which we might consider the city plan. The plan's appeal rests on a normative sense of being able *to know* that everything has its proper place, an appeal to a preferred model of land use. But the problematisation of the temporal and the cartographic disrupts the way in which technocratic forms of regulation configure land use and privilege a specific genre of metropolitan rationality.

In one sense the sheer scale of twenty-first-century global metropolitan expansion resurrects debates about planning that are inflected by our new ethical compass. Put crudely, the Keynesian welfare state nostrums of the post-1945 decades valorised land-use planning within a set of technocratic tools of social engineering whose beneficial use was privileged as part of the received wisdom and consensual political settlement of Europe and North America at the time. The Reagan–Thatcher neo-liberalism of the 1980s and 1990s vilified such a consensus and challenged the legitimacy of all forms of social engineering (including that of land-use planning). Significantly, the liberalism of the right shared elements of the critique of state-based social engineering with a liberalism of the left that also focused on the legitimacy of state-based identification of the will and the interest of the people and the city. Yet the scale of growth of twenty-first-century cities across the world highlights in Lagos, New York or Shanghai a need to consider simultaneously the economy of public goods, the provision of physical infrastructure and the ordering of the metropolis. So, for reasons that are as much ecological as ideological, the plan returns to capitalist New York and communist Shanghai, at times mediated through architectural languages and visual cultures of master-planning *parts* of the city as much as a will to rationalise the *whole* metropolis.

The 1940s attempts to plan a postwar London in many ways exemplify the scale of the social engineering ambitions of the Keynesian welfare state settlement, its detailed ambition and an unproblematic, unselfconscious articulation of the public good. In the *County of London Plan* and the *Greater London Plan* Patrick Abercrombie proposed that he would lend London 'order, efficiency and beauty and spaciousness' which would bring an end to 'violent competitive passion'.[32] In contrast, the tentative attempts of London's new mayor to create a new plan for twenty-first-century London are more limited in their ambition, though strikingly sanguine about the scale of change predicted for the capital in the short to medium term. *Towards the London Plan* suggests from the year 2001 that 'there could be an increase of around 700,000 people in the next fifteen years'.[33] The report also notes that because of changing lifestyle patterns and demographics this could translate into a demand for approximately 500,000 new households over approximately the same period of time.[34] This vision for the scale of change of London was endorsed by the Office of the Deputy Prime Minister in John Prescott's plan for creating 'Sustainable Communities' to the east of London on a scale as great or greater than those in the London Plan.[35]

Although it attracted little publicity at the time of publication, the London Plan also noted the significant probability that renewed growth in migrant flows would account for a significant fraction of this growing population, and that international in-migration was increasing rapidly and had already averaged about 56,000 people per year annually over the decade of the 1990s. The increasing cultural diversity of London was expected to result in an increase in 'non-white ethnic minorities' from 27 per cent of the population in 2001 to 31 per cent in 2011.[36]

The scale of growth and development envisioned like a photographic negative focuses on those spaces of the urban that are vulnerable to development pressures. Architecturally translated as voids, empty spaces or disused industrial lands, fragments of the city's morphology will be subjected to the designs and dreams of those who would reinvent the metropolis. The Chicago School depiction of zones of transition slips neatly into an increasingly transnational set of discourses about the city and incorporate practices exercised on the fabric of the city that fit within the rubric of *urban regeneration*. And in this process the representation of what might be, as well as what is and what once was in these parts of the city, will become central to narratives of urbanism that seek both to know through design and create new spaces for this extraordinary scale of growth.

In planning discourse such concerns are rationalised within a technocratic rhetoric that identifies a configuration of land uses that privileges an implicit – or at times explicit – appeal to the interest of the totality of the city. The putative essence of the metropolis becomes the spatial horizon of the political imaginary. In London, significantly, the growth is expected to focus on the eastern 'Thames Gateway' sector of the capital: 63 per cent of the capacity for development in London from 'very large sites' lies in the (largely post-industrial or 'brown-field') Gateway. And in positing the sort of urbanism that will be the result of such change the plan eschews the programmatic cartographies of Abercrombie's plot numbers and prefers instead to suggest that 'These sites offer particular scope for "urban village" type development.'[37]

Trends in urbanism that move between the strange and the familiar likewise reproduce the structural characteristics of the dialectical tension between sentiment and rationality. The importance of the urban realisation of the debate between liberals and communitarians in the structure of the cosmopolitan is consequently crucial to any thinking about how we might plan the multicultural urban.

Calls for an urban renaissance that were built into the British government's White Paper on the City,[38] and a plethora of consequent policy initiatives, are characteristically unsure about the degree to which the city can be *known* by its citizens, inhabitants and rulers. More profoundly, there is an ambivalence about the degree to which it is desirable that it should be known. More particularly, a progressive politics of urbanism that appeals to languages of citizenship and *la droit de la ville* may rest on a spatialised vocabulary that masks its incommensurability with a politics that takes as the city's fundamental ethical aspiration the creation of forms of engagement where strangers might meet in public.

The stranger has long been an ambivalent figure in narratives of the city. In thirteenth-century London:

> It is indicative of the close watch kept on upon all citizens that there were also regulations about private and social arrangements. Every aspect of life was covered by an elaborate network of law, ordinance and custom. No 'stranger' was allowed to spend more than one day and one night in a citizen's house, and no one might be harboured within a ward 'unless he be of good repute'.[39]

Much city thought can almost be classified by the degree to which the stranger is variously valorised or controlled. Specifically, there are two very different traditions of thinking about the city that – conflated within most social policy discussions of urban regeneration and renaissance – parallel distinctions between liberal and communitarian strands of argument already outlined. And whilst they are conflated within some kinds of writing about the city they may be less easily reconciled in their realisations in the multicultural metropolises of everyday life.

Using the development of public spaces as ways of involving all citizens of all incomes and classes, recent work by the mayor's Architecture and Urbanism Unit in London speaks to the possibility of the built form providing an active staging of urban civilisation. The refashioning of Trafalgar Square is just the most symbolically weighted such intervention. The overall register of speech within the celebration of the public space is in part an acknowledgement of the significance of the stranger for the city. At times this can sound like the murmuring of a privileged middle class that might be more at home in Periclean Athens than in Birkenhead, but it is important to consider the liberal philosophical convictions that underscore the occasionally aestheticised liberal sentiment that such structures of feeling bring into focus.

This register links intellectually to an agenda that draws on the work of Arendt, Bookchin, Habermas, Benhabib, Fraser and Sennett, and to a politics that relates to the liberal ethics that privileges notions of citizenship, rights and tolerance. The most recent government White Paper opens with the quote from Richard Rogers that 'People make cities but cities make citizens'.[40] The notion of the city treating alien strangers with dignity has similarly profound philosophical roots.[41] It is premised in part on a valorisation of the city as fundamentally unknowable, an invocation of urbanism that celebrates both the sensory overload of everyday life and the civic advantages of anonymity.[42] It correlates directly with both a liberal tradition that demands a categoric set of values at the heart of city citizenship and both a left- and right-wing notion of how the individual is figured within such a calculus. Both in the privileging of market relations between individuals and in its collective notions of human rights it speaks to a notion that in the public realm individuals should be treated according to abstract principles based on demonstrable argument rather than populist rendering of the will of the people.

Such a way of thinking contrasts with a writing about the city that sees each community providing a moral universe within the ecological mosaic of the whole. In this second register 'the community' becomes the source of moral value, and the ethical compass of the city needs to be set against the polar north of the known social unit of the neighbourhood. It links intellectually to an agenda that sees the promotion of the conduct of civil life at its heart. It has architectural correlates in the strong model of new urbanism that emanates from the Congress for New Urbanism that has assumed an almost ascendant ideological position in small-town USA, the practices of D/PZ (Duany/Plater-Zyberk),[43] and the legacies of urban villages and Prince Charles's Krier-inspired experiments in urban design. It has ethical correlates that valorise the 'knowability' of the neighbourhood and places the sociability of community above the anonymity of the civilised crowd.[44]

In programmes of neighbourhood renewal the plaintive appeal to bring local people into models of urban change simultaneously conjures up longstanding debates about the relative values of participatory and representative democracy. But, more significantly, this produces a different sort of politics. The privileging of an almost anthropological valorisation of community values also does not have a necessary correspondence with a politics of the right or the left. An authoritarian social reform agenda can at times be traced from the early Jane Jacobs through to the more recent communitarianism of Etzioni. In such metonymic readings of the city of bits, the politics of the metropolis can in part be seen through the logic of the fractal. Although each city is unique, the nature of the whole can be seen in the smallest part. Analytically this is not the way the world is. Ethically this is not the way we might want cities to be.

But equally an ethnographic relativism can privilege the plural (and incommensurable) moral worlds of difference and the corresponding autonomy of distinctive moral communities within the city. Such questions might seem arcane until they translate into the juxtaposition of 'bog standard' comprehensive education with a valorisation of church schools that immediately foregrounds the multiplicity of religious possibilities within the state-aided education sector. Similarly, the ready celebration of faith communities within the city may conveniently ignore the fact that the polis is characterised in most Enlightenment political philosophy precisely by its absence of theological debate. But most importantly these communitarianisms of both left and right are simply not reconcilable with the liberalisms (of left and right) outlined above.

It is at the boundaries between the secular and the religious, the private and the public, the neighbourhood and the metropolis, that very different cities begin to emerge in the normative theorising of contemporary urbanism. It is possible for Richard Rogers to quote Arendt and for the White Paper to invoke notions of citizenship. But to do either without seeing how alternative traditions of urbanism would project their preferred models of the city into alternative (and possibly incommensurable) formulations of the built form is to hide within the language of an urban renaissance a political debate about *la droit de la ville*.

City spaces 2: multiculture in the contact zone of the postcolonial city

Multiculturalism is both empirically incontestable and normatively contingent. As Stuart Hall has pointed out, it is the refusal of the latter alongside a blindness to the former that makes the contemporary a moment of such danger.[45]

Well over a quarter of London's population is already defined as coming from within ethnic minority groupings. Moreover, in places the fragility of the homogenising power of majoritarian whiteness falls apart under historical trajectories that contrast Jewish, Irish Catholic, Celtic Presbyterian and low-church legacies, the traces of which are part of the *objets trouvés* of the psycho-geographer's *dérive* through the city. In this context it is important to focus simultaneously on the truly complex disruptions to racial thinking that cartographies of the city might provide, alongside a sense of the persistence of singularly pre-modern articulations of intolerance and bigotry that remain.

In the wake of September 11, most parts of the United Kingdom reported a rise in violently Islamophobic attacks in British cities. In just one case, one of the poorest communities in London have together raised £60,000 to spend on two railway arches to create the Limehouse Mosque and Bangladeshi Cultural Association. On 14 January 2002 two fires were started deliberately within the mosque by a group of white men seen to break into the venue. The ensuing fire gutted the mosque and left little of the refurbishment work undamaged.

In East London, a few hundred metres away from the fire, a Victorian terrace of houses is now almost exclusively occupied by Lithuanian families. At the corner of Settle Street and Fordham Street a school named after the national poet of Bengal – Kobi Nazrul – stands opposite an unmarked shop which offers travel and welfare support to the Lithuanian community by day and at night in the summer sells beer and coffee, breaching all licensing laws. It is tempting to relapse into a Chicago School notion of succession, even though such a narrative obscures contingent processes and normalises change within a frame that represents parts of the city as the natural site of migrant settlement.

In East London in 2001 a survey examining the languages in most need of translation for public services other than English in Tower Hamlets demonstrated that when the numbers of Russian, Lithuanian, Albanian and Polish requests were aggregated, the demand for Eastern European language services collectively now exceeds that for Sylheti translation.[46] Though not reproduced within a demographic that includes several generations of British-born English-fluent citizens of Bangladeshi origin, the figures are significant. Multiculture in the UK becomes increasingly complex; whiteness likewise. London is increasingly witnessing new migrant flows from the former Soviet bloc that might disrupt the conventional race relations (paradoxically plural) binary framing of BME ('black and minority ethnic') and 'white' communities.[47]

So the configuration of race politics in the United Kingdom is changing rapidly. The categoric certainties of the couplet 'Black and Asian' (and its policy correlate 'BME') will increasingly be unable to address the complexity of the multicultural realities of tomorrow's London. The eugenicists' nightmare of 'race mixing' and the melanin rainbow of the new migrations of London's twenty-first century shatter such reassuring typologies. Straightforwardly, the debates about asylum seeking and refugee settlement barely conceal a pent-up demand for labour in the United Kingdom that is promoting new waves of migration, as the London Plan tacitly concedes. A recent Audit Commission report suggests that the numbers of people claiming asylum in the United Kingdom rose from '25,000 applications in 1990 to over 70,000 in both 1999 and 2000'.[48] The report identifies the fiscal advantages of moving from bed and breakfast accommodation into the provision of longer-term 'private sector accommodation'. Translated into the landscapes of London, the supply of these new forms of rental accommodation are often on the sink estates of the capital. Within the cost-cutting logic of the system there is commensurate pressure to concentrate asylum seekers in such sites. As the dry terms of the same Audit Commission report suggest, in some cases 'asylum seeking families have been able to stay with family or friends who have already settled into existing communities. This is the cheapest option as, in such cases, authorities have only provided subsistence, significantly reducing the overall cost of support.'[49]

Putting to one side the Jesuitical debate on the distinction between economic migrants and authentic asylum seekers, the administrative minutiae falsify two shibboleths that are pervasive in the common sense of the multicultural city.

The first is the notion of natural succession that invokes diagnostically liminal spaces of a city subjected to waves of cultural change that are mediated by the fabrication and reconstruction of the ghetto. Buried in the prosaic contemporary transformations of social housing, and the emergence of a new boom in the private rental sector in the contemporary UK, lies a mechanistic set of processes whereby the new migrations are being translated into housing classes that would make John Rex or Ray Pahl feel almost nostalgic. The new Rachmans appear through Margaret Thatcher's legacy of *right to buy* legislation that makes it entirely logical to buy up state-provided social housing in the name of empowering local residents, creating a residualised housing rental market characterised by long-term disinvestment and high rental values. Historically, the lodging houses and doss houses of Catholic Wapping in the mid nineteenth century, or the Jewish East End described in detail by Bill Fishman,[50] in part gave way to the ghetto of Michael Banton's coloured quarter, focusing on the red light district of Cable Street. Iconically this in turn was displaced by the perversely Weberian, bureaucratically rational segregations of state housing provision in the postwar era of social engineering that gave us Pruitt Igoe and Broadwater Farm. The ghetto is erased and reconstructed, but it is invariably a creation of specific moments of economic change and is mediated through particular regimes of regulation and control. Racialised cartographies of *residence* are always realised through the translation of governmental definitions of *settlement*. The banal minutiae of forms of rent control, allocations of tenure, the role of social landlords (registered social landlords, local authorities, housing associations), and the uncertain future of council housing structure the seemingly natural patterning of ethnic diversity of the city.

Second, the creation of 'community', a reflexively ethnic presence, is not now and has never been separated from the regimes of governmentality that not only circumscribe but also in part constitute both the new and the old formations of diasporic settlement. The structures of the state and the imperatives of government may appear to occupy the role of the constitutive outside that lends an imaginary horizon to the mobilisation of Kurdish marchers in the Strand, Somali communities demanding welfare rights in Whitechapel, or black communities demanding justice in the face of the institutional racism of the criminal justice system. But if in Foucauldian terms the boundary of state and civil society is invariably a transactional one, then the struggle for community is in part precisely a struggle about the nature of these transactions. From the decrees of 883 through which King Alfred foreshadowed apartheid when he allowed continuing Danish presence in London but confined it to the east of the River Lea, through to the explicitly geographical practices of SUS laws in the 1970s,[51] the governmental cartography of London has always been a racialised artefact.

When the two shibboleths that render the city visible as a natural plane of migrant settlement are dismissed, then two alternative (and relatively straightforward) organising principles can be seen to lie at the heart of the cosmopolitan city. The first principle is that political economy provides a material causality from which the cosmopolitan is fashioned. It is political in that it is inescapably located within particular regulatory regimes, and economic in that is invariably associated with *processes of commodification* that structure the contact zones of the urban.[52] The second organising principle is that in tracing the markers of race and ethnicity across the spaces of the city, the mapping of cultural difference brings with it the realisation of an iterative and at times *mimetic relationship* between place and the politics of identity.

First principle: commodification in the contact zone

It is a truism that migration is about the flow of one of the key factors of production as much as it is about the movement of people; that consequently multiculture needs always to be related to the flows of migrant labour and the multicultural city seen as patterned by the economic drivers of labour demand and the racial division of labour. Famously, the Communist Manifesto asserted that 'the bourgeoisie has through its exploitation of the world market given a cosmopolitan character to production and consumption in every country'.[53] In this context the contact zones of transnational flow are shaped out of relations that are simultaneously economic and cultural.

Much has been done to rescue the hidden histories of community struggles against racism and discrimination of diasporic communities settling in London and other major metropolises.[54] But these progressive stories of community building and resistance sit alongside less valorised tales that have a powerfully disruptive force that is no less significant in making sense of the simultaneous terms of trade of culture and commodity. It is in the hidden histories of the processes of racial-isation of London that the counterintuitive suddenly becomes visible, disrupting

the reassuring narratives of just-in-time production processes and cultural reproduction, the personifications of globalisation and a nuanced cosmopolitanism that
captures transnational realities.

In the East End of London and elsewhere a cast list of alternative historical
characters awaits discovery. Each in turn made money and reconfigured the
racialised labour markets of cosmopolitan capitalism in – respectively – the rag
trade, the restaurant sector and the sweated labour and development markets. Asil
Nadir was the chair of Polly Peck International and the nemesis of both Michael
Mates MP[55] and Deputy Assistant Commissioner Wyn Jones.[56] Nadir, who made
his fortune in the rag trade, was a high-profile casualty of the 1980s downturn and
his former headquarters was subsequently occupied by the East London and City
Health Authority. He sustained economic links and massive chains of formal and
informal employment that tied Turkish Cyprus to Sylheti leather traders in the
East End and major retail chains in the West End of the city throughout the early
1980s.[57] Musar Patel, whose life was plagiarised by Farukh Dhondy in the BBC
drama *King of the Ghetto*, and whose Pakistani origins were at times challenged in
Brick Lane's authenticity auction (because he was not Sylheti), was an early
promoter of the more up-market Indian cuisine that is now taken as a driving force
of cosmopolitan London (at the Clifton Restaurant) and who was famous for
borrowing electricity from the street-lighting circuits. Roy Sandhu's boom-and-
bust affluence generated both national press headlines and large business growth
that began in the UK but became a major corporate influence on the Indian
subcontinent. Roy – of the eponymous Roy's Corner in Aldgate – was famous in
the 1980s both for employing significant local white politicians and for his proposal
to build a tower almost as tall as César Pelli's 1 Canada Square[58] on the corner of
Aldgate roundabout that his employees were expected to deliver. These are just
three of numerous individuals pioneering survival in the niche economies of the
metropolis that provide an alternative – and often far less attractive – form of
cultural exchange that structures the emergence of migrant communities and
networks of association at any point in the history of the city.

These economic 'contact zones' may be less glamorous than fashion, less
cutting-edge than contemporary artistic expression. But they became part of the
cultural fabric that defines the constitutive heterogeneity of London and reveals
the creation of networks and engagements that were invariably commodified and
never free of the entangling but ever shifting boundary between state and civil
society. In this sense the political economy of migrant flows is always culturally
mediated through networks of labour demand, job recruitment and marketing of
the commodified differences implicit as much in old sources of employment in the
rag trade and the railways as in the new cultural industries that market difference
itself.

But it is also the categoric instability of the boundaries of ethnicity and the
subjects of racialisation that renders the spaces of the city singularly significant in
the articulation of both identity mimesis and political mobilisation. The city does
not merely mediate such relations, it becomes simultaneously both polis and arena
of communication.

Second principle: iconographies of certainty and cartographies of danger: mimetic urbanism

In the Arcades Project, Benjamin famously decried history for the ability of chronology to explain through 'flashing its Scotland Yard credentials'. Several decades after the peak of postwar Fordist labour migration it is similarly tempting to narrate London's cartography through commonsense mappings of the place names of multicultural Britain. Iconographies of contemporary London invoke their own racialised explanatory power; the very names of Brixton, Southall, Tottenham, Green Lanes, Eltham all resonate, freighted with cultural referents and self-confirming expectations of London's 'ethnic map'.

These iconographies both generate their own 'natural' repertoires of behaviour – the mimesis of the mirror dance – but also stand to be subverted in the performances of the everyday.[59] Promoted as 'boutique multiculture', the residents of such places may opt to turn cultural difference into scopohilic product or simultaneously undermine the certainties of their placing within London's geography. In this sense the role of Deptford networks within the diasporic resistance to the Abacha regime in 1990s Nigeria, or the presence of a transvestite Bengali dance troupe based just off Brick Lane, may equate to the more dangerous mappings of the multicultural that Benjamin would approve of. Echoes of history and the contingency of the present undermine the ambivalence of the cartographic certainty of some kinds of ethnic mapping of the city. In this sense the transnational realisations of diasporic cultures destabilise the categoric reassurance of ethnic monitoring.

In this context choosing between the celebration of the moment of hybridity or the cautionary rejection of a meeting of two purities becomes less germane than a recognition of how expressive cultures of both dominance and subordination are disrupted through what Paul Gilroy has described as the heterocultural vernacular of London life.[60] The contact zones of the city are thus a constitutive feature of the simultaneous and iterative reshaping of place and identity. They become Goffmanesque stages of contestation, subversion and disruption. In this way it may be that in hindsight we will see the Parekh Report's[61] noble attempt to reconstruct the nation in a particular kind of multicultural way as in some senses the high point of a particular kind of thinking that will soon become increasingly anachronistic. Because of both the sentimental implausibility of allegiance to the imagined nation and the empirical linking of transnational networks through the cities of the globe that become the commanding points of global flows, the metropolis is potentially displacing the nation state as both polis and site of dialogue. But even as this displacement occurs, the city itself is likewise contested, subverted and disrupted by the performance of the multicultural.

Contested

On the ley lines of London, in the park where the regicide of Charles I, Richard Brandon, is buried, many struggles define the nature of community life. Racists resist the renaming of the park in commemoration of the murdered garment worker Altab Ali in 1978, to this day painting out the sign with an extraordinary regularity. In the beginning of Bangladeshi nationalism was the word, the struggle for language recognition in the face of West Pakistani enforcement of Urdu. The site in East London is now appropriated through the presence – since 1999 – of a martyrs' memorial that cherishes the triumph of Sheikh Mujib's strand of secular left-wing nationalism over the Islamic state of Pakistan. It is simultaneously the site where in the early twenty-first century visiting imams hold seminars and the controversial Maulana Delwar Hossain Sayeedi – a former Jamaat MP in Bangladesh – has held public meetings that have been picketed by the secular-leaning Nirmul Committee. As Chapter 8 explored in greater detail, it is in short a stage where meaning is contested, dialogues of a sort between diasporic Bengali nationalism and plural forms of transnational Islam play out in the signs of graffiti, political demonstration, vernacular rumour and hidden histories. Without a reading of these signs of the street it is impossible to come to terms with very particular realisations of the juxtaposition of rationality and sentiment that render the postcolonial so contingent.

Subverted and disrupted

It is in the spatialisation of everyday practices that the continually contentious categories of identification are played out in the juxtaposition of new racisms and hybrid novelties described in exemplary fashion in the work of Les Back.[62] Likewise, in the traces of everyday life, different ethnographic projects recently completed at the Centre for Urban and Community Research in London uncover accidental archaeologies of community history that render comprehensible the particularly local moments in which identity is defined.[63]

In one South London interview a youth worker, born and brought up on what became the Milton Court Estate – identified in the Metropolitan Police's iconography of black London in the 1980s as the estate most likely to witness a repetition of the events on Broadwater Farm in 1985 – describes the archaeology of boundaries between the racialised public and the contingent interiors of sociality.[64] He describes both the exclusion of black communities from the policed public sphere and the development of cultures of the church-based network of voluntary-sector youth clubs:

> What I'm trying to say is that you had this, at the time it seems, it seems obvious but also ironic, that you had all these youth clubs that were heavily used by young black men whereas the guys you'd see on the street were white guys and you can only – it seems to me in retrospect – you can only put that down to the fact that at that point in this borough was that to be young and black and on the street was dangerous. The evidence of that is the fact that the anti SUS campaign started in Deptford and that the first conspiracy trials were in Deptford.

The notion of blackness negotiated through the musical vernaculars of the interior, and white masculinities resting their last claims to legitimacy in the streets of Deptford and New Cross in the 1980s, hardly accords with the commonsense rhetorics of that time, exemplified in Lord Scarman's notorious caricature of the British 'West Indian' community as a people of the street.[65] Likewise the hidden story of the fight against the SUS laws reveals links between black Communist Party activists exiled from South African apartheid after Sharpville and local black activists on the estates.[66]

In a corollary fashion, in the scramble for regeneration funds, racialised social policy initiatives directed towards the creation of ethnic enterprise, the participation of single parents in the workforce and the promotion of community safety create the subject positions to be inhabited by those aspiring to state funding. These fictive subjectivities echo themes explored in Chapters 5 and 9. The voluntary group that works within caricatures of black motherhood to extract state childcare support potentially may disrupt from 'inside' the caricature or merely reassert the primacy of the subjectifications of race thinking, but for community groups trying to get by in the city such nuances are less significant than the struggle for welfare provision in any name.

Nomadic practice and travelling theory in the politics of the magic carpet

So what kind of new city citizens can emerge in the cosmopolitan spaces between the strange and the familiar? To answer such a question it is perhaps best to return to the naming of racialised political subjects in the city.

The laboratory of urban interventions[67]

The architectural practice Stalker – drawing their name from Tarkovsky's film which focused on the discovery and exploration of magical zones of the city – have attempted to question what sorts of spatial practice might open up the border territories between the strange and the familiar.[68] Architectural critic Gil Doron has written extensively about the work of Stalker in his fascination with the potential of an architecture of transgression to learn from and draw on the practices of these transitional zones of the city.

Winners of the Prix Italia and exhibitors at the Venice Biennale in 2000, they toured cities of the Mediterranean with the exhibited 'Magic Carpet Project'. The project identifies the iconic significance of the Palatine Chapel in Palermo, 'originally built by Iranian craftsman in the style of an Islamic mosque'.[69] The creation of this installation piece drew together people of different origins in the construction of a combination of a sound sculpture and a mimetic object that recreated the devotional artefact as a magic carpet. According to the architects themselves, the intention was to disrupt the conventional categories of the political subject, recovering the historical links between Islam and Christianity but also reinserting new forms of political imaginary into the borderline architectural landscape of the city.[70] Stalker produced the Tappeto Volante, which they describe as:

> A re-elaboration, in rope and copper, of the wood ceiling of the Palatine Chapel in Palermo. It is accompanied by a sound travel towards the Iranic origin of the ceiling. The work is being done by a multicultural laboratory in Ararat.

Stalker have tried to concentrate on the manner in which the contradictions of capitalism are translated into the surprising geographies of the contemporary city. These are the parts of the city that are suddenly made visible by the restless gaze of capitalist growth. Concealed vernacular sites of rumour and alternative worlds, they become the acquisitive moment as well at the point of economic transformation in the land-use mappings of city planning. Stalker's work has consequently highlighted the architectural correlates of such transformation through notions of the nomadic university at Campo Boario, the shadowlands of the refugee and the situationist reappropriation of city spaces. Through such a frame of reference, what Gil Doron describes as spaces of suspension emerge in the privileged cultural contact zones of the city.

The elsewhere of postcolonial London

In his collection of essays *Means without ends*, Giorgio Agamben attempts a search for a new vocabulary of political subjectivity that can address the cosmopolitan present where national identity is rendered problematic in so many different ways. He considers a reconfiguration of the political imagination through a series of exercises that – following the 'ontological crisis' of political theory – attempt to invent new categories of political debate and discussion. Drawing on Hannah Arendt's 1943 essay 'We Refugees', he in particular has made a case for the centrality of the political subject position of the refugee:[71]

> given the now unstoppable decline of the nation state and the general corrosion of traditional political-juridical categories, the refugee is perhaps the only thinkable figure for the people of our time and the only category in which one may see today – at least until the process of dissolution of the nation state and of its sovereignty has achieved full completion – the forms and limits of a coming political community.[72]

Refiguring *the native* in the juridical order of the nation state Agamben draws on Arendt's link between the Rights of Man (and their decline) and the fate of the nation state in 'A call to build our political philosophy anew starting from the one and only figure of the refugee.'[73] He challenges both the nativity of communal sentiment and the erasure of governmental power in some received rhetorics of rationality and citizenship.

In a similar way, it is the constant iteration between the strange and the domestic that disrupts our own narratives of the city. Consciously deployed, this can be of particular significance in the translation of the incommensurability of the multicultural into the spaces of city life.[74] Agamben effectively critiques the roots of the nation state in the fiction of nativity:

> The fiction that is implicit here is that birth (nascita) comes into being immediately as nation so that there may not be any difference between the two moments. Rights, in other words, are attributed to the human being only to the degree to which he or she is the immediately vanishing presupposition (and in fact the presupposition must never come to light as such) of the citizen.[75]

In contrast, the city shares a similar fiction that connects directly with the genealogies of citizenship. The London folkmoot of 1216, which commodified the crown and which 'gave 1,000 marks to the French prince Louis in order that [he] might be consecrated as king in place of John',[76] took place at the same time as the city displayed its intense suspicion of the strange in its discipline of domestic life considered earlier, allowing only folk of good repute to stay for a night in a citizen's house. In other words the regulation of the social life of the urban was embedded in the codes and practices that were the orchestrating rules of everyday life, at the same time as a foreign prince was being manoeuvred in to displace King John by the merchants of London's square mile. In the city the strange and the familiar sit in an endlessly iterative relationship one with the other. Both the category of political citizen and the category of known neighbour are contingently constructed historically.

This sort of disruption of categories of the political subject resonates through an articulation of cultural rights in the arena of settlement and dwelling in the city. It resonates also in the transnational forms of solidarity, citizenship and belonging that form part of the multicultural present and must inform any new vocabularies of a cosmopolitan urbanism. In the UK, minority communities have based political campaigns for homes and articulated demands for recognition of housing rights through the establishment of BME Housing Associations, sometimes originating in squatting movements of the 1960s and 1970s, at other times products of a particular kind of 1980s identity politics.[77] As city multiculturalism becomes much more complex and such organisations evolve, the nature of rights and the focus of campaigns nuance likewise. In one such example, an attempt by The Monitoring Group (TMG) in Southall to intervene in policy debates and social housing provision around racial harassment in the United Kingdom draws directly on the experiences of the women's refuge movement and the notions of both recognition and equality to reconfigure the visible city.[78]

Campaigns for social housing neither necessarily reject nor necessarily accept a universalising philosophical narrative or the roots of ethnic specificity. Yet a fragmentary polis that recognises the legitimacy of identity politics potentially reifies categorically through institutions that may specify eligibility groups: gender, race, religion, sexuality, disability, (former) criminality may all become the plausible legitimate subjects through which universal provision is culturally inflected. In this sense the diversity of black and minority ethnic housing associations bears witness to both the struggles of specific communities and the acceptable manner through which race is rendered visible in the welfare provision of the means to life itself in contemporary Britain.

But it is through praxis that new spaces open up these categorisations. TMG and Asra Housing Association, along with a complex of partners and working with architects Penoyre and Prasad, have attempted to create a National Centre for Victims of Racial Harassment at the heart of Southall in West London. In the words of Sunand Prasad, the principal architect of the work, the category of *victimhood* at the heart of debates around racial harassment, made concrete through the architectural realisation of the centre, would self-consciously disrupt itself. The building is intended to intervene in the public realm but also reshape the territory of the public sphere itself. For Prasad the centre becomes simultaneously public and private, a forceful presence that makes a statement about the nature of racial violence but also provides a refuge that guarantees safety and privacy. The design drew on transcultural architectural traditions, raised gardens drawing on both the Indian vernacular and the British municipal tradition. The building was also to provide a meditative space and an aerial city panorama that goes against the grain, empowers through the masculinist politics of the view. The victimised are empowered to look down on the city from roof gardens that privilege their perspective.

But if the rendering of the city visible to the residents of the refuge attempts to reconfigure the position of the victim, the rendering of the refuge visible to the city as a public statement was consciously intended to disrupt conventional debates about racial harassment. For Prasad the proximity of Heathrow, the public profile of the centre and the ethos of the design all invoke parallels between conventional understandings of racial harassment and the treatment of victims of genocide and racial hatred who become refugees in the UK. In making connections between conventionally separated categories of *eligibility* the political subject positions of race in the multicultural city are likewise disturbed.

As practical intervention, the work of TMG, Penoyre and Prasad, and Asra Housing (never realised in bricks and mortar), disrupts the conventional categor-isations of the multicultural city. Ethically, it challenges the tensions between the knowable master-planning of multicultural difference and the privileged anony-mity of the urban. It highlights why a three-dimensional urbanism reconfigures the centrality of Arendt and Agamben's iconic *refugee*, and why a discourse of planning and technocratic intervention in the built form of the city becomes central to narratives of citizenship and belonging.

The manner in which access to dwelling and residence is racialised, and the manner in which BME housing associations respond to the new multicultures of London, echo the iterations between institutions of governance (residence and settlement in this case) and multicultural subject positions in earlier chapters of this volume. They are about much more than ethnicity but cannot be reduced to categories of race. The boundaries of inclusion and exclusion of eligibility potentially point towards broadening definitions of racialised subjectivity. This syncretism of architectural styles, the transgressing of the public and private spheres, and the disruption of conventional narratives of race was for Sunand inspired by thinking about the terms through which the *Asian* presence becomes visible in the cities of Britain. In a conscious moment of inverting the power relations of such scopic regimes, Sunand Prasad – unaware of the work of Stalker (which actually preceded chronologically Penoyre and Prasad's designs) – lit upon the metaphor of the *magic carpet* as the organising principle for the Southall project. The refuge was captured in an architectural plan sketch of a magic carpet that sits above contemporary Southall, looking down from on high, gazed at from the street yet integrated into the urban fabric from a position of scopophilic power.

Conclusion: beyond postcolonial melancholia and the cosmopolitan romance

The transnational and the global reconfigure the definition of metropolitan interest within the geographical scales of international, national and regional power. Forms of sovereignty and regimes of governmentality map uneasily on to these different geographical scales.[79] In this sense the liberal notions of the 'unknowability' of the metropolis (and deep-rooted urbanisms that privilege this 'unknowability') cannot erase the political imperative to plan it.[80] In terms of both our analytical and ethical problems of city multiculturalism, rather than reject such an imperative as dystopian in all its forms we need to consider the claims of the plan to know, to organise and to rationalise the city in the light of the *elsewhere of place* and the *global familiar* considered in this chapter. They are the product of both the commodification of the contact zone and the mimetic urbanism that are the defining characteristics of the multicultural metropolis, but they do not displace, subvert or discredit the social engineering of the city that might be central to a progressive politics of the cosmopolis.

In today's postcolonial London selective migrant affluence sits alongside racialised immiseration. The promise of the cosmopolitan is in no way irreconcilable with the perennial reinvention of racist intolerance. In moving beyond the binaries of domination and resistance, autonomy and subjection, state and civil society, there is a sense that in realising the banality of government and the potential of the plan we might adopt a more ambivalent positioning towards the contemporary city. In this sense a critical urbanism needs to recognise simultaneously both the aspiration of the cosmopolitan alongside the potential for the city to reproduce intense patterns of immiseration in the carceral spaces of the city that are most readily understood as a metropolitan version of Achille Mbembe's postcolony.[81]

The allure of generalisation, the coded trajectory of model minorities and the subtextual assimilatory dreams such models imply are refuted by the brutal everyday realities of today's London. But equally the city stages moments of communication, of uncertainty through which forces of ethnicised and racialised closure are challenged.

In this way the city itself disrupts reassuring narratives of triumph or despair; the spaces of contemporary London subvert either trite generalisation or Adorno's synthetic speculative theory. The fabric of London provides instead a much more ambivalent dialectical imagery for us to behold. Whilst some urbanists (such as Koolhaas) argue that the immensity of the twenty-first-century metropolis confounds planning and signals at times an end to the city as such, we come back to a search for forms of rationality precisely because there is no outside to power, because there is no space free of regimes of governmentality and because the tensions between the liberal and the communitarian cannot be erased.

This is explicitly not a privileging of the creative or Deleuzian cramped spaces of the vernacular city over the routinised territories of governance and subjectification. For precisely the reasons explored in earlier chapters on the ghetto and the cultural quarter, academic engagement will be inadequate if it either erases the banal omnipresence of structures of governance or (as with Wacquant) finesses the political in the catch-all omnibus of the neo-liberal state. Belatedly, the Arcades Project – many decades on – points to both the possibility and the danger of reflecting theoretically whilst simultaneously engaging with the empirically fluid quicksand of the configuration of the city. Indeed, Walter Benjamin's work is so essential precisely because of its restless movement between perspectives as well as its attention to the production of perspective itself. In refusing to allow theoretical categories to settle, Benjamin's constellatory epistemology spatialises movement between the strange and the familiar in configurations of power and people in the city. It is because the city is invariably a product of many representations that the politics of juxtaposition and shock becomes so powerful, of viewing from up close and from a distance, a perspectival simultaneity that lends force to Benjamin's axiomatic claim that he 'has nothing to say only to show'. In such a spirit the postcolonial provides an important lens through which London might be seen differently.

But, more significantly, it is precisely because the staging of city spaces becomes constitutive of the postcolonial moment that it demands both a critical intellectual engagement with the everyday realities of the multicultural city through an interpretative sociology *and also* a refusal of Adorno's speculative theory. The consequent perspectival dance between the view from up close (the ethnographically 'real') and the privileged heights of the ivory tower, the Bonaventure Hotel or a hill in Paris favours a continual disruption of the very categories of race and space through which the multicultural city is mapped. Rationality and sentiment must be spatialised through plural not singular visualisations and representations of the city. The baroque perspectives of such optics imply a self-consciousness of the processes of fabrication that underscore such categorisations.

This is important analytically because the city increasingly mediates circuits of political engagement and cultural reproduction at a post-national scale of analysis. It is important politically because the city becomes the disruptive force in the reproduction of cultural and political forms, the mediating field through which newness comes into the world after the cosmopolitan loses its populist gloss.

Notes

1 Introduction: Globalisation, urbanism and cosmopolitan fever

1 R. Koolhaas *et al.*, 2000, *Mutations* (Barcelona: ACTER), p. 2.
2 This is the argument of both A. Favell, 1998, *Philosophies of Integration: Immigration and the Idea of Citizenship in France and Britain* (London: Macmillan) and A. Favell, 2001, 'Multi-ethnic Britain: an exceptional case? Learning from cross national comparisons.', *Patterns of Prejudice*, 35 (1), pp. 35–57.
3 For example, see R. Koopmans and P. Statham (eds), 2000, *Challenging Immigration and Ethnic Relations Politics: Comparative European Perspectives* (Oxford: Oxford University Press) for some singularly egregious examples of the positivist fallacy that to measure all is to know all.
4 D. Held, 1995, *Democracy and the Global Order: From the Modern State to Cosmopolitan Governance* (Cambridge: Polity Press); see also W. Walters, 2002, 'Mapping Schengenland: denaturalising the border', *Environment and Planning D: Society and Space*, 20, pp. 564–80.
5 For just two of the more informative discussions, see P. Hirst and G. Thompson, 1996, *Globalization in Question: The International Economy and the Possibilities of Governance* (Cambridge: Polity Press) and R. Robertson, 1992, *Globalisation, Social Theory and Global Culture* (London: Sage).
6 C. Calhoun, 2003, 'The necessity and limits of cosmopolitanism: local democracy in a global context', http://www.ssrc.org/programs/calhoun/publications/limitsofcocmo3.doc.
7 D. Archibugi, 2000, 'Cosmopolitical democracy', *New Left Review*, 4, pp. 137–50 and D. Archibugi, 2002, 'Demos and cosmopolis', *New Left Review*, 13, pp. 24–38; D. Archibugi (ed.), 2003, *Debating Cosmopolitics* (London: Verso); T. Brennan, 2001, 'Cosmopolitanism and internationalism', *New Left Review*, 7, pp, 75–84; T. Brennan, 1997, *Cosmopolitanism Now. At Home in the World* (Cambridge, Mass.: Harvard University Press); D. Held, 1995, *Democracy and the Global Order: From the Modern State to Cosmopolitan Governance* (Cambridge: Polity Press); D. Held, 2004, *Global Covenant: The Social Democratic Alternative to the Washington Consensus* (Oxford: Polity Press).
8 *Public Culture*, 12 (3) (Fall 2000), and in particular S. Pollock, H. K. Bhabha and C. Breckenridge, 'Cosmopolitanisms', pp. 577–90.
9 U. Hannerz, 1992, 'Cosmopolitans and locals in world culture', in M. Featherstone (ed.), *Global Culture: Nationalism, Globalisation and Identity* (London: Sage).
10 S. Vertovec and R. Cohen (eds), 2002, *Conceiving Cosmopolitanisms: Theory, Context and Practice* (Oxford: Clarendon Press).
11 C. Bhatt, 2004, 'Contemporary geopolitics and "alterity" research', in M. Bulmer and J. Solomos (eds), *Researching Race and Racism* (London: Routledge).
12 So for Calhoun (drawing on Walzer) the tensions between identity politics of recognition and issues of solidarity suggest that 'actual conditions of membership are not restricted to a choice between thick but irrationally inherited identities on the one

hand and thin but rationally achieved ones on the other'. C. Calhoun, 2003, 'Imagining solidarity: cosmopolitanism, constitutional patriotism and the public sphere', *Public Culture*, 14 (1), pp. 147–71; J. Habermas, 2001, *The Postnational Constellation* (Oxford and Cambridge: Polity Press); J. Habermas, 2001, 'Constitutional democracy: a paradoxical union of contradictory principles?', *Political Theory*, 29 (6), pp. 766–81. See also D. Tambini, 2001, 'Post-national citizenship', *Ethnic and Racial Studies*, 24 (2), pp. 195–217.

13 See P. Cheah, 1999, 'The cosmopolitical – today', in P. Cheah and B. Robbins (eds), *Cosmopolitics: Thinking and Feeling Beyond the Nation* (Minneapolis, Minn. and London: University of Minnesota Press).

14 Bhatt, 'Contemporary geopolitics and "alterity" research'; A. Chua, 2003, *World on Fire: How Exporting Free Market Democracy Spreads Ethnic Hatred and Global Instability* (London: William Heinemann).

15 See, for example, D. Chakrabarty, 2000, *Provincialising Europe: Postcolonial Thought and Historical Difference* (Princeton, NJ: Princeton University Press).

16 See, for a very selective set of examples, D. Harvey, 1996, *Justice, Nature and the Politics of Difference* (Oxford: Blackwell); S. Sassen, 1991, *The Global City: London, New York, Tokyo* (Princeton, NJ: Princeton University Press); M. Mann, 2003, *Incoherent Empire* (London: Verso; Princeton, NJ: Princeton University Press); E. Soja, 2000, *Postmetropolis* (Oxford: Blackwell).

17 For Calhoun 'Political theory has surprisingly often avoided addressing the problems of political belonging in a serious analytic way by presuming that nations exist as the prepolitical bases of state-level politics.' Hence he suggests that cosmopolitan theory (which for Calhoun is liberal in its very formulation and in some senses hostile to the ethos of the communitarian) needs to consider the 'sociological' problem of solidarity and 'attend to one of the great lacunae of more traditional liberalism. This is the assumption of nationality as the basis for membership in states, even though this implies a seemingly illiberal reliance on inheritance and ascription rather than choice, and an exclusiveness hard to justify in liberal terms.' C. Calhoun, 2003, 'The class consciousness of frequent travellers: towards a critique of actually existing cosmopolitanism', in D. Archibugi (ed.), *Debating Cosmopolitics* (London: Verso), p. 92.

18 S. Ahmed, 1998, *Differences That Matter: Feminism and Postmodernism* (Cambridge: Cambridge University Press).

19 J. Derrida, 2001, *On Cosmopolitanism* (London: Routledge), p. 17. This is also in accord with Rabinow's suggestion that the problematisation of the contemporary world leads us back to Foucault's consideration of 'equipment', that is the medium of transformation of logos into ethos. P. Rabinow, 2003, *Anthropos Today: Reflections on Modern Equipment* (Princeton, NJ, and Oxford: Princeton University Press), pp. 1, 4–12 and 18.

20 This is best captured by McCarthy's powerful validation of the work of Max Horkheimer when he suggests that for Horkheimer 'Whatever the special demands of the different political situations however, there is a case to be made against any totalization of the classical critique of reason and for its continuation in the medium of sociocultural studies. The facts that contextualist and perspectivalist accounts of rationality invariably fall into the self referential or "performative" contradiction of having implicitly to presuppose what they want explicitly to deny, that the politics of otherness and difference makes sense only on the assumption of the very universalist values – freedom, justice, equality, respect, tolerance, dignity – that they seek to deconstruct, and that reported escapes into global ironising are given the lie in every situation of personal or political exigency suggest that it is important to attempt the latter.' T. McCarthy, 1993, 'The idea of critical theory and its relation to philosophy', in S. Benhabib, W. Bonss and J. McCole (eds), 1993, *On Max Horkheimer: New Perspectives* (London and Cambridge, Mass.: MIT Press), p. 133.

21 R. Beauregard and S. Body-Gendrot (eds), 1998, *The Urban Moment: Cosmopolitan Essays on the late 20th Century City. (Urban Affairs Annual Reviews)* (London and New York: Sage).

22 Drawing on a line of inquiry that can be loosely described as 'critical theory' and linked

to the work of both German thinkers of the mid-twentieth century such as Max Horkheimer, Walter Benjamin and Theodor Adorno, and their intellectual legacy in the New York political sociology of Calhoun, Benhabib and McCarthy, the volume takes it as axiomatic that city time and metropolitan space are themselves produced, narrated, multiple and complex rather than merely the media through which social, political and economic forms are realised. See M. Keith, 2002, 'Walter Benjamin, urban studies and the narratives of city life', in G. Bridge and S. Watson, 2000, *The Blackwell Companion to Urban Studies* (Oxford: Blackwell), pp. 410–29.

23 S. Ahmed, 1998, *Differences that Matter: Feminist Theory and Postmodernism* (Cambridge: Cambridge University Press); R. Braidotti, 1994, *Nomadic Subjects: Embodiment and Sexual Difference in Contemporary Feminist Theory* (New York: Columbia University Press).

24 K. Malik, 1996, *The Meaning of Race: Race, History and Culture in Western Society* (Basingstoke: Macmillan); M. Omi and H. Winant, 1994, *Racial Formation in the United States: From the 1960s to the 1990s* (New York: Routledge); H. Winant, 2001, *The World is a Ghetto: Race and Democracy since World War II* (New York: Basic Books).

25 D. T. Goldberg, 2001, *The Racial State* (Oxford: Blackwell).

26 J. Ifekunigwe, 1998, *Scattered Belongings: Cultural Paradoxes of Race, Nation and Gender* (London: Routledge).

27 P. Gilroy, 2000, *Between Camps: Nations, Culture and the Allure of Race* (London: Allen Lane).

28 L. Back, 1996, *New Ethnicities and Urban Culture* (London: UCL Press), Chapters 8–9.

29 In 2003 Tony White produced possibly the first novelistic description of a new London vernacular of *Benglish*, crossing East End cadence with 'urban' black slang and Sylheti. See T. White, 2003, *Foxy-T* (London: Faber and Faber).

30 H. Bhabha, 1994, *The Location of Culture* (London: Routledge); S. Rushdie, 1991, *Imaginary Homelands. Essays and Criticism 1981–1991* (London: Granta).

31 D. T. Goldberg, 1994, *Multiculturalism: A Critical Reader* (Oxford: Blackwell); B. Hesse, 2000, *Un/settled Multiculturalisms: Diasporas, Entanglements, Transruptions* (London: Zed Books); C. Joppke, 1999, 'How immigration is changing citizenship', *Ethnic and Racial Studies*, 22 (4), pp. 629–52; B. Parekh, 2000, *Rethinking Multiculturalism* (Basingstoke and London: Macmillan); Y. Soysal, 1994, *The Limits of Citizenship: Migrants and Postnational Membership in Europe* (Chicago, Ill.: University of Chicago Press). Cf. for a critique of the municipal model A. Kundnani, 2003, 'The death of multiculturalism', *Race and Class*, 43 (4), pp. 67–72.

32 B. Gidley, 2003, 'Citizenship and Belonging: East London Jewish Radicals 1903–1918' (Goldsmiths College, University of London, thesis submitted for the degree of Ph.D. in Sociology).

33 See Umberto Eco's analysis of the familial similarities and differences in defining fascism in the essays on 'Fascism' and 'Migration, tolerance and the intolerable' in U. Eco, 2001, *Five Moral Pieces* (London: Secker and Warburg).

34 Rabinow, *Anthropos Today: Reflections on Modern Equipment*, p. 12.

35 M. Banton, 2001, 'Progress in ethnic and racial studies', *Ethnic and Racial Studies*, 24 (2), pp. 173–94.

36 See P. Panayi, 2003, 'Cosmopolis: London's ethnic minorities', in J. Kerr and A. Gibson (eds), *London: From Punk to Blair* (London: Reaktion Books), pp. 67–73.

37 T. Osborne and N. Rose, 1999, 'Governing cities: notes on the spatialisation of virtue', *Society and Space*, 17, pp. 737–60; A. Amin and N. Thrift, 2000, *Cities: Reimagining the Urban* (Oxford: Polity Press).

38 See the chapter 'Boys Town', in R. Deutsche, 1996, *Evictions* (Cambridge, Mass.: MIT Press).

39 M. Heidegger, 1971 [1954], 'Building, dwelling, thinking', in M. Heidegger, *Poetry, Language, Thought* (New York: Harper and Row); H. Heynen, 2001, *Architecture and Modernity: A Critique* (Cambridge, Mass.: MIT Press).

40 The argument echoes Max Horkheimer, who argued that in the development of critical

theory there was 'no way of comprehending the structures of reason that does not involve sociohistorical inquiry' (McCarthy, 'The idea of critical theory and its relation to philosophy', p. 130). This volume argues that Horkheimer's comments and the general approach he adopted, epitomised in his celebrated inaugural lecture, are particularly apposite to an understanding of a contemporary city that changes empirically so rapidly but is invariably described through languages with deep cultural historical roots.

41 C. Taylor, 1985, *The Philosophy of the Human Sciences* (Cambridge: Cambridge University Press). See also C. Taylor and A. Gutman, 1992, *Multiculturalism and the Politics of Recognition* (Princeton, NJ: Princeton University Press).

42 See S. Hall, 2000, 'The multicultural question', in B. Hesse, *Un/settled Multiculturalisms: Diasporas, Entanglements, Transruptions* (London: Zed Books).

43 See the later chapters in this volume on ethnic enterprise and the rioter. The point being made here is that (after Foucault) we need to consider how regimes of governmentality map the transactional boundary state and civil society in ways that facilitate the emergence of some forms of social movements, domination and resistance but do not allow others. The refusal to recognise the inescapability of regimes of governmental power is at the heart of Sandercock's important work *Towards Cosmopolis* which is considered later in the volume.

44 P. Carey, 2001, *30 Days in Sydney: A Wildly Distorted Account* (London: Bloomsbury); P. Ackroyd, 2000, *London: A Biography* (London: Chatto and Windus).

45 R. Rorty, 1998, 'Justice as a larger loyalty', in P. Cheah and B. Robbins (eds), *Cosmopolitics: Thinking and Feeling Beyond the Nation* (Minneapolis, Minn. and London: University of Minnesota Press), pp. 45–58.

46 See, for example, C. Douzinas, 2000, *The End of Human Rights: Critical Legal Thought at the Turn of the Century* (Oxford: Hart); C. Douzinas, 2003, 'Humanism, military humanism and the new moral order', *Economy and Society*, 32 (2), pp. 159–83; P. Fitzpatrick, 1992, *The Mythology of Modern Law* (London: Routledge); P. Fitzpatrick, 2001, *Modernism and the Grounds of Law* (Cambridge: Cambridge University Press); D. Hirsch, 2003, *Law Against Genocide: Cosmopolitan Trials* (London: Glasshouse).

47 This notion is taken from Paul Gilroy's impressive use of Leroy Jones's term in Gilroy, *Between Camps*, p. 129.

48 Hesse, *Un/settled Multiculturalisms*.

49 Goldberg, *The Racial State*.

50 Contrast V. Ware and L. Back, 2002, *Out of Whiteness: Colour, Politics and Culture* (Chicago, Ill.: University of Chicago Press) with the white victimisation trope that runs through M. Collins, 2004, *The Likes of Us: A Biography of the White Working Class* (London: Granta).

51 K. Murji and J. Solomos (eds), 2005, *Racialisation* (Oxford: Blackwell); Gilroy, *Between Camps*.

52 C. Geertz, 2000, 'Anti anti-relativism', in C. Geertz, *Available Light: Anthropological Reflections on Philosophical Topics* (Princeton, NJ: Princeton University Press).

53 See M. Foucault, 1991, 'Governmentality', in G. Burchell, C. Gordon and P. Miller (eds), *The Foucault Effect: Studies in Governmentality* (Hemel Hempstead: Harvester Wheatsheaf) for the original, and N. Rose, 1999, *Powers of Freedom: Reframing Political Thought* (Cambridge: Cambridge University Press) for the most extensive discussion of this literature.

54 M. Hardt and A. Negri, 2000, *Empire* (Cambridge, Mass.: Harvard University Press), p. 51.

55 A. Mbembe, 2001, *On The Postcolony* (Berkeley: University of California Press).

56 N. Fraser, 1997, 'From redistribution to recognition?', in *Justice Interruptus: Rethinking Key Concepts of a Postsocialist Age* (London: Routledge); M. Yar, 2001, 'Beyond Nancy Fraser's "perspectival dualism"', *Economy and Society*, 30 (3), pp. 288–303.

57 E. Said, 1978, *Orientalism* (New York: Pantheon).

58 S. Buck Morss, 1978, *The Origin of Negative Dialectics* (Hassocks, Sussex: Harvester Press),

p. 156; D. Frisby, 1985, *Fragments of Modernity* (Oxford: Polity Press); T. Adorno and M. Horkheimer, 1997, *Dialectic of Enlightenment* (London: Verso).

59 In as much as Benjamin developed this notion systematically, his views are most clearly set down in W. Benjamin, 1972, 'Theses on the philosophy of history', in W. Benjamin, *Illuminations* (London: Fontana). He critiques an empty sense of the temporal: 'The concept of the historical progress of mankind cannot be sundered from the concept of its progression through a homogeneous, empty time. A critique of the concept of such a progression must be the basis of any criticism of the concept of progress itself' ('Theses', p. 252).

60 Chakrabarty, *Provincialising Europe*, p. 6. Chakrabarty calls for a scholarship in which 'The phenomenon of political modernity – namely the rule by modern institutions of the state, bureaucracy and capitalist enterprise – is impossible to think of anywhere in the world without invoking certain categories and concepts, the genealogies of which go deep into the intellectual and even theological traditions of Europe. Concepts such as citizenship, the state civil society, public sphere, human rights, equality before the law, the individual, distinctions between public and private, the idea of the subject, democracy, popular sovereignty, social justice, scientific rationality, and so on bear the burden of European thought and history' (*Provincialising Europe*, p. 4). The contextualising of a language of urbanism, making problematic the street, the tower block, the neighbourhood, the ghetto, the cultural quarter and the whole city identifies a problematic that is spatial in precisely the sense that Chakrabarty's project is historical.

61 See, for example, D. Gregory, 1994, *Geographical Imaginations* (Oxford: Blackwell); P. Jackson, 1989, *Maps of Meaning* (London: Unwin Hyman); J. Duncan and D. Ley, 1993, *Place, Culture, Representation* (London: Routledge).

2   The mirage at the heart of the myth? Thinking about the white city

1 It is certainly the case that the city has been transformed, and for some commentators the success of the project was identifiable at an early stage: 'Birmingham is replicating Glasgow's success in initiating a strategic, long-term process of regeneration. This is due to the sheer number of initiatives, now reaching a threshold of synergistic activity; to the broad scope of initiatives addressing the complex equation of urban renewal; to a history of pragmatic partnerships between the private sector and local government; and to a long-term strategic perspective shared between alternating Labour and Conservative controlled governments' (from M. Carley, 1991, 'Business in urban regeneration partnerships: a case study in Birmingham', *Local Economy*, 6, pp. 100–15). See also G. Kearns and C. Philo, 1993, *Selling Places: The City as Cultural Capital* (Oxford: Pergamon Press); M. Sorkin (ed.), 1992, *Variations on a Theme Park: The New American City and the End of Public Space* (New York: Hill and Wang).

2 Birmingham City Council, 1991, 'More than meets the eye'. The strapline was drawn from the verse by Rudyard Kipling, poet of Empire: 'Our England is a garden that is full of stately views, / Of borders beds and shrubberies and lawns and avenues, / With statues on the terraces and peacocks strutting by; / But the glory of the garden lies in more than meets the eye.'

3 J. Solomos and L. Back, 1995, *Race, Politics and Social Change* (London: Routledge).

4 P. Loftman, 1990, *A Tale of Two Cities: Birmingham, the Convention Centre and the Unequal City* (Birmingham: Birmingham Polytechnic).

5 Taken from the speech by Ken Livingstone, Mayor of London, to the Lord Mayor's Dinner on 'The Government of London' at the Mansion House in the City Corporation, 22 May 2000.

6 In Brixton, Brent, Lewisham, Greenwich and the East End of London a range of urban regeneration projects currently promote cultural diversity as one of the strengths of their locality. In 2004 the London Development Agency launched a programme designed to quantify the economic benefits of the diversity of the city.

7 J. Feagin, 1998, *The New Urban Paradigm: Critical Perspectives on the City* (Lanham, Md.: Rowman and Littlefield); D. Harvey, 1990, *The Condition of Postmodernity* (Oxford: Blackwell); I. Katznelson, 1992, *Marxism and the City* (Oxford: Clarendon Press); S. Lash and J. Urry, 1994, *Economies of Signs and Space* (London: Sage).

8 D. Goldberg, 1993, *Racist Culture. Philosophy and the Politics of Meaning* (Oxford: Blackwell); J. Solomos and L. Back, 1996, *Racism and Society* (Basingstoke: Macmillan).

9 J. Butler, E. Laclau and S. Zizek, 2000, *Contingency, Hegemony, Universality: Contemporary Dialogues on the Left* (London and New York: Verso).

10 D. Goldberg, 1993, *Racist Culture. Philosophy and the Politics of Meaning* (Oxford: Blackwell); M. Omi and H. Winant, 1987, *Racial Formation in the United States: From the Sixties to the Eighties* (London: Routledge); H. Winant, 1994, *Racial Conditions: Politics, Theory, Comparisons* (Minneapolis, Minn.: University of Minneapolis Press).

11 P. Gilroy, 2000, *Between Camps: Race, Identity and Nationalism at the End of the Colour Line* (London: Allen and Lane).

12 P. Saunders, 1981, *Social Theory and the Urban Question* (London: Hutchinson, 2nd edn, 1986); M. Savage and A. Warde, 1993, *Urban Sociology, Capitalism and Modernity* (Basingstoke: Macmillan), Chapters 5 and 6; A. Amin and N. Thrift, 2002, *Cities: Reimagining the Urban* (Oxford: Blackwell).

13 M. Keith, 2000, 'Walter Benjamin, urban studies and the narratives of city life', in G. Bridge and S. Watson, *The Blackwell Companion to Urban Studies* (Oxford: Blackwell).

14 T. Osborne and N. Rose, 1999, 'Governing cities: Notes of the spatialisation of virtue', *Environment and Planning D: Society and Space*, 17, pp. 737–60.

15 J. Der Derian, 1998, *The Virilio Reader* (Oxford: Blackwell); K. Robins and F. Webster, 1999, *Times of the Technoculture: From the Information Society to the Virtual Life* (London: Routledge).

16 R. Williams, 1973, *The Country and the City* (London: Chatto and Windus), p. 1.

17 Williams, *The Country and the City*, p. 7, emphasis added.

18 P. Hall, 1998, *Cities in Civilization* (London: Weidenfeld and Nicolson).

19 M. Castells, 1996–8, *The Information Age: Economy, Society, Culture*, vol. 1: *The Rise of the Network Society*, vol. 2: *The Power of Identity*, vol. 3: *End of Millennium* (Oxford: Blackwell).

20 A. Appiah and S. Sassen, 1999, *Globalisation and its Discontents: Essays on the New Mobility of People and Money* (New York: New Press); S. Sassen, 1999, *Guests and Aliens* (New York: New Press).

21 M. Davis, 2000, *Magical Urbanism: Latinos Reinvent the US Big City* (London: Verso); M. Davis, 1990, *City of Quartz: Excavating the Future in Los Angeles* (London and New York: Verso); E. Soja, 1989, *Postmodern Geographies* (London and New York: Verso); E. Soja, 1996, *Thirdspace: Journeys to Los Angeles and other Real-and-Imagined Places* (Oxford: Blackwell); E. Soja, 1999, *Postmetropolis: Critical Studies of Cities and Regions* (Oxford: Blackwell).

22 J. Donald, 1999, *Imagining the Modern City* (London: Athlone Press); S. Pile, 1996, *The Body and the City. Psychoanalysis, Space and Subjectivity* (London: Routledge).

23 A. Vidler, 1996, *The Architectural Uncanny* (Cambridge, Mass.: MIT Press), p. xiii.

24 P. Stallybrass and A. White, 1986, *The Politics and Poetics of Transgression* (London: Methuen).

25 M. Collings, 1997, *Blimey! From Bohemia to Britpop: The London Artworld from Francis Bacon to Damien Hirst* (Cambridge: 2), p. 2; Donald, *Imagining the Modern City*; Pile, *The Body and the City*; F. Moretti, 1998, *Atlas of the European Novel* (London and New York: Verso).

26 P. Rabinow, 1989, *French Modern. Norms and Forms of Social Environment* (Cambridge, Mass.: MIT Press), p. 5. For Rabinow 'social technicians were articulating a normative or middling modernism. In their discourses, society became its own referent, to be worked on by means of technical procedures which were becoming the authoritative arbiters of what counted as socially real' (*French Modern*, p. 13).

27 Rabinow *French Modern*, p. 358.

28 C. Boyer, 1986, *Dreaming the Rational City: The Myth of American City Planning* (Cambridge, Mass.: MIT Press).

29 M. Foucault, 1991, 'Governmentality', in G. Burchell, C. Gordon and P. Miller (eds), *The Foucault Effect: Studies in Governmentality* (Hemel Hempstead: Harvester and Wheatsheaf); R. Sennett, 1994, *Flesh and Stone: The Body and the City in Western Civilization* (New York and London: W. W. Norton and Company); G. Wright, 1991, *The Politics of Design in French Colonial Urbanism* (Chicago, Ill.: University of Chicago Press).

30 L. Barth, 1996, 'Immemorial visibilities: seeing the city's difference', in *Environment and Planning A*, 28 (3) (March), pp. 471–93; M. De Certeau, 1984, *The Practice of Everyday Life* (Berkeley: University of California Press); R. Deutsche, 1996, *Evictions* (Cambridge, Mass.: MIT Press).

31 H. Clinton, 1996, *It Takes a Village: And Other Lessons Children Teach Us* (New York: Touchstone Books); Social Exclusion Unit, 2000, *National Strategy for Neighbourhood Renewal: A Framework for Consultation. A Report by the Social Exclusion Unit* (London: HMSO).

32 European Commission, 1991, *Green Paper on the Urban Environment* (Brussels: European Commission), p. 7, emphasis added.

33 See Chapter 5 in this volume.

34 T. Osborne, 1998, *Aspects of Enlightenment: Social Theory and the Ethics of Truth* (London: UCL Press).

35 S. Buck-Morss, 1989, *The Dialectics of Seeing. Walter Benjamin and the Arcades Project* (London: MIT Press); M. Bullock and M. Jennings, 1996, *Walter Benjamin: Selected Writings*, vol. 1: *1913–1926* (Cambridge, Mass.: Harvard University Press); G. Gilloch, 1996, *Myth and Metropolis: Walter Benjamin and the City* (Oxford: Polity Press); Keith, 'Walter Benjamin, urban studies and the narratives of city life'; P. Missac, 1995, *Walter Benjamin's Passages* (Cambridge, Mass.: MIT Press); P. Szondi, 1995 [1962], 'Walter Benjamin's city portraits', in G. Smith (ed.), *On Walter Benjamin: Critical Essays and Recollections* (Cambridge, Mass.: MIT Press).

36 Again space prohibits an extensive examination here, but the cultural construction of gender draws on related diagnostic cartographies of the urban that both render a gendered analysis of the sites of the city equally germane and guarantee that the constructions of character examined later in this chapter are invariably simultaneously gendered and racialised; cf. G. Pollock, 1988, *Vision and Difference: Feminism, Femininity and the Histories of Art* (London: Routledge) with L. Heron, 1993, 'Women writing the city', in *Streets of Desire* (London: Virago); E. Wilson, 1992, 'The invisible flâneur', *New Left Review*, 191, pp. 90–110; J. Wolff, 1985, 'The invisible flâneuse: women and the literature of modernity', *Theory, Culture and Society*, 2 (3), pp. 37–48. The essay by Griselda Pollock, 1992, *Avant Garde Gambits: Gender and the Colour of Art History* (London: Thames and Hudson) provides a lucid realisation of the power of this approach for a consideration of 'the colour of art history'.

37 H. Bhabha, 1994, *The Location of Culture* (London: Routledge); M. L. Pratt, 1992, *Imperial Eyes: Travel Writing and Transculturation* (London and New York: Routledge).

38 R. Dyer, 1997, *White* (London: Routledge); R. Frankenberg, 1997, *Displacing Whiteness: Essays in Social and Cultural Criticism* (Durham, NC: Duke University Press); V. Ware, 1992, *Beyond the Pale: White Women, Racism and History* (London: Verso); V. Ware and L. Back, 2000, *Dark Thoughts On Whiteness* (Chicago, Ill. and London: University of Chicago Press).

39 L. Lokko (ed.), 2000, *White Papers, Black Marks: Architecture, Race, Culture* (Minneapolis, Minn.: University of Minnesota Press).

40 L. Kennedy, 2000, *Race and Urban Space in Contemporary Urban Culture* (Edinburgh: Edinburgh University Press).

41 G. Hage, 1998, *White Nation: Fantasies of White Supremacy in a Multicultural Society* (London: Pluto).

42 K. Mercer, 2000, 'A sociography of diaspora', in P. Gilroy, L. Grossberg and A. McRobbie (eds), *Without Guarantees: In Honour of Stuart Hall* (London: Verso), citing the work of Sarat Maharaj.

43 A. Abbott, 1999, *Department and Discipline* (Chicago, Ill.: University of Chicago Press); D. Goldberg, 1993, *Racist Culture. Philosophy and the Politics of Meaning* (Oxford: Blackwell); L. Harris, 2001, *Racism* (New York: Humanity Books).

44 Davis, *Magical Urbanism*; A. Y. Davis, 2000, *The Prison Industrial Complex* (CD ROM) (New York: AK Press).

45 F. Fanon, 1986, *Black Skin, White Masks* (London: Pluto Press); M. Wieviorka, 1998, 'Is multiculturalism the solution?', *Ethnic and Racial Studies*, 21 (5), pp. 881–910.

46 R. Rogers, 1997, *Cities for a Small Planet* (London: Faber and Faber).

47 I. M. Young, 1990, *Justice and the Politics of Difference* (Princeton, NJ: Princeton University Press); I. M. Young, 1997, *Intersecting Voices: Dilemmas of Gender, Political Philosophy and Policy* (Princeton, NJ: Princeton University Press).

48 C. Boyer, 1994, *The City of Collective Memory: Its Historical Imagery and Architectural Entertainments* (Cambridge, Mass.: MIT Press).

49 J. Butler, 1993, 'Endangered / Endangering schematic racism and white paranoia', in R. Gooding-Williams (ed.), *Reading Rodney King, Reading Urban Uprising* (London and New York: Routledge).

50 M. Jay, 1992, 'Scopic regimes of modernity', in S. Lash and J. Friedmann (eds), *Modernity and Identity* (Oxford: Blackwell); M. Jay, 1994, *Downcast Eyes* (Berkeley: University of California Press).

51 H. Lefèbvre, 1991, *The Production of Space* (Oxford: Blackwell).

52 E. Gellner, 1997, *Nationalism* (London: Weidenfeld and Nicolson).

53 Z. Bauman, 1989, *Modernity and the Holocaust* (Oxford: Polity Press).

54 See Rogers, *Cities for a Small Planet*, and for the continuation of this (in many ways laudable) project: http://www.london.gov.uk/mayor/auu/index.jsp.

55 S. Sassen, 1999, *Guests and Aliens* (New York: New Press).

56 The work of George Mosse provides an exemplary case of the intricate and contextual relationships between landscapes of nationalism and the configuration of the urban. G. Mosse, 1975, *The Nationalization of the Masses: Political Symbolism and Mass Movements in Germany from the Napoleonic Wars through the Third Reich* (New York: New American Library).

57 At one point in the novel the central protagonist, as ever with Ishiguro, gradually awakening to the fragile construction of his lifeworld, comments: 'And yet tonight, in the quiet of this room, I find that what really remains with me from this first day's travel is not Salisbury Cathedral, nor any of the other charming sights of this city, but rather that marvellous view encountered this morning of the rolling English countryside. Now, I am quite prepared to believe that other countries can offer more obviously spectacular scenery. Indeed, I have seen in encyclopaedias and the *National Geographic Magazine* breathtaking photographs of sights from various corners of the globe; magnificent canyons and waterfalls, raggedly beautiful mountains. It has never, of course, been my privilege to have seen such things at first hand, but I will nevertheless hazard this with some confidence: the English landscape at its finest – such as I saw it this morning – possesses a quality that the landscapes of other nations, however more superficially dramatic, inevitably fail to possess. It is, I believe, a quality that will mark out the English landscape to any objective observer as the most deeply satisfying in the world, and this quality is best summed up by the term "greatness". For it is true, when I stood on that high ledge this morning and viewed that land before me, I distinctly felt that rare, yet unmistakable feeling – the feeling that one is in the presence of "greatness". We call this land of ours *Great* Britain, and there may be those who believe this a somewhat immodest practice. Yet I would venture that the landscape of our country alone would justify the use of this lofty adjective.' Kazuo Ishiguro, 1989, *The Remains of the Day* (London: Faber and Faber), p. 28.

58 L. Back, 2000, 'Guess who's coming to dinner: investigating in the grey zone', in Ware and Back, *Dark Thoughts On Whiteness*.

59 J. M. Jacobs, 1996, *Edge of Empire: Postcolonialism and the City* (London: Routledge).

60 P. Bourdieu, 1999, 'Site effects', in P. Bourdieu *et al.*, *The Weight of the World* (London: Polity Press), p. 123.

61 D. Frisby, 1985, *Fragments of Modernity* (Oxford: Polity Press), Chapter 4.

62 Donald, *Imagining the Modern City*, p. xi.

63 L. Wacquant, 1998, 'Inside the zone: the social art of the hustler in the black American ghetto', *Theory, Culture and Society*, 15 (2), pp. 1–36, at p. 12.

64 R. Barthes, 1973, *Mythologies* (London: Granada); W. Benjamin, 1999, *The Arcades Project* (London: Verso); H. Caygill, 1998, *Walter Benjamin: The Colour of Experience* (London: Routledge); J. Raban, 1974, *Soft City* (London: Collins); P. Wright, 1992, *A Journey Through Ruins: The Last Days of London* (London: Radius).

65 Boyer, *The City of Collective Memory*.

66 U. Beck, 1992, *The Risk Society: Towards a New Modernity* (London: Sage).

3 After the cosmopolitan? The limits of the multicultural city and the mutability of racism

1 B. Gascoigne, 1971, *The Great Moghuls* (London: Jonathan Cape), p. 97.

2 A. Touraine, 2000, *Can We Live Together? Equality and Difference* (Original title: *Comment nous vivre ensemble?*), trans. David Macey (Oxford: Polity Press).

3 See also Chapter 7 of this volume.

4 The most obvious important exception to this is the recent work of David Goldberg, 2001, *The Racial State* (Oxford: Blackwell). See also L. A. Stoler, 1996, *Race and the Education of Desire: Foucault's 'History of Sexuality' and the Colonial Order of Things* (Durham, NC: Duke University Press), for a discussion of the significance of Foucault's lectures on the nature of racism, and also B. Hesse, 1997, 'White governmentality: urbanism, nationalism, racism', in S. Westwood and J. Williams (eds), 1997, *Imagining Cities* (London: Routledge). See Stoler, *Race and the Education of Desire* for other notable exceptions to this.

5 A. Mbembe, 2001, 'The aesthetics of vulgarity', in *On the Postcolony* (Berkeley: University of California Press).

6 It is precisely at the point where the hostility of conventionally economistic renderings of the 'global city' confront cultural theory that it becomes impossible to understand the multicultural nature of the contemporary urban condition. This chapter in part attempts to undermine the narrative that subsumes a new order of global cities within a hierarchy of deterministically described capitalist globalisation.

7 A. Appadurai, 2002, 'Deep democracy: urban governmentality and the horizon of politics', *Public Culture*, 14 (1), pp. 21–47. See also, for example, D. Massey, 2001, 'Debates', *City*, 5 (1), pp. 77–105. However, the notion of 'globalisation from below' invokes a Manichean evil of power (from above) and the implicit heroism of its resistance. Such thinking in all its binary formations is equally problematic for all the reasons argued throughout this chapter. This theme is returned to in Chapter 7.

8 Stuart Hall identifies the possibility of vernacular modernities as sites of alternative politics: 'Within these interstices lies the possibility of a disseminated set of vernacular modernities. Culturally these cannot frontally stem the tide of westernising techno-modernity. However, they continue to inflect, deflect and "translate" its imperatives from below. They constitute the basis for a new kind of "localism" that is not self sufficiently particular, but which arises within, without being simply a simulacrum of the global. This "localism" is no mere residue of the past. It is something new – globalising's accompanying shadow.' S. Hall, 2001, 'The multicultural question', in B. Hesse (ed.), *Un/settled Multiculturalisms: Diasporas, Entanglements, Transruptions* (London: Zed Books), p. 216. Consequently the western city for Hall has a privileged position: 'Only in such a context can we understand why what threatens to become the moment of the West's global closure – the apotheosis of its global universalising mission – is at the same time the moment of the West's slow, uncertain, protracted de-centring' (p. 217).

9 M. P. Smith, 2001, *Transnational Urbanism: Locating Globalization* (Oxford and New York: Blackwell).

10 See J. Friedmann, 1986, 'The world city hypothesis', *Development and Change*, 17 (1), pp. 69–84; J. Friedmann, 1995, 'Where we stand: a decade of world city research', in P. Knox and P. J. Taylor (eds), *World Cities in a World System* (Cambridge: Cambridge University Press), pp. 21–47; S. Sassen, 1991, *The Global City: London, New York, Tokyo* (Princeton, NJ: Princeton University Press); S. Sassen, 1998, *Globalization and its Discontents* (New York: New York Press); A. Giddens, 2000, *The Reith Lecture*: www.bbc.co.uk/reith.html.

11 As Ian Gordon has argued, the 'global cities' narrative can overstate the degree to which cities such as London 'see themselves'. For Gordon the Economic Development Strategy adopted by Ken Livingstone in London understates the degree to which the city depends on national trading far more than international forms of exchange. Ian Gordon, 'Capital needs, capital growth and global city rhetoric in Mayor Livingstone's London plan', paper presented in session on 'The Production of Capital Cities', Association of American Geographers' Annual Meeting, New Orleans, 7 March 2003.

12 P. Hirst and G. Thompson, 1996, *Globalization in Question* (London: Polity Press).

13 K. Cox (ed.), 1997, *Spaces of Globalization* (New York: Guilford Press). See also the working papers series on Global and World Series available at GAWC, University of Loughborough.

14 J. K. Gibson-Graham, 1996–7, 'Querying globalisation', *Rethinking Marxism*, 9 (1) (Spring), pp. 1–27.

15 Smith, *Transnational Urbanism*, pp. 18–20 and Chapter 8.

16 L. Sandercock, 1998, *Towards Cosmopolis* (London: Wiley); J. Holston, 2001, 'Spaces of insurgent citizenship', in L. Sandercock (ed.), *Making The Invisible Visible: Insurgent Planning Histories* (Berkeley: University of California Press); M. J. Dear, 2000, *The Postmodern Urban Condition* (Oxford: Blackwell), pp. 8–9.

17 Sandercock, *Towards Cosmopolis*.

18 Sandercock, *Towards Cosmopolis*: language, p. 207; an epistemology of multiplicity, p. 216; and a transformative politics of difference, p. 217.

19 Sandercock, *Towards Cosmopolis*, p. 212.

20 Sandercock, *Towards Cosmopolis*, p. 212.

21 Holston, 'Spaces of insurgent citizenship', p. 47, emphasis added.

22 It is in this sense that Chapters 4, 6 and 7 of this volume map the multicultural governmental territorialisations of the *ghetto*, the *street* and the *cultural quarter*; Chapters 5 and 8 the speaking positions of the *ethnic entrepreneur*, the *rebel*, the *single parent* and the *tagger*; and Chapters 9 and 10 the governmental technologies of *community safety* and *land use planning*.

23 See A. Barry, 2001, *Political Machines. Governing a Technological Society* (London and New York: Athlone Press), pp. 3 and 7 and Chapters 8 and 10.

24 As the argument in this chapter develops, this is not to argue for an *anti-essentialist* notion of race. It is instead the case that the historicity and spatiality of racial subjects lend racial practices a concretised horror that allows P. Gilroy, 1993, *The Black Atlantic* (London: Verso) – after C. Geertz, 2000, 'Anti anti-relativism', in C. Geertz, *Available Light: Anthropological Reflections on Philosophical Topics* (Princeton, NJ: Princeton University Press) – to argue for an *anti-anti-essentialism* that refutes the roots of incommensurable difference but does not endorse the myth of a liberal universalism.

25 See T. Osborne and N. Rose, 1999, 'Governing cities: notes on the spatialisation of virtue', *Society and Space*, 17, pp. 737–60. The argument that the discovery of 'the social' as a territory of analysis and a field of power relations was historically tied to the emergence of the industrial city has been a commonplace in many histories of social theory. More significantly, Osborne and Rose stress that the emergence of regimes of governmentality that take the city as a central organising theme determine quite different political subject positions for the city itself. See also M. Valverde, 2003, 'Police

science, British style: pub licensing and knowledges of urban disorder', *Economy and Society*, 32 (2), pp. 234–52.

26 D. Wilson, M. Game, S. Leach and G. Stoker, 1994, *Local Government in the United Kingdom (Government Beyond the Centre)* (Palgrave: Macmillan); G. Stoker, 2003, *Transforming Local Governance: From Thatcherism to New Labour* (Basingstoke: Macmillan).

27 Molotch H. Logan, 1987, *Urban Fortunes: The Political Economy of Place* (Berkeley: University of California Press); A. Harding, 2004, 'Theories of governance and urban economic and social change', in N. Buck, I. Gordon, A. Harding and I. Turok (eds), *City Matters* (Basingstoke: Palgrave).

28 A. Cochrane, 1993, *The End of Local Government* (Oxford: Oxford University Press); N. Jewson and S. Macgregor (eds), 1997, *Transforming Cities: Contested Governance and New Spatial Division* (London and New York: Routledge); D. King and G. Stoker (eds), 1996, *Rethinking Local Democracy* (Basingstoke: Palgrave); T. Travers, 2004, 'Labour's local record', *New Economy*, 11 (2), pp. 90–4.

29 K. Crenshaw, N. Gotanda, G. Peller and K. Thomas (eds), 1995, *Critical Race Theory* (New York: New Press).

30 N. Rose, 1999, *Powers of Freedom: Reframing Political Thought* (Cambridge: Cambridge University).

31 N. Brenner, 2000, 'The urban question as a scale question: reflections on Henri Lefèbvre, urban theory and the politics of scale', *International Journal of Urban and Regional Research*, 24, pp. 362–78; K. Gibson, 2001, 'Regional subjection and becoming', *Environment and Planning D: Society and Space*, 19, pp. 639–67; G. McCleod and M. Jones, 2001, 'Renewing the geography of the regions', *Environment and Planning D: Society and Space*, 19, pp. 669–95; E. Soja, 1999, *Postmetropolis: Critical Studies of Cities and Regions* (Oxford: Blackwell).

32 C. Skelcher, 2004, 'Beyond the sovereign council: the new governance of local communities', in G. Stoker and D. Wilson (eds), *British Local Government in the 2000s* (Basingstoke: Palgrave).

33 For a broad overview see Jewson and Macgregor, *Transforming Cities*.

34 See, for example, the work of John Keane in J. Keane, 1998, *Democracy and the Civil State* (London: University of Westminster Press); J. Keane, 1998, *Civil Society: Old Images, New Visions* (Cambridge: Polity Press); J. Keane (ed.), *Civil Society and the State: New European Perspectives* (London: University of Westminster Press).

35 M. Keith and S. Pile (eds), 1993, *Place and the Politics of Identity* (London and New York: Routledge), Chapters 1–2.

36 The constitutive outside of identity in J. Butler, E. Laclau and S. Zizek, 2000, *Contingency, Hegemony, Universality: Contemporary Dialogues on the Left* (London and New York: Verso); Keith and Pile, *Place and the Politics of Identity*, Chapters 1–2.

37 Oskar Negt and Alexander Kluge, 1993, *Public Sphere and Experience: Towards an Analysis of the Bourgeois and Proletarian Public Sphere*, foreword Miriam Hansen, trans. Peter Labanyi, Jamie Daniel and Assenka Oksiloff (Minneapolis, Minn.: University of Minnesota Press).

38 L. Back, M. Keith, A. Khan, K. Shukra and J. Solomos, 2001, 'Democratic governance and ethnic minority political participation', ESRC Conference, University of Manchester, 22 March, 'Democratic Governance and Ethnic Minority Political Participation in Contemporary Britain', in ESRC Final Report, forthcoming, *Struggles for Racialised Democracy* (Cambridge: Cambridge University Press).

39 M. Keith, 2005, 'Racialisation and the public spaces of the city', in K. Murji and J. Solomos (eds), *Racialisation* (Oxford: Blackwell).

40 See J. Dean, 2001, 'Cybersalons and civil society: rethinking the public sphere in transnational technoculture', *Public Culture*, 13 (2), pp 243–65.

41 L. Back, 1996, *New Ethnicities and Urban Culture* (London: UCL Press), Chapters 5 and 6.

42 J. Anim-Addo, 1995, *Longest Journey: A History of Black Lewisham* (London: Deptford Forum Publishing).

43 P. Ackroyd, 2000, *London: The Biography* (London: Chatto and Windus).

44 Negt and Kluge, *Public Sphere and Experience*.

45 B. P. Gidley, 2002, 'Citizenship and Belonging: East London Jewish Radicals 1903–1918' (University of London, Ph.D. thesis).

46 H. Bhabha, 1997, 'Minority culture and creative anxiety', in British Council, 2003, *Reinventing Britain* (London: British Council, Virtue Broadcasting); S. Pollock, H. Bhabha, C. Breckenridge and D. Chakrabarty, 2000, 'Cosmopolitanisms', *Public Culture*, 12 (3) (Fall), pp. 577–91.

47 S. Rushdie, 1991, *Imaginary Homelands. Essays and Criticism 1981–1991* (London: Granta).

48 M. Davis, 2000, *Magical Urbanism. Latinos Reinvent the US City* (London and New York: Verso).

49 For example, J. Feagin, 1998, *The New Urban Paradigm: Critical Perspectives on the City* (Lanham, Md.: Rowman and Littlefield), N. Smith, 1996, *The New Urban Frontier. Gentrification and the Revanchist City* (London and New York: Routledge).

50 For example, Janet L. Abu-Lughod, 1999, *New York, Chicago, Los Angeles: America's Global Cities* (Minneapolis, Minn.: University of Minnesota Press).

51 N. Rose and P. Miller, 1992, 'Political power beyond the state: problematics of government', *British Journal of Sociology*, 43 (2), pp. 173–205; Osborne and Rose, 'Governing cities: notes on the spatialisation of virtue'.

52 Importantly for these purposes there is no necessary relationship between the fiscally minimal state and the degree to which the state regulates the nature of social conduct. Clearly there are some neo-liberal regimes where a prescription of fiscal minimalisation has been accompanied by an increasingly interventionist role in the conduct of human behaviour.

53 L. Back, M. Keith, M. Khan, K. Shukra and J. Solomos (forthcoming), 'Islam and the new political landscape: faith communities and political participation in contemporary Britain', in *Struggles for Racialised Democracy*.

54 P. Hirst, 1994, *Associational Democracy: New Forms of Economic and Social Governance* (Cambridge: Polity Press).

55 A. Etzioni, 1988, *The Essential Communitarian Reader* (Lanham, Md.: Rowman and Littlefield).

56 B. Fine, 2001 *Social Capital or Social Theory: Political Economy and Social Science at the Turn of the Millennium* (London: Routledge).

57 M. R. Warren, 2001, *Dry Bones Rattling: Community Building to Revitalize American Democracy* (Princeton, NJ: Princeton University Press).

58 This refers to more than a notion of land-use planning. It captures also the valorisation of political mobilisations and the role of institutions of power in late liberal structures of governance. See Chapter 10 of this volume for the development of this argument.

59 Weber in H. H. Gerth and C. Wright Mills, 1991, *From Max Weber: Essays in Sociology*, ed. and intro. by H. H. Gerth and C. Wright Mills, new preface by Bryan S. Turner (London: Routledge), p. 214. All quotes are taken from the section 'Bureaucracy', pp. 196–245.

60 The most lucid discussion of these issues is to be found in P. Du Gay, 1994, 'Making up managers: bureaucracy, enterprise and the liberal art of separation', *British Journal of Sociology*, 45 (4), pp. 655–74. A more detailed and powerful exploration of the dangerous conflations of debates around rationality organisation and bureaucracy is found in P. Du Gay, 2000, *In Praise of Bureaucracy: Weber, Organisation, Ethics* (London: Sage).

61 'Thereby democracy inevitably comes into conflict with the bureaucratic tendencies, which by its fight against notable rule, democracy has produced' (Gerth and Mills, *From Max Weber*, p. 226).

62 It is also relevant to theorisations of modernity (and reflexive modernisation) that question the unitary logics of nation state and society, the homology of space and time, the identity of space and people, and the equivalence of past and future. See U. Beck, W.

Bons and C. Lau, 2003, 'The theory of reflective modernisation', *Theory, Culture and Society*, 20 (2), pp. 1–33, at p. 12. See also S. Lash, 1999, *Another Modernity, a Different Rationality* (London: Sage).

63 R. Rorty, 1998, 'Justice as a larger loyalty', in P. Cheah and B. Robbins (eds), *Cosmopolitics: Thinking and Feeling beyond the Nation* (Minneapolis, Minn.: University of Minnesota Press), pp. 45–59.

64 W. Kymlicka, 1995, *Multicultural Citizenship: A Liberal Theory of Minority Rights* (Oxford: Clarendon Press); B. Parekh, 2000, *Rethinking Multiculturalism* (Basingstoke and London: Macmillan); contributions by Taylor, Appiah, Habermas and Walzer in A. Gutman (ed.), 1994, *Multiculturalism* (Princeton, NJ: Princeton University Press); A. Appiah, 2001, 'Liberalism, individuality and identity', *Critical Inquiry*, 27 (Winter), pp. 305–32.

65 R. Sennett, 2003, *Respect: The Formation of Character in an Age of Inequality* (London: Allen Lane).

66 G. Baiocchi, 2003, 'Emergent public spheres. talking politics in participatory governance', *American Sociological Review*, 68, pp. 52–74.

67 C. Mouffe (ed.), *The Challenge of Carl Schmitt* (London: Verso).

68 Hence, for Weber, 'The demos itself, in the sense of an inarticulate mass, never "governs" larger associations; rather it is governed, and its existence only changes the way in which the executive leaders are selected and the measure of influence which the *demos*, or better, which social circles from its midst are able to exert upon the content and the direction of administrative activities by supplementing what is called "public opinion". Democratisation in the sense here intended, does not necessarily mean an increasingly active share of the governed in the authority of the social structure. This may be a result of democratisation, but it is not necessarily the case' (*From Max Weber*, p. 226).

69 This is famously the key point at the heart of Bauman's work on the Holocaust in Z. Bauman, 1989, *Modernity and the Holocaust* (Cambridge: Polity Press).

70 See N. Papergstergiadis, 2000, *The Turbulence of Migration: Globalization, Deterritorialization and Hybridity* (Cambridge: Polity Press), for an overview of the centrality of migration to global economic transformation.

71 C. Hall, 2002, *Civilising Subjects: Metropole and Colony in the English Imagination 1830–1867* (Oxford: Polity Press).

72 S. Castles, 1989 *Migrant Workers and the Transformation of Western Societies* (Ithaca, NY: Cornell University Press); S. Castles, 2003, *The Age of Migration: International Population Movements in the Modern World*, 3rd edn (Basingstoke: Macmillan); C. Peach, 1968, *West Indian Migration to Britain: A Social Geography* (Oxford: Oxford University Press).

73 P. Gilroy, 2000, *Between Camps. Race, Identity and Nationalism at the End of the Colour Line* (London: Allen Lane), p. 21.

74 D. Harraway, 1991, *Simians, Cyborgs and Women: The Reinvention of Nature* (London and New York: Routledge); D. Harraway, 1997, *Modest_Witness@Second_Millennium: FemaleMan©_Meets_OncoMouse* (London and New York: Routledge); S. Franklin, C. Lury and J. Stacey, 2000, *Global, Nature, Global Culture: Gender, Race and Life Itself* (London: Sage).

75 Gilroy, *Between Camps*, p. 104.

76 Hesse, *Un/settled Multiculturalism*s, Chapter 1.

77 A. Sivanandan, 2001, *Globalism and the Left* (London: IRR) http://www.irr.org.uk/a_sivanandan/.

78 A. Rattansi and C. O'Cinneide, 2002, *Our House: Race and Representation in British Politics* (London: Institute for Public Policy Research); L. Back, M. Keith, A. Khan, K. Shukra and J. Solomos, 2002, 'New Labour's white heart: politics, multiculturalism and the return of assimilation', *Political Quarterly*, 73 (4), pp. 445–54; R. Brubaker, 2001, 'The return of assimilation? Changing perspectives on immigration and its sequels in France, Germany and the United States', *Ethnic and Racial Studies*, 24 (4), pp. 531–48.

79 Runnymede Trust, 2000, *Islamophobia* (London: Runnymede Trust); L. Back, M. Keith,

A. Khan, K. Shukra and J. Solomos, forthcoming, *Power, Identity and Representation: Race, Governance and Political Mobilisation in British Society* (Cambridge: Cambridge University Press).

80 Samuel P. Huntington, 1996, *The Clash of Civilizations and the Remaking of World Order* (New York: Simon and Schuster); Samuel P. Huntington, 2004, *Who Are We? The Challenge to America's National Identity* (New York: Simon and Schuster).

81 Back *et al.*, *Power, Identity and Representation*.

82 S. Benhabib, 1993, 'Models of Public Space: Hannah Arendt, the liberal tradition and Jürgen Habermas', in C. Calhoun (ed.), *Habermas and the Public Sphere* (Cambridge, Mass.: MIT Press), p. 83.

4 The ghetto: Knowing your place and the performative cartographies of racial subordination

1 *La Haine* (Hate) Director: Matthieu Kassiewitz, 1995; *Ciudad del Dios* (City of God) Director: Fernando Meirelles, 2002. According to Konstantarakos, *La Haine* was originally to be titled *Droit de Cité*. This piece highlights both the continuities and the discontinuities in the representational politics of the ghetto, the interplay between the spatially marginal and the symbolically central. M. Konstantarakos, 2000, 'The *film de banlieue*: renegotiating the representation of urban space', in M. Balshaw and L. Kennedy (eds), 2000, *Urban Space and Representation* (London: Pluto).

2 L. Wacquant, 1997, Three pernicious premises in the study of the American ghetto', *International Journal of Urban and Regional Research*, 20 (2), pp. 341–53.

3 Wacquant persuasively suggests that in the study of urban immiseration 'both its generic mechanisms and the specific forms it assumes become intelligible once they are linked firmly to the historical matrix of class, state and place characteristic of each society. It follows that we need to develop more complex and differentiated images of the "damned of the city" if we are to properly capture their social state and explain their collective fate in different national contexts'. Hence 'one must maintain a clearcut separation between the folk concepts used by state managers, city authorities and residents to designate neighbourhoods of exile and the analytical concepts that the social research must construct in order to account for their evolving makeup and position in the sociospatial structure of the metropolis'. Both quotes taken from L. Wacquant, 2001, Preface to *Os Condenados da cidade* (Rio de Janeiro: Revan), pp. 1 and 3.

4 For Wacquant, 'the social sciences have failed to develop a robust *analytic concept* of the ghetto; instead they have been content to borrow the *folk concept* current in popular and political discourse on each epoch'. L. Wacquant, 2000, 'The new peculiar institution: on the prison as surrogate ghetto', *Theoretical Criminology*, 4 (3), pp. 377–89.

5 M. Duneier, 1999, *Sidewalk* (New York: Farrar, Strauss and Giroux); E. Anderson, 1999, *Code of the Street: Decency, Violence and the Moral Life of the Inner City* (New York: W. W. Norton); K. Newman, 1999, *No Shame in My Game: The Working Poor in the Inner City* (New York: Russell Sage Foundation and Knopf).

6 L. Wacquant, 2002, 'Scrutinizing the street: poverty, morality and the pitfalls of urban ethnography', *American Journal of Sociology*, 107 (6), pp. 1468–532, at 1521.

7 Adorno once criticised Benjamin similarly for 'the astonished presentation of simple facts'. The final chapter of this volume discusses such a critique of the empirical.

8 Wacquant, 'The new peculiar institution'.

9 The ghetto for Wacquant is 'a distinct space, containing an ethnically homogeneous *population*, which finds itself forced to develop within a set of interlinked *institutions* that duplicates the original framework of the broader society from which that group is banished and supplies the scaffolding for the construction of its specific "style of life" and social strategies'. The notion of scrutiny used in the title of Wacquant's piece highlights the nature of the visual that might problematise the manner in which objects of social inquiry are brought into vision, as well as the academic rigour of any particular

optic. Wacquant, 'Scrutinizing the street'. See also Chapter 6 on 'The street' in this volume.

10 A. Hirsch, 1998, *Making the Second Ghetto: Race and Housing in Chicago 1940–1960* (Chicago, Ill.: University of Chicago Press); T. Sugrue, 1998, *The Origins of the Urban Crisis* (Princeton, NJ: Princeton University Press).

11 Wacquant appeals to 'the agency of the state' (Wacquant, 'Scrutinizing the street', p. 1521), simplifying the plural regimes of governmentality, social control and governmental practice that criss-cross the everyday lives of the urban.

12 R. Sennett, 1998, *The Corrosion of Character* (New York: W. W. Norton).

13 M. Heidegger, 1971 [1954], 'Building, dwelling, thinking', in M. Heidegger, *Poetry, Language, Thought* (New York: Harper and Row); H. Heynen, 2001, *Architecture and Modernity: A Critique* (Cambridge, Mass.: MIT Press); A-Maliq Simone, 2002, 'Globalizing urban economies', in O. Enwezor, H. Ander, H. Fietzek and N. Rottner (eds), 2002, *Documenta_11Platfordm 5: Exhibition* (Kassel: Dr. Cantz'sche Druckerei).

14 As has been pointed out in one of the responses to Wacquant, the use of state-based folk categories such as the underclass was to some extent characteristic of his earlier working association with William Julius Wilson. K. Newman, 2002, 'No shame: the view from the left bank', *American Journal of Sociology*, 107 (6), pp. 1577–99. See also the robust and lucid response of M. Duneier, 2002, 'What kind of combat sport is sociology?', *American Journal of Sociology*, 107 (6), pp. 1551–76. See also A. Gupta and J. Ferguson, 1999, *Culture, Power, Place: Explorations in Critical Anthropology* (Durham, NC: Duke University Press).

15 J. Rex, 1973, *Race, Colonialism and the City* (London: Routledge and Kegan Paul).

16 M. Banton, 1955, *The Coloured Quarter: Negro Immigrants in an English City* (London: Jonathan Cape).

17 S. J. Smith, 1989, *The Politics of 'Race' and Residence: Citizenship, Segregation and White Supremacy in Britain* (Cambridge: Polity Press).

18 Smith, *The Politics of 'Race' and Residence*; P. Ambrose, 1994, *Urban Process and Power* (London: Routledge); A. Power, 1997, *Estates on the Edge: The Social Consequences of Mass Housing in Northern Europe* (Basingstoke: Macmillan).

19 Social Exclusion Unit, 2000, *National Strategy for Neighbourhood Renewal: A Framework for Consultation* (London: Cabinet Office); M. Keith, 2004, 'Knowing the city? 21st century urban policy and the introduction of Local Strategic Partnerships', in C. Johnstone and M. Whitehead (eds), 2004, *New Horizons in British Urban Policy: Perspectives on New Labour's Urban Renaissance* (London: Ashgate), pp. 185–97.

20 The principal projects referred to are the Deptford City Challenge Evaluation Project (1992–7); the ESRC-funded 'Finding the Way Home' project (1998–2001) and the Pepys Estate Action Research project (2000–6). These research projects were conducted at the Centre for Urban and Community Research (CUCR) in Goldsmiths College, University of London. For further details see www.goldsmiths.ac.uk/cucr.

21 See L. Back, 1995, *New Ethnicities and Urban Culture* (London: UCL Press), Appendix 2, for a description of the increased numbers of West Africans on the estate between 1981 and 1991.

22 See M. Stone, 2003, *Social Housing in the UK and the US: Evolution, Issues and Prospects* (British Council Atlantic Fellowship Mimeos).

23 Smith, *The Politics of 'Race' and Residence*; D. A. Phillips, 1986, *What Price Equality? A Report on the Allocation of GLC Housing in Tower Hamlets* (London: GLC Housing Research and Policy), Report 9; P. Sarre, D. Phillips and R. Skellington, 1989, *Ethnic Minority Housing: Explanations and Policies* (Ashgate: Gower).

24 For both a description of the diagnostic policing cartographies of London's ghetto estates in terms of their likelihood to generate 'disorder' and a description of police black confrontation, see M. Keith, 1993, *Race, Riots and Policing: Policing a Multi-Racist Society* (London: UCL Press), Chapters 10 and 11.

25 In the ESRC-funded project 'Finding the Way Home' (see www.goldsmiths.ac.uk/cucr)

young adolescents described their imagined geographies of the neighbourhood, their cartographies of the ghetto and the link between the Milton Court Estate and the gangs within a rubric of *ghetto boys*. See Chapter 9 of this volume for a development of some of these themes.

26 W. J. Wilson, 1988, *The Truly Disadvantaged: The Inner City, the Underclass and Public Policy* (Chicago, Ill. and London: University of Chicago Press); W. J. Wilson (ed.), *The Ghetto Underclass: Social Science Perspectives* (New York: Sage); and W. J. Wilson, 1997, *When Work Disappears: The World of the New Urban Poor* (New York: Random House).

27 For example, in Tower Hamlets in the 1990s, estates that were majority white appeared to demonstrate both low electoral participation rates and a ready willingness to support stock transfer. In contrast, some of the estates that witnessed the highest levels of residential segregation, and were dominated by as much as 80 per cent Bengali tenure, almost universally rejected stock transfer – at least initially – when offered the choice to vote on the issue.

28 See L. Back, P. Cohen and M. Keith, 2001, *Finding the Way Home Project Final Report* (London: CNER and CUCR).

29 SUS was the bylaw which until the mid-1980s allowed people to be arrested for being 'about to commit a crime': an 'offence' that targeted and consequently criminalised large sections of London's young black Caribbean communities: see Keith, *Race, Riots and Policing*; C. Demuth, 1978, *Sus: A Report on Section 4 of the Vagrancy Act 1924* (London: Runnymede Trust). See also J. Steel, 1993, *Turning the Tide. The History of Everyday Deptford* (London: Deptford Forum Publishing), for a powerful description of Deptford's history.

30 In the late 1990s sustained ethnography in a school adjacent to the Milton Court Estate in the ESRC-funded 'Finding the Way Home' project by Les Back, Phil Cohen, Michael Keith, Landé Pratt and Sarah Newlands worked through the cartographies of the real and imagined ghettos that young adolescents used in everyday narratives and to make sense of their own lives. The project discussed with young people their landscapes of racialised fear and danger in the mapping of the ghetto.

31 E. Laclau and C. Mouffe, 1985, *Hegemony and Socialist Strategy* (London: Verso), p. 113.

32 Instead, as Zizek has commented, Laclau and Mouffe's work 'articulates the contours of a political project based on an ethics of the real'. S. Zizek, 2000, 'Da capo senza fine', in J. Butler, E. Laclau and S. Zizek, 2000, *Contingency, Hegemony, Universality: Contemporary Dialogues on the Left* (London and New York: Verso), p. 259.

33 A. Mbembe, 2001, *On The Postcolony* (Berkeley: University of California Press).

34 S. Hall, C. Critcher, T. Jefferson, J. Clarke and B. Roberts, 1978, *Policing The Crisis* (London: Macmillan), Chapter 10.

35 Hall *et al.*, *Policing the Crisis*, p. 329.

36 Hall *et al.*, *Policing the Crisis*, p. 329.

37 S. Hall, 1979, *Drifting into a Law and Order Society* (The Cobden Lecture, London: The Cobden Trust), p. 3.

38 Hall, *Drifting into a Law and Order Society*, p. 13.

39 Hall, *Drifting into a Law and Order Society*, p. 13.

40 A. Gamble, 1988, *The Free Economy and the Strong State: The Politics of Thatcherism* (London: Macmillan), p. 16.

41 P. Gilroy, 1987, *There Ain't no Black in the Union Jack* (London: Hutchinson); P. Gilroy and J. Sim, 1985, 'Law, order and the state of the left', *Capital and Class*, 25, pp. 15–21.

42 Gilroy, *There Ain't no Black in the Union Jack*, p. 74.

43 Gilroy, *There Ain't no Black in the Union Jack*, p. 76.

44 Keith, *Race, Riots and Policing*, Chapters 10 and 11.

45 Most famously, see H. Becker, 1971, *Outsiders* (New York: Free Press); E. Goffman, 1963, *Stigma* (Harmondsworth: Penguin).

46 See E. Said, 1978, *Orientalism* (London: Peregrine).

47 R. Young, 1990, *Colonial Desire: Hybridity in Theory, Culture and Race* (London: Routledge), p. 127.

48 Young, *Colonial Desire*, p. 128.
49 Although the distinction between representations of space and spaces of representation in Lefèbvre is useful, the heuristic distinctions used here between the literal, the dramaturgical and the imagined do not equate with his threefold typology of the perceived, the conceived and the lived and the accompanying Eurocentric notion of the transformation of absolute to abstract space.
50 M. Keith and A. Rogers (eds), 1991, *Hollow Promises: Rhetoric and Reality in the Inner City* (London: Mansell).
51 R. Ardrey, 1961, *The Territorial Imperative* (London: Fontana).
52 D. Harvey, 1989, *The Condition of Postmodernity* (London: Blackwell), p. 355.
53 In a similar vein Sharon Zukin has reiterated this appeal to reality in her suggestion that 'circuits of cultural capital are formed in real spaces'. S. Zukin, 1991, *Landscapes of Power: From Detroit to Disneyworld* (Berkeley: University of California Press), p. 266.
54 R. Sennett, 1977, *The Fall of Public Man* (London: Faber and Faber).
55 All quotes in this section are taken from the transcription of the Scarman Inquiry which is placed in the Public Records Office at Kew.
56 See Keith, *Race, Riots and Policing*.
57 D. Howe, 1981, *From Bobby to Babylon* (London: Race Today Collective).
58 Keith, *Race, Riots and Policing*.
59 S. Pile and G. Rose, 1992, 'All or nothing. Politics and critique in the modernism/postmodernism debate', *Society and Space*, 10, pp. 123–36.
60 F. Fanon, 1963/1965, *The Wretched of the Earth* (London: MacGibbon and Kee), p. 41.
61 P. Stallybrass and A. White, 1986, *The Politics and Poetics of Transgression* (London: Methuen), p. 131.
62 E. Wilson, 1991, *The Sphinx and the City* (London: Verso), p. 8.
63 See E. Laclau, 1990, *New Reflections on the Revolution of our Time* (London: Verso); and also Butler *et al.*, *Contingency, Hegemony, Universality*.
64 S. Hall, 1987, 'Minimal selves', in L. Appignanesi (ed.), *The Real Me: Postmodernism and the Question of Identity* (London: ICA), p. 45.
65 S. Hall, 1990, 'Cultural identity and cinematic representation', *Framework,* 36, pp. 68–80, at p. 74.
66 Hall, 'Minimal selves', p. 44.
67 See the series of reports on the Deptford City Challenge programme published by CUCR at Goldsmiths College, University of London (www.goldsmiths.ac.uk/cucr).
68 Steele, *Turning the Tide: The History of Everyday Deptford.*
69 J. Conrad, 1988 [1899] *Heart of Darkness* (London and New York: W. W. Norton), pp. 8–9.
70 B. Hesse, 1993, 'Black to front and Black again: racialization through contested times and spaces', in M. Keith and S. Pile (eds), 1993, *Place and the Politics of Identity* (London: Routledge), where Hesse problematises the dominance of 'Windrush narratives' that temporalise the black presence in the UK through the dominant metaphoric originary point of the *SS Empire Windrush*'s landing in London, bringing Caribbean migrant labour to the UK in the postwar era.
71 See Keith, *Race, Riots and Policing*.
72 See J. Anim-Addo, 1995, *Longest Journey: A History of Black Lewisham* (London: Deptford Forum Publishing).

5 Ethnic entrepreneurs and street rebels: Looking inside the inner city

1 See S. Pile and N. Thrift (eds), 1995, *Mapping the Subject* (London: Routledge).
2 In the work on social capital the landmark study is clearly that of R. D. Putban, 2000, *Bowling Alone? The Collapse and Revival of American Community* (London and New York: Simon and Schuster). The most powerful critique of this literature is to be found in B. Fine, 2001, *Social Capital or Social Theory: Political Economy and Social Science at the Turn of the Millennium* (London: Routledge). In terms of the invocation of this literature, see

B. Rothstein, 2001, 'Social capital and the social democratic welfare state', *Politics and Society*, 29 (2), pp. 207–41.

3 Drawing on a more general sense of governance, this is sometimes understood as the 'quango state', alluding to the growth of quasi-autonomous non-governmental organisations. The role of forms of regulation that frame action draws on the analytical frame of reference already developed in Chapter 3.

4 T. Osborne and N. Rose, 1999, 'Governing cities: notes of the spatialisation of virtue', *Environment and Planning D: Society and Space*, 17, pp. 737–60.

5 M. Keith and A. Rogers, 1991, 'Hollow promises: policy, theory and practice in the inner city', Chapter 1 of *Hollow Promises: Rhetoric and Reality in the Inner City* (London: Mansell).

6 Much of the work for this chapter is based on work by the author as part of the Deptford City Challenge Evaluation Project (DCCEP) at the Centre for Urban and Community Research, Goldsmiths College, from 1992 to 1998. The DCCEP consisted of Elsa Guzman-Flores, Michael Keith, Aileen O'Gorman, Nikolas Rose and Philippa Superville. Thanks are due to all of the team and the many individuals working within the City Challenge Process who were so cooperative in the conduct of the five-year ethnography from which this work is drawn.

7 Deptford City Challenge Evaluation Project, 1993, *Deptford City Challenge Baseline Study* (London: CUCR/DCCEP, Goldsmiths College).

8 R. Atkinson and G. Moon, 1994, *Urban Policy in Britain* (Basingstoke: Macmillan).

9 I. Light, 1972, *Ethnic Enterprise in America* (Berkeley and Los Angeles: University of California Press); I. Light and E. Bonacich, 1988, *Immigrant Entrepreneurs* (Berkeley and Los Angeles: University of California Press); I. Light and C. Rosenstyn, 1995, *Race, Ethnicity and Entrepreneurship in Urban America* (New York: Aldyne de Gruyter); A. Portes and R. Bach, 1985, *Latin Journey* (Berkeley: University of California Press); A. Portes and L. Jensen, 1987, 'What is an ethnic enclave? The case for conceptual clarity', *American Sociological Review*, 52, pp. 768–71; R. Waldinger, 1993, 'The ethnic enclave debate revisited', *International Journal of Urban and Regional Research*, 17, pp. 444–52; R. Ward and R. Jenkins, 1984, *Ethnic Communities in Business; Strategies for Economic Survival* (Cambridge: Cambridge University Press); P. Werbner, 2001, 'Metaphors of spatiality and networks in the plural city: a critique of the ethnic economy debate', *Sociology*, 35 (3), pp. 671–93.

10 All quoted material in this chapter is drawn from the reports in the work of the Deptford City Challenge Evaluation Project.

11 Training and Enterprise Councils were created in the United Kingdom in 1990 to control central government programmes for business support and labour supply management. They also gained access to specific funds for the promotion of 'ethnic enterprise' and in several cities either participated in urban regeneration partnerships or led programmes of urban regeneration through bids for central government and/or European monies. Training and Enterprise Councils were replaced by Learning and Skills Councils in 2000.

12 After the completion of this chapter a compromise was reached between different parties and the new Business Association was launched, but the institutional realisation of the subject position of 'ethnic enterprise' remained uncertain.

13 Runnymede Trust, 1993, *Race Relations in Tower Hamlets* (London: Runnymede Trust); Tower Hamlets Homeless Families Campaign (THHFC), 1993, *Tower Hamlets Policies on Homelessness* (London: THHFC).

14 Lord Lester (chair), 1993, *Political Speech and Race Relations in a Liberal Democracy: Report of an Inquiry into the Conduct of the Tower Hamlets Liberal Democrats in Publishing Allegedly Racist Election Literature between 1990 and 1993* (London: Liberal Democratic Party).

15 J. Mohan, 1992, *Financial Pressure on the Voluntary Sector in Tower Hamlets* (Queen Mary and Westfield College, University of London: Department of Geography Working Paper).

16 CAPA Legal Advice and Support Group, Centre for Bangladeshi Studies, Queen Mary and Westfield College, Tower Hamlets Race Equality Council (THREC), 1993, *Young*

Bengalis and the Criminal Justice System: Proceedings of a Conference Held at QMW, University of London (London: QMW).

17 *The Independent*, 20 April 1992, p. 4.

18 M. Keith, 1993, *Race, Riots and Policing: Lore and Disorder in a Multi-racist Society* (London: UCL Press).

19 S. Hall, C. Critcher, T. Jefferson, J. Clarke and B. Robert, 1978, *Policing the Crisis* (London: Macmillan).

20 Bethnal Green City Challenge, 1991, 'Bethnal Green City Challenge Action Plan: Working Together to Unlock Opportunities' (mimeo submitted to the DoE).

21 Bethnal Green City Challenge, 1993, 'Action Plan 1994–95' (mimeo submitted to the DoE).

22 C. Gordon, 1991, 'Governmental rationality: an introduction', in G. Burchell, C. Gordon and P. Miller (eds), *The Foucault Effect: Studies in Governmentality* (Hemel Hempstead: Harvester Wheatsheaf), p. 8.

23 H. Bhabha, 1993, *The Location of Culture* (Oxford: Blackwell), p. 218.

24 Gordon, 'Governmental rationality: an introduction', p. 47.

6 The street: Street sensibility?

1 The original version of this chapter was given at a conference on 'Social Justice and fin de siècle Urbanism', on 14 and 15 March 1994, at the School of Geography in the University of Oxford, in celebration of the twentieth anniversary of the publication of David Harvey's *Social Justice and the City*. Many thanks are due to Eric Swyngedouw and Andy Merrifield for organising the conference, for their responses to an earlier draft of this chapter, and for their patience in waiting for me to complete the revisions. First published as 'Street sensibility? Negotiating the political by articulating the spatial', in A. Merrifield and E. Swyngedouw (eds), 1995, *The Urbanisation of Injustice* (London: Lawrence and Wishart).

2 The area referenced in this chapter is a small patch of East London in the London borough of Tower Hamlets, bounded by the Highway in the south, Bethnal Green Road in the north, Spitalfields market in the west and Burdett Road in the east. London's own Ellis Island, it is an area that has been inscribed with the presence of Huguenot, Jewish, African, Afro-Caribbean, Irish and Somali migrants, along with countless other dispossessed and displaced minorities, tracked, traced and explored by generations of urban explorers, spectators, philanthropists, walkers and academics.

3 In the three cases I am trying to follow Stallybrass and Whyte's contention that 'what is socially peripheral is so frequently symbolically central'. P. Stallybrass and A. Whyte, 1986, *The Politics and Poetics of Transgression* (London: Methuen), p. 5.

4 Whitechapel Art Gallery flier, 1992.

5 Whitechapel Art Gallery flier.

6 Patricia C. Philips, 1992, in the exhibition catalogue, 'Republica de Chile Pasaporte', n.p.

7 J. Bird, 1992, in the 'catalogue'. There was no conventional catalogue as such for the exhibition but instead a commentary by John Bird, three of Jaar's maps in his 'new cartography' and an essay on Jaar's work by Patricia C. Philips inside a replica Chilean passport. It is this 'package' that is referred to here as the 'catalogue'.

8 A article from the journal *Capital and Class* almost ten years before was pointed to in the gallery for 'background reading'.

9 Bird in the 'catalogue'.

10 Paradoxically, given the fuss that the exhibition prompted, the accompanying essay by John Bird in the exhibition 'catalogue', which in the main gives a valuable theoretical frame of reference for the installation, closes with a quote from Spivak: 'It's all very well to theorise cultural practices and institutions as potential sites for discursive intervention into the construction of social meaning, but this has also to take account of

discrepant audiences, different agendas and modalities of resistance – of the necessity of "doing our homework properly".' It is surely around precisely this notion of doing 'one's homework properly' that the installation, provoking though it was, ultimately failed.

11 Taken one way, the image of Spivak and the pool of water was a clever and very witty way of ironising some of the debates around masculinism, narcissism and the lust for knowledge, and in particular the feminist cut on these debates. See L. Irigaray, 1985, *Speculum of the Other Woman* (Ithaca, NY: Cornell University Press); J. Mitchell, 1974, *Feminism and Psychoanalysis* (London: Allen Lane); J. Rose, *Sexuality in the Field of Vision* (London: Verso); all in marked contrast to C. Lasch, 1978, *The Culture of Narcissism: American Life in an Age of Diminishing Expectations* (New York: Norton).

12 Walter Benjamin's term (1971), coined in *Charles Baudelaire: A Lyric Poet in the Era of High Capitalism* (London: Harry Zohn), p. 36.

13 Brick Lane lies at the heart of Spitalfields and is dominated by small Bengali businesses, particularly restaurants and shops. It is also the site of a mosque in an old Jewish synagogue that was once famously a Huguenot church. In many ways it is both the symbolic heart of Bengali settlement in Britain and an iconic site of city transition. The work in this section of the chapter is based in part on a series of interviews conducted by the author and Denise Jones with restaurant owners and workers in the immediate aftermath of the 'Brick Lane rampage'. The interview material was used locally to consider the potential legal case the restaurant owners had for compensation for the extensive damage to their shops.

14 It is important to stress that in this and the subsequent example there is no attempt to provide an authoritative account of these events or to represent the perceptions or feelings of the Bengali community at this time. For such accounts see the bulletins produced by Tower Hamlets Against Racism, Tower Hamlets Anti-Racist Committee and the interview with Kumar Murshid in *Regenerating Cities*, no. 6 (1994). It is instead the case that I am trying to work through how these and other practices are 'placed' within the racialised frame of everyday life in the East End.

15 It is surely no coincidence that a postmodern displacement of metanarrative certainty with little narratives and local knowledges has found a narrative echo in the renewed fascination with the personal memoir, the wanderings of the contemporary *flâneur* – Davis and Sieff in Los Angeles, Fitch in New York, Patrick Wright, Iain Sinclair and Elizabeth Wilson in London. There are also epistemological equivalents of such developments, which might owe their lineage principally to the urban mythologies of Roland Barthes, tracing the indeterminacy of the signs of the streets and the celebrations of the poets of the street by Michel de Certeau. For such a valorisation see, for instance, R. Deutsche, 1991, 'Boys town', *Environment and Planning D: Society and Space*, 9, pp. 5–30; M. Keith, 1999, 'Walter Benjamin, urban studies and the narratives of city life', in G. Bridge and S. Watson, 1999, *The Blackwell Companion to Urban Studies* (Oxford: Blackwell).

16 It is in this context that D. Frisby, 1994, 'The flaneur in social theory', in K. Tester (ed.), *The Flâneur* (London: Routledge), has argued for the relevance of the lessons of the *flâneur* to be taken on board in a reconsideration of the work of figures such as Robert Park and that the work of Walter Benjamin should be reinstated in mainstream social science, for 'In so doing we are compelled to recognise that in . . . his Arcades Project and in his many other writings, Benjamin revealed himself to be not merely an outstanding literary critic and writer in his own right, nor merely a subtle philosopher of history, nor indeed merely a stimulating and often unorthodox Marxist – and all of these groupings have claimed Benjamin as their own – but also a *sociologist*' (p. 82, emphasis in original). This is notwithstanding Benjamin's own warnings of 'the euphemistic whisperings of sociology'.

17 Liz Heron, 1994, Introduction to *Streets of Desire* (London: Virago). See also how Judith Walkowitz has described the manner in which the changing configuration of late Victorian capitalism 'rendered the streets of London an enigmatic and contested site for

class and gender encounters'. J. Walkowitz, 1992, *City of Dreadful Delight: Narratives of Sexual Danger in Late-Victorian London* (London: Virago), p. 41.

18 Cf. I. M. Young, 1990, 'The ideal of community and the politics of difference', in L. J. Nicholson, *Feminism/Postmodernism* (London: Routledge).

19 This is not to say that these properties are necessary properties of an essential urbanism – only that vocabularies of urbanism are constitutive organising principles of them. See M. Keith and M. Cross, 1993, 'Racism and the postmodern city', in M. Cross and M. Keith (eds), *Racism, the City and the State* (London: Routledge).

20 Cf. L. Mulvey, 1989, *Visual and Other Pleasures: Language, Discourse, Society* (London: Macmillan); G. Pollock, 1988, *Vision and Difference: Feminism, Femininity and the Histories of Art* (London: Routledge); J. Wolff, 1989, 'The invisible flaneuse: women and the literature of modernity', in A. Benjamin, 1989, *The Problems of Modernity: Adorno and Benjamin* (London: Routledge).

21 L. Davidoff and C. Hall, 1987, *Family Fortunes: Men and Women of the English Middle Class, 1780–1850* (London: Hutchinson).

22 E. Wilson, 1991, *Sphinx in the City: Urban Life, the Control of Disorder and Women* (London: Virago).

23 Walkowitz, *City of Dreadful Delight*.

24 See S. Marcus, 1973, 'Reading the illegible', in H. J. Dyos and M. Wolff (eds), *The Victorian City: Images and Realities* (London: Routledge).

25 As John Rignall has pointed out, Benjamin himself was not consistent; on the one hand Benjamin's *flâneur*, who revels in the gaze, never really challenges the idea that to see is to know. Indeed 'the transformation of the street into a kind of interior is one of the ways in which he makes the alien urban world bearably familiar . . . the flaneur also combines the casual eye of the stroller with the purposeful gaze of the detective. His vision is thus both widely ranging and deeply penetrating at the same time.' J. Rignall, 1979, 'Benjamin's flaneur and the problem of realism', in Benjamin, *The Problems of Modernity*, p. 119. However, the *flâneur*'s position remains a precarious one, not because of a crisis of aesthetics, but because with the changing form of the capitalist city he (sic), through immersion, becomes identified with the commodity caught in the maelstrom of the capitalist urban. Consequently 'the narrator has come finally to admit that the heart of the world cannot be known' (Rignall, 'Benjamin's flâneur', p. 119), pointing a way to the crisis of the realist narrative form.

26 Benjamin in *Charles Baudelaire*.

27 In losing oneself on the streets only to find oneself and an identity within the matrices of contemporary capitalism, Benjamin's uncertain *flâneur* predates Jameson's project of 'cognitive mapping' and in his doubt pre-empts Jameson's notion of 'incommensurability-vision'.

28 See K. Robins, 1993, Prisoners of the city: whatever could a postmodern city be?', in E. Carter, J. Donald and J. Squires (eds), *Space and Place: Theories of Identity and Location* (London: Lawrence and Wishart).

29 G. Deleuze and F. Guattari, 1988, 'The rhizome', in *A Thousand Plateaus: Capitalism and Schizophrenia* (London: Athlone).

30 There is one caveat here. On the one hand the more optimistic characterisations of cross-cultural identification disrupt the metanarrative certainties of history with a spatially nuanced vocabulary – space subverts time, geography is the modality through which third space is articulated. On the other hand, celebrations of the city, be it the city as lived or the city as signed, tend to slide towards an assessment of the immanent properties of the essential urban, something that is not suggested here.

31 The reference here and later in the chapter is to Sennett's 1977 celebration of 'the publick' throughout his work *The Fall of Public Man* (London: Faber and Faber).

32 I. Chambers, 1990, *Border Dialogues* (London: Routledge).

33 These are the central values at the heart of Sennett's analysis of *The Fall of Public Man*, pp. 238–40.

34 One striking example of this particular representation was seen in the title given to an edition of the journal *Race and Class* at around this time – 'Black America: the street and the campus', *Race and Class*, 35 (1) (July–September 1993) – an explicit contrast easily slipping into an implicit binary opposition.

35 Fanon's opening of *Black Skin, White Masks* captures the subjectification of the black body through the white gaze. Taken together with his axiomatic notion that 'the black man's soul is a white man's artefact' and the memorably epigrammatic comment that 'The Black man is not. Any more than the White man', Fanon's work has become increasingly important in cultural studies projects that trace back the construction of processes of racialisation to the social context in which the formative experiences of identification and identity formation take place. It is this *taking place* element of this process that makes an understanding of the spatialities of a sophisticated urbanism indispensable to anti-racist theory and practice. F. Fanon, 1967 [1952], *Black Skin, White Masks* (London: Pluto).

36 An illustrated version of this chapter with the images from the press stories appeared in A. Merrifield and E. Swyngedouw, 1995, *The Politics of Injustice* (Brighton: Harvester Wheatsheaf).

37 See M. Keith, 1993, *Race, Riots and Policing* (London: UCL Press), Chapter 12, for a fuller elaboration of the manner in which 'blackness' becomes a sign of criminal otherness in a manner that allows the tropes of criminalisation that have blighted the lives of British Afro-Caribbean communities to work across the 'Black/Asian' distinction of popular British racial discourse in a manner which narrates the experiences of young Bengali men and young Afro-Caribbean men through the same vocabulary.

38 See bell hooks, 1992, *Black Looks: Race and Representation* (London: Turnaround).

39 In discussing the framing of images of the beating of Rodney King, Judith Butler has made precisely this point forcefully with the comment that 'The visual field is not neutral to the question of race; it is itself a racialised formation, an episteme, hegemonic and forceful.' J. Butler, 1993, 'Endangered/endangering schematic racism and white paranoia', in R. Gooding-Williams, *Reading Rodney King, Reading Urban Uprising* (London: Routledge), pp. 15–22 at p. 17.

40 The most impressive exposition of this is found in Michael Taussig's 1987 *Shamanism, Colonialism and the 'Wild Man'* (Chicago, Ill.: University of Chicago Press), developed theoretically in 1993 in *Mimesis and Alterity* (London: Routledge).

41 See S. Hall, 1982, 'The lessons of Lord Scarman', *Critical Social Policy*, 2, pp. 66–72.

42 See, for instance, how in E. Laclau, 1990, *New Revolution for Our Times* (London: Verso), 'the political' is defined in terms of contestable practices.

43 It is precisely this sort of slippage that lies at the heart of M. Berman, 1970, *The Politics of Authenticity* (Oxford: Oxford University Press).

44 In particular see Laclau, *New Revolution*, but also M. Keith and S. Pile, 1993, 'The politics of place', Chapter 2 of M. Keith and S. Pile (eds), *Place and the Politics of Identity* (London: Routledge).

45 H. Bhabha, 1994, *The Location of Culture* (London: Routledge), pp. 228, 231. It is perhaps not insignificant that the demands to speak to the authenticity of territory is not equivalent across the range of the new cultural politics of difference. For example, the nuances of sexualised and gendered territorial authenticity contrast strikingly with those of race and class.

46 Although Bhabha himself talks about the 'the contradictory and ambivalent space of enunciation' (*The Location of Culture*, p. 37), he appears reluctant to tie this in to sophisticated understandings of political economy. Powerfully exposing the narrative form through which Frederic Jameson ultimately resorts to the optical ontology of class categories, to enable him to 'see to the bottom of the stream' and resolve the problems of 'incommensurability vision' (*The Location of Culture*, pp. 216–24), Bhabha remains reluctant to examine the imbrication of class and culture, always preferring to cite colonialism without ever representing colonialism itself as a productive system, a silence

that is surely a weakness of much of postcolonial cultural studies. See, for instance, P. Williams and L. Chrisman (eds), 1993, *Colonial Discourse and Postcolonial Theory* (London: Routledge).

47 See M. Berman, 1982, *All That Is Solid Melts into Air* (London: Verso), Part V.

48 Bhabha, *The Location of Culture*, p. 241.

49 D. Harvey, 1973, *Social Justice and the City* (London: Edward Arnold), p. 22.

50 Where representation necessarily misrepresents we find the political moment when the strategic nature of closure is revealed. Such closures are moments in a politics of articulation, an echo of something Fanon reflected on while listening to the radio in the midst of anti-colonial war: 'The Arabic channel was of course jammed. But the scraps of sound had an exaggerated effect. Like rumours, they were constructively heard, and listening to them became an act of participation in revolutionary victories which might never have occurred. To quote Fanon, "the radio receiver guaranteed this true lie".' In S. Feuchtwang, 1985, 'Fanon's politics of culture: the colonial situation and its extension', *Economy and Society*, 14 (4), pp. 450–73.

51 The Tower Hamlets 9 were nine Asian youths arrested at the vigil outside the London Hospital for Quddus Ali. The Tower Hamlets 9 Defence Campaign was set up by local youth in Tower Hamlets to campaign on their behalf.

7 The cultural quarter: Globalisation, hybridity and curating exotica

1 S. Zukin, 2001, 'How to make a cultural capital: reflections on urban markets and places', in I. Blazwick (ed.), *Century City* (London: Tate Modern), pp. 258–64.

2 W. Benjamin, 1999, *The Arcades Project*, trans. Rolf Tiedemann (Cambridge, Mass.: Belknap Press.

3 In an article for the *New Yorker* in September 1998, Toni Morrison famously suggested that 'Clinton displays almost every trope of blackness: single-parent household, born poor, working-class, saxophone-playing, McDonald's-and-junk-food-loving boy from Arkansas.'

4 See S. Shukla, 2002, 'Cross-cultures in twentieth century Harlem', paper given at 'Re-imagining Communities', Institute for Women's Studies, Lancaster University, 23–25 May 2002.

5 Michael Powell, 'Bill Clinton homeboy: as the ex-president opens his new office, Harlem (mostly) opens its arms', *Washington Post*, 31 July 2001.

6 In S. Zukin, 1995, *The Cultures of Cities* (Oxford: Blackwell), p. 9.

7 However, important issues of definition surround those forms of activity which are or are not included within the notion of the cultural industries. To take one recent example used by the prestigious urban regeneration consultants AEA in a study of the future of East London, the cultural industries are taken to include the six core subsectors of performing arts, visual arts, audio-visual, music, design and publishing. The business structure, economies of scale and scope, vertical and horizontal integration, internal logics, economic imperatives and finance and capital norms clearly range enormously across small, medium and multinational companies within these economic areas. This does not challenge the central and organising importance of the symbolic and the aesthetic in their constitution, but it does raise questions about where the generalised category of cultural industries is useful in providing explanation and the moments at which it becomes conceptually chaotic.

8 C. Leadbeater, 1999, *Living on Thin Air: The New Economy* (London: Penguin); C. Leadbeater and K. Oakley, 1999, *The Independents* (London: Demos); C. Landry, 2000, *The Creative City: A Toolkit for Urban Innovators* (London: Earthscan Publications Ltd).

9 R. Florida, 2002, *The Rise of the Creative Class* (New York: Basic Books), p. 201.

10 For a comprehensive and helpful overview of the growth in both the cultural industries themselves and the related literature, see D. Hesmondhalgh, 2002, *The Cultural Industries* (London: Sage). See also the introduction and contributions to P. du Gay and M. Pryke

(eds), 2002, *Cultural Economy* (London: Sage), for a consideration of the *culturalisation* of the economy, including A. MacRobbie, 'From Holloway to Hollywood: happiness at work in the new cultural economy'.

11 Comedia, 1996, *The Art of Regeneration* (London: Comedia); F. Tonkiss, 2002, 'Between markets, firms and networks: constituting the cultural economy', in S. Metcalfe and A. Warde (eds), *Market Relations and the Competitive Process* (Manchester: Manchester University Press), pp. 114–29; A. Pratt, 2002, 'Managing creativity in the cultural industries', *Creativity and Innovation Management* 11 (4), pp. 225–33 (editorial, and Special Guest Editor with Paul Jeffcutt); A. Pratt, 2002, 'Hot jobs in cool places: the material cultures of new media product spaces: the case of South of the Market, San Francisco', *Information, Communication and Society*, 5 (1), pp. 27–50; A. Pratt, 2000, 'New media, the new economy and new spaces', *Geoforum*, 31, pp. 425–36.

12 See Zukin, *The Culture of Cities*.

13 R. Kitchin, 2002, 'Sexing the city: The sexual production of non-heterosexual space in Belfast, Manchester and San Francisco', *City*, 6 (2), pp. 205–18; J. Binnie and B. Skeggs, 2004, 'Cosmopolitan knowledge and the production and consumption of sexualized space: Manchester's gay village', *Sociological Review*, 52 (1), pp. 39–61.

14 Wun Fung Chan, 2003, 'Chinese Identities: Official Representations and New Ethnicities' (Ph.D. thesis, Department of Geography, University of Birmingham); K. Anderson, 1991, *Vancouver's Chinatown: Racial Discourse in Canada 1875–1980* (Montreal and Buffalo: McGill-Queen's University Press).

15 J. M. Jacobs, 1996, *Edge of Empire: Postcolonialism and the City* (London and New York: Routledge).

16 J. Urry, 1995, *Consuming Places* (London: Routledge).

17 See material around the *Creative London* programme on the LDA website at http:// www.creativelondon.org.uk/about.php.

18 See Jacobs, *Edge of Empire*; also H. Begum, 2002, 'The East End: a multicultural mosaic or cosmopolitan conundrum', paper given at ESRC 'Transforming London: rethinking regeneration through commerce, planning and art' seminar programme; G. Mavromatis, 2003, 'Race, Gentrification and Difference' (Ph.D. thesis, Goldsmiths College, University of London).

19 Like the subject positions of ethnic entrepreneur, street rebel or single mother dealt with in Chapter 5, the cartographic marker of the cultural quarter cannot be separated from its cultural signifier. This is neither to decry the study of ethnic enterprise nor to challenge the power of the cultural industries in reshaping the urban. It is instead to argue that the cultural signification of the cartographies of the metropolis and its visible subjects need to be understood as causally related to the material configurations of property values, economic activity and labour markets.

20 A. Amin, 1997, 'Postfordism: models, fantasies and phantoms of transition', in A. Amin, *Postfordism: A Reader* (Oxford: Blackwell), p. 31.

21 P. Gilroy, 1993, *The Black Atlantic: Modernity and Double Consciousness* (London: Verso); P. Gilroy, 2000, *Between Camps: Race, Identity and Nationalism at the End of the Colour Line* (London: Penguin).

22 See also D. Basu and P. Werbner, 2001, 'Bootstrap capitalism and the culture industries: a critique of invidious comparisons in the study of ethnic entrepreneurship', *Ethnic and Racial Studies*, 24 (2), pp. 236–62.

23 C. Harris, 1987, 'British capitalism, migration and relative surplus-population', *Migration*, 1 (1), pp. 21–46; R. Miles, 1993, *Racism after 'Race Relations'* (London: Routledge).

24 C. Peach, 1968, *West Indian Migration to Britain* (Oxford: Oxford University Press).

25 M. Cross (ed.), 1992, *Ethnic Minorities and Industrial Change in Europe and North America* (Cambridge: Cambridge University Press).

26 Policy Studies Institute, 1996, *Trends in Ethnic Minority Labour Market Involvement* (London: PSI); Parekh Report, 2001, *The Future of Multiethnic Britain* (London: Profile

Books); K. Malik, 1996, *The Meaning of Race: Race, History and Culture in Western Society* (Basingstoke: Macmillan).

27 N. Jewson and D. Mason, 1986, 'Modes of discrimination in the recruitment process: formalisation, fairness and efficiency', *Sociology*, 20 (1), pp. 43–63.

28 R. Jenkins and J. Solomos, 1987, *Racism and Equal Opportunity Policies in the 1980s* (Cambridge: Cambridge University Press); J. Wrench, 1996, *Preventing Racism in the Workplace: A Report on 16 European Countries* (Dublin: European Foundation for the Improvement of Living and Working Conditions).

29 C. Peach (ed.), 1996, *Ethnicity in the 1991 Census*, vol. 2: *The Ethnic Minority Populations of Great Britain* (London: HMSO).

30 J. Solomos, 2003 (revised original 1989), *Race and Racism in Britain* (London: Macmillan).

31 A. Pratt, 2000, 'New media, the new economy and new spaces', *Geoforum*, 31, pp. 425–36.

32 See, for example, the work by Calvin Taylor and others at the University of Leeds on www.creativeyorkshire.com.

33 C. Boyer, 1994, *The City of Collective Memory* (Cambridge, Mass.: MIT Press); G. Kearns and C. Philo (eds), 1993, *Selling Places: The City as Cultural Capital* (Oxford: Pergamon Press); M. Sorkin (ed.), 1992, *Variations on a Theme Park* (New York: Hill and Wang); J. Urry, 1995, *Consuming Places* (London: Routledge).

34 J. Lash and S. Urry, 1994, *Economies of Signs and Space* (London: Sage).

35 H. Bhabha (ed.), 1990, *Nation and Narration* (London: Routledge); Jacobs, *Edge of Empire*.

36 N. Smith, 1996, *The New Urban Frontier: Gentrification and the Revanchist City* (London: Routledge), p. 37.

37 Smith, *The New Urban Frontier*.

38 See D. Slater and F. Tonkiss, 1998, *Markets, Modernity and Social Theory* (London: Polity Press).

39 P. Hirst and J. Zeitlin (eds), 1989, *Reversing Industrial Decline?* (Oxford: Berg).

40 See Landry, *The Creative City*, and C. Landry, 2001, *Creative Lewisham: Report of the Lewisham Culture and Urban Development Commission* (London: London Borough of Lewisham).

41 A. D. Sorenson, 1981, 'Towards a market theory of planning', *Planner*, 69 (3), pp. 4–14.

42 J.-P. Le Dantec, 1991, 'For a baroque approach to cities and architecture', *Architecture and Behaviour*, 7 (4), pp. 467–78; L. Sandercock, 1998, *Towards Cosmopolis* (London: Wiley); J. Holston, 2001, 'Spaces of insurgent citizenship', in L. Sandercock (ed.), *Making The Invisible Visible: Insurgent Planning Histories* (Berkeley: University of California Press).

43 The notion of *the quarter* is important here. Space prevents too extensive a digression, but the notion of the city fragment implicit in the *quarter* (or neighbourhood, or district) appeals to an uncertain metonymy. The whole that is its logical and linguistic corollary might be identified with the totality of the city or the totality of the cultural network or the universal. It is the incomplete nature of the constitution of the cultural quarter that questions what lies beyond its boundaries and how its constitutive outside is constituted.

44 See C. Lury, 1996, *Consumer Culture* (Cambridge: Polity Press); S. Franklin, C. Lury and J. Stacey, 2000, *Global Nature, Global Culture* (London: Sage).

45 A. Appadurai, 2001, *Globalisation* (Durham, NC: Duke University Press); A. Appadurai, 2002, 'Deep democracy: urban governmentality and the horizon of politics', *Public Culture*, 14 (1), pp. 21–47.

46 See D. Archibugi and D. Held (eds), 1995, *Cosmopolitan Democracy* (Oxford and Cambridge: Polity Press); U. Beck, 2001, 'Cosmopolis and risk: a conversation with Ulrich Beck', *Theory, Culture and Society*, 18 (4), pp. 47–63; J. Habermas, 2001, *The Postnational Constellation: Political Essays* (Oxford and Cambridge: Polity Press).

47 T. Finkelpearl, 2000, 'The city as site', in T. Finkelpearl (ed.), *Dialogues in Public Art* (Cambridge, Mass.: MIT Press); M. Miles, 1997, *Art, Space and the City* (London: Routledge); W. J. T. Mitchell, 1990, *Art and the Public Sphere* (Chicago, Ill.: University of Chicago Press).

48   Benjamin, *The Arcades Project*, p. 533. For a helpful discussion of many related arguments see I. Karp and S. D. Lavine, 1991, *Exhibiting Cultures: The Poetics and Politics of Museum Display* (London and Washington: Smithsonian Press).

49   The principal curator of Documenta 11 – Okwui Enwezor – impressively refers to the aim of both deterritorialising the hegemonic placing of Documenta in the German city of Kassel and explicitly intervening in specifically local situations, as enlarging 'the space of the critical debates of contemporary artistic discourse today'. O. Enwezor, 2002, 'Preface', in *Documenta 11_Platform 5: Exhibition Catalogue* (Kassel, Ostfildern-Ruit: Hatje Cantz Publisher), p. 40.

50   H. Bhabha, 1997, 'Minority culture and creative anxiety', in British Council, 2003, *Reinventing Britain* (British Council website).

51   S. Hall, 1999, 'Whose heritage?', keynote address at 'Whose Heritage? The Impact of Cultural Diversity on Britain's Living Heritage', national conference at G-Mex, Manchester, 1–3 November.

52   The Parekh Report attempted to describe the state of multicultural Britain that followed on from the 1960s IRR project, which tried to provide a defining portrait of multiracial Britain in N. Deakin, 1970, *Colour, Citizenship and British Society* (London: Fontana). See Parekh Report, *The Future of Multiethnic Britain*.

53   For Beck: 'The nation state is a zombie category because it cannot handle the cosmopolitanization which has been taking place within the containers it labels.' Beck, 'Cosmopolis and risk', p. 47.

54   It is important to stress that neither Hall nor Bhabha confuses debates over an ethics of recognition with the belated acknowledgment of some of the major arts funders of the racialised institutional biases of their own practice. However, the figuring of this problematic – not least in the epigraph by Sharon Zukin with which the chapter starts – and some of the more Benetton moments of the Century City exhibition that christened the opening of Tate Modern in London at the millennium do precisely this.

55   Benjamin, *The Arcades Project*, p. 531.

56   S. Hall, 1997, 'The nub of the argument', in British Council, *Reinventing Britain*. See also the collection of essays in F. Jameson and M. Miyoshi, 1998, *The Cultures of Globalization* (Durham, NC: Duke University Press).

57   N. Glazer and D. P. Moynihan, 1970 [1963], *Beyond the Melting Pot* (Cambridge, Mass.: MIT Press).

58   K. Mercer, 1994, *Welcome to the Jungle: Essays in Black Cultural Studies* (London: Routledge). In this fashion the debate of 2003 in which Monica Ali's novel *Brick Lane* was systematically celebrated by a white literary élite and denounced by certain sections of the Sylheti population in East London is paradigmatic. Both the quality of the literature and the right to narrate such lives were the subject of controversy; frequently the calculus of the former was said (quite wrongly) to depend on the validity of the latter.

59   Bhabha, 'Minority culture and creative anxiety'.

60   Bhabha, 'Minority culture and creative anxiety'.

61   See Chapter 10 of this volume for a more detailed consideration of precisely these problems.

62   See M. Keith, 1999, 'Walter Benjamin, urban studies and the narratives of city life', in G. Bridge and S. Watson, 1999, *The Blackwell Companion to Urban Studies* (Oxford: Blackwell).

63   Boyer, *The City of Collective Memory*.

64   H. Haacke, 2001, 'Mixed messages', in *Give and Take* (London: Serpentine Gallery and Victoria and Albert Museum), p. 47.

65   Haacke, 'Mixed messages', p. 52.

66   The link between curation, collection and a mythic city whole is captured in Benjamin's typically epigrammatic comment: 'What is decisive in collecting is that the object is detached from all its original functions in order to enter into the closest conceivable

relation to things of the same kind. This relation is the diametric opposite of any utility, and falls into a peculiar category of completeness. What is this "completeness"? It is a grand attempt to overcome the wholly irrational character of the object's mere presence at hand through its integration into a new, expressly devised historical system: the collection.' Benjamin, *The Arcades Project*, pp. 204–5.

67 See T. Eagleton, 2000, *The Idea of Culture* (Oxford: Blackwell), for one of the more recent discussions of this debate and R. Williams, 1963, *Culture and Society* (Harmondsworth: Penguin), for what remains one of the ground-breaking works in this area.

68 Florida, *The Rise of the Creative Class*, p. 200 onwards. Florida's thesis, whilst expanding the boundaries of the cultural in certain (fairly 'pro-capital') directions, is keen to insert (fairly arbitrary and slightly reactionary) boundaries elsewhere. His claim that 'Many cultural theorists like to see cultural forms such as graffiti art and rap as political movements expressing the voices of the oppressed. This absurd notion does a disservice to both politics and art' (p. 203) is one example of this.

69 P. Hall, 2000, *Cities in Civilization* (London and New York: Weidenfeld and Nicolson).

70 J. Hutnyk, 2000, *Critique of Exotica: Music, Politics and the Culture Industry* (London: Pluto).

71 Lash and Urry, *Economies of Signs and Space*; C. Dwyer and P. Jackson, 2003, 'Commodifying difference: selling EASTern fashion', *Environment and Planning D: Society and Space*, 21, pp. 269–91.

72 See Anderson, *Vancouver's Chinatown*; Jacobs, *Edge of Empire*.

73 S. Fish, 1997, 'Boutique multiculturalism, or why liberals are incapable of thinking about hate speech', *Critical Inquiry*, 23 (Winter), pp. 378–95.

74 See M. Hardt and A. Negri, 2000, *Empire* (Boston, Mass.: Harvard University Press).

75 Zukin, 'How to make a cultural capital', p. 264.

76 A. Abbott, 1999, *Department and Discipline: The Chicago School at One Hundred* (Chicago, Ill.: Chicago University Press).

77 There is no space to explore the ethical questions that confront the production of ethnographic texts by established academics in the multicultural metropolises of today, but for a lucid exploration of this question see L. Back and J. Solomos, 1993, 'Doing research, writing politics: the dilemmas of political intervention in research on racism', *Economy and Society*, 22 (2), pp. 178–99; M. Bulmer and J. Solomos (eds), *Researching Race and Racism* (London: Routledge).

78 See the arguments around the nature of inner city space and the street in Chapters 5 and 6 for a more detailed exploration of these issues.

79 D. Massey, 1994, 'A global sense of place', in D. Massey, *Space, Place, Gender* (Oxford: Blackwell).

80 See C. Geertz, 2000, 'Anti anti-relativism', in C. Geertz, *Available Light: Anthropological Reflections on Philosophical Topics* (Princeton, NJ: Princeton University Press), pp. 42–67. Geerz's notion of anti-anti-relativism is clearly important in its own right. It is also influential in structuring the anti-anti-essentialism that informs Paul Gilroy's seminal routing of the black Atlantic and the turn to notions of *travel* and *translation* espoused in the work of James Clifford and the anthropology of multisite ethnography. See J. Clifford, 1997, *Routes: Travel and Translation in the Late Twentieth Century* (London and Boston, Mass.: Harvard University Press); P. Gilroy, 1993, *The Black Atlantic: Double Consciousness and Modernity* (Boston and Cambridge, Mass.: Harvard University Press); S. Marcus, 1995, 'Ethnography in/of the world system: the emergence of multi-sited ethnography', *Annual Review of Anthropology*, 24, pp. 95–117.

81 This is written in the spirit of James Clifford's observation that contemporary multisited ethnography generates a sense in which 'the good news and the bad news presuppose each other'. Clifford, *Routes*, p. 10.

82 E. Burke, 1958, *A Philosophical Enquiry into the Origin of our Ideas of the Sublime and the Beautiful* (London: Routledge and Kegan Paul).

83 I. Kant, 1990 [1764], *Critique of Judgement*, trans. James Creed Meredith (Oxford: Oxford University Press).

84 J. Thompson, 1999, 'The sublime moment: the rise of the critical watchman', in Arts Council, *Sublime: The Darkness and the Light* (London: Hayward Gallery Publications), p. 25.

85 J.-F. Lyotard, 1971, *Discours, figure* (Paris: Editions Klincksiek).

86 Thompson, 'The sublime moment', p. 27.

87 O. Enwezor, 2002, 'The black box', in *Documenta 11_Platform 5*.

88 See S. Pile, 1996, *The Body and the City. Psychoanalysis, Space and Subjectivity* (London: Routledge); J. Donald, 1999, *Imagining the Modern City* (London: Wiley); I. Rogoff, 2000, *Terra Infirma: Geography's Visual Culture* (London: Routledge).

8 Tagging the city: Graffiti practice and transcultural communication

1 The research on which this chapter is based was supported by a grant from the Harry Frank Guggenheim Foundation for a project on 'The cultural mechanisms of racist expression: a study of racism and anti-Semitism in graffiti, pamphlets, style and body symbolism.' We are grateful to them for their support.

2 We have noted elsewhere how the Nazis used graffiti as both a weapon in the persecution of the Jews and as a form of propaganda within occupied territories. See L. Back, M. Keith and J. Solomos, 1996, 'Technology, race and neo-fascism in a digital age: the new modalities of racist culture', *Patterns of Prejudice*, 30 (2), pp. 3–27.

3 J. Ferrell, 1993, *Crime of Style: Urban Graffiti and the Politics of Criminality* (New York and London: Garland Publishing), p. 197.

4 P. Hagopian, 1988, 'Reading the indecipherable: graffiti and hegemony', *Polygraph*, 1, pp. 105–9, at p. 109.

5 See A. Dundes, 1966, 'Here I sit', *Kroeber Anthropological Society*, 34, pp. 91–105; R. Reynolds, 1975, *Magic Symbols. A Photographic Study of Graffiti* (Portland, Ore.: Graphic Arts Centre Pub Co.); R. Perry, 1976, *The Writing on the Wall: The Graffiti of London* (London: Elm Tree Books); N. Rees, 1979, *Graffiti Lives, OK* (London: Unwin Paper Backs); S. Henderson, 1981, *Billboard Art* (London: Angus and Robertson).

6 J. Lindsay, 1960, *The Writing on the Wall: An Account of Pompeii in its Last Days* (London: Frederick Muller); R. Reisner, 1974, *Graffiti: Two Thousand Years of Wall Writing* (London: Frederick Muller).

7 E. L. Abel and B. E. Buckley, 1977, *The Handwriting on the Wall: Towards a Sociology and Psychology of Graffiti* (London: Greenwood Press); E. Cockcroft, 1977, *Towards a People's Art* (New York: E. P. Dutton).

8 The notion of *détournement* was first developed by the Belgian surrealist Marcel Mariën and its meaning is connected to spontaneous moments of subversion or diversion in which conventions are played with and thus revealed. Sadie Plant, in her excellent study of the Situationist International, describes the role of graffiti: 'Anonymous, cheap and immediate, the use of graffiti in the May events epitomised the avant-garde dream of art realised in the practice of everyday life. A transformation of its environment as a larger *détournement* of the city it inspired and reported.' S. Plant, 1992, *The Most Radical Gesture: The Situationist International in a Postmodern Age* (London and New York: Routledge), p. 104.

9 J. Bushnell, 1990, *Moscow Graffiti: Language and Subculture* (London: Unwin Hyman); T. Cresswell, 1996, *In Place/Out of Place: Geography, Ideology and Transgression* (Minneapolis, Minn.: University of Minnesota Press); Ferrell, *Crime of Style*.

10 J. Q. Wilson and G. Kelling, 1982, 'Broken windows: the police and neighbourhood safety', *Atlantic Monthly*, March, pp. 29–38.

11 N. Glazer, 1974, 'On subway graffiti in New York', *Public Interest*, 54, pp. 3–11 at p. 4.

12 R. Sennett, 1991, *The Conscience and the Eye* (New York: W. W. Norton), p. 126.

13 Sennett, *The Conscience and the Eye*, p. 127.

14 Sennett, echoing situationist *détournement*, favours the suggestive wall writing of Parisian graffiti which juxtaposes images and slogans which 'intrigue pedestrians who slow down and look'. Sennett, *The Conscience and the Eye*, p. 211.

15 G. Cesaretti, 1975, *Street Writers: A Guided Tour of Chicano Graffiti* (New York: Acrobat Books); M. Cooper and H. Chalfant, 1980, *Subway Art* (London: Thames and Hudson).

16 Cited in C. Castleman, 1982, *Gettin Up: Subway Graffiti in New York* (Cambridge, Mass.: MIT Press), pp. 86–7.

17 See particularly R. Ricard, 1981, 'The radiant child', *Artforum*, 20 December, pp. 35–43.

18 E. Sussman, 1997, 'Songs of innocence at the nuclear pyre', in E. Sussman (ed.), *Keith Haring* (New York: Whitney Museum of Modern Art), p. 10.

19 D. Hebdige, 1993, 'Welcome to the Terrordome: Jean Michel Basquiat and the dark side of hybridity', in R. Marshall (ed.), *Jean Michel Basquiat* (New York: Whitney), p. 64.

20 Hebdige, 'Welcome to the Terrordome', p. 65.

21 M. Cooper and J. Sciorra, 1994, *R.I.P.: New York Spray Can Memorials* (London: Thames and Hudson), p. 7.

22 M. Berman, 1987, 'Take it to the streets: conflict and community in public space', *Dissent*, Winter, pp. 476–85.

23 Jill Posner's insightful study of feminist graffiti shows how the spray can has also been used by women activists to deface offensive public representations of femininity. One example graphically challenged the advertiser to 'Get Your Ads off my Body!' Graffiti, she suggests, offers the means to overwrite the dominant gendered imagery presented in advertising and other public texts. J. Posner, 1982, *Spray it Loud* (London: Polity Press). Here the act of defacement is perhaps another example of a momentary attempt to open up patriarchal imagery to public scrutiny.

24 J. Borja and M. Castells, 1997, *Local and Global* (London: Earthscan), p. 4. A similar point is made by Benjamin Barber about the coincidence of globalism and tribalism. He argues that we are caught between 'Babel and Disneyland, the planet is falling precipitously apart and coming reluctantly together at the very same moment'. B. Barber, 1995, *Jihad vs. McWorld: How Globalism and Tribalism are Reshaping the World* (New York: Ballentine Books).

25 For an extended and illustrated version of the argument in this chapter, see L. Back, M. Keith and J. Solomos, 1998, 'Reading the writing on the wall: graffiti in the racialised city', in D. Slayden and R. K. Whillock, 1998, *Soundbite Culture: The Death of Discourse in a Wired World* (London and New York: Sage), pp. 69–102, which also draws more extensively on material from the English city of Birmingham.

26 See Bethnal Green Trades Council, 1979, *Blood on the Streets* (London: Stepney Books).

27 D. Ley and R. Cybrinski, 1974, 'Urban graffiti as territorial markers', *Annals of the Association of American Geographers*, 64, pp. 491–505.

28 P. Corrigan, 1976, 'Doing nothing', in T. Jefferson and S. Hall (eds), *Resistance through Rituals: Youth Subcultures in Post-War Britain* (Birmingham, UK: Centre for Contemporary Cultural Studies).

29 L. Back, M. Keith and J. Solomos, 1996, 'Technology, race and neo-fascism in a digital age: the new modalities of racist culture', *Patterns of Prejudice*, 30 (2), pp. 3–27.

30 J. W. Moore, 1978, *Homeboys: Gangs, Drugs and Prison in the Barrios of Los Angeles* (Philadelphia, Pa.: Temple University Press).

31 H. D. Lomas, 1973, 'Graffiti: some observations and speculations', *Psychoanalytic Review*, 68, pp. 70–5.

32 Lomas, 'Graffiti: some observations and speculations', p. 71.

33 H. Lefèbvre, 1991, *The Production of Space* (Cambridge: Polity Press).

34 M. Jay, 1992, 'Scopic regimes of modernity', in S. Lash and J. Friedman (eds), *Modernity and Identity* (Oxford: Blackwell).

35 W. Wimsatt, 1994, *Bomb the Suburbs* (Chicago, Ill.: The Subway and Elevated Press Company), p. 10.

36 This research was developed out of a project conducted with Anoop Nayak which examined racism in the suburbs. See L. Back and A. Nayak, 2000, *The New Frontiers of Racism: Youth, Community and Conflict in the Suburbs* (Coventry: University of Warwick, Centre for Research in Ethnic Relations).

37　G. Mosse, 1991, *The Nationalization of the Masses: Political Symbolism and Mass Movements in Germany from the Napoleonic Wars through the Third Reich* (London and New York: Cornell University Press).

38　Malcolm Quinn, in his excellent history of the swastika, points out that it is a symbol that cannot be subverted because of the overburdening legacy of Nazi violence and genocide. M. Quinn, 1994, *The Swastika: Constructing the Symbol* (London: Routledge). See also J. Solomos and L. Back, 1996, *Racism and Society* (Basingstoke: Macmillan).

39　A. M. Oliver and P. Steinberg, 1994, 'The graffiti of the Intifada: a brief survey' (mimeo), p. 5.

9　The cartographies of community safety: Mapping danger and rumours of risk

1　U. Beck, 1992, *Risk Society: Towards a New Modernity* (London: Sage); and for consideration of this work and its impact on notions of reflexive modernisation 10 years on, see U. Beck, W. Bons and C. Lau, 2003, 'The theory of reflective modernisation', *Theory, Culture and Society*, 20 (2), pp. 1–33.

2　This research was funded by the Economic and Social Research Council (Project number: R000236301) and carried out by a research team that also included Les Back, Phil Cohen, Tim Lucas, Tahmina Maula, Sarah Newlands and Lande Pratt. The research involved extensive ethnographic engagement with two schools over a one-year period in 1997–8, supplemented by work with artists, policy makers and educational professionals considering the generation of racist landscapes of racial danger and intercultural dialogue in East and South London. The work produced by this project was clearly collaborative, although the faults and flaws of this chapter are entirely my own.

3　G. Mulgan, 1994, *Politics in an Anti-Political Age* (Oxford: Polity Press).

4　A. Giddens, 1998, *The Third Way* (London and Cambridge: Polity Press), p. 77.

5　Giddens, *The Third Way*, p. 85.

6　Giddens, *The Third Way*, p. 78.

7　C. Gordon, 1991 'Governmental rationality: an introduction', in G. Burchell, C. Gordon, and P. Miller (eds), *The Foucault Effect: Studies in Governmentality* (Brighton: Harvester Wheatsheaf), pp. 1–53; N. Rose, 1989, *Governing the Soul: The Shaping of the Private Self* (London: Routledge); N. Rose, 1999, *Powers of Freedom: Reframing Political Thought* (Cambridge: Cambridge University Press).

8　D. Mitchell, 2003, *The Right to the City: Social Justice and the Fight for Public Space* (New York: Guilford); N. Smith, 1996, *The New Urban Frontier: Gentrification and the Revanchist City* (London: Routledge).

9　See, for example, Department of Environment, Transport and the Regions, 1997, *Building Partnerships for Prosperity* (London: HMSO, Cm 3814).

10　L. Johnston, 2000, *Policing Britain: Risk, Security and Governance* (Harlow, Essex: Pearson Education).

11　L. Lees, 2004, *The Emancipatory City: Paradoxes and Possibilities* (London: Sage).

12　S. Driver and L. Martell, 1997, 'New Labour's communitarianisms', *Critical Social Policy*, 52, pp. 27–46.

13　L. Back, 1995, *New Ethnicities and Urban Culture: Racisms and Multiculture in Young Lives* (London: UCL Press).

14　Interesting mappings of the local areas of safety and danger by young white students at George Green School identified a barrier of 'Bengali danger' across the north of the Isle of Dogs that corresponded closely with these estates.

15　R. Sennett, 2000, 'Reflections on the public realm', in G. Bridge and S. Watson (eds), *A Companion to the City* (Oxford: Blackwell), pp. 380–8, at p. 382.

16　P. Cohen, 1997, *Rethinking the Youth Question* (London: Macmillan).

17　Back, *New Ethnicities and Urban Culture*.

18　S. Kripke, 1980, *Naming and Necessity* (Oxford: Blackwell).

19 L. Back and M. Keith, 1999, 'Rights and wrongs: youth, community and narratives of racial violence', in P. Cohen (ed.), *New Ethnicities, Old Racisms* (London: Zed Books), pp. 131–62.

20 C. Alexander, 2001, *The Asian Gang* (London: Berg).

21 D. Hayden, 1995, *The Power of Place: Urban Landscapes as Public History* (Cambridge, Mass.: MIT Press); D. Hayden, 2000, 'In search of the American cultural landscape', in A. Alanen and R. Melnick, *Preserving Cultural Landscapes in America* (Baltimore, Md., and London: Johns Hopkins University Press); L. Sandercock, 1997, *Towards Cosmopolis: Planning for Multicultural Cities* (New York: Wiley); S. Zukin, 1991, *Landscapes of Power: From Detroit to Disney World* (Berkeley: University of California Press).

22 The most articulate version of this is probably to be found in Hayden, *The Power of Place*.

23 For Sue Clifford of Common Ground, 'The plea is for *Local Distinctiveness*. Places are not just physical surroundings, they are a web of rich understandings between people and nature, peoples and their histories, people and their neighbours. People understand places and value them because they mean something to them. Little things (detail) and overlapping clues to previous lives and landscapes (patina) may be the very things which breathe significance into the streets or fields. Try to define these things from the outside or at a grand scale and the point is lost; better to ensure that local culture has sufficient self knowledge and self esteem to be confident in welcoming new people and new ideas.' S. Clifford, 1996, 'How many common streams? Places, cultures and local distinctiveness', in R. Jaijee and K. Thomas (eds), *Getting in Touch with the Thames* (London: London Rivers Association), pp. 16–20, at p. 18. Common Ground is a charity which emphasises the value of everyday surroundings and positive investment people can make in their own localities. The organisation forges links between the arts, the conservation of nature and cultural landscapes, offering ideas, inspiration and information. See http://www.commonground.org.uk/.

24 Clifford, 'How many common streams?'.

25 D. Massey, 1993, *Space, Place and Gender* (Cambridge: Polity Press).

26 R. Sennett, 1990, *The Conscience of the Eye* (New York: Norton).

27 G. Robson, 2000, *No-One Likes Us, We Don't Care: The Myth and Reality of Millwall Fandom* (London: Berg).

28 R. Sennett, 1970, *The Uses of Disorder: Personal Identity and City Life* (New York: Norton), p. 109.

29 Sennett, R. *The Uses of Disorder*, p. 111.

30 P. Cohen, 1997, 'Out of the melting pot into the fire next time: imagining the East End as city, body, text', in S. Westwood and J. Williams (eds), *Imagining Cities* (London: Routledge), pp. 73–86.

31 D. Chakraborty, 2000, *Provincialising Europe* (Princeton, NJ: Princeton University Press).

10 The plan: Knowing urbanism: between the allure of the cosmopolitan and the horror of the postcolony

1 The term 'postcolonial melancholia' is taken from the work of Paul Gilroy describing the malaise of contemporary Britain, the notion of 'the postcolony' from the work of Achille Mbembe. See, for example, P. Gilroy, 2003, 'A London Sumtin Dis . . .', *AAFiles*, 49, pp. 7–14; A. Mbembe, 2001, *On The Postcolony* (Berkeley: University of California Press).

2 S. Buck Morss, 1978, *The Origin of Negative Dialectics* (Hassocks, Sussex: Harvester Press), p. 150.

3 Buck Morss, *The Origin of Negative Dialectics*, p. 156.

4 H. Lonitz (ed.), 1999, *Theodor W. Adorno and Walter Benjamin: The Complete Correspondence 1928–1940*, trans. Nicholas Walker (Cambridge: Polity Press). Adorno's critique of the astonished presentation of simple facts is echoed in Wacquant's critiques of ghetto ethnographies considered in Chapter 4.

5 G. Simmel, 'Excurs über den Fremden', in G. Simmel, 1923, *Soziologie* (Munich and Leipzig: Duncker und Humblot).

6 The work is also useful in prefiguring an understanding of how the tension between the familiar and the strange links closely to a Freudian exploration of the uncanny and a psychoanalytic reading of the city. The focus of this chapter is on the parallelism between the spatialisation of the familiar and the strange and the changing configurations of city ethics and urban knowledges. This is not to devalue such psychoanalytic insights. For an exploration of such 'warped spaces' see A. Vidler, 2001, 'Spaces of passage: the architecture of estrangement: Simmel, Kracauer, Benjamin', in A. Vidler, *Warped Space: Art, Architecture and Anxiety in Modern Culture* (Cambridge, Mass.: MIT Press), pp. 65–81.

7 See W. Benjamin, 1999, 'A little history of photography', in W. Benjamin, *Selected Writings*, vol. 2: *1927–34*, ed. M. W. Jennings, H. Eiland and G. Smith (Cambridge, Mass.: Belknap Press of Harvard University Press), pp. 507–30; and W. Benjamin, 1973, 'The work of art in the age of its technological reproducibility', in H. Arendt, *Illuminations*, ed. and with an 'Introduction' by Hannah Arendt, trans. Harry Zohn (London: Fontana).

8 See M. Keith, 2000, 'Walter Benjamin, urban studies and the narratives of city life', in G. Bridge and S. Watson, 2000, *The Blackwell Companion to Urban Studies* (Oxford: Blackwell).

9 See R. Koolhaas *et al.*, 2001, *Mutations* (Paris: ACTAR); R. Koolhaas, 1997, *Delirious New York: A Retroactive Manifesto for Manhattan* (New York: Monacelli Press); S. Kwinter, 2001, *Architectures of Time: Towards a Theory of the Event in Modernist Culture* (Cambridge, Mass.: MIT Press), Chapter 2. In part the iconography of the lexicon of urbanism described in Chapter 3 and explored throughout this volume may accord with the notion of an archive of the infrastructure of urbanism that Kwinter describes in S. Kwinter, 2001, 'Urbanism: an archivist's art?', in Koolhaas *et al.*, *Mutations*, pp. 494–504.

10 See S. Boeri, 2004, *Uncertain States of Europe: Multiplicity (USE). A Trip Through a Changing Europe* (Rome: Skira Editore).

11 Although these tensions themselves need to be both spatialised and historicised; their conceptual vocabulary cannot be taken for granted, e.g. M. Poovey, 2002, 'The liberal civil subject and the social in eighteenth century British moral philosophy', *Public Culture*, 14 (1), pp. 124–45.

12 For extensive discussion around both the theorisation of the notion and for its more literary invocations see, for example, the special issue on 'Cosmopolitanism' in *Public Culture*, 12 (3) (Fall 2000), and in particular S. Pollock, H. Bhabha and C. Breckenridge, 'Cosmopolitanisms', pp. 577–90. For a variety of perspectives, see S. Vertovec and S. Cohen (eds), 2002, *Conceiving Cosmopolitanism: Theory, Context and Practice* (Oxford: Oxford University Press).

13 A. Ong, 1999, *Flexible Citizenship. The Cultural Logics of Transnationality* (Durham, NC, and London: Duke University Press).

14 See M.-L. Pratt, 1992, *Imperial Eyes: Travel Writing and Transculturation* (London and New York: Routledge).

15 S. Hall, 2001, 'The multicultural question', in B. Hesse (ed.), *Un/settled Multiculturalisms: Diasporas, Entanglements, Transruptions* (London: Zed Books), pp. 209–38. Even in the political theory the city is commonly invoked as much as analysed; hence for Calhoun, 'the great imperial cities stood as centres of diversity. Enjoying this diversity was one of the marks of a sophisticated modern urbanite by contrast to the "traditional hick". To be a cosmopolitan was to be comfortable in heterogeneous public space.' C. Calhoun, 2003, 'The class consciousness of frequent travellers: towards a critique of actually existing cosmopolitanism', in D. Archibugi (ed.), *Debating Cosmopolitics* (London: Verso), p. 106.

16 See P. Cheah, 1999, 'The cosmopolitical – today', in P. Cheah and B. Robbins (eds), *Cosmopolitics: Thinking and Feeling Beyond the Nation* (Minneapolis, Minn. and London: University of Minnesota Press).

17 In part the chapter is attempting to respond to some of the writing in the planning literature of the late twentieth century, which, whilst politically progressive and sympathetic to notions of cosmopolitan urbanism, was – I believe – deeply flawed in its theorisation of city power and romantic about the nature of the ethnographic realities of the city grassroots. See Chapter 3 of this volume and L. Sandercock, 1998, *Towards Cosmopolis* (London: Wiley), J. Holston, 2001, 'Spaces of insurgent citizenship', in L. Sandercock (ed.), *Making The Invisible Visible: Insurgent Planning Histories* (Berkeley: University of California Press); M. J. Dear, 2000, *The Postmodern Urban Condition* (Oxford: Blackwell), pp. 8–9.

18 'All so-called modern, liberal nation states thus combine the so-called rational, reflective, civic form of allegiance to the state with a so-called intuitive, instinctual ethnic or allegiance to the nation' (Hall, 'The multicultural question', p. 229).

19 M. Hardt and A. Negri, 2000, *Empire* (Cambridge, Mass.: Harvard University Press), parts 1–2.

20 L. Back, M. Keith, A. Khan and L. Solomos (forthcoming), 'Islam and the new political landscape of London after September 11'.

21 See M. Warren, 2001, *Dry Bones Rattling: Community Building to Revitalize American Democracy* (Princeton, NJ, and Oxford: Princeton University Press).

22 P. Gilroy, 2002, 'Diving into the tunnel: the politics of race between old and new worlds', *Open Democracy* (web journal), July.

23 P. Cohen, L. Back and M. Keith, 2001, *Finding the Way Home*, ESRC Final Report (London: Goldsmiths College, Centre for Urban and Community Research).

24 For the most concise summary of these debates see R. Rorty, 1998, 'Justice as a larger loyalty', in Cheah and Robbins, *Cosmopolitics*, pp. 45–59, and C. Harris, 2001, 'Beyond multiculturalism?: difference, recognition and social justice', *Patterns of Prejudice*, 35 (1), pp. 13–34, and in interesting contrast C. Taylor, 2002, 'Modern social imaginaries, *Public Culture*, 14 (1), pp. 91–124.

25 See S. Rushdie, 1988, *Satanic Verses* (London: Penguin), p. 314. Also H. Bhabha, 1993, *The Location of Culture* (London: Routledge).

26 F. Engels, 1999, *Condition of the English Working Class* (Harmondsworth: Penguin), p. 276. Engels' anticipation of the corporeality of an ethics of recognition is more than felicitous and in many ways prefigures the concerns of Emmanuel Levinas.

27 I. Borden *et al.* (eds), 1996, *Strangely Familiar: Narratives of Architecture in the City* (London: Routledge).

28 Hall, 'The multicultural question', pp. 209–38.

29 Hall, 'The multicultural question', p. 235.

30 C. Mouffe, 1993, *The Return of the Political* (London: Verso).

31 Hall, 'The multicultural question', p. 237, and P. Gilroy, 2000, *Between Camps: Race, Identity and Nationalism at the End of the Colour Line* (London: Penguin).

32 In P. Ackroyd, 2000, *London: The Biography* (London: Vintage), p. 755.

33 GLA, 2001, *Towards the London Plan. Initial Proposals for the Mayor's Spatial Development Strategy* (London: Greater London Authority), p. 21.

34 GLA, *Towards the London Plan*, p. 21. This figure would amount to approximately 30–35,000 new households needed in London per year for the next 15 years.

35 Office of the Deputy Prime Minister (ODPM), 2003, *Sustainable Communities: Building for the Future* (London: HMSO).

36 GLA, *Towards the London Plan*, p. 22. The rhetorical focus on 'non-white migration' is significant.

37 GLA, *Towards the London Plan*, p. 78.

38 Department of Environment, Transport and the Regions (DETR), 2000, *The Urban White Paper: Towards an Urban Renaissance* (London: HMSO).

39 In Ackroyd, *London: The Biography*, pp. 60–1.

40 DETR, *The Urban White Paper*, p. 7.

41 They are roots that contrast starkly with much in contemporary debate about asylum seekers and refugees in the United Kingdom, mainland Europe, Australia and the USA.

42 I. Borden, J. Jerr, J. Rendell and A. Pivaro, 2001, 'Things, flows, filters, tactics', and S. Pile, 2001, 'The un(known) city . . . or, an urban geography of what lies buried below the surface', both in I. Borden, J. Jerr, J. Rendell with A. Pivaro (eds), *The Unknown City: Contesting Architecture and Social Space* (Cambridge, Mass.: MIT Press).

43 For the evangelical espousal of new urbanism and the lexicon of new urbanism, see http://www.dpz.com.

44 D. McCannell, 1999, 'New urbanism and its discontents', in J. Copjec and M. Sorkin (eds), *Giving Ground: The Politics of Propinquity* (London and New York: Verso).

45 Hall, 'The multicultural question', pp. 209–38.

46 Tower Hamlets Language Line (interpreting requests from council departments in Tower Hamlets 2000 (April) – 2001 (March)). London: London Borough of Tower Hamlets Cabinet Papers (available to the public): Bengali/Sylheti 6549, Albanian 2384, Polish 3100, Farsi 2105, Russian 212, Romanian 1178, Kurdish 850, Vietnamese 507, Somali 1824, Turkish 1424.

47 S. Hunt and N. Lightly, 2001, 'The British black Pentecostal "revival": identity and belief in the "new" Nigerian churches', *Ethnic and Racial Studies*, 24 (1), pp. 104–24; C. Nagel, 2002, 'Constructing difference and sameness: the politics of assimilation in London's Arab communities', *Ethnic and Racial Studies*, 25 (2), pp. 258–87.

48 Audit Commission, 2001, *Halfway Home: An Analysis of the Variation in the Cost of Supporting Asylum Seekers* (London: Audit Commission Management Paper), p. 5.

49 Audit Commission, *Halfway Home*, pp. 19–20.

50 W. J. Fishman, 1888, *East End 1888: A Year in a London Borough amongst the Labouring Poor* (London: Duckworth), pp. 25–48.

51 The offence of SUS (short for 'suspicion') was based on a Victorian bylaw that allowed two men of good faith to arrest and charge an individual who was about to commit a crime. People could consequently be convicted for an offence that had quite literally not yet occurred. In the 1970s SUS was seen to be used almost entirely in London and in a massively disproportionate way against young British black men, particularly in specific parts of the city. SUS was repealed following Lord Scarman's inquiry into the Brixton disorders of 1981. The inquiry highlighted the racialised injustice perpetrated through the twentieth-century use of the SUS laws.

52 Pratt, *Imperial Eyes*.

53 K. Marx and F. Engels, 1986 [1848], *Manifesto of the Communist Party* (Moscow: Progress), p. 31.

54 For just four examples of very different genres of historical account, see C. Adams, 1987, *Across Seven Seas and Thirteen Rivers* (London: Stepney Books); B. Alleyne, 2002, *Radicals Against Race: Black Activism and Cultural Politics* (London: Berg); J. Anim-Addo, 1995, *Longest Journey: A History of Black Lewisham* (London: Deptford Forum Publishing); A. Ashgar, 1996, *Bangladeshi Community Organisations in East London* (London: Bangla Heritage).

55 Interestingly, Michael Mates returned to the public eye in 2004 as an elder statesman, sitting as one of two cross-party representatives on the Butler Inquiry into the 'WMD' claims that informed the invasion of Iraq.

56 DAC Wyn Jones left the Metropolitan Police after newspaper coverage of his links with Nadir.

57 On 3 September 2003 the *Guardian* reported that 'Asil Nadir, the Polly Peck tycoon who fled to northern Cyprus in 1993 to avoid charges involving theft totalling £34m, yesterday astonished friends, Turkish politicians and the serious fraud office by pledging to return to Britain to clear his name.'

58 1 Canada Square – built by Canary Wharf Group in London's Docklands – was the tallest building in Europe for much of the 1990s.

59 The emphasis on mimesis is taken particularly from the work of Michael Taussig, 1987, *Shamanism, Colonialism and the Wild Man: A Study in Terror and Healing* (Chicago, Ill. and London: University of Chicago Press); and M. Taussig, 1993, *Mimesis and Alterity: A*

Particular History of the Senses (London and New York: Routledge). Paul Gilroy's exploration of a supplement to the vocabulary of diaspora is also powerfully helpful here through his notion (after Leroi Jones) of the 'changing same' where 'neither the mechanistic essentialism that is too squeamish to acknowledge the possibility of difference within sameness nor the lazy alternative that animates the supposedly strategic variety of essentialism can supply keys to the untidy workings of diaspora identities. They are creolized, syncretised, hybridized and chronically impure cultural forms, particularly if they were once rooted in the complicity of rationalised terror and racialised reason . . . Iteration is the key to this process.' Gilroy, *Between Camps*, p. 129.

60 Gilroy, *Between Camps*, p. 121.

61 The Parekh Report, 2001, *The Future of Multiethnic Britain* (London: Profile Books).

62 L. Back, 1995, *New Ethnicities and Urban Culture* (London: UCL Press).

63 See Goldsmiths College Centre for Urban and Community Research: www.goldsmiths. ac.uk/cucr.

64 In 1985 the most serious city uprising seen in the latter half of the twentieth century took place on Broadwater Farm Estate in Tottenham when police fought with the local black community after the death of the black mother of a local community worker in a police search.

65 Lord Scarman, 1982, *The Scarman Report: The Brixton Disorders of 10–12 April 1981* (Harmondsworth: Penguin).

66 In the 'Finding the Way Home' project based at CUCR and CNER, University of London, in the late 1990s a local activist described the evolution of the alternative public sphere of black clubs in South London: the sites of the development of expressive black culture and a new form of vernacular black urbanism in South London, framed by the politics of police criminalisation of British black communities and transnational resistance. See also Anim-Addo, *Longest Journey*.

67 *Stalker*, director Andrey Tarkovsky, 1979, based on the novel *Roadside Picnic* by Arcady and Boris Strugatsky. 'The framework of their story was relatively explicit: extraterrestrials had created a number of "zones" during their brief visits to earth where mysterious forces remained at play. The attraction of these is that they contain many strange and valuable things, including a golden sphere which can grant wishes – though only *unconscious* ones – but they are guarded by fantastic booby traps. The profession of "Stalker" has developed to guide those brave enough to run the risk.' I. Christie, 2000, 'Landscape and location: reading filmic space historically', *Rethinking History*, 4 (2), pp. 165–74.

68 I am grateful to Gil Doron, who attended courses at CUCR, for drawing my attention to the work of Stalker in his fascinating work on the Dead Zone: see G. Doron, 2000, 'The Dead Zone and the architecture of transgression', *City*, 4, pp. 246–63. I am also grateful to members of the Stalker practice for personal discussions about their political and theoretical provenance that took place on the top of a hill watching the midnight sun as part the Game of Tromsø ('Spillet om Tromsø'), part of the Norwegian Day for Architecture, 2001.

69 G. Doron, 2001, 'Leaps and boundaries: Rassegna Stampa', *Building Design*, 27 April.

70 Personal communication with Stalker architectural practice.

71 G. Agamben, 2000, *Means Without Ends: Notes on Politics* (Minneapolis, Minn.: University of Minnesota Press).

72 Agamben, *Means Without Ends*, 16.6.

73 Agamben, *Means Without Ends*, p. 15.

74 Derrida has made a similar, if less explicit, consideration of the relationship between city, state and the cosmopolitan which also draws on Arendt's work. For Derrida (similarly to Agamben) the right of visitation for the stranger is at the heart of contemporary political debate, and Kant's notions of universal hospitality need to be linked to the *public* nature of public space and its regulation by forms of government. In a political world where the fate of minorities provides a litmus test 'if we look to the city,

rather than to the state it is because we have given up hope that the state might create a new image for the city'. J. Derrida, 2001, *On Cosmopolitanism* (London: Routledge), p. 6.

75 Agamben, *Means Without Ends*, p. 20.

76 In Ackroyd, *London: The Biography*, p. 58.

77 L. Back, M. Keith, A. Khan, K. Shukra and J. Solomos, forthcoming 2006, *Power, Identity and Representation: Race, Governance and Political Mobilisation in British Society* (Cambridge: Cambridge University Press). Based on ESRC-funded research as part of the Democracy and Participation Programme.

78 This example draws on ESRC-funded research in the Democracy and Participation Programme. See Back *et al.*, *Power, Identity and Representation*.

79 See M. Keith and M. Cross, 1993, 'Racism and the postmodern city', in M. Cross and M. Keith (eds), *Racism, the City and the State* (London: Routledge).

80 I. M. Young, 1997, *Intersecting Voices: Dilemmas of Gender, Political Philosophy and Policy* (Princeton, NJ: Princeton University Press); I. M. Young, 2001, 'Activist challenges to deliberative democracy', *Political Theory*, 29 (5), pp. 670–90.

81 Achille Mbembe characterises the postcolony as chaotically pluralistic. Drawing on a Foucauldian framing of the problem of government – via Castoriadis – he is interested in the manner in which state power creates a world of meanings, institutionalised in the common sense of a socio-historical world. The effect is similar to the processes of mimesis described in this chapter, and Mbembe suggests that 'the postcolonial relationship is not primarily a relationship of resistance or collaboration but can best be characterised as convivial, relationship fraught by the fact of the *commandement* and its "subjects"'. A. Mbembe, 2001, 'The aesthetics of vulgarity', in A. Mbembe, *On The Postcolony* (Berkeley: University of California Press), p. 104.

Index

eBooks – at www.eBookstore.tandf.co.uk

A library at your fingertips!

eBooks are electronic versions of printed books. You can store them on your PC/laptop or browse them online.

They have advantages for anyone needing rapid access to a wide variety of published, copyright information.

eBooks can help your research by enabling you to bookmark chapters, annotate text and use instant searches to find specific words or phrases. Several eBook files would fit on even a small laptop or PDA.

NEW: Save money by eSubscribing: cheap, online access to any eBook for as long as you need it.

Annual subscription packages

We now offer special low-cost bulk subscriptions to packages of eBooks in certain subject areas. These are available to libraries or to individuals.

For more information please contact webmaster.ebooks@tandf.co.uk

We're continually developing the eBook concept, so keep up to date by visiting the website.

www.eBookstore.tandf.co.uk